CATHOLIC RECORD SOCIETY
PUBLICATIONS
(RECORDS SERIES) VOLUME 71

Editorial Committee: *A. F. Allison*
D. M. Rogers
P. R. Harris
M. Hodgetts

RECUSANTS IN THE EXCHEQUER PIPE ROLLS 1581-1592

Extracted by
DOM HUGH BOWLER, O.S.B., F.S.A.

Edited by
TIMOTHY J. McCANN, B.A.

CATHOLIC RECORD SOCIETY
1986

© The Catholic Record Society

ISBN 0 902832 10 7

Printed in Great Britain by
Hobbs the Printers of Southampton

INTRODUCTION

The present volume is the fourth to be published by the Catholic Record Society devoted to the business of the Exchequer in dealing with the offence of recusancy. Some fifty years ago, the Society published the Latin text of the first Recusant Roll of the Exchequer[1], and, in recent years, it has published an abstract in English of the second, third and fourth Recusant Rolls[2]. Dom Hugh Bowler, in a pioneer article in *Recusant History*[3], which he later enlarged in his definitive introduction to the second Recusant Roll[4], pointed out that the earliest records of prosecutions for failure to attend the new Anglican church services, under the Act of 23 Eliz., c.l, were entered in the annual Great Pipe Rolls of the Exchequer. These began to appear during the period 16 Jan.—18 March 1580/1, and continued to be recorded on the Pipe Rolls until the opening of the Recusant Rolls at Michaelmas 1592. The aim of the present volume is to rescue the important recusancy material scattered through the Pipe Rolls during the first twelve years of the working of the 1581 Act, and to present it in a clear and simple form.

The parliamentary legislation responsible for the appearance of material relating to the offence of recusancy on the Pipe Rolls was formulated in two Acts of 1581 and 1587. The 1581 Act—'An Act to retain the Queen's Majesty's subjects in their due obedience' (23 Eliz., c.l)—dealt with three types of offences. The first offence—that of reconciling or of being reconciled to the Catholic Church—was henceforth punishable by death. The second offence—the saying and hearing of mass—was punishable by fines of 200 marks and 100 marks respectively. The Act provided penalties of imprisonment until the fines were paid in the case of the celebrant, and imprisonment for one year in the case of the hearer. The third offence—the failure to attend the new Anglican church services—now carried a fine of £20 a month, in place of the twelve-pence fine under the Act of Uniformity. Moreover, the fines were declared to be forfeitures of the Crown, and, as a result, the offence of recusancy came under the cognisance of the Exchequer, and the accounts connected with the levying of these fines by the sheriffs began to appear on the Pipe Rolls.

It soon became clear, however, that there were inadequacies in the 1581 Act, irregularities in its execution, and that recusants were able to evade its penalties. Accordingly a second Act was passed in 1587. This 'Act for the more speedy and due execution of certain branches of a statute made in the 23rd. year of the Queen's Majesty's reign' (28, 29 Eliz., c.6) was passed to overhaul the whole procedure. The importance of the new Act as far as the Exchequer was concerned, was that henceforth the liability for debts was

---

1. M.M.C. Calthrop, *Recusant Roll no. 1:1592–1593. C.R.S.*, vol. XVIII, (1916).
2. Hugh Bowler, *Recusant Roll no. 2:1593–1594. C.R.S.*, vol. LVII, (1965), and Hugh Bowler, *Recusant Roll no. 3: 1594–1595 and Recusant Roll no. 4:1595–1596. C.R.S.*, vol. LXI, (1970).
3. Hugh Bowler, 'Some Notes on the Recusant Rolls of the Exchequer', in *R.H.*, vol. 4, (1958), pp. 182–198.
4. *CRS*, LVII, pp. vii–cxiv.

cumulative. For the five years of the 1581 Act, the convicted recusant's total liability had been taken to be limited to the fines specified in his indictment. Under the new Act, any single conviction was regarded as sufficient to involve the individual recusant in a continual series of monthly fines until he conformed. Secondly, the Exchequer staff were required to calculate all pre-1587 debts deemed to have accumulated, in addition to the £260 annual fine, and to arrange to collect them in two payments, one half by the end of Trinity Term 1587, and the other half by the end of Hilary Term 1588. Naturally, the vast majority of recusants proved incapable of settling their arrears on this basis, and so, the new Act provided thirdly, that henceforth, in every case, all the goods of the defaulting recusant and two-thirds of his property were to be regarded as forfeit to the Crown. The record of these forfeitures, like the fines under the 1581 Act, appeared on the Pipe Rolls.

The annual Great Pipe Rolls of the Exchequer were the official registers of sheriffs' accounts, setting forth, under the various county titles, the itemised revenues due to the Crown, which it was the duty of the sheriff in each case to collect during his term of office. Every roll, therefore, contains the current charge against the individual sheriff, with brief annotations showing the measure of his achievement, and the statement of the final audit of his arrears. Among the various items enrolled were fines imposed by the local courts of law, and profits of lands, tenements, goods and chattels seized by the Crown for statutory offences. Among these items the recusancy material is to be found. The Pipe Roll covering the year Michaelmas 1580 to Michaelmas 1581[5] shows that Judges and local Justices soon applied the new laws and certified convictions of recusants to the Exchequer. For the next twelve Exchequer years, the Pipe Rolls continued to include the fines and forfeitures of recusants under the two Acts of Parliament.

By the end of 1591, however, recusancy business resulting from these two Acts, which had increased each year, had become altogether too great to incorporate with other debts in the Pipe Rolls. All the recusancy business was therefore transferred to the new separate Recusant Rolls from Michaelmas 1592, and all accounts relating to this offence continued to be entered in these new rolls for the next one hundred years. It is important to remember, however, that the Recusant Rolls were created purely as an administrative convenience after the Exchequer had gained several years experience in dealing with the offence of recusancy, and not as a result of parliamentary legislation. As sheriff's account rolls, the Recusant Rolls have the same provenance as the Pipe Rolls, which they supplement, and they share common features of physical composition, content and procedure. The body of material now written on the subject of the Recusant Rolls[6], should more

---

5. P.R.O., E. 372/426.
6. Apart from the work of Dom Hugh Bowler noted above, see, for example, J. Anthony Williams, 'Recusant Rolls: Short Guides to Records, No. 11', in *History,* vol. 50, (1965), pp. 193–196, and Frank H. Pugh, 'Monmouthshire Recusants in the Reigns of Elizabeth and James I', in *South Wales and Monmouth Record Society,* vol. 4, (1957), pp. 59–110.

appropriately belong as an introduction to the recusancy business contained on the Pipe Rolls, which predate the Recusant Rolls by twelve years.

The filling of this twelve year gap between the inception of Exchequer recusancy and the start of the Recusant Rolls is the purpose of this present volume. The reason why it has not been attempted before, is, perhaps, because of the very scattered nature of the recusancy material in the Pipe Rolls. Clearly the methods of approach would need to be radically different from those employed in the publication of the early Recusant Rolls by the Society. A transcript of the varied entries (whether in Latin or in English) would not have been an economic proposition, and would have been a well-nigh impossible undertaking for even the most assiduous student. Accordingly, a compromise has been adopted. The original Pipe Roll entries have been radically truncated and here present merely the bare bones of the business. This present volume is designed to be an index to the recusant content of the twelve consecutive Pipe Rolls concerned. These rolls are, as follows:—

I = Pipe Roll listed at the PRO as E.372/426, dated Mich. 22–23 Eliz. 1580–1581.
II = Pipe Roll listed at the PRO as E.372/427, dated Mich. 23–24 Eliz. 1581–1582.
III = Pipe Roll listed at the PRO as E.372/428, dated Mich. 24–25 Eliz. 1582–1583.
IV = Pipe Roll listed at the PRO as E.372/429, dated Mich. 25–26 Eliz. 1583–1584.
V = Pipe Roll listed at the PRO as E.372/430, dated Mich. 26–27 Eliz. 1584–1585.
VI = Pipe Roll listed at the PRO as E.372/431, dated Mich. 27–28 Eliz. 1585–1586.
VII = Pipe Roll listed at the PRO as E.372/432, dated Mich. 28–29 Eliz. 1586–1587.
VIII = Pipe Roll listed at the PRO as E.372/433, dated Mich. 29–30 Eliz. 1587–1588.
IX = Pipe Roll listed at the PRO as E.372/434, dated Mich. 30–31 Eliz. 1588–1589.
X = Pipe Roll listed at the PRO as E.372/435, dated Mich. 31–32 Eliz. 1589–1590.
XI = Pipe Roll listed at the PRO as E.372/436, dated Mich. 32–33 Eliz. 1590–1591.
XII = Pipe Roll listed at the PRO as E.372/437, dated Mich. 33–34 Eliz. 1591–1592.

The original entries of recusancy material on the Pipe Rolls have been abstracted, and are reproduced in the present volume as abbreviated entries in English. Approximately 2,500 recusants are mentioned in the rolls, and the material relating to their recusancy has been arranged as an alphabetical index, which gives the name of each recusant, his parish, his occupation, and the details of his recusancy, with the reference to the original Pipe Roll and individual rotulet in each case. This method is intended to provide enough information to enable historians to trace their quarry in the Pipe Rolls themselves. Where appropriate, reference is also made to the Memoranda Rolls of the Lord Treasurer's Remembrancer, and, in particular, to the 'Recorda' section of these rolls, which contain not only authoritative statements of proceedings relating to the seizure of recusant property, but also the cancellation of such seizures and the surrender of the royal claims in their regard. As well as being a record of the discharging of petitioners from the penalties incurred under the recusancy laws, the Memoranda Rolls are a record of each recusant's convictions, and of the proceedings leading up to the seizure of his property.

The recusancy material recorded on the Pipe Rolls that has been abstracted in this alphabetical index gives information on the subject of convictions for recusancy, fines, records of debts, and the seizure of lands and goods. The present work records first, after the name, parish of domicile and description of each individual recusant, the date of inception of his recusancy as given in the rolls. Secondly it notes the date of his conviction for recusancy as forwarded to the Exchequer. However, since the date of conviction is often omitted in the early rolls, the date here given is that of the earliest recorded period of recusancy, and such periods are sometimes dated by the day of their termination rather than that of their inception. The entries record the seizure of recusants' goods for the non-payment of fines, Ann Barton being the earliest[7] recorded entry. Thirdly the abstracts record the various types of entries relating to the seizure of property for the non-payment of fines. These include the record of lands seized, the rental of lands seized, and details of the leasing of such seized lands. Details of the seizure of lands of 266 recusants had accumulated on the Pipe Rolls by the time of the opening of the Recusant Rolls. Finally, the present work records the fines and debts enrolled on the Pipe Rolls. The abstracts contain summaries of all debts for recusancy, and, after the provisions of the 1587 Act, a re-enrollment of all pre-1587 debts, and also of all other debts for recusancy offences.

The Pipe Rolls record a series of fines for different offences. First, they record a number of fines for contempt. Thomas Barnaby[8], for example, was fined £50 by the High Commissioners for contempt of court in 1585/6, in refusing to bring his wife before the High Commission on a charge of refusing to attend the new Anglican services. Richard Hobson[9] was fined £40 by the Bishop of London at St. Paul's for 'a contempt against the church'. John Brummell[10] was the first of many recusants who were fined for the contempt in ignoring the sheriff's summons after excommunication. The index includes a number of instances of priests being fined for saying mass, as in the case of James Bell[11], and for the offence of hearing mass, as in the case of Francis Bastard, who was one of many recusants who managed to hear mass

---

7. Earliest in the order of the present volume, rather than earliest in date. See p. 16.
8. See p. 15.
9. See p. 84.
10. See p. 29.
11. See p. 19.

while they were in prison. Finally, there are occasionally to be found examples of fines for offences committed prior to the 1581 Act. For example, Humphrey Comberford's £20 fine imposed by the High Commissioners in 1577 for obstinate recusancy lasting several years[12], was recorded in the Pipe Rolls, as was Richard Owen's[13] fine of £40, imposed by the High Commissioners in St. Paul's on 28 June 1577 for a similar offence.

Although recognisable recusants occur in the Pipe Rolls for non-religious offences (for example—failure in payment of lay subsidies), all such entries are here omitted. Only entries of offenders specifically connected with religion are included.

---

12. See pp. 40, 41.
13. See p. 129.

ACKNOWLEDGMENTS

Dom Hugh Bowler began transcribing the recusant material on the Pipe Rolls in December 1952, but he did the majority of the work during the winter of 1966/1967. He transferred the material he had abstracted onto cards, allotting one card to each recusant named in the Rolls, and arranged the cards in an alphabetical sequence. He then began typing up his material, but, it became clear during the last years of his life, that he would never complete the task of editing this volume, which would have completed his lifetime study of the workings of the Exchequer Departments in dealing with the offence of recusancy. By the time of his death in February 1978, Fr. Hugh had more or less completed the alphabetical list of recusants in the form in which it appears in this volume, and had drafted some suggestions for the annotations he wished to make, which mainly concerned the large number of priests and prisoners who were recorded in the Rolls. It has been my task to annotate the material, to write the introduction, and to prepare the material for publication.

Scholars familiar with the work of Dom Hugh Bowler, know that 'by years of dedicated study, with almost no outside help, he had arrived at an unparalleled knowledge of the penal legislation which successive English governments had enacted against their Catholic fellow-citizens, and of the complicated network of legal and fiscal procedures which the implementation of these laws required. His hundred-page preface to volume 57 of the Catholic Record Society's publications, *Recusant Roll* no.2, combines such technical mastery of the whole subject with such precision of statement and clarity of presentation that it has become universally recognised as the definitive treatment of its subject'[14]. It was, therefore, an easy decision to determine to produce this volume in a form, as near as possible to that which Fr. Hugh would have produced had he lived to complete the task. The drafts for footnotes that Fr. Hugh left, reveal to the careful student his particular knowledge of Berkshire recusancy, and the extent of his current reading in the literature of recusant history. I have consciously maintained these slight emphases in his knowledge, and resisted the temptation to balance his knowledge of Berkshire recusants with any knowledge I might have of their counterparts in Sussex.

I am extremely grateful to Fr. Abbot and the Community at Douai, who have encouraged me to complete Fr. Hugh's work, and who have helped me greatly with their hospitality at Douai, and with their generosity in making available to me much of Fr. Hugh's library. I am greatly indebted to the Editorial Committee of the Catholic Record Society for their advice and encouragement. Most of all, however, I am indebted to Fr. Hugh Bowler himself, for his friendship, his encouragement, and, above all, for his example.

Timothy J. McCann
July 1981

---

14. A.F. Allison and D.M. Rogers, in *R.H.*, vol. 15, (1979), p.1.

LIST OF ABBREVIATIONS

*	An asterisk signifies more than one reference on a rotulet
Anstruther I	Godfrey Anstruther, *The Seminary Priests, vol.I: 1558 – 1603* (1960)
CRS	*Catholic Record Society Publications*
CRS I	*Miscellanea I* (1905)
CRS II	*Miscellanea II* (1906)
CRS V	John Hungerford Pollen, *Unpublished Documents relating to the English Martyrs, vol. I: 1584 – 1603* (1908)
CRS X,XI	Edwin H. Burton and Thomas L. Williams, *The Douay College Diaries. Third, Fourth and Fifth, 1598 – 1654.* 2 vol. (1911)
CRS XVIII	M.M.C. Calthrop, *Recusant Roll no. 1: 1592 – 1593* (1916)
CRS XXII	*Miscellanea XII* (1921)
CRS XXXII	*Miscellanea XV* (1936)
CRS LVII	Hugh Bowler, *Recusant Roll no. 2: 1593 – 1594* (1965)
CRS LX	Anthony G. Petti, *Recusant Documents from the Ellesmere Manuscripts* (1968)
CRS LXI	Hugh Bowler, *Recusant Roll no. 3: 1594 – 1595, and Recusant Roll no. 4: 1595 – 1596* (1970)
Challoner	Richard Challoner, *Memoirs of Missionary Priests* (1924)
DNB	*Dictionary of National Biography*
Foley	H. Foley, *Records of the English Province of the Society of Jesus.* 7 vol. (1877 – 83)
Jeaffreson	J. Cordy Jeaffreson, *Middlesex County Records, 1549 – 1688.* 4 vol.
Knox	T.F. Knox, *First and Second Diaries of the English College, Douay* (1878)
LTR	Lord Treasurer's Remembrancer
Morris	John Morris, *The Troubles of our Catholic Forefathers* (1872, 1877)
MR	Memoranda Roll
Pollen	John Hungerford Pollen, *Acts of the English Martyrs* (1891)
PRO	Public Record Office
QR	Queen's Remembrancer
RH	*Recusant History*
RR	Recusant Roll
Venn	J. and J.A. Venn, *Alumni Cantabrigienses* (1922)
VCH	*Victoria County History*
Wark	K.R. Wark, *Elizabethan Recusancy in Cheshire* (1971)

ABINGTON, Richard, esq., of Bromyard, Herefords. 12 months recusancy from 1 Sept. 1586: convicted 18 Mar. 1587/8.—VIII(30). Rental of lands seized 1588.—IX(25v), X(28), XI(28), XII(28).

ABRAHAM, Thomas, 'yom'', of Harrow, Middx. 3 mths recusancy from 6 June 1587: conv. 1 Dec. 1587.—VIII(38v).

ACTON, Joan, wife of Edmund Acton, 'yeoman', of Albie [Aldeby], Norf. 3 mths recusancy from 13 Apr. 1587: conv. 1 Apr. 1588.—VIII(54).

ADAM, David, [ ], of Raglan, Mon. 5 mths recusancy from 24 Mar. 1586/7: conv. 13 Mar. 1587/8.—VIII(48).

ADAM, Margaret, [ ], (of same parish: same period and conviction date).—VIII(48).

ADAM, Thomas Philip William, 'yoman' (of same par.: same period & conviction date).—VIII(48). Record of land-seizure, 24 Oct. 1588.— IX(42v). Rental of seized lands.—IX(42v), X(50), XI(45).

ADAMS, Elizabeth, wife of Thomas Adams, 'yom'', of Winterbourne [St.] Martin, Dorset. 2 mths recusancy from 1 May 1587: conv. 4 Mar. 1587/8.—VIII(19).

ADAMS, John, 'clericus'[1], of Southwark, Surrey [prisoner]. 6 mths recusancy ending 18 Feb. 1584/5, when convicted.—V(52v).

ADYN, Robert, yom', of Southwark, Surrey [prisoner]. 4 mths recusancy ending 22 July 1583, when convicted.—IV(49v). Debt re-enrolled.—VI(51),

ALDWORTHE, Alice, wife of [ ] Aldworthe, [ ], of 'Longe Coome', Oxfords. 12 mths recusancy from 26 Sept. 1586: conv. 7 Mar. 1587/8.—VIII(35v).

ALFORDE, Thomas, gent., of St. Bride par., Farringdon Ward Without, London. 3 mths recusancy from 25 Mar. 1587: conv. 10 July 1587.—VIII(38v).

ALKINTON, Alkington, Mary, 'spinster', of St. Dunstan par., Canterbury, Kent, wife of Samuel Alkinton, [ ], of the City of Canterbury. 9 mths recusancy ending 4 Mar. 1582/3, when convicted; and one later conviction dated 15 July 1583.—III(28v)*. Debts re-enrolled. V(30)*.

ALLEN, Thomas, 'yeoman', of Bedhampton, Hants. 2 mths recusancy from 25 Feb. 1586/7: conv. 26 Feb. 1587/8.—VIII(67).

ALLENSON, Isabel, 'spinster', of Wyresdale, Lancs. 12 mths recusancy from 20 Sept. 1589: conv. 22 Mar. 1590/1.—X(39v).

ALLETT, William, 'clericus'[2], of Southwark, Surrey [prisoner]. 4 mths recusancy ending 20 July 1584, when convicted. V(50v).

ALLOTT, Thomas, gent., of Stanfeild [Stainfield], Lindsey, Lincs. 10 mths recusancy from 9 Sept. 1586: conv. 28 Mar. 1588.—VIII(44v). Debt re-enrolled.—X(16v). Record of land-seizure, 12 Aug. 1588.— IX(40v). Rental of seized lands—IX(9), X(42), XI(42), XII(41). John Bendbow's lease of seized lands from 4 June 1590—X(16), XI(42), XII(41v).

---

1. John Adams (Cf. Anstruther I, pp. 1, 2)
2. William Allett (Cf. Anstruther I, p. 6, under Allot)

ALMON, Ann, spinster, of Whilpshire [Wilpshire], Lancs. 12 mths recusancy from 20 Sept. 1589: conv. 22 Mar. 1590/1—X(40v).

ALMOND, Robert, 'Taleor', of Dinckeley, Lancs. (same recusancy period and conviction date)—X(40v).

ALMOND, Margaret, his wife (same par., period and conviction date)— X(40v).

ALSOPP, Isabel, wife of Richard Alsopp, [ ], of Hamstall Ridware, Staffs. 8 mths recusancy from 1 Aug. 1585: conv. 13 Mar. 1585/6—VI(63v).

ALSTON, James, 'taleor', of Whalley, Lancs. 12 mths recusancy from 20 Sept. 1589: conv. 22 Mar. 1590/1—X(40).

ALTE, Aulte, Margaret, 'spinster', of Bubton [Bupton], Derbys. 10 mths recusancy from 9 Sept. 1586: conv. 22 Mar. 1587/8—VIII(21).

ALTE, Aulte, Mary, 'spinster' (same par., period & conviction date)— VIII(21).

ALTE, Aulte, Ralph, [ ], of Spital, par. of Barton [Blount], Derbys. (same period of conviction date)—VIII(21). Goods value £2 – 9 – 8 seized 27 Jan. 1588/9.—IX(17v).

ANDERTON, Alice, wid., of Euxton, Leyland par., Lancs. 4 mths recusancy from 18 Mar. (?)1585/6: conv. 8 Aug. 1586: and one later conviction dated 25 Mar. 1588—X(35), VIII(21v).

ANDERTON, Jane, 'spinster', of Westby, Lancs. 12 mths recusancy from 20 Sept. 1589: conv. 22 Mar. 1590/1—X(39v).

ANDROES, Gilbert, gent., of Ledbury, Herefords. 12 mths recusancy from 1 Sept. 1586: conv. 18 Mar. 1587/8—VIII(30).

ANNE, Alice, [ ], of Brotherton, W.R. Yorks. 6 mths recusancy from 3 July 1587: conv. 18 Mar. 1587/8—VIII(27). Goods value £20 seized 8 Apr. 1589.—IX(22v).

ANNE, George, esq., of Frickley, W.R. Yorks. 12 mths recusancy from 1 Apr. 1588: conv. [?]—XI(10v). Record of land-seizure, 25 Jan. 1590/1. (*ibid.*). Rental of seized lands—XII(24).

ANNE, Gervase, gent., of Frickley, Yorks. Rental of lands seized 28 Aug. 1591—XI(10v), XII(24). Seized lands let to John Twiste and George Hill from Mich. 1591—XII(11v).

ANSLOWE, Katherine, wid., of Castleton [Chastleton], Oxfords. 12 mths recusancy from 26 Sept. 1586: conv. 7 Mar. 1587/8—VIII(35). See ONSLOWE.

APPRICE, Elizabeth, 'spinster', of Tansor, Northants. 12 mths recusancy from 31 July 1587: conv. 4 Mar. 1588/9—IX(47).

APPRICE, John, gent., of Astwicke, Beds. 12 mths recusancy from 6 July 1587: conv. 12 Mar. 1588/9—IX(1v).

APPRICE, William, gent., of Higham Gobion, Beds. 3 mths recusancy from 29 Mar. 1587: conv. 20 Mar. 1587/8—VIII(1).

APRICE, Robert, esq., [of Washingley, Hunts.] 6 mths recusancy from 31 Mar. 1587. Fine (£120) paid 28 Nov. 1588—VIII(7v). Annual fine (£260) from 27 Sept. 1588 paid. Quit—IX(5v), X(6v), XI(6v), XII(6v).

APRICE, *alias* DAVIE, Richard, 'yeom", of Windlebury [Wendlebury], Oxfords. 12 mths recusancy from 26 Sept. 1586: conv. 7 Mar.

1587/8—VIII(35). See PRICE *alias* DAVIE, Alice, (wife).
ARDEN, Ann, wife of John Arden, gent., of Cottesford [Cottisford], Oxfords. 12 mths recusancy from 26 Sept. 1586: conv. 7 Mar. 1587/8—VIII(35).
ARDEN, Mary, wid., of Coughton, Warwicks. 3 mths recusancy from 12 May 1587: conv. 15 Mar. 1587/8—VIII(76).
ARDEN, Thomas, gent., of St. George's par., Southwark, Surrey. 5 mths recusancy from 17 Feb. 1586/7: conv. 17 July 1587—IX(54).
ARDINGTON, Beatrice, wife of Henry Ardington, gent., of West Ashall, Yorks. 2 mths recusancy from 4 Jan. 1585/6: conv. 14 Mar. 1585/6—VI(20v).
ARDINGTON, Katherine, wid., of Ardington [Arthington], W.R. Yorks. (same recusancy period and conviction date)—VI(20v). See ARTHINGTON.
ARMIGER, Grace, wid., of Swilland, Suff. 3 mths recusancy from 8 Apr. 1587: conv. 27 Mar. 1588—VIII(73).
ARNETT, Joan, wife of Roger Arnett, 'yom''', of Winterbourne [St] Martin, Dorset. 2 mths recusancy from 1 May 1587: conv. 4 Mar. 1587/8—VIII(19).
ARNOLD, Margery, wife of Thomas Arnold, 'yoman', of Hamstall Ridware, Staffs. 8 mths recusancy from 1 Aug. 1585: conv. 13 Mar. 1585/6: and a later conviction dated 1 Aug. 1586—VI(63v)*.
ARROWSMITHE, Jane, 'spinster', of Heydock [Haydock], Winwick par., Lancs. 12 mths recusancy from 30 July 1587: conv. 17 Mar. 1588/9—X(35).
ARROWSMITHE, Thurstan, 'husb', (of same par.) 3 mths recusancy from 10 Oct. 1581: conv. 18 Jan. 1581/2—II(38v). Debt re-enrolled—VIII(46).
ARROWSMITHE, Thurstan, 'husband''', of Salford, par. of Manchester, Lancs. [prisoner] 3 mths recusancy from 18 Jan. 1581/2: conv. 2 May 1582: and two later convictions, ending 22 Jan. 1583/4—II(38v)*, IV(37). Debts re-enrolled—IV(42v), VI(39), VIII(46)*.
ARRUNDELL, Sir John, knt, [of Cornwall] 14 mths recusancy from 1 Jan. 1586/7 to 29 Oct. 1588: fine (£280) paid. Quit—VIII(8). One year's recusancy from 29 Oct. 1588: fine (£260) paid. Quit—IX(6).
ARRUNDELL, John, esq., of London, *alias* of Lanherne, Cornwall. 3 mths recusancy from 1 Nov. 1591 to 7 Apr. 1592: fine (£60) paid. Quit—XI(7v). 6 mths recusancy from 7 Apr. 1592 to 22 Sept. 1592: fine (£120) paid. Quit—XII(7v).
ARTHINGTON, Rosamund, wife of Serill Arthington, esq., of Arthington, W.R. Yorks. 6 mths recusancy from 3 July 1587: conv. 18 Mar. 1587/8.—VIII(27). See ARDINGTON.
ASHEBURNHAM, John, esq., of Ashburnham, Sussex. 3 mths recusancy from 1 Nov. 1588: conv. 27 June 1589—IX(53). Record of land-seizure, 13 Apr. 1590—X(67). Summary of debts for recusancy, 22 Sept. 1589 to 18 Oct. 1592: 27 mths (£510)—XI(57).
ASHEBURNHAM, William, esq., of Ashburnham, Sussex. 2 mths

recusancy from 17 Apr. 1587: conv. 26 Feb. 1587/8—VIII(63v).
Record of land-seizure, 17 Jan. 1588/9—IX(54v). Rental of seized
lands—X(65v), XI(55v). Seized lands let to Thomas Palgrave and
John Murfyne from 2 Dec. 1590—X(67), XI(55v), XII(56v).

ASHECOMBE, 'Marthea', wife of Oliver Ashecombe, gent., of Liforde
[Lyford], Berks. 12 mths recusancy from 1 Sept. 1586: conv. 4 Mar.
1587/8—VIII(5).

ASPINWALL, Richard, 'schoolmaster', of Salford, par. of Manchester,
Lancs. [prisoner] 12 mths recusancy from 20 Feb. 1582/3: conv.
22 Jan. 1584/5—IV(37). Debt re-enrolled—IV(42v), VI(39).

ASPINWALL, Richard, 'scolem[aster]', of Lathom, Ormskirk par., Lancs.
12 mths recusancy from 30 July 1587: conv. 17 Mar. 1588/9—X(35).

ASPINWALL, Richard, 'husb'', of Bickerstaff, Ormskirk par., Lancs.
(same recusancy period and conviction date)—X(35).

ASSHETON, Margaret, of Bamfurlong, Lancs., wife of Richard Assheton,
[   ]. 12 mths recusancy from 20 Sept. 1589: conv. 22 Mar.
1590/1—X(38).

ASTELL, Henry, 'yoman', of St. George's par., Southwark, Surrey
[prisoner]. 5 mths recusancy from 17 Feb. 1586/7: conv. 17 July
1587—IX(54).

ASTON, William, gent., of Orforth [Orford], Warrington par., Lancs. 12
mths recusancy from 20 Sept. 1589: conv. 22 Mar. 1590/1—X(38).

ATKINS, Robert, 'yoman', of Borstall [Boarstall], Bucks. 3 mths recusancy
from 27 Mar. 1587: conv. 18 Mar. 1587/8—VIII(3).

ATKINSON, Alison, 'spinster', of Weeton, Lancs. 12 mths recusancy from
20 Sept. 1589: conv. 22 Mar. 1590/1—X(39).

ATKINSON, Margery, wid., of Exelby, N.R. Yorks. 13 mths recusancy
from 3 Sept. 1586: conv. 4 Sept. 1587—VIII(25v).

ATKYNSON, William, 'yom'', of Richmond, Yorks. (same recusancy
period and conviction date)—VIII(25v).

ATWOOD, Ann, wid., of Rowington, Warwicks. 7 mths recusancy from
12 July 1586: conv. 15 Mar. 1587/8—VIII(76).

ATWOOD, Margaret, wid., of Rockington [? Rowington], Warwicks. 1 mth
recusancy from 27 June 1588: conv. 5 Mar. 1588/9—IX(11v).

AUBERY, John, 'husb'', of Whiteparish, Wilts. 3 mths recusancy from
16 Apr. 1588: conv. 11 July 1588—VIII(74v).

AULTE, see ALTE.

AVIS, Thomas, 'fletcher', of Bury St. Edmund, Suff. 3 mths recusancy from
8 Apr. 1587: conv. 27 Mar. 1588—VIII(73).

AWDECOCK, Alice, wife of Thomas Awdecock, [   ], of the city of York. 4
mths recusancy from 28 Mar. 1581: conv. 17 July 1581—I(8). Debt re-
enrolled—III(10), V(8), VII(8), IX(8).

AWDLEY, Elizabeth, 'spinster', of Sporle, Norf. 2 mths recusancy from
24 Jan. 1588/9: conv. 7 July 1589—IX(45v). Debt re-enrolled—
XI(48).

AWDLEY, Margaret, wife of Philip Awdeley, esq., of Stowe Bedon, Norf. 3
mths recusancy from 13 Apr. 1587: conv. 1 Apr. 1588—VIII(54).

AWSTYNE, Roger, 'yoman', of Westminster, Middx [? prisoner]. 1 mth recusancy from 6 Oct. 1587: conv. 29 Jan. 1587/8—VIII(38v).

BABTHORPE, Grace, wife of Ralph Bapthorpe, esq., of Osgarbye [Osgodby], E.R. Yorks. 6 mths recusancy from 3 July 1587: conv. 18 Mar. 1587/8—VIII(25v).
BACHE, Katherine John, 'spinster', of Raglan, Mon. 5 mths recusancy from 24 Mar. 1586/7: conv. 13 Mar. 1587/8—VIII(48).
BACKWELL, Margaret, 'spinster', of Langford [Longford], Derbys. 10 mths recusancy from 9 Sept. 1586: conv. 22 Mar. 1587/8—VIII(21).
BACKWELL, Richard, 'husb'', (same par., recusancy period & conviction date)—VIII(21).
BACKWELL, Robert, 'husb'', (same par., recusancy period & conviction date)—VIII(21).
BADGER, Eleanor, wife of John Badger, gent., of Hanley Castle, Worcs. 6 mths recusancy from 29 Sept. 1587: conv. 25 July 1588—VIII(80v).
BADGER, William, 'yeoman', of Yeastley [Iffley], Oxfords. 12 mths recusancy from 26 Sept. 1586: conv. 7 Mar. 1587/8—VIII(35v).
BAILIE, Anthony, [ ], of Ashby Magna, Leics. 9 mths recusancy ending 10 Aug. 1587, when convicted—VIII(45v).
BAILIE, Katherine, wife of Thomas Bailie, 'yeom'', of Brodwell [Broadwell], Oxfords. 12 mths recusancy from 26 Sept. 1586: conv. 7 Mar. 1587/8—VIII(35).
BAKEN, Alice, 'spinster', of Langford [Longford], Derbys. 10 mths recusancy from 9 Sept. 1586: conv. 22 Mar. 1587/8—VIII(21).
BAKER, James, 'yom'', of Dorchester, Dorset. 5 mths recusancy from 23 Mar. 1583/4: conv. 24 Aug. 1584—IV(16v): and one later conviction dated 28 Feb. 1585/6—VI(16).
BAKER, John, 'yom'', of Yeatmister [Yetminster], Dorset. 10 mths recusancy from 1 May 1583: conv. Lent 1583/4—IV(16v).
BAKER, Philip, 'sacre theolog' doctor'[3], of St. Botolph's par., Bishopsgate Ward, London. 3 mths recusancy from 6 Oct. 1583: conv. 30 Dec. 1583—IV(32v). Debt re-enrolled—VI(34).
BAKER, Doctor, 'clericus'[3], of St. Mary Magdalene par., borough of Southwark, Surrey. 3 mths recusancy (period not specified): conv. 5 July 1588—VIII(63).
BAKER, Philip, gent., [3], of Stepney, London. 3 mths recusancy from 20 Mar. 1587/8: conv. 28 June 1588—IX(37).
BAKEWELL, Robert, 'husb'', of Hamstall Ridware, Staffs. 6 mths recusancy from 6 Sept. 1587: conv. 22 July 1588—VIII(58).

---

3. Philip Baker (Cf. *DNB* III, p. 14). Ordained deacon at Norwich, but no further ecclesiastical advancement traced (Cf. Venn). He was imprisoned in the Poultry Counter in Apr. 1584, and was three times indicted for recusancy in London, twice as a cleric (beginning 30 Dec. 1583), and finally (on 28 June 1588) as a layman. He was buried at St. Margaret's, Friday St., London on 12 Aug. 1590. A copy of his will (in which he describes himself as a 'preist') is PCC. Drury 57.

BALDWYNE, Alexander, 'milner', of Swynden [Swinden, nr Colne], Lancs. 12 mths recusancy from 20 Sept. 1589: conv. 22 Mar. 1590/1—X(40).

BALL, Robert, 'yom'', par. of St. Giles in the Fields, Middx. 3 mths recusancy from 21 Jan. 1586/7: conv. 31 May 1587—VIII(38v).

BAMBER, George, [ ], of Westby, Lancs. 12 mths recusancy from 20 Sept. 1589: conv. 22 Mar. 1590/1—X(39v).

BAMBER, [ ], his wife (same par., recusancy period & conviction date)— X(39v).

BAMFORD, Agnes, 'spinster', of Kircklangeley [Kirk Langley], Derbys. 10 mths recusancy from 9 Sept. 1586: conv. 22 Mar. 1587/8—VIII(21).

BAMFORD, Elizabeth, 'spinster', of West Hallam, Derbys. (same recusancy period & conviction date)—VIII(21).

BANCK, Elizabeth, wid., of Wrightington, Eccleston par., Lancs. 12 mths recusancy from 1 Aug. 1587: conv. 17 Mar. 1588/9—X(35).

BANCK, John, 'husb'' (same par., recusancy period & conviction date)— X(35).

BANISTER, Bannester, Ann, wid., of Hurstewood [Burnley par.], Lancs. 12 mths recusancy from 20 Sept. 1589: conv. 22 Mar. 1590/1—X(40).

BANISTER, Edward, gent., of Idsworth, Hants. 2 mths recusancy from 18 Mar. 1580/1: conv. 15 May 1581: and one later conviction dated 24 Apr. 1582—III(50v)*. Debts re-enrolled—V(56), VI(54). Record of land-seizure in Hants, 30 Oct. 1587—VIII(68v). Rental of lands seized in Hants—VIII(68v), X(69). Record of land-seizure in Hants, 22 Apr. 1588—VIII(67). Lands seized in Hants let to William Style from Mich. 1588—VIII(68v), IX(57v), X(68v), XI(59v), XII(60v). Record of land-seizure in Sussex, 20 Sept. 1587—VIII(63). Rental of seized lands in Sussex—VIII(64). Arrearage of rent: Sussex lands— X(66v), XI(57). Seized lands in Sussex let to Richard Bellingham from 6 Mar. 1588/9—X(65v), XI(55v), XII(56v).

BANISTER, James, gent., of Parkehill, [Whalley par.], Lancs. 12 mths recusancy from 20 Sept. 1589: conv. 22 Mar. 1590/1—X(40).

BARBOR, Ann, wife of John Barbor, 'yeoman', of St. Mary Magdalen par., Oxford City. 12 mths recusancy from 26 Sept. 1586: conv. 7 Mar. 1587/8—VIII(35v).

BARBOR, Thomas ap John, 'yoman', of Tregaier [Tregare], Mon. 12 mths recusancy from 3 July 1582: conv. 12 July 1583—III(45): and two later convictions ending 31 July 1584—IV(38v)*. Debts re-enrolled— II(38), V(40v), VI(40v)*.

BARBOR, Thomas John, 'yom'', of Tregaier [Tregare], Mon. 8 mths recusancy from 19 July 1585: conv. 1 Mar. 1585/6—VI(40v): and two later convictions ending 20 Mar. 1586/7—VI(40), (40v).

BARBOR, William, 'labourer', of Great Malvern, Worcs. 2 mths recusancy from 7 Apr. 1588: conv. 6 Mar. 1588/9—IX(70v).

BARHAM, Eliz., 'spinster', of par. of St. Dunstan, Canterbury, Kent [? prisoner]. 9 mths recusancy from 18 Mar. 1580/1, conviction undated—II(28): and three later convictions ending 22 Feb.

1583/4—III(28v)*, IV(12), V(30). Debt re-enrolled—VI(12).
BARKELEY, Lady Alice, wid., of Holborne, Middx. 2 mths recusancy from 2 July 1589: conv. 3 Dec. 1589—IX(37).
BARKER, Ann, 'spinster', of Dore, in Dron(e)feild par., Derbys. 10 mths recusancy from 9 Sept. 1586: conv. 22 Mar. 1587/8—VIII(21).
BARKER, John, 'husb'', of Charnock Richard, Lancs. 12 mths recusancy from 20 Sept. 1589: conv. 22 Mar. 1590/1—X(38).
BARKER, Laurence, 'clericus',[4] of Swinnerton [Swynnerton], Staffs. 12 mths recusancy from 6 Sept. 1586: conv. 25 Mar. 1588—VIII(78v).
BARLEY, Thomas, gent., of [   ] in Hathersage par., Derbys. 10 mths recusancy from 9 Sept. 1586: conv. 22 Mar. 1587/8—VIII(21).
BARLOWE, Alexander, esq., of Salford, Manchester par., Lancs. [prisoner] 13 mths recusancy from 6 May 1583: conv. 18 Mar. 1584/5—IV(46v). Debt re-enrolled—VI(39).
BARLOWE, Thomas, recusant, of Hathersedge [Hathersage], Derbys. Goods value £4 – 5 – 8 seized 27 Jan. 1588/9—IX(17v).
BARLOWE, Walter, 'clericus',[5] of Rydware Hamstall [Hamstall Ridware], Staffs. 4 mths recusancy from 31 Mar. 1582: conv. 2 Aug. 1582—II(14). Debt re-enrolled—IV(62), VI(63).
BARLOWE, Barloth, Walter, 'clericus', of Southwark, Surrey [prisoner].[5] 6 mths recusancy ending 18 Feb. 1584/5, when convicted—V(52v).
BARLOWE, Walter, 'clericus', 'lately of Stafford' [entry under 'Staff''].[5] 4 mths recusancy from 13 Mar. 1585/6: conv. 1 Aug. 1586—VI(63v).
BARMBYE, Beatrice, wife of Thomas Barmbye, gent., of Calthorne [Cawthorne], W.R. Yorks. 6 mths recusancy from 3 July 1587: conv. 18 Mar. 1587/8—VIII(25v). [See Barnabye, Barneby]
BARNABYE, Thomas, gent., of Barnabye Hall, W.R. Yorks. Fined £50 by High Commissioners for 'contempt of court', 1585[6]—V(23v).
BARNARD, Joan, wid., of Staunton Harecourt [Stanton Harcourt], Oxfords. 12 mths recusancy from 26 Sept. 1586: conv. 7 Mar. 1587/8—VIII(35v).
BARNEBY, Beatrice, wife of Thomas Barneby, esq., of Barneby [Barnby-upon-Don: W.R.], Yorks. 2 mths recusancy from 4 Jan. 1585/6: conv. 14 Mar. 1585/6—VI(20v).

---

4. Laurence Baker Unidentified. Possibly one of the priests serving the Fitzherberts of Swynnerton, Staffs.
5. Walter Barlow A pre-Elizabethan priest, he was imprisoned for four months in the Marshalsea in 1582 (Cf. *CRS* II, p. 240.). He seems to have been domiciled in Staffs., and was apparently another chaplain often employed by the Fitzherberts.
6. Three Yorkshire Catholics had been ordered to bring their wives before the High Commissioners on Monday after Michaelmas Day (4 Oct. 1585) to answer for their continuous refusal to attend the Anglican church services. They were John Palmes of Naburne, ER Yorks, esq., (Cf. footnote 228), Thomas Barnabye, and George Fowbery of Newbald, ER Yorks., (Cf. footnote 89). Neither Palmes, nor his wife appeared. Barnabye and Fowbery both appeared, but without their wives... 'quia uxores suas divinis officiis in ecclesia interesse recusantes et abhorrentes, tunc secum introducere neglexerunt'. When the High Commission met at Bishopthorpe on Tuesday 2 Nov. 1585 (Cf. M.R., Q.R., 28 Eliz., Hilary Term, 'recorda'.— E.159/390, rotulet 207.) under Edwin Sandys, Archbishop of York, Palmes was fined £100 for this 'manifest contempt and contumacy'. Barnaby and Fowberry were fined £50 each (q.v.)

BARNES, 'Avis', 'spinster', of Hanley Castle, Worcs. 12 mths recusancy from 20 Sept. 1586: conv. 28 Mar. 1588—VIII(77).
BARNES, Margaret, 'spinster' (same parish, period, and conviction date)—VIII(77).
BARNES, Thomas, 'yeoman' (same parish, period, and conviction date)—VIII(77).
BARNES, Margaret, his wife (same parish, period, and conviction date)—VIII(77).
BARNEY, Ralph, gent., of Marten [Merton], Norfolk. 3 mths recusancy from 13 Apr. 1587: conv. 1 Apr. 1588.—VIII(54). Record of land-seizure, 18 Oct. 1588—IX(45). Rental of lands seized 18 Oct. 1588—IX(45)*, X(52v), XI(46v), XII(47v).
BARON, Isabel, [   ], of Charnock Richard, Lancs. 12 mths recusancy from 20 Sept. 1589: conv. 22 Mar. 1590/1—X(38v).
BARON, Laurence, 'laborer', of Great Crosby, Lancs (same recusancy period and conviction date)—X(38).
BARRETT, Eliz., 'spinster', of Chippenham, Cambs. 10 mths recusancy from 1 Sept. 1586: conv. 24 Mar. 1587/8—VIII(7v).
BARRETT, Ursula, 'spinster', of Kirtleton [? Kirtlington], Oxfords. 12 mths recusancy from 26 Sept. 1586: conv. 7 Mar. 1587/8—VIII(35v).
BARROWE, Henry, gent., of St. Sepulchre par., Farringdon Ward Without London [prisoner][7]. 12 mths recusancy from 18 Apr. 1587: conv. 30 Apr. 1588—VIII(38v).
BARROWE, Henry, gent., of Thornage, Norfolk. 3 mths recusancy from 13 Apr. 1587: conv. 1 Apr. 1588—VIII(54).
BARROWE, Jane, wife of James Barrowe, esq., of Bullingham, in the par. of St. Martin, Hereford. 12 mths recusancy from 26 June 1581: conv. 26 June 1582—II(64). And 9 later convictions, ending 3 Aug. 1584—II(64)*, III(27), IV(64v)*, V(26), (26v)*.
BARROWE, Jane, wid., of Bullingham, in the par. of St. Martin, Hereford. 2 mths recusancy from 2 Jan. 1584/5: conv. ult. Feb. 1584/5—V(26v). And 2 later convictions, ending 25 July 1586—V(26v), VI(25).
BARROWE, Jane, wid., of the par. of St. Nicholas, Hereford. 2 mths recusancy from 13 Dec. 1585: conv. 10 Feb. 1585/6—VI(25). And one later conviction dated 18 Mar. 1586/7—VI(25).
BARTON, Ann, wid., of Barton Roo, Lancs. 4 mths recusancy from 18 Mar. 1580/1: conviction undated—VI(40v). Goods value £40 – 10s seized 24 Oct. 1587—X(40v). Record of lands seized 24 Oct. 1587—X(40v). Rental of lands seized 24 Oct. 1587—XII(44).
BARTON, Godfrey, 'yoman', of Westminster [prisoner]. 3 mths recusancy from 20 Mar. 1587/8: conv. 28 June 1588—IX(37).

---

7. Henry Barrowe A founder of Congregationalism (Cf. *DNB*.), he was executed at Tyburn, 6 Apr. 1593, for publishing seditious tracts. See footnote 104.

BARTON, John, 'son of Richard Barton, esq., deceased', of Barton, Broughton par., Lancs. 3 mths recusancy from 21 May 1587: conv. 25 Mar. 1588—VIII(21v).

BARTON, Sybil, 'spinster', of Hanley, Worcs. 2 mths recusancy from 7 Apr. 1588: conv. 6 Mar. 1588/9—IX(70v).

BASSETT, Joan, wid., of the par. of Chishull [? Cheesehill St. Peter, Winchester], Hants. 2 mths recusancy from 18 Mar. 1580/1: conviction undated—III(50v). And one later conviction, ? in Oct. 1582. Debts re-enrolled—V(56)*.

BASTERD, Bastard, Francis, gent., of Newington, Middx. 12 mths recusancy from 2 Jan. 1582/3: conv. 20 Jan. 1583/4—IV(32v). On same day[8], convicted also of hearing Mass on 1 Dec. 1583 in St. Bride's par., Farringdon Ward Without London (fined 100 marks).— IV(32v). Both debts re-enrolled—VI(34).

BASTION, Eliz., wife of William Bastion of Saunderton, Bucks., 'yeoman'. 3 mths recusancy from 27 Mar. 1587: conv. 18 Mar. 1588—VIII(3).

BAUGHE, Leonard, 'yoman', of Cumberton [? Comberton], Worcs. 2 mths recusancy from 7 Apr. 1588: conv. 6 Mar. 1588/9—IX(70v).

BAXTER, Francis, gent., of Marten [Merton], Norfolk. 3 mths recusancy from 13 Apr. 1587: conv. 1 Apr. 1588—VIII(54).

BEAKE, John, gent., of par. of St. Dunstan, Canterbury, Kent [? prisoner]. 9 mths recusancy from 18 Mar. 1590/1, conviction undated—II(28): and three later convictions, ending 22 Feb. 1583/4—III(28v)*, IV(12), V(30). Debt re-enrolled—VI(12).

BEAND [? Beavan], Merrick, 'yoman', of Llanthewy Skirrid, Mon. 5 mths recusancy from 24 Mar. 1586/7: conv. 13 Mar. 1587/8—VIII(48v).

BEANE [? Beavan], Joan David Powell, wife of John Morgan Beane, [   ], of Usk, Mon. (same recusancy period and conviction date)—VIII(49).

BECKETT, Robert, esq./gent., of Southwark, Surrey [prisoner]. 10 mths recusancy ending 11 Mar. 1582/3, when convicted: and 2 later convictions, ending 20 July 1584—IV(49v)*, V(52v). Debt re-enrolled—VI(51).

BECKETT, Robert, esq., of Cortider [Cartuther manor house], Cornwall. Goods value 18s seized 11 Jan. 1588/9—X(8). Rental of lands seized 11 Jan. 1588/9—X(8). John Wingfeild's lease, dated Ladyday 1589, of seized lands—IX(6), X(8), XI(7), XII(7).

BECKWITH, Katherine, wife of Thomas Beckwith, gent., of Killinghall, Ripley par., W.R. Yorks. 13 mths recusancy from 3 Sept. 1586: conv. 4 Sept. 1587—VIII(25v).

BECONSHAWE, John, gent., of Southwark, Surrey [prisoner]. 10 mths recusancy ending 11 Mar. 1582/3, when convicted: and 2 later convictions, ending 20 July 1584—IV(49v)*, V(50v). Debt re-enrolled—VI(51).

---

8. Francis Basterd was committed to Newgate, 10 Jan. 1583/4, and was still there 30 Sept. 1584. (Cf. *CRS* II, pp. 237, 284.)

BECONSHAWE, Beconsawe, William, gent., of the Soke of Winton, par. of Chishull [Cheesehill] St. Peter, Hants. 18 mths recusancy from 15 May 1581, conviction undated—III(50v): and three later convictions ending (? Sept.) 1584—IV(53), V(56v)*. Debts re-enrolled—V(56), VI(54).

BEDINGFEILD, Bedingefeild, Bedingfeld, Adam, gent., of Felmingham, Norfolk. 3 mths recusancy from 13 Apr. 1587: conv. 1 Apr. 1588—VIII(54).

BEDINGFEILD, Edmund, gent., of Oxeborough [Oxborough], Norf. (same recusancy period and conviction date)—VIII(54).

BEDINGFEILD, Edmund, gent., of Westleton, Suffolk. 3 mths recusancy from 8 Apr. 1587: conv. 27 Mar. 1588—VIII(73).

BEDINGFEILD, Eliz., wid., of Holme Hale, Norf. 3 mths recusancy from 13 Apr. 1587: conv. 1 Apr. 1588—VIII(54). Record of land-seizure, 18 Oct. 1588—IX(45). Rental of lands seized 18 Oct. 1588—X(52v), XI(46v), XII(47v).

BEDINGFEILD, Henry, esq., of Oxborough, Norf. 9 mths recusancy from 1 July 1582: conv. 10 Mar. 1583/4—IV(44v).

BEDINGFEILD, Henry, gent., of Oxborough, Norf. 3 mths recusancy from 13 Apr. 1587: conv. 1 Apr. 1588—VIII(54).

BEDINGFEILD, Humphrey, esq., of Depeham [Deopham], Norf. 11 mths recusancy from 1 Aug. 1581: conv. 23 July 1582—II(40). Debt re-enrolled—III(72v), IV(40).

Four fines, each of 100 marks, incurred for hearing Mass said by William Richar, alias Gardiner[9], at Quidenham, Norfolk, in the 'mansion house' of Anthony Twaites, gent., on the following dates, 6 May 1583, 1 July 1583, 2 Sept. 1583 and 16 Sept. 1583, 'against the form of the statute' [23 Eliz., c. 1 (1581)]; convictions undated—IV(44v).

8 mths recusancy from 12 July 1583: conv. Lent 1583/4—IV(44v), and three later convictions, ending Lent 1586/7—V(46v)*, VI(25v). Debts (for recusancy) re-enrolled—V(41v), VI(41v), VII(41)*. Record of land-seizure, 26 Sept. 1587—VIII(51). Rental of lands seized 26 Sept. 1587—VIII(6v), IX(43v), X(52v), XI(46v). Richard Weston's lease, from 29 May 1590, of seized lands—X(81), XI(46v), XII(47v).

BEDINGFEILD, John, esq., of Redlingfeld [Redlingfield], Suffolk. 35 mths recusancy ending 7 July 1583, when convicted—VI(58): and two later convictions, ending 10 July 1588—VI(58)*, VIII(73). Debt re-enrolled—X(64). Lands seized and let by Crown to William Dunston, as from 14 June 1588—VIII(72), IX(63), X(63), XI(65), XII(66).

BEDINGFEILD, Margaret, his wife. 3 mths recusancy from 8 Apr. 1587: conv. 27 Mar. 1588—VIII(73).

BEDINGFEILD, Laurence, gent., of Holme Hale, Norf. 3 mths recusancy from 13 Apr. 1587: conv. 1 Apr. 1588—VIII(54).

---

9. Humphrey Bedingfield (Cf. *CRS* XXII, p. 56 footnote.)

BEDINGFEILD, 'Nazarena', 'spinster', of Oxborough, Norf. (same recusancy period and conviction date)—VIII(54).
BEDINGFEILD, Thomas, gent., of Felmingham, Norf. (same recusancy period and conviction date)—VIII(54).
BEE, Robert, 'carpenter', of Barnacre [Garstang], Lancs. 12 mths recusancy from 20 Sept. 1589: conv. 22 Mar. 1590/1—X(39).
BEISLEY, Richard, 'yoman' (same parish, recusancy period and conviction date)—X(39).
BELL, James, 'clericus'[10], of Salford in the parish of Manchester, Lancs. [prisoner]. 12 mths recusancy from 20 Feb. 1582/3: conv. 22 Jan. 1583/4—IV(37). Debt re-enrolled—IV(42v), VI(39).
   [11]Fine of 200 marks incurred for saying a private Mass on 27 Dec. 1583 at Golburne [Golborne], Lancs., 'in the house of a certain Lucy; against the form of a statute of the first year [sic] of the said Queen's reign, upon which he was convicted'—IV(37). Debt re-enrolled—IV(42v), VI(39).
BELLAMY, Ann, 'spinster', of Harrow(e), Middx. 3 mths recusancy from 6 June 1587: conv. 1 Dec. 1587—VIII(38v).
BELLAMY, Faith ('Fides'), 'spinster' (same parish, recusancy period and conviction date).—VIII(38v).
BELLAMY, Katherine, wife of Richard Bellamy, gent., of Harrowe, Middx. (same recusancy period and conviction date).—VIII(38v).
BELLAMY, Mary, 'spinster' (same parish, recusancy period and conviction date).—VIII(38v).
BELLAMY, Robert, gent., of St. Botolph's par., Bishopsgate Ward Without London. Fine of 100 marks incurred for hearing Mass in his house, situated in the above parish of St. Botolph, said on 30 Jan. 1585/6 by William Thomson, alias Blackborn, lately of London, 'clericus'[12]. Bellamy was convicted and fined for this offence at the Old Bailey, London, on 18 Apr. 1586. With him were similarly convicted and fined, for hearing the same Mass, the following five laymen (*q.v.*): Richard Webster, Roger Lyne, Richard Reighnoldes, Benjamin Stockwithe and William Higham.—VI(34v).
BELLAMY, Thomas, gent., of Harrowe, Middx. 3 mths recusancy from 6 June 1587: conv. 1 Dec. 1587—VIII(38v).
BELLOUS, 'Jenetta', 'spinster', of Ledston, W.R. Yorks. 6 mths recusancy from 3 July 1587: conv. 18 Mar. 1587/8—VIII(27).
BELSON, Ann, wid., of Ixill [Ixhill] Lodge, Okeley [Oakley], Bucks. 3 mths recusancy from 27 Mar. 1587: conv. 18 Mar. 1587/8—VIII(3).
BELSON, Augustine, gent., of Okeley [Oakley], Bucks. (same recusancy period and conviction date)—VIII(3).

---

10. James Bell (Cf. Challoner, pp. 100, 101.)
11. A clerical error is evident here. The amount of the fine imposed for saying Mass (200 marks) indicates that the Statute upon which he was convicted was not 'I Eliz. c.1', but '23 Eliz. c.1'. The trial took place at the Sessions of the Peace, Manchester, on 22 Jan. 1583/4.
12. Robert Bellamy sheltered William Thomson, *alias* Blackburn, who was martyred at Tyburn in 1586, for saying mass in his house. (Cf. Anstruther I, p. 351, under Thomson.)

BELSON, Eleanor, 'spinster', of Oakley, Bucks. (same recusancy period and conviction date)—VIII(3).
BELSON, Isabel, 'spinster', wife of William Belson of Brill, Bucks. (same recusancy period and conviction date)—VIII(3).
BELSON, Margaret, wife of Augustine Belson of Brill, Bucks. (same recusancy period and conviction date)—VIII(3).
BELSON, Thomas, gent., of Oakley, Bucks.[13] 12 mths recusancy from 18 Mar. 1587/8: conv. 23 June 1589—IX(70).
BELSTONE [BELSON], Augustine, gent., of Okeley [Oakley], Bucks., with Ann Belstone [Belson], wid., of Ixhill Lodge, Bucks., recusants.
    Two-thirds of lands at Ixhill Lodge, Brill and Oakley seized [date not mentioned], and let by Crown to Richard Brewster, gent., from 4 Jan. 1589/90. Lease cancelled in Hilary term 1589/90. Brewster discharged; ref. in annotation[14]—IX(1v).
BENCE, Richard, 'husb''', of Stonehouse, Gloucs. 5 mths recusancy from 26 Mar. 1587: conv. 11 Mar. 1587/8—VIII(82).
BENNETT, Ann, 'spinster', of Westby, Lancs. 12 mths recusancy from 20 Sept. 1589: conv. 22 Mar. 1590/1—X(39v).
BENNETT, Eliz., of Westby, Lancs., wife of William Bennett, (same recusancy period and conviction date)—X(39v).
BENNETT, Ellen, of Westby, Lancs., wife of George Bennett, 'husb''', (same recusancy period and conviction date)—X(39v).
BENNETT, Jane, wife of Thomas Bennett, 'husb''', (same parish, recusancy period and conviction date)—X(39v).
BENTLEY, Katherine, of Bentley in the par. of Langford [Longford], Derbys., wife of Edward Bentley [ ]. 10 mths recusancy from 9 Sept. 1586: conv. 22 Mar. 1587/8—VIII(21).
BERISFORD, Humphrey, gent., of Fennibentlie [Fenny Bentley], Derbys. 10 mths recusancy from 9 Sept. 1586: conv. 22 Mar. 1587/8—VIII(21). Record of property seized 13 Apr. 1588 for the satisfaction of a 'pre-1587' debt of £1,220 for recusancy (cf. statute 28 Eliz., cap. 6): i.e. two-thirds of an annuity of £5 granted to Berisford, 'during the term of his imprisonment', by the will of Francis Rolston of Mayfeild, Staffs., esq., defunct, the executors being Mary, relict of the said Francis Rolston, and John Vernon of Sudbury, Derbys., esq.— VIII(20v), (21v).

---

13. Thomas Belson, third son of Augustine Belson, gent., of Brill, Bucks., and Margaret Scarning, his wife, was executed, 5 July 1589, for assisting two priests in Oxford—George Nichols and Richard Yaxley—who were executed immediately before him. (Cf. *CRS* X, p. 254 footnote.)

14. A fuller specification of the seized lands shows 'one messuage called Ixhill Lodge and 40 acres of arable land, lying in the common fields of the neighbouring towns (Brill and Oakley), and 30 acres of meadow and pasture which they occupy in demesne to the said Lodge, with the keeping of Her Majesty's game in Ixhill and Titherslade parcel of Her Majesty's forest of Barnewood, being worth yearly by estimation £13 – 6 – 8. William, second son of Augustine, claimed that the said lands had been granted to him by indenture dated 20 Apr. 1582. William was not a convicted recusant. Sir John Popham, Attorney General, agreed that the lands should be returned to William. This was done by the Barons of the Exchequer. (Cf. M.R., L.T.R., 31 Eliz., Hilary Term, 'Recorda' section—E.368/454, mem. 133.)

BERKELEY, William, 'laborer', of Wendlebury, Oxfords. 12 mths recusancy from 26 Sept. 1586: conv. 7 Mar. 1587/8—VIII(35v).

BESLYN, Thomas, 'yoman', of Wilton, Wilts. 3 mths recusancy from 16 Apr. 1588: conv. 11 July 1588—VIII(74v).

BETHAM, Joan, 'spinster', of Adwell, Oxfords. 12 mths recusancy from 26 Sept. 1586: conv. 7 Mar. 1587/8—VIII(35v).

BETHAM, Nicholas, gent., (of same parish, same recusancy period and conviction date)—VIII(35v).

BETHAM, Robert, gent. (same parish, recusancy period and conviction date)—VIII(35v).

BETTAIN, Margery, wife of Christopher Bettain, gent., of Adwell, Oxfords. (same recusancy period and conviction date)—VIII(35).

BEZANTE, Eliz., 'spinster', of St. Saviour's par., Southwark, Surrey [? prisoner]. 3 mths recusancy [undated]: conv. 5 July 1588—VIII(63).

BICKARDICK, Eliz., [ ], of Kirke Dighton [Kirk Deighton], W.R. Yorks. 6 mths recusancy from 3 July 1587: conv. 18 Mar. 1587/8—VIII(27).

BICKERSON, Anthony, 'yeoman', of Bidford [-on-Avon], Warwicks. 3 mths recusancy from 12 May 1587: conv. 15 Mar. 1587/8—VIII(76).

BICKERSON, [ ], 'spinster', his wife (same parish, recusancy period and conviction date)—VIII(76).

BIDDOLPHE, Richard, gent., of Biddulph(e), Staffs. 6 mths recusancy from 6 Sept. 1587: conv. 22 July 1588.—VIII(58).

BIGGE, Cicily, [ ], of Cromarshe [Crowmarsh], Oxfords. 12 mths recusancy from 26 Sept. 1586: conv. 7 Mar. 1587/8.—VIII(35v).

BIRCHE, Burche, Edward, 'husb'', of Malsall [? Walsall], Staffs. 6 mths recusancy from 6 Sept. 1587: conv. 22 July 1588—VIII(58). Goods value £33 – 3s seized 4 Sept. 1589—X(14). Record of land-seizure, 4 Sept. 1589—X(78v). Rental of lands seized 4 Sept. 1589—X(7v), XI(64v), XII(65v).

BIRCHE, *alias* of COWPER, Thomas.

BIRCHELL, Edmund, [ ], of Etwall, Derbys. 10 mths recusancy from 9 Sept. 1586: conv. 22 Mar. 1587/8.—VIII(21).

BLACK, Edward, 'yoman', of Bledlowe, Bucks. 3 mths recusancy from 27 Mar. 1587: conv. 18 Mar. 1587/8.—VIII(3).

BLACKWALL, James, 'laborer', of Padley, Hatherseche [Hathersage] parish, Derbys. 12 mths recusancy from 1 July 1587: conv. 14 Mar. 1588/9.—IX(17v).

BLAKEY, John, 'batcheler', of Colne, Lancs. 12 mths recusancy from 20 Sept. 1589: conv. 22 Mar. 1590/1.—X(40).

BLEASDALE, Henry, 'husb'', of Chipping, Lancs. (same recusancy period and conviction date)—X(39).

BLENKYNSOPP, Henry, esq., of 'Burghe subtus Staynmore' [Brough under Stainmore], Westmld. 1 mth recusancy from 1 June 1588: conv. 5 Aug. 1588.—IX(69).

BLENKYNSOPP, Margery, wid., (same parish, recusancy period and conviction date)—IX(69).

BLISSARD, Ann, wife of William Blissard, 'husb'', of Evesham, Worcs. 6 mths recusancy from 29 Sept. 1587: conv. 25 July 1588.—VIII(80v).

BLOCKEWOOD, Richard, 'yeoman', of Charsfeild, Suff. 3 mths recusancy from 8 Apr. 1587: conv. 27 Mar. 1588.—VIII(73).

BLOMER, Martha, wife of William Blomer, gent., of Hatherop(p), Gloucs. 5 mths recusancy from 26 Mar. 1587: conv. 11 Mar. 1587/8.— VIII(82).

BLUNDELL, Eliz., wid., of Preston, Lancs. 13 mths recusancy from 30 July 1587: conv. 17 Mar. 1588/9.—X(35).

BLUNDELL, Ellen, wife of Thomas Blundell, 'yoman', of Carreside, Lancs. 12 mths recusancy from 20 Sept. 1589: conv. 22 Mar. 1590/1.—X(38).

BLUNDELL, Henry, 'servingman', of Much Crosby, Lancs. (same recusancy period and conviction date)—X(38).

BLUNDELL, Margery, Margaret, 'spinster', of Crosbie, parish of Sefton, Lancs. 13 mths recusancy from 30 July 1587: conv. 17 Mar. 1588/9: and one later conviction dated 22 Mar. 1590/1.—X(35), (38).

BLUNDELL, Margery, wid., of Carreside, relict of William Blundell. 12 mths recusancy from 20 Sept. 1589: conv. 22 Mar. 1590/1.—X(38).

BLUNDELL, Mary, wife of Robert Blundell, gent., of Inceblundell [Ince Blundell], Lancs. (same recusancy period and conviction date)—X(38).

BLUNDELL, Richard, esq., of Crosbie, Sephton [Sefton] par., Lancs. 13 mths recusancy from 14 Aug. 1596: conv. 25 Mar. 1588: and one later conviction dated 22 Mar. 1590/1.—VIII(21v), X(38). Richard Urmeston's lease, from 12 Nov. 1591, of lands seized 1 Sept. 1591.— XII(44).

BLUNDELL, Ann, his wife, of Crosby, Lancs. 12 mths recusancy from 20 Sept. 1589: conv. 22 Mar. 1590/1.—X(38).

BLUNDELL, Richard, junior, gent., of Crosbie, Sefton par., Lancs. 13 mths recusancy from 30 July 1587: conv. 17 Mar. 1588/9: and one later conviction dated 22 Mar. 1590/1.—X(35), (38).

BLUNDELL, Robert, 'husb'', of Ince Blundell, Lancs. 12 mths recusancy from 20 Sept. 1589: conv. 22 Mar. 1590/1.—X(38).

BLUNDELL, 'Jenetta', his wife (same parish, recusancy period and conviction date)—X(38).

BLUNDELL, William, gent., of Crosbye, parish of Sefton, Lancs. 13 mths recusancy from 14 Aug. 1586: conv. 25 Mar. 1588: and one later conviction dated 17 Mar. 1588/9.—VIII(21v), X(35)*.

BLUNDELL, 'Evelina', of Crosby, Lancs., wife of William Blundell. 12 mths recusancy from 20 Sept. 1589: conv. 22 Mar. 1590/1.—X(38).

BLUNDELL, William, of Crosby, Lancs., son of Richard Blundell, esq. (same recusancy period and conviction date as preceding entry)— X(38).

BLUNTE, Eliz., 'spinster', of Asteley [Astley], Worcs. 12 mths recusancy from 20 Sept. 1586: conv. 28 Mar. 1588: and one later conviction dated 25 July 1588.—VIII(77), (80v).

BLUNTE, Francis, gent., of Alchurch [Alvechurch], Worcs. 6 mths recusancy from 29 Sept. 1587: conv. 25 July 1588.—VIII(80v).

BLUNTE, Isabel, wid., of Blithebury [Blithbury], Staffs., 'supposed recusant and fugitive'. Record of land-seizure, 4 Sept. 1589—X(78v). Rental of lands seized 4 Sept. 1589—X(7v), XI(64v), XII(65v)[15].

BLUNTE, Thomas, gent., of Alchurche [Alvechurch], Worcs. 2 mths recusancy from 7 Apr. 1588: conv. 6 Mar. 1588/9.—IX(70v).

BLUNTE, Thomas, gent., of Astley, Worcs. 7 mths recusancy from 1 July 1589: conv. [26 Feb.?] 1589/90. Record of land-seizure, 16 Oct. 1590.—X(75v). Rental of lands seized 16 Oct. 1590.—X(51v), XI(70), XII(71).

BLUNTE, Frances, wife of Thomas Blunte, gent., of Astley, Worcs. 12 mths recusancy from 1 Apr. 1587: conv. 28 Mar. 1588: and one later conviction dated 15 July 1588.—VIII(80), (80v).

BLUNTE, Walter, gent., of Southwark, Surrey [prisoner]. 10 mths recusancy ending 11 Mar. 1582/3, when convicted; and 6 later convictions ending 16 Feb. 1586/7.—III(58v), IV(49v)*, V(50v), (52v)*, VI(49v), (50)*, (51). Lands at Kinston [? Kingstone], Utceter [Uttoxeter], Staffs., seized and let by Crown to Hugh Cuffe, gent., from Michaelmas 1585—VI(33v), VIII(16v), XI(64v), XII(65v).

BOBINSON, William, 'yeoman', of Watlington, Oxfords. 12 mths recusancy from 26 Sept. 1586: conv. 7 Mar. 1587/8.—VIII(35v).

BOBINSON, Margery, his wife (same parish, recusancy period and conviction date)—VIII(35v).

BOLBETT, Richard, 'yoman', of St. Saviour's par., Southwark, Surrey [prisoner]. 5 mths recusancy ending 17 Feb. 1586/7, when convicted.—VI(50).

BOMIELL, Agnes, wid., of Eynsham, Oxfords. 12 mths recusancy from 26 Sept. 1586: conv. 7 Mar. 1587/8.—VIII(35v).

BOLTE, Hugh, gent., of Church Eaton, Staffs. 12 mths recusancy from 6 Sept. 1586: conv. 25 Mar. 1588.—VIII(78v).

BOLTON, Adam, 'yoman', of Salebury [Salesbury], Blackburn par., Lancs. 1 mth recusancy from 30 June 1588: conv. 17 Mar. 1588/9: and 1 later conviction dated 22 Mar. 1590/1.—X(35), (40).

BOLTON, Jane, his wife (of same parish). 12 mths recusancy from 20 Sept. 1589: conv. 22 Mar. 1590/1.—X(40v).

BOLTON, 'Adria', wid., of Overhilton [Over Hulton], Deane par., Lancs. 2 mths recusancy from 2 June 1588: conv. 17 Mar. 1588/9.—X(35).

BOLTON, Frances, 'spinster', of Dinckley, Lancs. 12 mths recusancy from 20 Sept. 1589: conv. 22 Mar. 1590/1.—X(40v).

BOLTON, John, 'clericus'[16], of St. George's par., Southwark, Surrey [prisoner]. 5 mths recusancy from 17 Feb. 1586/7: conv. 17 July 1587.—IX(54).

---

15. The seized lands of Isabel Blunte at Blithbury, Staffs., were discharged in 1591. (Cf. M.R., L.T.R., 35 Eliz., Michaelmas Term, 'Recorda' section.)

16. John Bolton (Cf. Anstruther I, p. 43.)

BOLTON, Lancelot, 'yoman', of Salesbury, Blackburn par., Lancs. 1 mth recusancy from 30 June 1588: conv. 17 Mar. 1588/9.—X(35).

BOLTON, Nicholas, gent., of Salesbury, Blackburn par., Lancs. 3 mths recusancy from 2 May 1588: conv. 17 Mar. 1588/9.—X(35). Record of lands seized 18 Sept. 1590—X(37). Richard Bolton's lease, from 19 Nov. 1590, of lands seized 1 Oct. 1590.—XII(44).

BOLTON, Nicholas, 'yoman', of Salesbury, Lancs. 12 mths recusancy from 20 Sept. 1589: conv. 22 Mar. 1590/1.—X(40).

BOLTON, Richard, 'husbandman', of Litherland, Lancs. 12 mths recusancy from 20 Sept. 1589: conv. 22 Mar. 1590/1.—X(38).

BOLTON, Thomas, 'taleor', of Blackburn, Lancs. 12 mths recusancy from 20 Sept. 1589: conv. 22 Mar. 1590/1.—X(40v).

BOLTON, Ann, his wife (same parish, recusancy period and conviction date)—X(40v).

BOOTIE, Richard, 'yeoman', of Burgate, Suffolk. 3 mths recusancy from 8 Apr. 1587: conv. 27 Mar. 1588.—VIII(73).

BORANI, Martha, wife of Thomas Borani, gent., of Morley, Norfolk. 3 mths recusancy from 13 Apr. 1587: conv. 1 Apr. 1588.—VIII(54).

BOST, 'Jenetta', wid., of Duston [Dufton], Westmld. 1 mth recusancy from 1 June 1588: conv. 5 Aug. 1588.—IX(69).

BOTOMLEY, Alice, wid., of Arkendal(e), Knarisburghe [Knaresborough] parish, W.R. Yorks. 13 mths recusancy from 3 Sept. 1586: conv. 4 Sept. 1587.—VIII(25v).

BOURNE, Borne, John, gent., of Chesterton, Oxfords. 12 mths recusancy from 26 Sept. 1586: conv. 7 Mar. 1587/8.—VIII(35).

BOURNE, Winifrid, his wife (same parish, recusancy period and conviction date).—VIII(35v).

BOURNE, William, gent., of Wendlebury, Oxfords. 8 mths recusancy from 4 July 1583: conv. 27 Feb. 1583/4: and 6 later convictions, ending 7 Mar. 1587/8.—IV(29)*. V(47)*. VI(30v), (47v)*. VIII(35). Richard Ferris' lease, from 27 July 1591, of lands seized 17 Apr. 1591.—XII(54).

BOURNE, Margery, his wife (of same parish). 12 mths recusancy from 26 Sept. 1586: conv. 7 Mar. 1587/8.—VIII(35v).

BOWATER, Richard, 'yeoman', of St. Michael's parish, Lewes, Sussex [? prisoner]. 7 mths recusancy ending 8 Mar. 1582/3, when convicted.—III(58v). Debt re-enrolled—V(52v).

BOWES, Joan, wife of William Bowes, gent., of Upsall, N.R. Yorks. 6 mths recusancy from 3 July 1587: conv. 18 Mar. 1587/8.—VIII(25v).

BOWLINGE, Constance, of Charnock Richard, Lancs., wife of Hugh Bowlinge, 'husb". 12 mths recusancy from 20 Sept. 1589: conv. 22 Mar. 1590/1.—X(38v).

BOWLINGE, John, [   ], son of Hugh Bowlinge, 'husb", of Charnock Richard, Lancs. (same recusancy period and conviction date)—X(38v).

BOWMAN, William, of the city of York, 'lockesmith'. 4 mths recusancy from 26 Mar. 1582: conv. (?) July 1582.—II(8). Debt re-enrolled

V(8). VII(8). IX(8).

BOWMAN, Isabel, his wife (same city, recusancy period and conviction date).—II(8).

BOWMER, Katherine, [ ], of Yorkshire. 7 mths recusancy from 3 July 1587: conv. 18 Mar. 1587/8. Record of property-seizure dated 10 Apr. 1589—IX(8v). Rental of property seized 10 Apr. 1589—IX(21v). X(21v). XI(24v). XII(23v). [See BULMER, Katherine].

BOXE, Jane, wife of William Boxe of Marcham, Berks., esq. 12 mths recusancy from 1 Sept. 1586: conv. 4 Mar. 1587/8.—VIII(5).

BOYSE, Edward, gent., of St. Bride's par., Farringdon Ward Without, London. 3 mths recusancy prior to 20 April 1588, when convicted.— VIII(38v).

BRADBURY, Bradburie, John, 'laborer', of Tiddeswell [Tideswell], Derbys. 10 mths recusancy from 9 Sept. 1586: conv. 22 Mar. 1587/8.—VIII(21).

BRADBURY, John, 'clericus'[17], of Stone, Staffs. 8 mths recusancy from 22 July 1588: conv. 21 July 1589.—IX(69v).

BRADFORD, Ann, wife of Thomas Bradford, gent., of Cirencester, Gloucs. 5 mths recusancy from 26 Mar. 1587: conv. 11 Mar. 1587/8.—VIII(82).

BRADLEY, Eliz., of Thornley in Wheatley, Lancs., wife of Thomas Bradley, 'yoman'. 12 mths recusancy from 20 Sept. 1589: conv. 22 Mar. 1590/1.—X(39).

BRADLEY, Hugh, 'husbandman' (same parish, recusancy period and conviction date).—X(39).

BRADLEY, John, 'husb'' (same parish, recusancy period and conviction date).—X(39).

BRADLEY, Margaret, of Bryning, Lancs., wife of John Bradley, gent. 12 mths recusancy from 20 Sept. 1589: conv. 22 Mar. 1590/1.—X(39v).

BRADOCKE, George, 'yeoman', of Coley Hall, Knowsall [Gnosall] parish, Staffs. 12 mths recusancy from 6 Sept. 1586: conv. 25 Mar. 1588.— VIII(78v).

BRADSHOFFE, *alias* BRADSHOWE, Richard, 'weaver', of St. Mary's parish, Bury St. Edmunds, Suffolk. 6 mths recusancy from 20 Sept. 1588: conv. 2 July 1589.—IX(64). Debt re-enrolled—XI(72v).

BRADSTOCK, Brodstock, 'Idea', wife of William Brodstock, 'yoman', of Hanley Castle, Worcs. 6 mths recusancy from 29 Sept. 1587: conv. 25 July 1588.—VIII(80v).

BRADSTOCKE, Joan, 'spinster', of Eldersfeild, Worcs. 12 mths recusancy from 1 Apr. 1587: conv. 28 Mar. 1588.—VIII(80).

---

17. John Bradbury Unidentified. A convicted, but unpenalised recusant; probably a pre-Elizabethan priest.

BRADSTOCK, Brodstock, John, 'yeoman', of Southwark, Surrey [prisoner[18]]. 10 mths recusancy ending 11 Mar. 1582/3, when convicted; and 5 later convictions, ending 16 Feb. 1586/7.—III(58v). IV(49v). V(52v). VI(49v), (50). Debts re-enrolled—V(52v). VI(51). Lands in Worcs. seized by Crown 12 Jan. 1589/90, and let to John Chare from 3 Apr. 1590 for an annual rent of £12 per ann. [entries under 'Worcs.']—X(51v). XI(70). XII(71).

BRADSTOCK, Brodstocke, William, gent., of Corse, Gloucs. 5 mths recusancy from 26 Mar. 1587: conv. 11 Mar. 1587/8.—VIII(82). Record of land-seizure, 14 Jan. 1588/9.—X(27v). Rental of lands seized 14 Jan. 1588/9.—X(82). XI(27). XII(27).

BRADSTOCK, [ ], his wife (same parish, recusancy period and conviction date).—VIII(82).

BRADWIN, John, 'yeoman', of West Hallam, Derbys. 10 mths recusancy from 9 Sept. 1586: conv. 22 Mar. 1587/8.—VIII(21).

BRAKENBURY, Anthony, 'yom'', of Tottenham, Middx. 3 mths recusancy from 5 Apr. 1587: conv. 1 Sept. 1587.—VIII(38v).

BRAMPTON, Richard, gent., of West Dereham, Norfolk. 3 mths recusancy from 13 Apr. 1587: conv. 1 Apr. 1588.—VIII(54).

BRAMPTON, Bramston, Thomas, 'clericus', of St. George's parish, Southwark, Surrey [prisoner][19]. 5 mths recusancy from 17 Feb. 1586/7: conv. 17 July 1587.—IX(54).

BRANKAR, Brankard, Alice, 'spinster', wife of Robert Brankar(d), 'yoman', of Aylesham, Norfolk. 11 mths recusancy from 1 Aug. 1582: conv. 8 July 1583.—III(72v). Debt re-enrolled—V(46v).

BRAUNCH, Thomas, 'yom'', of Ukerbye [Uckerby], par. of Bolton [on Swale], N.R. Yorks. 13 mths recusancy from 3 Sept. 1586: conv. 4 Sept. 1587.—VIII(25v).

BRAWNE, Richard, 'horsekeper', of Bryning, Lancs. 12 mths recusancy from 20 Sept. 1589: conv. 22 Mar. 1590/1.—X(39v).

BRAWNE, [ ], his wife (same parish, recusancy period and conviction date)—X(39v).

BRAYBROOKE, Brabroke, Braibrook, James, gent., of Westminster, Middx [prisoner][20] [entry under 'Berks']. 3 mths recusancy from

---

18. John Bradstock was in the Clink from 2 May 1581 to Feb. 1587/8. (Cf. *CRS* II, pp. 235, 252, 283.), and six times indicted. His seized lands in Worcs., were two-thirds of two messuages or tenements called 'Woodend' and 'Pleistowe', with appurtenances at Queenhill in Ripple. The lands were discharged in 1593. (Cf. M.R., L.T.R., 36 Eliz., Michaelmas Term, 'Recorda' section. And *CRS* LVII, p. 190 (6) and p. 192 (11).)

19. Thomas Bramston (Cf. Anstruther I, pp. 47–49.)

20. James Braybrooke, gent., born in Abingdon, Berks., was a lawyer by profession, and one of the earliest recusants. He was imprisoned in the Gatehouse by the Bishop of London and the High Commissioners in 1581 (Cf. *CRS* II, p. 225.) He married Martha, dau. of John Yate of Lyford, Berks., and died on 8 May 1588, seised of a moiety of Marleston Manor, and of other properties in Berks. Two-thirds of these lands were sequestered for recusancy and let by the Crown to Sir William Bruncker and Richard Hide from Michaelmas 1593 (Cf. *VCH* Berks III; and *CRS* LVII, pp. 4, 5.) The earliest record of Martha Braybrooke's recusancy occurs in *CRS* XVIII, p. 9, where she is described as a widow of Brickleton (Bright Walton), Berks., convicted on 12 Mar. 1592/3, of 13 months recusancy, beginning 28 Sept. 1591 and ending 9 Apr. 1593. This computation of a year's

24 Mar. 1580/1: conv. 18 June 1581.—III(5). And 8 later convictions ending 18 Aug. 1583.—I(3v). II(65v)*. IV(46)*. Debts re-enrolled—II(65v). IV(46). V(3v). VI(3v)*. VII(3v). VIII(4v). Summary of debts for recusancy (£180) at date of land-seizure in Berks.—IX(51v). Crown lease to William Brunker and Richard Hide, dated Ladyday 1589, of lands in Berks seized 10 July 1584.—X(3v). XI(4). XII(4).

BRAYE, Henry, 'yoman', lately of Bloxford [? Bloxworth (Blocheshorde), Dorset], 'inhabiting St. Clement's parish, Winchester, Hants'. 2 mths recusancy ending 16 May 1581, when convicted.—V(56).

BRAYE, Henry, 'yom'', of St. Clement's par., Winchester, Hants [? prisoner]. 5 mths recusancy from 6 May 1581; conv. 1 Oct. 1581: and 2 later convictions, ending 24 Apr. 1582.—I(55)*. III(50v). Debts re-enrolled.—III(62)*.

BRAYE, William, 'yoman', of Stepney, Middx. 3 mths recusancy from 5 Apr. 1587: conv. 1 Sept. 1587.—VIII(38v).

BRAYE, William, 'yoman', of Westminster, Middx [prisoner][21]. 3 mths recusancy from 20 Mar. 1587/8: conv. 28 June 1588.—IX(37).

BREDMAN, Edith, wid., of Tingrith, Beds. 3 mths recusancy from 29 Mar. 1587: conv. 20 Mar. 1587/8.—VIII(1).

BRETT, Richard, gent., of Marten [Merton], Norfolk. 12 mths recusancy from 10 July 1587: conv. 20 July 1588: and one later conviction dated 7 July 1589.—IX(45), (45v). Debts re-enrolled—XI(48)*.

BRETTEN, Bretton, George, gent., of Petworth, Sussex. 2 mths recusancy from 17 Apr. 1587: conv. 26 Feb. 1587—VIII(63v).

BRETTON, Ann, his wife (same parish, recusancy period and conviction date)—VIII(63v).

BRETTON, Brettaine, Britton, John, gent., of Salford in the parish of Manchester, Lancs. [prisoner][22]. 4 mths recusancy from 3 Sept. 1584: conv. 27 Dec. 1584.—VI(40v).

20—Continued
recusancy 'at a rate of 28 days per month' cost her £260. James Braybrooke had two sons by Martha: William, who died o.s.p., and Richard, who married Katherine, a dau. of William Eyston of Catmore, Berks., and who died in 1651, leaving a dau. Lucy. (Cf. *Harleian Visitations, Berks.* II, pp. 82, 83 (Braybrooke)). On 16 July 1600 Martha yielded to the Queen three other messuages in Long Crendon, Bucks., *viz.*, 'Lovedens' (the capital messuage) for which she was due to pay £16 Long Crendon, Bucks., *viz.*, 'Lovedens' (the capital messuage) for which she was due to pay £16 rent and £14 p.a. for appurtenances; and two smaller houses, 'Fitzwaters' and 'Digbies' which she was renting for £6 and £4 respectively. These were taken and seized into the hands of the late Queen by Francis Goodwin and other commissioners, as is stated in R.R., 42 Eliz., under 'Buck'. And £131 of the year 6 James I. Total debt: £147. 'But she ought not to be summoned for £56 which is the same rent as on the feast of the Annunciation B.V.M. in the King's 6th. year. Nor ought she to be further charged with the rent of the (   ) day of May or June, when Martha Braybrooke died; by consideration of the Barons annotated in the M.R., L.T.R., 10 James, Hilary Term, 'Recorda' section. And she owed £91. And it is answered in R.R., 10 James I, under 'Buck'.

21. William Braye, also named Charles, was probably imprisoned in the Tower of London for a period from 30 Nov. 1586, among some 50 other persons arrested by Walsingham on suspicion of having connection with the Babington Plot. Braye was referred to as 'a common conveyor of priests and recusants'; and was said to have 'been taken when carrying the Earl of Arundell overseas'. Was committed to the Gatehouse, 19 Aug. 1588. (Cf. *CRS* II, pp. 261, 269, 284.)

22. John Bretton (Cf. Hugh Bowler, 'Exchequer Dossiers 2: The Recusancy of Venerable John Bretton, gentleman, and of Frances his wife', in *RH* vol. 2, (1953), pp. 116 – 134, and 'Further Notes on the Venerable John Bretton', in *RH* vol. 15, (1979), pp. 1 – 10.)

BRETTON, John, recusant (same person as preceding entry), of West
    Bretton, W.R. Yorks. 6 mths recusancy from 3 July 1587: conv.
    18 Mar. 1588. Record of land-seizure, 8 Apr. 1589—IX(22v). Goods
    value £30 seized 8 Apr. 1589—IX(22v). Rental of lands in West
    Bretton and Dewsbury seized 8 Apr. 1589—IX(21v). X(21v). XI(24v).
    XII(23v). Seized lands let by Crown to Cuthbert Stillingfleet from
    Ladyday 1590—X(13v). XI(24v). XII(24).
BREWSTER, Breuster, George, gent., of Southwark, Surrey [prisoner][23]. 12
    mths recusancy ending 15 Feb. 1583/4, when convicted.—IV(49v).
    Debt re-enrolled—VI(51). Goods value £60 seized 12 May
    1585—V(52v). £60 paid 2 Mar. 1585/6: Quit.—VII(51v).
BRINDELEY, Mary, of Charnock Richard, Lancs., wife of John Brindeley,
    'husb''. 12 mths recusancy from 20 Sept. 1589: conv. 22 Mar.
    1590/1.—X(38v).
BRINDELEY, Robert, 'shomaker' (same parish, recusancy period and
    conviction date).—X(38).
BRINDELEY, Margaret, his wife (same parish, recusancy period and
    conviction date).—X(38).
BRINDLEY, John, 'wever', of Langford [Longford], Derbys. 10 mths
    recusancy from 9 Sept. 1586: conv. 22 Mar. 1587/8.—VIII(21).
BRITON, Richard, 'clericus'[24], of Kirkeham [Kirkham], Lancs. 13 mths
    recusancy from 14 Aug. 1586: conv. 25 Mar. 1588.—VIII(21v).
BRITTEN, George, gent., of Wraxall [Wraxhall], Wilts. 3 mths recusancy
    from 2 Apr. 1587: conv. 1 Mar. 1587/8.—VIII(74v).
BROCKE, Katherine, 'spinster', of Fladburie, Worcs. 2 mths recusancy
    from 7 Apr. 1588: conv. 6 Mar. 1588/9.—IX(70v).
BROCKES, Humphrey, 'yoman', of Rocester, Staffs. 6 mths recusancy
    from 25 Mar. 1588: conv. 14 Mar. 1588/9.—IX(69v).
BROKEHOLES, Dorothy, of Claughton [-on-Brock], Lancs., wife of
    Thomas Brockeholes, esq. 12 mths recusancy from 20 Sept. 1589:
    conv. 22 Mar. 1590/1.—X(39).
BROKESBY, Bartholomew, gent., of Marten [? Merton, Surrey]. 3 mths
    recusancy from 25 Mar. 1587: conv. 13 Feb. 1587/8.—VIII(63).
BROKESBY, Margaret, 'spinster' (same parish, recusancy period and
    conviction date).—VIII(63).
BROMELEY, Hugh, esq., of Hamptone, Malpas parish, Cheshire. 13 mths
    recusancy from 25 Sept. 1586: date of conviction omitted.—
    VIII(58v).
BROOKE, *alias* of COBBE, James (q.v.)
BROWNE, Agnes, 'spinster', of Whalley, Lancs. 12 mths recusancy from
    20 Sept. 1589: conv. 22 Mar. 1590/1.—X(40).
BROWNE, Eliz., 'spinster', of Ewell, Surrey. 3 mths recusancy from
    24 June 1588: conv. 30 June 1589.—IX(53).

---

23. George Brewster was imprisoned in the White Lion on 23 Mar. 1583/4. (Cf. *CRS* II, pp. 234, 237.)
24. Richard Briton Unidentified. Probably a pre-Elizabethan priest.

BROWNE, Eliz., wid., of Beltofte, Lincs. 9 mths recusancy in 1582 (dates omitted).—III(54v). Debt re-enrolled—V(9v).
BROWNE, Francis, gent., of Stepney, Middx. 3 mths recusancy from 28 June 1587: conv. 1 Dec. 1587.—VIII(38v). Goods value £2 – 9 – 10 seized Trinity term 1590.—X(46). Debt for recusancy re-enrolled and cancelled, Easter term 1592[25]—X(47).
BROWNE, Margaret, 'spinster', of West Hallam, Derbys. 10 mths recusancy from 2 Sept. 1586: conv. 22 Mar. 1587/8.—VIII(21).
BROWNE, Margery, wife of Thomas Browne, 'husb''', of Wendlebury, Oxfords. 12 mths recusancy from 26 Sept. 1586: conv. 7 Mar. 1587/8.—VIII(35v).
BROWNE, Mary, of Scales in Newton, Lancs., wife of Henry Browne, gent. 12 mths recusancy from 20 Sept. 1589: conv. 22 Mar. 1590/1.— X(39v).
BROWNE, Richard, 'yeoman', of East Harling, Norfolk. 3 mths recusancy from 13 Apr. 1587: conv. 1 Apr. 1588.—VIII(54).
BROWNE, Timothy, 'laborer', of Hampstall [Hamstall] Ridware, Staffs. 6 mths recusancy from 25 Mar. 1588: conv. 14 Mar. 1588/9.—IX(69v). Goods value £2 – 12 – 10 seized 4 Sept. 1589—X(14).
BROWNE, William, esq., of Parva [Little] Fakenham, Suffolk. 8 mths recusancy from 15 July 1588: conv. 2 July 1589.—IX(64). Debt re-enrolled—XI(72v).
BROWNELEY, William, 'yeom''', of Horeseley [Horsley], Derbys. 10 mths recusancy from 9 Sept. 1586: conv. 22 Mar. 1587/8.—VIII(21).
BROWNEWELL, 'Gratianus', gent., of St. Saviour's parish, Southwark, Surrey [prisoner][26]. 5 mths recusancy ending 16 Feb. 1586/7, when convicted.—VI(50).
BRUERTON, John, 'yoman', of Langton in Lindsey, Lincs. 12 mths recusancy from 7 July 1588: conv. 7 July 1589.—IX(9). Debt re-enrolled—XI(11).
BRUMELL, John, of Webley [Weobley], Herefords. Two fines of £20 imposed for ignoring sheriffs summonses after excommunication, 4 Apr. and 27 May 1581.—III(28)*. Debts re-enrolled—V(26)*.
BRUSTER, Katherine, wid., of Llantilio Pertholey, Mon. 5 mths recusancy from 24 Mar. 1586/7: conv. 13 Mar. 1587/8.—VIII(48v).
BRYNE, Brine, John, [   ], lately of Chideock, Dorset [entry under 'Hants']. 2 mths recusancy ending 16 May 1581, when convicted— V(56).
BRYNE, Brine, John, 'clericus', of St. Clement's parish, Winchester, Hants [? prisoner][27]. 5 mths recusancy from 6 May 1581: conv. 1 Oct. 1581:

---

25. Francis Browne's debt for recusancy was discharged. (Cf. M.R., L.T.R., 34 Eliz., Easter Term, 'Recorda' section.)
26. Gratian Brownewell was imprisoned 'in and about London', 30 Sept. 1588, for not taking the oath administered at Court Leets, nor 'will take the Queen's part against the Pope's army'. (Cf. CRS II, p. 283.)
27. John Bryne's clerical character remains doubtful up to 24 Apr. 1582, when he disappears from the Pipe Rolls. He has not been identified.

and two later convictions, ending 24 Apr. 1582.—I(55)*. III(50v). Debts re-enrolled—III(62). V(56).

BRYNE, Brine, John, 'yom'', 'clericus'' [sic], of the city of Winchester, Hants. 5 mths recusancy from 6 May 1581: conv. 1 Oct. 1581.—III(62).

BUCK, Eliz., wid., of Westby, Lancs. 13 mths recusancy from 14 Aug. 1586: conv. 25 Mar. 1588.—VIII(21v).

BUCKLEY, Alice, wid., of Aston, near Birmingham, Warwicks. 7 mths recusancy from 12 July 1586: conv. 15 Mar. 1587/8.—VIII(76).

BUCKLEY, Robert, 'clericus', of Southwark, Surrey [prisoner][28]. 10 mths recusancy ending 11 Mar. 1582/3, when convicted: and one later conviction dated 18 Feb. 1584/5.—III(58v). V(52v). Debts re-enrolled—V(52v).

BULKELEY, Rowland, [entry under 'Salop']. Fined £20 at St. Paul's Cathedral, London, by High Commissioners, 6 June 1577 (offence unspecified).—V(58v). Debt re-enrolled—VI(13).

BULKELEY, Rowland, gent., of Drayton, Salop. 12 mths recusancy from 24 Feb. 1586/7: conv. 18 July 1588.—VIII(16v). Record of land-seizure, 8 Apr. 1589—IX(13v). Rental of lands seized 8 Apr. 1589—IX(69v). X(59v). XI(62v). XII(63). Lease of seized lands by Crown to Isaac Burges & George Dickenson from 30 Nov. 1590—XII(64v).

BULL, James, 'yoman', of Steyning, Sussex. 3 mths recusancy from 1 Apr. 1588: conv. 3 Mar. 1588/9.—IX(53).

BULL, Richard, 'yeoman', of Feltwell, Norfolk. 3 mths recusancy from 13 Apr. 1587: conv. 1 Apr. 1588.—VIII(54).

BULLACAR, 'Edbora', wid., of Warblington, Hants. 7 mths recusancy from 16 Sept. 1583: conv. ? Apr. 1584.—V(56v).

BULLEIN, Bulleyn, Bullin, Bullyne, John, gent., of Hardwick, Oxfords. 4 mths recusancy from 25 Feb. 1582/3: conv. 4 July 1583—III(4): and six later convictions ending 17 Mar. 1586/7.—IV(29). V(47)*. VI(11v), (47v)*. Debts re-enrolled—V(31v). VI(30v).

BULLEIN, John, 'yom'', of Hardwick, Oxfords. 8 mths recusancy from 29 June 1581: conv. 15 Feb. 1581/2—III(4); and three later convictions ending 27 Feb. 1583/4.—III(4)*. IV(29). Debts re-enrolled—V(31v)*. Crown lease of seized lands to Hugh Cuffe from Michaelmas 1585—VI(33v). VIII(16v). X(79v). XI(53v). XII(53v).

BULLEIN, Joyce, wife of John Bullin, 'yeom'', of Hardwick, Oxfords. 12 mths recusancy from 26 Sept. 1586: conv. 7 Mar. 1587/8.—VIII(35v).

BULMER, Anthony, gent., of Gaterley [Gatherley], Middleton Tyas parish, N.R. Yorks. 13 mths recusancy from 3 Sept. 1586: conv. 4 Sept. 1587.—VIII(25v).

---

28. Dom Siegbert Buckley was the link between the old and the restored Benedictine Congregations. (Cf. Stephen Marron, 'Dom Siegbert Buckley and his brethren', in the *Douai Magazine*, vol. 7, (1933), pp. 130–138, and David Lunn, *The English Benedictines, 1540–1688*, (1980), pp. 92–97.)

BULMER, Henry, gent., (same parish, recusancy period and conviction date)—VIII(25v).
BULMER, Katherine, wid. (same parish, recusancy period and conviction date: and one later conviction dated 18 Mar. 1587/8)—VIII(25v), (27). [See BOWMER, Katherine]
BUNCKLEY, William, 'yeoman', of Lydgers Ashebye [Ashby St. Ledgers], Northants. 12 mths recusancy from 31 July 1587: conv. 4 Mar. 1588/9.—IX(47).
BUNDY, Bundaye, Roger, 'husband", of Crodeley [Cradley], Herefords. Two fines of £20 imposed for ignoring sheriff's summonses after excommunication, 4 Apr. and 27 May 1581.—III(28)*. Debts re-enrolled—V(26)*.
BURD, Judith, wid., of St. Bride's parish, Farringdon Ward Without, London. 13 mths recusancy from 19 Jan. 1586/7: conv. 19 Jan. 1587/8.—VIII(38v).
BURGHE, John, [   ], of Garstange, Lancs. 10 mths recusancy from 18 Mar. 1580/1: conv. 18 Jan. 1581/2.—II(38v). Debt re-enrolled—VIII(46).
BURGHE, John, 'clericus'[29], of Salford in parish of Manchester, Lancs. [prisoner] 3 mths recusancy from 17 Jan. 1581/2: conv. 2 May 1582.—II(38v). Debt re-enrolled—VIII(46).
BURGHE, John, schoolmaster ('ludimagister'), of Salford in parish of Manchester, Lancs. [prisoner]. 4 mths recusancy from 2 Sept. 1582: conv. 16 Jan. 1582/3—II(38v): and one later conviction dated 22 Jan. 1583/4.—IV(37). Debts re-enrolled—IV(42v). VI(39). VIII(46).
BURGOYNE, Dorothy, wife of George Burgoyne, esq., of Clothall, Herts. 12 mths recusancy from 12 July 1586: conv. 1 Mar. 1587/8.—VIII(31).
BURLEY, Burleighe, Burghley, William, gent., of Middleton *alias* Longparish, Hants. 2 mths recusancy from 18 Mar. 1580/1: conv. 24 Apr. 1582—III(50v)*; and four later convictions ending ? Sept. 1584.—IV(53). V(56v)*. Debts re-enrolled—V(56)*. VI(54). VII(54)*. VIII(68). IX(59)*. Crown lease of seized lands to Hugh Cuffe from 2 Mar. 1583/4—IV(52). Lease transferred to George Burley as from Ladyday 1584—IV(52). V(55v). VI(53v). VII(53v). VIII(66v). IX(57v). X(68v). George Burley's lease revised by a new commission dated 5 May 1590—X(69), (71). XI(59v), (60). XII(60v).
BURINGTON, Eliz., wife of Francis Burington, gent., of Yarkill [Yarkhill], Herefords. 12 mths recusancy from 1 Sept. 1586: conv. 18 Mar. 1587/8.—VIII(30).
BURLOWE, Sibyl, wife of William Burlowe, 'yeoman', 'in the aforesaid county' [Worcs]. 12 mths recusancy from 20 Sept. 1586: conv. 28 Mar. 1588.—VIII(77).

---

29. John Burghe Unidentified. His clerical status is uncertain, and he was probably a Catholic schoolmaster.

BURTE, Burton, Agnes, 'spinster', of Longparish, Hants. 5 mths recusancy from 6 May 1581: conv. ? 1 Oct. 1581—I(55): and two later convictions ending 24 Apr. 1582.—I(55). III(50v). Debt re-enrolled—III(62)*. V(56)*.

BURTE, Eliz., 'spinster' (same parish, recusancy periods and conviction dates).—I(55). III(50v). Debts re-enrolled—III(62)*. V(56)*.

BURTE, Joan, wid., (same parish, recusancy periods and conviction dates).—I(55). III(50v).

BURTE, Joan, 'spinster' (same parish, recusancy periods and conviction dates).—III(62). V(56).

BURTON, Katherine, 'spinster', of St. Bride's parish, Farringdon Ward Without, London. 12 mths recusancy from 2 Jan. 1582/3: conv. 20 Jan. 1583/4.—IV(32v). Debt re-enrolled—VI(34).

BURTON, Katherine, 'spinster' (of same parish and ward, London). Fine of 100 marks imposed for hearing Mass on 24 Dec. 1583 'in the said parish and ward': convicted 20 Jan. 1583/4.—IV(32v). Debt re-enrolled—VI(34).

BUTCHER, *alias* WRATHE, Adrian, [   ], of Kirkeby [? Kirkby Mallory], Leics. 10 mths recusancy from 9 Sept. 1586: conv. 19 Mar. 1587/8.—VIII(45v).

BUTCHER, *alias* WRATHE, [   ], his wife (same parish, recusancy period and conviction date).—VIII(45v).

BUTLER, Alban, gent., of Natebie, Garstang parish, Lancs. 4 mths recusancy from 18 Mar. 1580/1: conv. ? July 1581.—VI(40v).

BUTLER, James, gent., of Cirencester, Gloucs. 8 mths recusancy from 25 July 1586: conv. 5 Mar. 1586/7.—VII(47v). Debt re-enrolled—XI(27v).

BUTLER, Jane, of Kirkeland [nr. Garstang], Lancs., wife of John Butler, esq. 12 mths recusancy from 20 Sept. 1589: conv. 22 Mar. 1590/1.—X(39).

BUTLER, John, junior, 'yeoman', of Brill, Bucks. 3 mths recusancy from 27 Mar. 1587: conv. 18 Mar. 1587/8 - -VIII(3).

BUTLER, John, senior, 'yeoman' (same parish, recusancy period and conviction date).—VIII(3).

BUTLER, Butlar, Ann, wife of John Butlar, senior, gent. [*sic*], of Brill, Bucks. (same recusancy period and conviction date).—VIII(3).

BUTLER, Michael, gent., of Droytwiche [Droitwich], Worcs. 2 mths recusancy from 7 Apr. 1588: conv. 6 Mar. 1588/9.—IX(70v).

BUTLER, Mary, his wife (same parish, recusancy period and conviction date)—IX(70v).

BUTLER, Richard, gent., of Rawclyff, parish of Michaelles [St. Michael-on-Wyre], Lancs. 13 mths recusancy from 14 Aug. 1586: conv. 25 Mar. 1588.—VIII(21v).

BYSHOPP, Thomas, 'yeoman', of St. Sepulchre parish, Northampton, Northants. 12 mths recusancy from 31 July 1587: conv. 4 Mar. 1588/9.—IX(47).

CABLE, Richard, esq., of Whiteparish, Wilts. 8 mths recusancy from
  25 June 1583: conv. Lent 1584.—IV(59v).
CABLE, Richard, 'yeoman', of Whiteparish, Wilts. 7 mths recusancy from
  20 Aug. 1584: conv. ? Apr. 1585.—V(63). Debts re-enrolled—
  VI(59v). VII(60v). Seized lands let by Crown to John Lovelaike and
  Thomas Hayter from 26 Aug. 1584—V(62v). VI(59). VI(60). IX(65).
  X(76). XI(67). XII(68v).
CADWALITER, Alice, wife of David Cadwaliter, 'husb'', of Hardwick,
  Oxfords. 12 mths recusancy from 26 Sept. 1586: conv. 7 Mar.
  1587/8.—VIII(35v).
CALCOTE, Thomas, gent., of Orwell, Cambs. 12 mths recusancy from
  20 July 1583: conv. 21 July 1584.—VI(5v). Debt re-enrolled—
  VIII(13v).
CALIE, Robert, 'yeoman', of Horsham St. Faith, Norfolk. 3 mths
  recusancy from 13 Apr. 1587: conv. 1 Apr. 1588.—VIII(54).
CALLENGWOOD, Henry, junior, [   ], of Tucksford [Tuxford], Notts.
  2 mths recusancy from 3 Jan. 1588/9: conv. 11 July 1589.—IX(48v).
CALVERLEY, William, gent., of Calverley, Yorks. [W.R.]. 4 mths
  recusancy from 28 Mar. 1581: conv. 17 July 1581—I(21v): and one
  later conviction dated 18 Mar. 1587/8.—VIII(25v). Debt re-
  enrolled—III(24). V(22). Lands seized 8 Apr. 1589 and let by Crown
  to Richard Maunsell from 11 July 1590—X(13v). XI(24v). XII(23v).
CALVERLEY, Katherine, his wife (of same parish). 6 mths recusancy from
  3 July 1587: conv. 18 Mar. 1587/8.—VIII(27). [see CAVERLEY]
CAMPE, John, 'husb'', of Cowley, Gloucs. 5 mths recusancy from 26 Mar.
  1587: conv. 11 Mar. 1587/8.—VIII(82).
CAMPION, Edward, 'clericus', of St. George's parish, Southwark, Surrey
  [prisoner][30]. 2 mths recusancy: convicted 17 July 1587.—IX(54).
CANTERTON, Caunterton, Thomas, 'yeoman', of Kingesomborne [King's
  Somborne], Hants. 6 mths recusancy from 26 Oct. 1587: conv.
  26 Feb. 1587/8—VIII(67). Goods value £2 – 13 – 4 seized 8 Nov.
  1588—IX(58).
CAPELL, Thomas, 'yoman', of Westminster, Middx [? prisoner]. 1 mth
  recusancy from 6 Oct. 1587: conv. 29 Jan. 1587/8.—VIII(38v).
CAPPER, Francis, junior, 'yom'', of Didlaston [Dudleston], Salop. 12 mths
  recusancy from 24 Feb. 1586/7: conv. 18 July 1588.—VIII(16v).
CARDEN, Ann, 'spinster', of Salesbury, Lancs. 12 mths recusancy from
  20 Sept. 1589: conv. 22 Mar. 1590/1.—X(40v).
CARDWELL, Cuthbert, 'husb'', of Wesham, Lancs. 12 mths recusancy
  from 20 Sept. 1589: conv. 22 Mar. 1590/1.—X(39).
CARDWELL, Margaret, his wife (same parish, recusancy period and
  conviction date)—X(39).
CARELES, John, 'yom'', of Drayton, Salop. 12 mths recusancy from
  24 Feb. 1586/7: conv. 18 July 1588.—VIII(16v).

---

30. Edward Campion's true name was Gerard Edwards. He was martyred at Canterbury, 1 Oct. 1588. (Cf. Anstruther I, p. 109 under Edwards.)

CAREWE, Carey, Peter, gent., of Southwark, Surrey [prisoner][31].
    Condemned for 10 mths recusancy ending 22 Mar. 1582/3, when
    convicted,—III(58v); and 4 later convictions ending 18 Feb.
    1584/5—IV(49v). V(50v), (52v). Debts re-enrolled—VI(51).
CARLETON, Margaret, 'spinster', of Marten [Merton], Norfolk. 3 mths
    recusancy from 13 Apr. 1587: conv. 1 Apr. 1588.—VIII(54).
CARLETON, Richard, 'yeoman', of Linton, Cambs. 10 mths recusancy
    from 1 Sept. 1586: conv. 24 Mar. 1587/8.—VIII(7v).
CARPENTER, Constance, 'spinster', of Stoughton, Sussex. 3 mths
    recusancy from 1 Apr. 1588: conv. 3 Mar. 1588/9.—IX(53).
CARRE, John, 'servingman', of Crosby, Lancs. 12 mths recusancy from
    20 Sept. 1589: conv. 22 Mar. 1590/1.—X(38).
CARRINGTON, Anthony, 'yeoman', of Harrowden, Northants. 12 mths
    recusancy ending 2 May 1587: conv. 12 Mar. 1587/8.—VIII(52v).
CARRINGTON, George, 'yeoman', of Little Harrowden, Northants. 12
    mths recusancy from 31 July 1587: conv. 4 Mar. 1588/9.—IX(47).
CARROLL, 'Tadus', 'tailor', of Christ Church parish, Farringdon Ward
    Within, London [? prisoner]. 3 mths recusancy from 18 Mar. 1580/1:
    conv. 28 July 1581.—I(32v). Debt re-enrolled—III(38v). V(35).
CARTER, John, 'yom'', of Wesham, parish of Kirkham, Lancs. 13 mths
    recusancy from 14 Aug. 1586: conv. 25 Mar. 1588—VIII(21v): and
    one later conviction dated 22 Mar. 1590/1.—X(39).
CARTWRIGHTE, Humphrey, schoolmaster, of Salford in the parish of
    Manchester, Lancs [prisoner]. 12 mths recusancy from 20 Feb.
    1582/3: conv. 22 Jan. 1583/4.—IV(37). Debt re-enrolled—IV(42v).
    VI(39).
CARYE, Henry, esq., of Tadford [Taddiford, near Milford], Hants. 10 mths
    recusancy from 1 Apr. 1589: conv. 17 Aug. 1590[32]. Rental of lands in
    Hants and Dorset seized 6 Aug. 1591—XI(61).

---

31. Peter Carewe or Carey was among 30 prisoners in the Marshalsea from 20 Oct. 1578 to 22 Mar. 1582/3. (Cf. *CRS* II, p. 240.)

32. The proximity of the south coast made Tadford a dangerous site for recusant users. The three manors constituting it, were carefully watched, especially at the time of the Armada. Henry Carye's lands are referred to under 'Hants' in the M.R., L.T.R., 33 Eliz, Hilary Term. E.368/465, mem.63., which begins with Hordle Bremor, its capital messuage and appurtenances, some 3 miles north of the coast; next comes Keyhaven Manor at the S.E. corner of the site, on the coastal road to Southam *alias* Hamworthy near Poole Harbour, Dorset, the third manor. The commissioners at Fordingbridge on 6 Aug. 1591, valued Hordle Bremor at £5 – 10 – 0. (two-thirds at £3 – 3 – 4). Keyhaven Manor, including Milford-on-Sea, Tadford and Christchurch-Twinham, they valued at £6 – 2 – 0. (two-thirds at £4 – 1 – 4); and the Manor of Hamworthy, Dorset, at £6 – 3 – 5. (two-thirds at £4 – 2 – 3). The total value of the Carye property amounted to £17 – 15 – 5¾ (two-thirds of which, claimed by the Crown, yielded £11 – 16 – 11¾ .) The three leasees responsible for delivering to the Crown the rental sum of £11 – 17 – 0, in two payments of £5 – 18 – 6, were John Goyte, William Bake and John Thomas. Beginning on 15 Dec. 1591, they fulfilled this duty regularly for nine years, ending 10 Nov. 1599. They never functioned together again; although Goyte made several attempts to do so with other associates. The fullest statement of their financial proceedings will be found in *CRS* XVIII, pp. 285, 286, and *CRS* LVII, p. 38 (19).

CATCHMAYE, Matilda, wife of Edmund Catchmaye, gent., of Newland, Gloucs. 5 mths recusancy from 26 Mar. 1587: conv. 11 Mar. 1587/8.—VIII(82).

CATHERICK, Catt(e)rick, George, esq., of Carleton, parish of Stanwick [St. John], N.R. Yorks. 13 mths recusancy from 3 Sept. 1586: conv. 4 Sept. 1587.—VIII(25v).

CATHERICK, Cattrick, George, gent., of Catton, N.R. Yorks. 6 mths recusancy from 3 July 1587: conv. 18 Mar. 1587/8.—VIII(27). Goods value £130 seized 10 Apr. 1589—IX(8v). Record of land-seizure, 10 Apr. 1589—IX(8v). Rental of lands seized—IX(21v). X(21v). XI(24v). XII(23v). Seized lands let by Crown to William Steare from 11 Oct. 1589—X(13v). XI(24v). XII(23v).

CATTERALL, Caterall, Margaret, wid., of Milton, Whalley parish, Lancs. 4 mths recusancy from 18 Mar. 1580/1: conv. ? 31 July 1581.—VI(40v).

CAVERLEY, Edward, 'clericus', of St. George's parish, Southwark, Surrey [prisoner][33]. 5 mths recusancy from 17 Feb. 1586/7: conv. 17 July 1587.—IX(54). [See CALVERLEY]

CEICILT, Hoell David, 'yoman', of Grosmont, Mon. 5 mths recusancy from 24 Mar. 1586/7: conv. 13 Mar. 1587/8.—VIII(49v).

CEICILT, Margaret David [   ] (same parish, recusancy period and conviction date)—VIII(49v).

CHADERTON, Henry [See SHATTERTONE, Henry, gent.], recusant, of Sussex. Goods value £1 – 13 – 4 seized 13 Jan. 1588/9.—IX(54v). £10 owed to Henry Chaderton, recusant, by William Chaderton, gent., of Garneley [Earnley], Sussex, seized by Queen's Commissioners 13 Jan. 1588/9, for Henry's recusancy.—IX(54v).

CHADICKE, John, [   ], of Much Crosby, Lancs. 12 mths recusancy from 20 Sept. 1589: conv. 22 Mar. 1590/1.—X(38).

CHALENOR, Ellen, 'spinster', of Wigan, Lancs. 3 mths recusancy from 10 Oct. 1581: conv. ? 18 Jan. 1581/2.—II(38v). Debt re-enrolled—VIII(46).

CHALENOR, Ellen, 'spinster', of Salford in parish of Manchester, Lancs. [prisoner]. 3 mths recusancy from 17 Jan. 1581/2: conv. 2 May 1582: and one later conviction dated 16 Jan. 1582/3.—II(38v)*. Debts re-enrolled—VIII(46)*.

CHAMBERS, Mary, 'spinster', of Torrisholme, Lancs. 12 mths recusancy from 20 Sept. 1589: conv. 22 Mar. 1590/1.—X(39v).

CHANDELER, Chaundler, John, 'carpenter', of Hindringham, Norfolk. 2 mths recusancy from 15 May 1588: conv. ? 20 July 1588;—IX(45): and one later conviction dated 7 July 1589.—IX(45v). Debts re-enrolled—XI(48)*.

CHAPMAN, John, 'clericus', of Southwark, Surrey [prisoner][34]. 3 mths recusancy ending 15 Feb. 1583/4, when convicted;—IV(49v): and two

---

33. Edward Caverley (Cf. Anstruther I, p. 62 under Calverley.)
34. John Chapman, a Marian priest, was arrested in the house of Edberrow Bullaker (*qv.*), great aunt of the Venerable Thomas Bullaker OFM. (Cf. Anstruther I, pp. 72, 73.)

later convictions, ending 18 Feb. 1584/5.—V(50v), (52v). Debt re-enrolled—VI(51).

CHARLES, Eliz., 'spinster', of Llangattock Vibon Avel, Mon. 5 mths recusancy from 24 Mar. 1586/7: conv. 13 Mar. 1587/8.—VIII(48v).

CHARLES, Henry, 'yoman' (same parish, recusancy period and conviction date).—VIII(48v).

CHARNELEY, George, 'yoman', of Torrisholme, Lancs. 12 mths recusancy from 20 Sept. 1589: conv. 22 Mar. 1590/1.—X(39v).

CHARNELEY, 'Jenetta', wid., of Weeton, Lancs. (same recusancy period and conviction date)—X(39).

CHARNEY, Richard, 'taleor', of Graunge [-over-Sands], Lancs. (same recusancy period and conviction date)—X(40).

CHARNOCK, 'Jenetta', of Wesham, Lancs., wife of William Charnock, 'husb''. (same recusancy period and conviction date)—X(39).

CHARTON, Charlton, William, gent., of Harley, Salop. 12 mths recusancy from 24 Feb. 1586/7: conv. 18 July 1588.—VIII(16v). Goods value £45 – 10s. seized 9 Oct. 1589—IX(13v). Debt re-enrolled—X(58v). XI(63v). Record of land-seizure, 9 Oct. 1589—IX(13v). Rental of lands seized—IX(69v). XI(62v). XII(63v). Arrearage of rent—X(58v).

CHARTON, Carleton, William, gent., of Hartley [Harley], Salop. Seized lands let by Crown to Isaac Burges & George Dickenson from 30 Nov. 1590.—XII(64v).

CHATHMAY [CATCHMAY?], *alias* of JAMES, Philip.

CHATTELTON, Chatleton, Chedleton, Thomas, 'clericus', of Southwark, Surrey [prisoner][35] 5 mths recusancy ending 11 Mar. 1582/3, when convicted.—III(58v). Debt re-enrolled—V(52v).

CHAUNCE, Richard, 'taylor', of Castle Frome, Herefords. Two fines of £20 imposed for ignoring sheriff's summonses after excommunication, 4 Apr. and 27 May 1581.—III(28)*. Debts re-enrolled—V(26)*.

CHAUNSEY, Juliana, wid., of Lugwardine, Herefords. 6 mths recusancy from 1 Sept. 1588: conv. 14 July 1589.—IX(25v). Debt re-enrolled—XI(29).

CHAWE, Edward, 'servingman', of Butterworthe in Billington, Lancs. 12 mths recusancy from 20 Sept. 1589: conv. 22 Mar. 1590/1.—X(40v).

CHENEY, Ann, wid., of West Woodhaie [Woodhay], Berks[36]. 12 mths recusancy from 1 Sept. 1586: conv. 4 Mar. 1587/8.—VIII(5). Goods value £10 seized 4 Oct. 1588—IX(4v). Debt re-enrolled—X(4v). Rental of lands seized 4 Oct. 1588—IX(4v). X(3).

CHENEY, Giles, gent., of Irtlingbourghe [Irthlingborough], Northants. 12 mths recusancy ending 2 May 1587: convicted 12 Mar. 1587/8.—VIII(52v).

---

35. Thomas Chattelton, a pre-Elizabethan priest, was probably the man deprived as V. Worfield, Salop.; V. St Mary's, Stafford; and Prebend of Pipa Parva in Lichfield Cathedral. He was reported to the Privy Council in 1577, as one 'who comes not to church to hear divine service'. In the Marshalsea in Nov. 1582. (Cf. *CRS* II, p. 231). Buried at St. Mary's Stafford on 20 June 1589.

CHENEY, Robert, gent., of West Woodhaie [Woodhay], Berks.[36] 12 mths
  recusancy from 1 Sept. 1586: conv. 4 Mar. 1587/8.—VIII(5). Goods
  value £5 seized 4 Oct. 1588.—IX(4v). Debt re-enrolled—X(4v).
CHEPMANE, Christiana, wid., of Munckton [Monckton], Dorset. 2 mths
  recusancy from 2 Jan. 1587/8: conv. 15 July 1588.—VIII(19v).
CHEPMANE, Mary, wife of William Chepmane, 'husb'', of [   ] Dorset
  (same recusancy period and conviction date).—VIII(19v).
CHEISWES, Chesus, Chessous, Alice, 'spinster', of Chester Castle,
  Cheshire [prisoner]. 13 mths recusancy from 14 Sept. 1585: conv.
  3 Oct. 1586.—X(35v).
CHEISWES, Alice, wid., of St. Mary's parish, Chester [? prisoner]. 8 mths
  recusancy from 1 Sept. 1584: conv. ? 26 Apr. 1585.—VI(48v).
CHEISWES, Richard, 'laborer', of St. Mary's parish, Chester [? prisoner].
  13 mths recusancy from 21 Sept. 1583: conv. ? Sept. 1584: and one
  later conviction dated 26 Apr. 1585.—VI(48v)*.
CHEISWES, Richard, 'yoman', of Chester Castle, Cheshire [prisoner]. 13
  mths recusancy from 14 Sept. 1585: conv. 3 Oct. 1586:—X(35v): and
  one later conviction dated 24 Apr. 1587—VIII(58v).
CHEISWES, William, 'laborer', of St. Mary's parish, Chester [? prisoner].
  13 mths recusancy from 21 Sept. 1583: conv. ? Sept. 1584; and one
  later conviction dated 26 Apr. 1585.—VI(48v)*.
CHEISWES, William, 'yoman', of Chester Castle, Cheshire [prisoner]. 13
  mths recusancy from 14 Sept. 1585: conv. 3 Oct. 1586.—X(35v).
CHIDDEN, Chydden, Richard, 'tailor', of Romsey, Hants. Fine of 100
  marks imposed for hearing Mass. Convicted at Winchester, 7 Jan.
  1583/4.—IV(53). Debt re-enrolled—VI(54).
CHILSON, Richard, 'tanner', of Wigan, Lancs. 3 mths recusancy from
  1 May 1588: conv. 17 Mar. 1588/9.—X(35).
CHOLMELEY, Thomasina, wife of Richard Cholmeley, esq., of Benham
  [Bentham], W.R. Yorks. 13 mths recusancy from 3 Sept. 1586: conv.
  4 Sept. 1587.—VIII(25v).
CHOWE, 'Jennetta', 'spinster', of Billington, parish of Blackburn, Lancs.
  13 mths recusancy from 30 July 1587: conv. 17 Mar. 1588/9.—X(35).
CHRICHELOWE, Crichelowe, *alias* of CRISLEY, Roger.
CLARCKSON, Margaret, of Blumpton [Plumpton ?], parish of Kirkham,
  Lancs., wife of William Clarckson, 'husb''. 12 mths recusancy from
  20 Sept. 1589: conv. 22 Mar. 1590/1.—X(39v).
CLARKE, Alice, junior, servant of Roger Vaughan, esq., of Kynnersley
  [Kinnersley], Herefords. 6 mths recusancy from 1 Sept. 1588: conv.
  14 July 1589.—IX(25v). Debt re-enrolled—XI(29).

---

36. Robert Cheyney's widow, Ann, had a very tenuous hold on the Cheyney property at West Woodhay, Berks. (Cf. *VCH* Berks, IV, p. 243–244.), her rivals for the lands being the local family of Darrell. She appealed to the Exchequer against the seizure of her goods and chattels, as did her son Robert (see below). Their case was heard together on 4 Oct. 1588. Both were discharged, she of £10 and Robert of £5. (Cf. M.R., L.T.R., 31 Eliz., Michaelmas Term. 'Recorda' section.) Ann was still in possession in 1594. The manor was sold to Sir Benjamin Rudyerd in 1634.

CLARKE, Edward, gent., of All Saints parish, Hereford. 1 mth recusancy
from 27 May 1583: conv. 15 July 1583—III(27): and 7 later
convictions, ending 27 Mar. 1587.—IV(64v). V(26v)*. VI(25)*. Debt
re-enrolled—V(26).

CLARKE, Edward, gent., of Willington [Wellington], Herefords. 19 mths
recusancy from 18 Mar. 1580/1: conv. ? 20 Sept. 1582—II(64)*: and 4
later convictions, ending 8 Aug. 1586.—VI(25). Debts re-enrolled—
III(27). IV(64v)*. V(26). Seized lands let by Crown to Hugh Cuffe
from Michaelmas 1585—VI(33v).

CLARKE, Richard, gent., of Willington [Wellington], Herefords. 12 mths
recusancy from 1 Sept. 1586: conv. 18 Mar. 1587/8.—VIII(30).
Record of land-seizure 23 Aug. 1588—IX(25v). Rental of lands seized
23 Aug. 1588—IX(25v). X(28). XI(28). XII(28). Rental of lands
seized 18 Sept. 1591—XI(30).

CLARKE, William [*sic*], of Herefords. Seized lands let by Crown to Hugh
Cuffe from Michaelmas 1585 [entry under 'Staffs'].—VIII(16v).
X(29). XI(28). XII(28).

CLEYTON, William, [   ], of Tyddeswall [Tideswell], Derbys. 12 mths
recusancy from 1 July 1587: conv. 14 Mar. 1588/9.—IX(17v).

CLIFFORD, Thomas, 'yeom", of [   ] in North Wingfeild parish, Derbys.
10 mths recusancy from 9 Sept. 1586: conv. 22 Mar. 1587/8.—
VIII(21).

CLIFTON, Alice, wid., of Westby, Lancs. 12 mths recusancy from 20 Sept.
1589: conv. 22 Mar. 1590/1.—X(39v).

CLIFTON, Alice, wid., relict of Cuthbert Clifton, gent., deceased, of
Westby, parish of Kirkham, Lancs. Lands seized 15 Apr. 1591 and let
by Crown from 25 June 1591 to Edward Bradshawe.—XII(44).

CLIFTON, Joan, wid., of Cocklclaie [Cockley Cley], Norfolk. 3 mths
recusancy from 13 Apr. 1587: conv. 1 Apr. 1588.—VIII(54).

CLIFTON, Mary, wid., of the city of Canterbury, Kent [? prisoner]. 3 mths
recusancy from 18 Mar. 1580/1: conv. 10 Jan. 1581/2.—II(12).

CLIFTON, Clyfton, Thomas, 'clericus', of St. George's parish, Southwark,
Surrey [prisoner][37]. 5 mths recusancy from 17 Feb. 1586/7: conv.
17 July 1587.—IX(54).

CLIFTON, Clyfton, William, gent., of Ballam, Kirkham parish, Lancs. 13
mths recusancy from 30 July 1587: conv. 17 Mar. 1588/9.—X(35).
Lands seized 1 Sept. 1591 and let by Crown from 12 Nov. 1591 to
Richard Urmeston.—XII(44).

CLIFTON, Clyfton, William, gent., of Westby, Lancs. 13 mths recusancy
from 14 Aug. 1586: conv. 25 Mar. 1588,—VIII(21v): and one later
conviction dated 22 Mar. 1590/1.—X(39v).

CLIFTON, Clyfton, [   ], his wife (of same parish). 12 mths recusancy
from 20 Sept. 1589: conv. 22 Mar. 1590/1.—X(39v).

CLYBBORNE, Richard, esq., of Southwark, Surrey [prisoner]. 6 mths
recusancy ending 18 Feb. 1586: when convicted.—V(52v).

---

37. Thomas Clifton (Cf. Anstruther I, pp. 80, 81.)

COBBE, *alias* BROOKE, James, gent., of Stoke, Suffolk. 3 mths recusancy from 8 Apr. 1587: conv. 27 Mar. 1588.—VIII(73).

CODRINGTON, Coddrington, Cowdrington, John, gent., of Fyfeild [Fifield Bavant], Wilts. 3 mths recusancy from 2 Apr. 1587: conv. 1 Mar. 1587/8.—VIII(74v). Record of land-seizure 8 Oct. 1588—IX(66). Rental of lands seized 8 Oct. 1588—IX(66). X(76v)*. XI(67v). XII(68v). Seized lands let by Crown from 13 July 1590 to Robert Penruddock—X(77). XI(67v). XII(68v).

COLBECKE, Thomas, gent., of Temesford [Tempsford], Beds. 12 mths recusancy from 6 July 1587: conv. 12 Mar. 1588/9.—IX(lv).

COLE, Alice, 'spinster', of Heston, Middx. 3 mths recusancy from 3 Oct. 1588: conv. 14 Feb. 1588/9.—IX(36v).

COLE, Mary, 'spinster' (same parish, recusancy period and conviction date)—IX(36v).

COLLES, William, gent., of Tenbury, Worcs. 6 mths recusancy from 29 Sept. 1587: conv. 25 July 1588.—VIII(80v).

COLLES, Mary, his wife (same parish, recusancy period and conviction date)—VIII(80v).

COLLIER, Collyer, John, 'husb'', of Hampstall [Hamstall] Ridware, Staffs. 6 mths recusancy from 6 Sept. 1587: conv. 22 July 1588.—VIII(58). Goods value £7 – 1s. seized 4 Sept. 1589—X(14).

COLLIER, Collyer, Ralph, 'clericus', of Westminster, Middx [prisoner][38] [entry under 'Yorks']. 3 mths recusancy from 27 June 1581: conv. 26 Sept. 1581: and three later indictments, ending 16 Mar. 1581/2.—II(22v)*. Debts re-enrolled—VI(22)*.

COLLIER, Thomas, 'clericus', of Hamstall Ridware, Staffs[39]. 8 mths recusancy from 1 Apr. 1588: conv. 21 July 1589.—IX(69v).

COLLIER, Collyer, Thomas, [ ], 'supposed recusant & fugitive' of Staffs. Goods value £4 seized 4 Sept. 1589—X(14). Records of land-seizure, 4 Sept. 1589—X(78v). Rental of lands seized 4 Sept. 1589—X(7v). XI(64v). XII(65v).

COLLIER, Thomas, 'clericus', of Staffs. Lands seized 4 Sept. 1589 let by Crown to Edward Thorne from 22 Dec. 1591—XII(72v).

---

38. Ralph Collier was an "ould preste", ordained *temp.* Henry VIII. Convicted of a *praemunire*, he was a prisoner in the Gatehouse, and later in the King's Bench Prison on 28 Jan. 1582/3. (Cf. *CRS* II, pp. 225, 226, 230, 231.)

39. Thomas Collier was a pre-Elizabethan priest. Educated at St. John's, Cambridge, he was deprived as V. Uppingham, Rutland and Prebend of Holywell *alias* Finsbury in St. Paul's Cathedral in 1560. He then returned to Staffs., where he obtained (? from Richard Fitzherbert) a small farm called 'Bancroft' presumably in the vicinity of Hartesmeare, the Fitzherbert residence in Hamstall Ridware, for which he owed a rent of £3 – 6 – 8 yearly. He eventually became involved prominently in recusant activity in Staffs., and after having been convicted for his recusancy in 1588 (see the present entry), became publicly known as a recusant 'fugitive' for having, with nine other neighbours, gone into hiding when the pursuivants came to investigate his financial status (Cf. *CRS* LVII, pp. 146, 147, for their names Knolles to Wade). The man responsible for this investigation was one Edward Thorne, a bitter anti-papist, who had obtained from the Crown on 22 Dec. 1591, a lease of the lands of Fitzherbert and Collier for £10 – 6 – 8 *per annum*, with a further commission to collect and, if necessary, to drive away their cattle, and seize all other possessions ostensibly for the Queen's use. A sum of £125 – 13 – 8 was collected in this way, and was carefully

COLLINGWOOD, Robert, gent., of Fawdon, Northumberland. 12 mths recusancy from 1 Aug. 1582: conviction date omitted.—III(52). Debt re-enrolled—VIII(57v).

COLLINS, Brisingham, Brislingham, 'joyner', of Meanestoke [Stoke Meon], Hants. 2 mths recusancy ending 16 May 1581, when convicted—V(56): and three later convictions, ending 24 Apr. 1582—I(55)*. III(50v). V(56). Debts re-enrolled—III(62)*.

COLLINSON, Robert, 'poticarie' [apothecary], of St. Mary's parish, Nottingham. 10 mths recusancy from 9 Sept. 1586: conv. 25 Mar. 1588.—VIII(80).

COLLYNES, William, 'yoman', of Raglan, Mon. 5 mths recusancy from 24 Mar. 1586/7: conv. 13 Mar. 1587/8.—VIII(48).

COMBE, Frances, wife of Walter Combe of Dorchester, Dorset, 'yom''. 6 mths recusancy from 1 Jan. 1587/8: conv. 15 July 1588.—VIII(19v).

COMBE, Walter, 'yoman', of Ashemeare [Ashmore], Dorset. 6 mths recusancy from 7 Jan. 1586/7: conv. 21 July 1587.—IX(16v). Debt re-enrolled—XII(78v).

COMBERFORD, Cumberford, Humphrey, gent., of Watford, Northants. £20 fine imposed by High Commissioners in 1577 for prolonged 'contempt' in refusing to comform in religion. (See text below)[40] [entry under 'Northants'].—I(42v). Debt re-enrolled—II(41v). IV(41v). VI(43v).

39—Continued
allotted to the Queen in the records of the Exchequer. In the meantime, on 9 June 1595 Richard Fitzherbert died, and shortly afterwards also the notorious Edward Thorne. (for Thorne's death, Cf. *CRS* LXI, p. 86 (10) last postscript ('Diem clausit extremum'), and p. 88 footnote. For Fitzherbert's death, Cf. R.R., Staffs., 39 Eliz., quoting the above date as given in the M.R., L.T.R., 40 Eliz., 'Recorda' section. (He left a debt of £18 – 9 – 8).) In the next entry, Thorne, now in charge of the farm, proceeds to bring Collier's 'Bancroft' property up to date by adding a further £20 as unpaid arrears, making a final rent of £23 – 6 – 8, the authority for which was the M.R., L.T.R., 39 Eliz., Michaelmas Term, 'Recorda' section. The entry ends: 'And he (Thorne) is quit'. These long standing debts are briefly referred to from time to time in the Staffs. section of the R.Rs., e.g., in 1600, 1603, 1607 and 1611, consisting merely of short notes relating to diminishing remnants of Fitzherbert's debt, and particularly to the aforesaid sum of £125 – 13 – 8, the safe-keeping of which was entrusted to Agnes Knolles, a widow of Sandbarrow, Staffs., herself one of the original 'fugitives'.

40. The earliest Pipe Roll entry, unique in form, of a prosecution for recusancy prior to the Statute of 1581. This lengthy entry is repeated at each re-enrolment of Cumberford's case of this date. (Text of I (42v).:- 'Humfridus Cumberford de Watford in Com' Northt' gen' (deb') £20 de quodam fine super ipsum imposit' pro contemptu suo commisso viginti lib', pro eo quod dictus Humfridus per nonnullos annos elapsos religion' servicio dei et principis et nostro beneficio in hoc regno Anglie agnite & professe non conformavit, nec adhuc suam obedienc' in ea parte praebere velit aut divinor' celebrac' interesse aut sacram communio' recipere, sed id facere pertinaciter et obstinate recusavitet recusat in praesenti. Nichilominus ad suam obedienciam in praemissis praebend' publice & legitime mandat' in omni lenitate iussa, ac eciam longo deliberand' spacio ad conferrend' et Communicand' pro eius reformacione in praemissis cum piis et doctis viris ex verbo divino et orthodoxo' part' scriptis concedebatur, dictus tamen Humfridus Cumberford persuasionibus, consiliis vel mandatis praedictis nullo modo acquiescere aut parere voluit sed pocius obstinato et indurato animo in ea parte persistere videbatur, in manifesto contempt' iuris et mandat' praedict'. Et eo praetextu dictus Humfridus Cumberford pronunciat' erat contumax et contemptor tam legibus in hac parte stabilit' quam mandatis in ea parte ei datis, et in penam contumacie' et contempt sue huiusmodi fin' sive mulcta viginti lib' ad usum domine Regine super

COMBERFORD, Cumberford, Humphrey, gent., of St. Margaret's parish, Westminster [prisoner]⁴¹ [entry under 'Northants']. 1 mth recusancy from 18 May 1581: conv. 26 June 1581.—I(42v). Debt re-enrolled—II(41v). IV(41v). VI(43v).

COMBERFORD, Cumberford, Humphrey, gent., of Westminster, Middx [prisoner]. [entries under 'Warwicks']⁴². 3 mths recusancy from 17 June 1581: conv. 26 Sept. 1581—II(llv); and eleven later convictions, ending 17 Nov. 1583—II(llv)*. IV(60v)*. Debts re-enrolled—VI(61)*.

COMBERFORD, Cumberford, Katherine, 'spinster', of Stone [? or Stoue (Stowe)], Staffs. 4 mths recusancy from 31 Mar. 1582: conv. 23 July 1582—VI(63): and seven later convictions, ending 13 Mar. 1585/6—IV(62v)*. V(66)*. VI(63), (63v)*.

CONBERFORD, Cumberford, Katherine, 'spinster', of Aston, Staffs. 5 mths recusancy from 3 Apr. 1587: conv. 25 Mar. 1588—VIII(78v).

CONIERS, Conyers, Samuel, 'yeoman', of Southwark, Surrey [prisoner]⁴³. 1 mth recusancy ending 11 Mar. 1582/3, when convicted—III(58v).

CONIERS, Conyers, Samuel, 'clericus', of Southwark, Surrey [prisoner]⁴⁴. (same recusancy period and conviction date)—V(52v).

CONYERS, Thomas [entry under 'Yorks']. Fine of £20 imposed by High Commissioners (? 1585 – 6)—VI(22). Debt re-enrolled—VIII(26). X(23).

CONSTABLE, John, gent., of Martham, Norfolk. 8 mths recusancy from 20 July 1588: conv. 7 July 1589.—IX(45v). Debt re-enrolled—XI(48).

40—Continued

ipsum prout supra in dicto suo manifest' contempt' imponebatur: viz. pro Edmundo Brudenell, milite, nuper vicecomite de anno 19 (Eliz.) (1577/8). (Annotation of payment) De quibus vic' respondet de Cs. Et deb' £15'. English Translation of Pipe Roll I (42v).:- 'Humfrey Cumberford of Watford, Northants., gent., (owes) £20 of a certain fine imposed on himself for contempt, in that the said Humfrey has for several years shunned the religious service of God, of his Queen and our benefit in this realm, by openly and publicly refusing to be present at divine celebration or to receive holy communion, but has obstinately refused the same, and still continues to do so.

Notwithstanding calls for his obedience, publicly yet mildly delivered urging him to confer for his reformation with pious and learned men, versed in Holy Writ and the orthodox fathers, the said Humfrey Cumberford would in no way consent and acquiesce and obey, but with an obstinate and hardened heart persisted in manifest contempt of the aforesaid injunctions. For this reason the said Humfrey Cumberford was pronounced contumacious and contemptuous, not only of established laws, but also of injunctions given to him personally, and in punishment for his stubborness, a fine or mulct of £20 was imposed on him, the Queen's use, for his said manifest contempt'. (Annotation) for which the Sheriff answers for 100s. And Cumberford owes £15.

41. Humphrey Cumberford was in the Gatehouse from 1578 to 1586. He was convicted on 26 June 1581, at the Old Bailey, of one month's recusancy from 18 May 1581—one of the earliest statutory convictions for this offence under the Act of 1581, c.I. (Cf. CRS I, p. 62, and CRS II, pp. 225, 245, 253.)

42. Comberford Hall, the family residence, was in the parish of Tamworth, two miles north of that town, and then regarded by the Exchequer as being situated in Warwicks. and not Staffs.

43. Samuel Coniers (Cf. Anstruther I, p. 86.)

44. Coniers was not the only priest to gain by the inaccuracy of a legal scribe in the 1580s. The same error appears in the entry of William Hartley—a well-known priest—in the same list, here likewise given the safer, but false, title of 'yoman', instead of 'clericus'. But if Coniers was saved by this error, it was not allowed to save Hartley, who was executed for his priesthood on 5 Oct. 1588.

CONSTABLE, Lady Margaret, wife of Sir Henry Constable, knt., of Constable Burton, E.R. Yorks. 6 mths recusancy from 3 July 1587: conv. 18 Mar. 1587/8.—VIII(27).

CONWEY, John, 'husb''', of Leighe, Staffs. 12 mths recusancy from 6 Sept. 1586: conv. 25 Mar. 1588—VIII(78v): and one later conviction dated 22 July 1588—VIII(58).

CONWEY, Ellen, his wife (of same parish). 4 mths recusancy from 13 Mar. 1585/6: conv. 1 Aug. 1586.—VI(63v).

COOKE, Ann, wife of Ambrose Cooke, of the city of York. 4 mths recusancy from 28 Mar. 1581: conv. 17 July 1581.—I(8). Debt re-enrolled—III(10). V(8). VII(8). IX(8). Goods value £10 seized from husband, 6 Feb. 1582/3—II(8).

COOKE, Eliz., wid., of Thistleton, parish of Kirkham, Lancs. 13 mths recusancy from 30 July 1587: conv. 17 Mar. 1588/9.—X(35).

COOKE, George, 'husb''', of Hamstall Ridware, Staffs. 6 mths recusancy from 25 Mar. 1588: conv. 14 Mar. 1588/9.—IX(69v). Goods, value £5 – 0 – 4, seized 4 Sept. 1589—X(14).

COOKE, Henry, esq., of Milton, Cambs. 10 mths recusancy from 1 Sept. 1586: conv. 24 Mar. 1587/8.—VIII(7v). Rental of lands seized 3 June 1588—IX(5v). Seized lands let by Crown to John Hutton from 28 June 1588—X(6). XI(6). XII(6).

COOKE, Ann, 'spinster', his wife (same parish, recusancy period and conviction date)—VIII(7v).

COOKE, John, [   ], of Kennington, Lambeth parish, Surrey. 3 mths recusancy from 15 Sept. 1588: conv. 30 June 1589.—IX(53).

COOKE, Laurence, 'husb''', of Westby, Lancs. 13 mths recusancy from 14 Aug. 1586: conv. 25 Mar. 1588.—VIII(21v).

COOKE, William, 'yoman', of Bunbury, Cheshire. 13 mths recusancy from 25 Sept. 1586: date of conviction omitted.—VIII(58v).

COPESTACKE, Anthony, 'yeom''', of [   ] in Chesterfeild parish, Derbys. 10 mths recusancy from 9 Sept. 1586: conv. 22 Mar. 1587/8.—VIII(21).

COPLEY, Katherine, Lady, 'spinster', of Horsham, Sussex. 3 mths recusancy from 1 Apr. 1588: conv. 3 Mar. 1588/9.—IX(53).

COPLEY, Katherine, Lady, wid., of Horsham, Sussex. Record of land-seizure, 13 Apr. 1590—X(67). Seized lands let by Crown to John Wattes from 29 July 1590—X(67)*. XI(55v). XII(56v).

CORMORTHE, John, 'clericus', of Westminster, Middx [prisoner][45]. [entries under 'Staffs'] 3 mths recusancy from 26 June 1581: conv. 26 Sept. 1581—II(14): and nine later convictions ending 25 Nov. 1583—II(14)*. IV(62), (62v)*. Debts re-enrolled—VI(63)*, (63v)*.

CORRIDEN, Eliz., 'spinster', of Checkley, Staffs. 4 mths recusancy (undated): convicted 21 July 1589.—IX(69v).

---

45. John Cormoth was a pre-Elizabethan priest who was deprived as V. North Weald Basett, Essex. He was imprisoned in the Gatehouse, 1581 – 1584. (Cf. *CRS* II, p. 235.)

CORSE, Thomas, 'husband'', of Asperton [Ashperton], Herefords. Two fines of £20 imposed for ignoring sheriff's summonses after excommunication, 4 Apr. and 27 May 1581.—III(28)*. Debts re-enrolled—V(26)*.

COSEN, Thomas, 'waterman', of St. Saviour's parish, Southwark, Surrey [? prisoner]. 4 mths recusancy ending 17 July 1587, when convicted.—IX(54).

COSYE, Ellen, wid., of Worthington, Lancs., relict of Alexander Cosye. 12 mths recusancy from 20 Sept. 1589: conv. 22 Mar. 1590/1.—X(38v).

COTSMORE, Cottesmore, Thomas, 'clericus', of St. Margaret's parish, Westminster, Middx [prisoner][46] [entry under 'Sussex']. One month recusancy from 18 May 1581: conv. 26 June 1581. Debt re-enrolled—VII(51). IX(55). XII(58). [Entries under 'Oxfords'], 3 mths recusancy from 27 June 1581: conv. 26 Sept. 1581—II(29v); and four later indictments, ending 16 Mar. 1581/2—II(29v), (44)*. Debts re-enrolled—IV(29v)*. VI(30v)*.

COTTON, George, esq., of St. Bride's parish, Farringdon Ward Without, London [prisoner][47]. 3 mths recusancy from 18 Mar. 1580/1: conv. 28 July 1581.—I(32v). Debt re-enrolled—III(38v). V(35).

COTTON, Sir George, knt., of St. Bride's parish, Farringdon Ward Without, London [entry under 'Hants']. 7 mths recusancy from 13 June 1582: conv. 18 Jan. 1582/3.—II(52). Debt re-enrolled—IV(52). VI(54).

COTTON, George, esq., of Warblington, Hants. Annual fine for recusancy (£260) paid from 28 Oct. 1587.—VII(54). VIII(67). IX(58). X(70v). XI(60). XII(62). Summary of pre-1587 debts for recusancy.—VII(54). VIII(66v). Remainder of pre-1587 arrears (£333 – 6 – 8) paid 21 Nov. 1590. Quit.[48]—X(69).

---

46. Thomas Cottesmore was a pre-Elizabethan priest. Deprived as V. Poynings, Sussex, in 1560, he is mentioned as living with the Gage family at Firle Place, Sussex, in 1567. (*VCH* Sussex, II, p. 25.) He may have been 'an old massing priest, taken at Arundel coming over from beyond the seas, and committed by the Privy Council to the Gatehouse prison, Westminster, two years since', in 1583. (Cf. *CRS* II, pp. 224, 230, 235.) His experience of prosecution for recusancy was confined to the period of his imprisonment. There were six periods in all:—
  (1) (1 month) 18 May 1581 to 26 June 1581 (his earliest recusancy)
  (2) (3 months) 27 Jun 1581 to 26 Sept. 1581
  (3) (1 month) 16 Oct. 1581 to 20 Nov. 1581
  (4) (1 month) 19 Nov. 1581 to 18 Dec. 1581
  (5) (1 month) 18 Dec. 1581 to 18 Jan. 1581/2
  (6) (3 months) 18 Jan. 1581/2 to 16 Mar. 1581/2
No further prosecution for recusancy occurs against him.

47. George Cotton was imprisoned in the Fleet from 18 Mar. 1580/1 to 28 July 1581. (Cf. *CRS* II, pp. 223, 229.) Being a wealthy man, he was persuaded by the Exchequer to adopt the full scheme of the Statute of 1586/7 (section III) for the payment of his recusancy debts, and of his pre-1587 arrears. (Cf. *CRS* LVII, Appendix.)

48. George Cotton's paid debts, upon examination, were found to amount to £1,199 – 6 – 8 out of £3,600 for recusancy from 28 July 1581 to 20 Oct. 1586 (68 months). He was required to render to the Exchequer, in the Michaelmas Term of 1587, £199 – 6 – 8, and at Michaelmas 1588, £333 – 6 – 8, and thereafter, in every Michaelmas term, £333 – 6 – 8, until payment was completed, by the sureties of the said George Cotton, *viz.* Thomas Onley esq., of Catesby, Northants.; John

COTTON, John, gent., of Warblington, Hants. 7 mths recusancy from 12 Sept. 1586: conv. 26 Feb. 1587/8.—VIII(67).
COTTON, Mary, 'spinster', of Brickles [Breckles] Magna, Norfolk. 3 mths recusancy from 13 Apr. 1587: conv. 1 Apr. 1588.—VIII(54).
COTTON, Thomas, gent., of Grindon, Staffs. 12 mths recusancy from 6 Sept. 1586: conv. 25 Mar. 1588.—VIII(78v).
COURTNEY, James, esq., of Cheriton Fitzpayne [Fitzpaine], Devon. 3 mths recusancy from 7 Jan. 1581/2: conv. 31 Aug. 1584.—IV(14v). Debt re-enrolled—VI(14v). Record of land-seizure, 6 Oct. 1587—VIII(18). Rental of seized land—VIII(18v). IX(15). X(19). XI(17). Seized lands let by Crown to John Clapham & Thomas Culliford from 25 Mar. 1590—X(19v). XI(17). XII(18).
COWHAPPE, John, 'laborer', of [   ] in North Wingfeild parish, Derbys. 10 mths recusancy from 9 Sept. 1586: conv. 22 Mar. 1588.—VIII(21).
COWPER, [   ], 'laborer', of Lee in the parish of Ashber [? Ashover], Derbys. 10 mths recusancy from 9 Sept. 1586: conv. 22 Mar. 1588.—VIII(21).
COWPER, [   ], his wife (same parish, recusancy period and conviction date)—VIII(21).
COWPER, Joan, 'spinster', of St. Jones [John's], Southover, E. Sussex. 2 mths recusancy from 17 Apr. 1587: conv. 26 Feb. 1587/8.—VIII(63v).
COWPER, Richard, 'yeoman', of Pittlesthorne [Pitstone], Bucks. 3 mths recusancy from 27 Mar. 1587: conv. 18 Mar. 1587/8.—VIII(3).
COWPER, *alias* BIRCHE, Thomas, [   ], of Meaddowes [? nr. Pemberton], Lancs. 12 mths recusancy from 20 Sept. 1589: conv. 22 Mar. 1590/1.—X(38).
COXE, Ann, Wid., of Chilton, Berks. 12 mths recusancy from 1 Sept. 1586: conv. 4 Mar. 1587/8.—VIII(5).
COXE, Katherine verch John, wife of John Coxe, [   ], of Llantilio Crossenny, Mon. 5 mths recusancy from 24 Mar. 1586/7: conv. 13 Mar. 1587/8.—VIII(49v).
COXE, Richard, 'brickmaker', of Otterbo(u)rne, Hants. 6 mths recusancy from 1 Aug. 1587: conv. 8 July 1588.—VIII(68v).
COXE, Richard, 'yeoman', of St. Sepulchre parish, Northampton, Northants. 12 mths recusancy from 31 July 1587: conv. 4 Mar. 1588/9.—IX(47).
COXON, Gertrude, 'spinster', of Hamstall Ridware, Staffs. 4 mths recusancy [undated]: convicted 21 July 1589.—IX(69v).

48—Continued
Chamberlen, esq., of Beaulieu, Hants.; and John Wakeham, gent., of Beckford, Gloucs. His arrears were paid off on 21 Nov. 1590, by the delivery of the final £333 – 6 – 8 into the Treasury (Cf. Item South' VII (54)). He now concentrated on the regular yearly payment of his fine of £260, which he continued to pay till his death on 13 Nov. 1609. By that date he had contributed, in all, £3,539 – 6 – 8. Only eight recusants were confident enough to tackle such debts in the 1580s. (Cf. *CRS* LVII, Introd., pp. xxx – xxxii, xliii – xliv, lxxxiv – lxxxv.) By the end of Elizabeth's reign, however, the number had risen to 15, but never surpassed it.

COXON, Henry, 'laborer', of Hamstall Ridware, Staffs. 6 mths recusancy from 25 Mar. 1588: conv. 14 Mar. 1588/9.—IX(69v).
CRABBE, William, 'yoman', of Southwark, Surrey [prisoner][49]. 8 mths recusancy ending 16 Feb. 1586/7, when convicted.—VI(50).
CRAGGE, Alice, 'spinster', of Milwiche, Staffs. 4 mths recusancy [undated]: convicted 21 July 1589.—IX(69v).
CRAGGE, Crage, Ralph, gent., of Gaiton, Gaton [Gayton], Staffs. 6 mths recusancy from 6 Sept. 1587: conv. 22 July 1588.—VIII(58).
CRAGGE, Crage, Margaret, his wife (same parish, recusancy period and conviction date).—VIII(58).
CRANE, Christiana, 'spinster', of Holmehall, Norfolk, wife of John Crane, 'yom''. 8 mths recusancy from 12 July 1583: conv. Lent 1583/4—IV(44v).
CRANE, Nicholas, 'clericus', of St. Sepulchre parish, Farringdon Ward Without, London [prisoner][50]. 13 mths recusancy from 18 Apr. 1587: conv. 30 Apr. 1588.—VIII(38v).
CRAWLEY, Thomas, esq., of Manweden [Manuden], Essex. 3 mths recusancy from 25 Mar. 1588: conv. 13 Mar. 1588/9.—IX(27v). Record of land-seizure, 22 May 1589—IX(27v). Rental of lands seized 22 May 1589—IX(49). X(25). XI(21). XII(20v). Seized lands let by Crown to Robert Seale from 11 June 1589.—X(26v). XI(21v). XII(20v).
CRESSEY, Christopher, gent., of Twiford [Twyford], Bucks. 12 mths recusancy from 12 Mar. 1587/8: conv. 23 June 1589.—IX(70).
CRISLEY, alias CRICHELOWE, Roger [ ], son of Edward Crichlow [ ], of Charnock Richard, Lancs. 12 mths recusancy from 20 Sept. 1589: conv. 22 Mar. 1590/1.—X(38v).
CRISLEY, alias CRICHELOWE, Eliz., wife of the said Roger (same parish, recusancy period & conviction date)—X(38v).
CRISLOWE, Ralph, 'webster', of Charnock Richard, Lancs. (same recusancy period and conviction date)—X(38v).
CRISPE, Grace, [ ], of Debenham, Suffolk. 3 mths recusancy from 1 Jan. 1587/8: conv. 10 July 1588.—VIII(73). Debt re-enrolled—X(64).
CROCKET, Ralph, 'clericus' of St. Georges Parish, Southwark, Surrey [prisoner][51]. 5 mths recusancy from 17 Feb. 1586/7: conv. 17 July 1587—IX(54).
CROFT, Thomas, esq., of Wigmore, Herefords. 19 mths recusancy from 24 Mar. 1580/1: conv. 8 Jan. 1581/2—II(64), and 10 later convictions ending 18 Mar. 1587/8—IV(64)*. V(26), (26v)*. VIII(30). Debts re-

---

49. William Crabbe was arrested in Chichester Haven and imprisoned in the Marshalsea on 25 Apr. 1586. (Cf. *CRS* II, pp. 242, 244, 252, 254.)

50. Nicholas Crane (?1522–?1588), presbyterian 'cleric' of Christ's College, Cambridge. (Cf. *DNB*, XIII, p. 11.)

51. See footnote 244A. The Pipe Office Clerk regularly confused Ralph Crocket with George Potter.

enrolled—III(27). 'Chattels real' value £100, seized Michaelmas 1585 by Hugh Cuffe, commissioner—X(29v). Goods value £2 seized 23 Aug. 1588—XI(29). Record of land-seizure, 23 Aug. 1588—IX(25v). Rental of lands seized 23 Aug. 1588—IX(25v). X(28). XI(28).

CROFT, Thomas, gent., of Wigmore, Herefords. 3 mths recusancy from 22 Sept. 1582: conv. 5 Jan. 1582/3, and one later conviction dated 4 Mar. 1582/3.—II(64)*. Debts re-enrolled—III(27). V(26).

CROMBLEHOLME, William, 'yom''', of Southwark, Surrey [? prisoner]. 4 mths recusancy ending 17 Feb. 1585/6, when convicted—VI(49v).

CROMPTON, William, 'wariner', of Litherland, Lancs. 12 mths recusancy from 20 Sept. 1589: conv. 22 Mar. 1590/1.—X(38).

CRONE, Margaret, of Weeton, Lancs., wife of Robert Crone, 'husb''. (same recusancy period and conviction date)—X(39).

CROOKE, [   ], of Westby, Lancs., wife of Richard Crooke. (same recusancy period and conviction date)—X(39v).

CROOKE, Eliz., wid., of Thistleton, Lancs. 12 mths recusancy from 20 Sept. 1589: conv. 22 Mar. 1590/1.—X(39).

CROOKE, Eliz., wid., of Grenhalgh [Greenhalgh], Kirkham parish, Lancs. 13 mths recusancy from 14 Aug. 1586: conv. 25 Mar. 1588.—VIII(21v).

CROOKE, Evanc', 'yeoman', of East Harling, Norfolk. 3 mths recusancy from 13 Apr. 1587: conv. 1 Apr. 1588.—VIII(54).

CROOKE, Laurence, [   ], of Westby, Lancs. 12 mths recusancy from 20 Sept. 1589: conv. 22 Mar. 1590/1.—X(39v).

CROOKE, Margaret, wife of John Crooke, 'yoman', of Bryning, Lancs. (same recusancy period and conviction date)—X(39v).

COOKE, Thomas, [   ], of Westby, Lancs. (same recusancy period and conviction date)—X(39v).

CROSDALE, Thomas, 'yeoman', of Sheringham, Norfolk. 3 mths recusancy from 13 Apr. 1587: conv. 1 Apr. 1588.—VIII(54).

CROWCHER, Eliz., recusant (of Sussex). Goods, value £21 – 6 – 8, seized 17 Jan. 1588/9.—IX(54v).

CROWTHER, Crowder, Thomas, 'clericus', of Southwark, Surrey [prisoner][52]. 9 mths recusancy ending 11 Mar. 1582/3, when convicted—III(58v); and one later conviction dated 20 July 1584—V(50v). Debt re-enrolled—V(52v).

CUFFIELDE, Cuffald, Cuffall, Simon, gent., of Basing, Hants. 18 mths recusancy from 18 Mar. 1580/1: conv. ? Sept. 1582—III(50v): and one later conviction dated 7 Jan. 1583/4—IV(53). Lands seized by Crown and let to Hugh Cuffe from 2 Mar. 1583/4—IV(52).

CULPAGE, John, priest ('sacerdos'), of Salford in the parish of Manchester, Lancs. [prisoner][53]. 3 mths recusancy from 10 Oct. 1581:

---

52. Thomas Crowther (Cf. Anstruther I, p. 95.)
53. John Cuppage or Coppage (Cf. Wark, pp. 174–175.)

conv. 18 Jan. 1581/2, and two later convictions ending 16 Jan. 1582/3.—II(38v)*. Debts re-enrolled—VIII(46)*.
CUMBER, John, 'bruer', of St. Ebbes parish, Oxford city. 7 mths recusancy from 23 July 1584: conv. 5 Feb. 1584/5.—V(47): and three later convictions ending 17 Mar. 1586/7.—V(47). VI(11v), (47v).
CUMBERFORD, see COMBERFORD.
CURROR, Eliz., wife of Peter Curror, gent., of Clint, in parish of Ripley, W.R. Yorks. 13 mths recusancy from 3 Sept. 1586: conv. 4 Sept. 1587.—VIII(25v).
CURWINE, Curwyne, Nicholas, gent., of Nappa Hall [Aysgarth parish], N.R. Yorks. 13 mths recusancy from 3 Sept. 1586: conv. 4 Sept. 1587.—VIII(25v).
CURWINE, William, gent., (same place, recusancy period and conviction date).—VIII(25v).

DALE, Nicholas, 'laborer', of Wiswell, Lancs. 12 mths recusancy from 20 Sept. 1589: conv. 22 Mar. 1590/1.—X(40).
DALE, Agnes, his wife (same parish, recusancy period and conviction date)—X(40).
DALLYSON, John, gent., of Laughton, Lincs. 1 mth recusancy from 23 Mar. 1580/1: conv. ? Apr. 1581, and one later conviction dated 22 Sept. 1581.—I(49)*.
DALTON, James, 'yoman', of Kirkland [Garstang], Lancs. 12 mths recusancy from 20 Sept. 1589: conv. 22 Mar. 1590/1.—X(39).
DALTON, Robert, 'taleor', of Duxbury, Lancs. (same recusancy period and conviction date)—X(38v).
DANBIE, Christopher, gent., of Scruton, N.R. Yorks. 13 mths recusancy from 3 Sept. 1586: conv. 4 Sept. 1587.—VIII(25v).
DAND, Henry, [   ], of St. Mary's parish, Nottingham, Notts. 3 mths recusancy from 1 Apr. 1588: conv. 17 Mar. 1588/9.—IX(70). Debt re-enrolled—XII(75).
DANE, Margaret, 'spinster', of Hanley Castle, Worcs. 12 mths recusancy from 1 Apr. 1587: conv. 28 Mar. 1588.—VIII(80).
DANIELL, Ann, 'spinster', of Acton, Suffolk. 3 mths recusancy from 8 Apr. 1587: conv. 27 Mar. 1588.—VIII(73).
DANIELL, Danyell, John, gent., of Acton, Suffolk (same recusancy period and conviction date as preceding entry)—VIII(73). Record of land-seizure in Suffolk, 10 Sept. 1589—IX(64). Rental of lands seized in Suffolk—IX(45v). X(63v). XI(65v). Lands seized in Suffolk let by Crown to Matthew Cripes from Michaelmas 1589—X(80v). XI(65v). XII(66v). Record of land-seizure in Essex, 3 Feb. 1589/90—X(26v). Lands seized in Essex let by Crown to Henry Marwood from 20 Mar. 1589/90—XI(21v). XII(20v).
DANIELL, Danyell, John, esq., of Acton, Suffolk. Lands seized in Suffolk and Essex on 12 June 1590 let by Crown to Richard Brewster from 16 July 1590—X(80v). XI(65v). XII(66v).

DANIELL, Margaret, wid., of Acton, Suffolk. 3 mths recusancy from
  8 Apr. 1587: conv. 27 Mar. 1588.—VIII(73). Goods, value £5, seized
  7 Oct. 1588—IX(64). Rental of lands seized 7 Oct. 1588—IX(64).
  Seized lands let by Crown to Matthew Crispe [sic] from 10 Mar.
  1588/9—IX(64). X(63v). XI(65v).
DANIELL, Danyell, William, gent., of Acton, Suffolk (same recusancy
  period and conviction date)—VIII(73). Record of land-seizure in
  Acton, 7 Oct. 1588—IX(64). Rental of seized lands—IX(45v).
  X(63v). XI(65v). Seized lands at Acton let by Crown to Matthew
  Cripes [sic] from Michaelmas 1589—X(80v). XI(65v). XII(66v).
DARCEY, 'Collinbra', wife of Thomas Darcey, esq., of Hornebie [Hornby],
  N.R. Yorks. 13 mths recusancy from 3 Sept. 1586: conv. 4 Sept.
  1587—VIII(25v).
DARCYE, 'Colabrea', wife of Thomas Darcye, esq., of Hornebye [Hornby],
  N.R. Yorks. 6 mths recusancy from 3 July 1587: conv. 18 Mar.
  1587/8—VIII(25v).
DARNELL, Katherine, wid., of the city of Hereford. 12 mths recusancy
  from 26 June 1581: conv. 26 June 1582—II(64), and three later
  convictions, ending 4 Mar. 1582/3—II(64)*.
DARNELL, Katherine, wid., of St. Owen's parish, Hereford. 1 mth
  recusancy from 27 May 1583: conv. 15 July 1583—III(27), and nine
  later convictions, ending 8 Aug. 1586—IV(64v)*. V(26v)*. VI(25)*.
  Debts re-enrolled—V(26)*.
DARRINGTON, William, [   ], of Etwall, Derbys. 10 mths recusancy
  from 9 Sept. 1586: conv. 22 Mar. 1587/8.—VIII(21).
DARWYN, Robert, 'husb'', of Ince Blundell, Lancs. 12 mths recusancy
  from 20 Sept. 1589: conv. 22 Mar. 1590/1.—X(38).
DAVID, Eliz. verch Hoell, wife of Richard John David, [   ], of
  Llangattock nigh Usk, Mon. 5 mths recusancy from 24 Mar. 1586/7:
  conv. 13 Mar. 1587/8.—VIII(49).
DAVID, 'Gwenliana', wife of 'Morice' David, [   ], of Llanvihangel
  Ystern Llewern, Mon. (same recusancy period & conv. date).—
  VIII(49v).
DAVID, Henry John, 'yoman', of Llanthewy Skirrid, Mon. (same recusancy
  period & conv. date).—VIII(48v).
DAVID, Isabel verch Hoell, wife of John William David, [   ], of
  Llangattock Vibon Avel, Mon. (same recy period & conv. date).—
  VIII(48v).
DAVID, John, senior, 'yoman', of Llanvihangel Crucorney, Mon. (same
  recy period & conv. date).—VIII(48v).
DAVID, John ap Jevan, 'yom'', of Raglan, Mon. 8 mths recusancy from
  12 Aug. 1586: conv. ? 20 Mar. 1586/7.—VI(40).
DAVID, John ap Jevan John, 'yoman', of Raglan, Mon. 12 mths recusancy
  from 1 July 1581: conv. 23 July 1582,—II(38): and eight later
  convictions, ending 20 Mar. 1586/7.—IV(38v)*. V(40v)*. VI(40v)*.
  Debt re-enrolled—III(45).
DAVID, 'Jonetta', his wife (same parish). 5 mths recusancy from 24 Mar.

1586/7: conv. 13 Mar. 1587/8.—VIII(48).
DAVID, Llewelyn, 'yoman', of Trostoe [Trostrey], Mon. (same recy period & conv. date).—VIII(49).
DAVID, 'Gwenliana', his wife (same parish, recy period & conv. date).—VIII(49).
DAVID, Margaret verch Harry, wife of Henry David, [ ], of Aburgavenny, Mon. (same recy period & conv. date).—VIII(48).
DAVID, Matilda, 'spinster', of Llanvihangel Tomegrose [Llantarnam], Mon. (same recy period & conv. date).—VIII(49).
DAVID, Matilda verch David, wife of Jevan Thomas David, [ ], of Raglan, Mon. (same recy period & conv. date).—VIII(48).
DAVID, Sybil, wid., (same parish, recy period & conv. date).—VIII(48).
DAVID, Thomas, 'yoman', of Llanthewy Skirrid, Mon. (same recy period & conv. date).—VIII(48v).
ap DAVID, John ap Jevan, [ ], of Raglan, Mon. 8 mths recusancy from 4 July 1583: conv. 6 Mar. 1583/4.—VI(40v).
verch DAVID, 'Alsona', wid., of St. Bride's [Wentiloog], Mon. 5 mths recusancy from 24 Mar. 1586/7: conv. 13 Mar. 1587/8.—VIII(48).
verch DAVID, Blanche, 'spinster', of Llangoven, Mon. (same recy period & conv. date).—VIII(49v).
verch DAVID, 'Crisilia', 'spinster', of Llanvair Kilgedin, Mon. (same recy period & conv. date).—VIII(49).
verch DAVID, 'Jonnetta', 'spinster', of Llangattock Vibon Avel, Mon. (same recy period & conv. date).—VIII(48v).
verch DAVID, Katherine, 'spinster', of Llanvihangel Ystern Llewern, Mon. (same recy period & conv. date).—VIII(49v).
verch DAVID, Margaret, 'spinster', of Llanthewy Rytherch, Mon. (same recy period & conv. date).—VIII(48).
verch DAVID, Margaret, 'spinster', of Llantilio Pertholey, Mon. (same recy period & conv. date).—VIII(48v).
verch DAVID, Matilda, 'spinster', of Llangattock Vibon Avel, Mon. (same recy period & conv. date).—VIII(48v).
verch DAVID, Matilda, 'spinster', of [? Usk], Mon. (same recy period & conv. date).—VIII(49).
DAVIE, *alias* of APRICE, Richard.
DAWBNEY, William, gent., of [ ], Worcs. 12 mths recusancy from 1 Apr. 1587: conv. 28 Mar. 1588.—VIII(80).
DAWES, Richard, gent., of Southwark, Surrey [prisoner][54] 10 mths recusancy ending 17 Feb. 1585/6, when convicted.—VI(49v).
DAWNEY, Cuthbert, gent., of West Hestlerton [Heslerton], E.R. Yorks. 9 mths recusancy from 25 Mar. 1582: conv. 17 May 1583.—IV(21). Debt re-enrolled—VI(22).

---

54. Richard Dawes, or Dowse or Dowce, was imprisoned in the Clink for 18 years, from 1583/4 to 1602. (Cf. *CRS* II, pp. 246, 252, 283, 285, 288) The same Pipe Roll (under 'Item Sussex') gives another prosecution against 'Richard Dowse, yeoman, of Southwark, Surrey' (The Clink prison) for 8 months recusancy ending 16 Feb. 1586/7, when he was again convicted and fined £160.

DAWNEY, Katherine, his wife (same parish, recusancy period and
    conviction date).—IV(21).
DAWSON, Frances, wife of Richard Dawson, gent., of [   ], Yorks. 6
    mths recusancy from 3 July 1587: conv. 18 Mar. 1587/8.—VIII(27).
DAWSON, George, [   ], of [   ], Yorks.[55] (same recusancy period and
    conviction date).—VIII(27).
DAYE, Daie, John, 'yom'', of Ensham [Eynsham], Oxfords. 8 mths
    recusancy from 25 July 1586: conv. 17 Mar. 1586/7.—VI(llv). Record
    of land-seizure, 21 Feb. 1587/8—VIII(59v). Rental of seized lands—
    VIII(35). IX(50). X(57). XI(53). XII(53). Seized lands let by Crown to
    Thomas Bostock & Edward Streete from 5 July 1589—IX(31v).
    X(57v). XI(53v). XII(53v).
DAYE, Daie, Thomas, 'yoman', of Rickenhall [Rickinghall], Suffolk. 3
    mths recusancy from 1 Jan. 1587/8: conv. 10 July 1588.—VIII(73).
    Debt re-enrolled—X(64).
DEANE, William, 'clericus', of Southwark, Surrey [prisoner][56] 5 mths
    recusancy ending 15 Feb. 1583/4, when convicted—IV(49v): and one
    later conviction, dated 20 July 1584—V(50v). Debts re-enrolled—
    VI(51).
DELVES, Margaret, 'spinster', of Warneham [Warnham], W. Sussex. 3
    mths recusancy from 1 Apr. 1588: conv. 3 Mar. 1588/9.—IX(53).
DENFORD, John, 'clericus'[57], of Stepney, Middx. 3 mths recusancy from
    1 July 1588: conv. 2 Dec. 1588.—IX(37).
DENNIS, [   ], wid., of Denbie in Horseley [Horsley] parish, Derbys,
    'spinster'. 10 mths recusancy from 9 Sept. 1586: conv. 22 Mar.
    1587/8.—VIII(21).
DENNIS, Ann, wife of William Dennis, gent., of Lekehampton
    [Leckhampton], Gloucs. 5 mths recusancy from 26 Mar. 1587: conv.
    11 Mar. 1587/8.—VIII(82).
DENNIS, Jane, 'spinster' (same parish, recusancy period and conviction
    date)—VIII(82).
DENNYS, Robert, 'laborer', of St. Jones [John's], Southover, Sussex. 2
    mths recusancy from 17 Apr. 1587: conv. 26 Feb. 1587/8.—
    VIII(63v).
DENTON, Susan, [   ], of All Saints parish, city of Oxford. 12 mths
    recusancy from 26 Sept. 1586: conv. 7 Mar. 1587/8.—VIII(35v).
DENTON, William, 'clericus', of Southwark, Surrey [prisoner][58]. 10 mths
    recusancy ending 11 Mar. 1582/3, when convicted—III(58v): and one
    later conviction dated 18 Feb. 1584/5.—V(52v).
DEREHAM, John, gent., of Cossey [Costessey], Norfolk. 3 mths recusancy
    from 13 Apr. 1587: conv. 1 Apr. 1588.—VIII(54).

---

55. George Dawson is not given a domicile in every roll of the series. However, he is described in R.R. no. 1, as of Hunsingore in Yorks. (Cf. *CRS* XVIII, p. 60.)
56. William Deane (Cf. Anstruther I, p. 100.)
57. John Denford An unidentified cleric.
58. William Denton (Cf. Anstruther I, p. 100.)

DEREHAM, William, gent., of Wingfeild, Suffolk. 3 mths recusancy from 8 Apr. 1587: conv. 27 Mar. 1588.—VIII(73).

DEWE, John, gent., of Southwark, Surrey [prisoner][59]. 3 mths recusancy ending 11 Mar. 1582/3, when convicted.—III(58v).

DEWE, John, 'yom'', of Southwark, Surrey [prisoner][59]. 4 mths recusancy ending 22 July 1583, when convicted—IV(49v); and three later convictions, ending 18 Feb. 1584/5—IV(49v), V(52v)*. Debts re-enrolled—VI(51)*.

DEWEY, Edward, 'yom'', of Dorchester, Dorset. 6 mths recusancy from 2 Jan. 1587/8: conv. 15 July 1588.—VIII(19v).

DEWHURSTE, Eliz., of Wiswall, parish of Whalley, Lancs., wife of Christopher Dewhurst [ ]. 10 mths recusancy from 18 Mar. 1580/1: conv. 25 Apr. 1582.—II(38v). Debt re-enrolled—VIII(46).

DEWHURSTE, Eliz., 'spinster', of Halselmore, Lancs. 12 mths recusancy from 20 Sept. 1589: conv. 22 Mar. 1590/1.—X(40v).

DEWHURSTE, Isabel, of Halselmore, Lancs., wife of John Dewhurste, 'husb''. (same recusancy period and conviction date)—X(40v).

DICCONSON, Eliz., 'spinster', of Swartbreck [Swarbrick], Kirkham parish, Lancs. 13 mths recusancy from 30 July 1587: conv. 17 Mar. 1588/9.—X(35).

DICCONSON, Ellen, of Weeton, Lancs., wife of Thomas Dicconson, gent. 12 mths recusancy from 20 Sept. 1589: conv. 22 Mar. 1590/1.—X(39).

DICONSON, Thomas, gent., of Swartbreck [Swarbrick], Kirkham parish, Lancs. 13 mths recusancy from 30 July 1587: conv. 17 Mar. 1588/9.—X(35).

DIGGES, William, 'husb'', of Langford [Longford], Derbys. 10 mths recusancy from 9 Sept. 1586: conv. 22 Mar. 1587/8.—VIII(21).

DINGLE, Henry, 'yoman', of Acton, Suffolk. 6 mths recusancy from 20 Sept. 1588: conv. 2 July 1589.—IX(64). Debt re-enrolled—XI(72v).

DIXSON, Agnes, wid., of Barford [Barforth] Dykes, in Gillinge parish [sic], N.R. Yorks. 13 mths recusancy from 3 Sept. 1586: conv. 4 Sept. 1587.—VIII(25v).

DOBSON, Humphrey, 'laborer', of Graunge [-over-Sands], Lancs. 12 mths recusancy from 20 Sept. 1589: conv. 22 Mar. 1590/1.—X(40).

DOD(D), Dood, John, 'yoman', of Denham, Bucks. 3 mths recusancy from 27 Mar. 1587: conv. 18 Mar. 1587/8.—VIII(3). Rental of lands seized 12 Oct. 1588 (discharge ref.)—IX(70). Goods, value £25 – 10 – 7, seized 12 Oct. 1588 (discharge ref.)[60]—IX(70).

DORRINGTON, Andrew, gent., of Muccleston [Mucklestone], Staffs. 12 mths recusancy from 6 Sept. 1586: conv. 25 Mar. 1588.—VIII(78v).

---

59. John Dewe was a servant of William Shelley at Michelgrove in Clapham, Sussex. He was in the Clink, 17 Aug. 1582. (Cf. *CRS* II, p. 227.)

60. John Dodd was discharge from his two debts—the £3 – 17 – 10 for two-thirds of his lands seized for recusancy at Southmead, 12 Oct. 1588, and the £25 – 10 – 7 for his goods and chattels. (Cf. M.R., L.T.R., 32 Eliz., Trinity Term, 'Recorda' section.)

DORRINGTON, Dorington, Ellen, wife of Thomas Dorington, gent., of Moleston [Mucklestone?], Staffs. 6 mths recusancy from 6 Sept. 1587: conv. 22 July 1588.—VIII(58).

DORRINGTON, Dorington, Thomas, gent., of Muccleston [Mucklestone], Staffs. 12 mths recusancy from 6 Sept. 1586: conv. 25 Mar. 1588.—VIII(78v).

DORRINGTON, William, gent. (same parish, recusancy period & conviction date).—VIII(78v).

DORRINGTON, John, 'yoman', of St. Mary Magdalene parish, borough of Southwark, Surrey [prisoner][61]. 12 mths recusancy from 10 Sept. 1586: conv. 5 July 1588[62].—VIII(63).

DOUGHTIE, *alias* ROBERTES, Jane (*q.v.*).

DOWNES, Francis, gent., of Acton, Suffolk. 3 mths recusancy from 8 Apr. 1587: conv. 27 Mar. 1588.—VIII(73).

DOWNES, John, gent., of Boughton, Norfolk. 9 mths recusancy from 1 Oct. 1581: conv. ? 1 July 1582—IV(44v): and one later conviction, dated 1 Apr. 1588.—VIII(54).

DOWNES, Mary, his wife (of same parish). 3 mths recusancy from 13 Apr. 1587: conv. 1 Apr. 1588.—VIII(54).

DOWNES, Margery, wife of George Downes, gent., of [Bishop's] Frome, Herefords. 12 mths recusancy from 1 Sept. 1586: conv. 18 Mar. 1587/8.—VIII(30).

DOWNES, Robert, esq., of Melton Magna, Norfolk. 11 mths recusancy from 1 Aug. 1581: conv. 23 July 1582—II(40): and five later indictments, ending 6 Apr. 1587—III(72v). IV(44v). V(46v)*. VI(25v). Debts re-enrolled—IV(40). V(41v). VII(41)*. Summary of pre-1587 debts—VI(41v), (42). Goods, value £26 – 13 – 4, seized 1585—V(41v). Goods, value £6 – 6 – 8, seized 1587—VII(41). Record of land-seizure 26 Sept. 1587—VIII(51). Rental of lands seized 26 Sept. 1587—VIII(6v). IX(43v). X(52v). XI(46v). XII(47v). Seized lands let by Crown to John Coleman & Peter White from 3 Mar. 1589/90[63]—X(8lv). XI(46v), (47). XII(47v). 12 acres of woods in Melton Magna, value £144 – 10s, seized by commissioners Richard Brewster & Thomas Felton in 1589—X(81v). XI(66).

Two fines, each of 100 marks, imposed for hearing Mass at Melton Magna in his own house on 11 Aug. and 26 Aug. 1583[64].—IV(44v)*.

DOWSE, Richard, 'yoman', of Southwark, Surrey [prisoner]. 8 mths recusancy ending 16 Feb. 1586/7, when convicted—VI(50). Cf. DAWES, Richard.

---

61. John Dorrington of Staffs., was probably a prisoner in the Wood Street Counter.
62. 'Mr. Dorrington' was suspected of complicity in the Babington Plot. (Cf. *CRS* II, p. 258.)
63. Robert Downes's lands in Great Melton consisted of the Manor of Peverelles and Haggines, which was seized by the Crown on 26 Sept. 1586. On 3 Mar. 1589/90 this property was let by the Crown to John Coleman and Peter White for a rent of £111 – 8 – 9½ *per annum*. It was taken over at Easter 1598 by Henry Clarck, gent., who continued in charge until the death of Robert Downes in 1611. Ann Downes, Robert's widow continued her recusancy at a cost of £14 – 4s. *per annum*.
64. (Cf. Pipe Roll, 5 James I: Robert Downes is again acquitted.)

DRAYCOTT, Draicote, Alban, gent., of Draicote [Draycott], Staffs. 6 mths recusancy from 6 Sept. 1587: conv. 22 July 1588.—VIII(58).

DRAYCOTT, Dracote, Edmund, gent., of Stone [? or Stoue], Staffs. 6 mths recusancy from 25 Mar. 1588: conv. 14 Mar. 1588/9.—IX(69v).

DRAYCOTT, Draicotte, Edward, gent., of Uttoxator [Uttoxeter], Staffs. 12 mths recusancy from 6 Sept. 1586: conv. 25 Mar. 1588—VIII(78v).

DRAYCOTT, Draycote, John, esq., of Draycott, Staffs. 12 mths recusancy; convicted Easter 1582 by informer's suit[65].—III(64v). Debt re-enrolled—V(66). VII(64). IX(69). XI(71v).

DRAYCOTT, Draicote, John, esq., of Paynesley, Draycott parish, Staffs. 4 mths recusancy from 31 Mar. 1582: conv. ? 3 Aug. 1582;—IV(62v): and five later convictions, ending 25 Mar. 1588.—IV(62v)*. VIII(78v). Debts re-enrolled—VI(63)*, (63v)*. XI(71v). Summary of unpaid debts for recusancy, Mar. 1582 to Aug. 1584, (£600), granted to William Ashbye[66]—VIII(16v). X(78v). Annual fines of £260 p.a., beginning 19 Apr. 1591, enrolled and discharged [in favour of William Ashbye][67].—X(7v). XI(71v).

DRAYCOTT, Dracote, John, [ ], of Denbie, in Horseley [Horsley] parish, Derbys. 10 mths recusancy from 9 Sept. 1586: conv. 22 Mar. 1587/8.—VIII(21).

DRAYCOTT, Dracote, Philip, gent., of Magna Over, Derbys. (same recusancy period and conviction date)—VIII(21).

DRAYCOTT, Dracotte, Philip, gent., of Stone [? or Stoue], Staffs. 12 mths recusancy from 6 Sept. 1586: conv. 25 Mar. 1588.—VIII(78v).

DREWRYE, Drury, Eliz., wid., of Lawshall, Suffolk. 8 mths recusancy from 15 July 1588: conv. 2 July 1589.—IX(64). Debt re-enrolled XI(72v). Lands seized, 12 Apr. 1591, let by Crown to William Hunnys from 11 Nov. 1591.—XII(66v).

---

65. In *Qui Tam* actions for recusancy, the informer was due to obtain one third of the total penalty, viz. £80, of the £240 in the present case. (Cf. *CRS* LVII, Introd. pp. xiv, and xv – xx.)

66. A special interest attaches to the treatment of John Draycott in that he is seemingly the earliest instance of the payment of crown servants by the grant of recusants' forfeitures—a practice not uncommon in the first seven years of the next reign. On 18 Mar. 1585/6, the Exchequer authorities were notified, by warrant under the privy seal, that the Queen, to whom Draycott owed £600 for recusancy between 31 Mar. 1582/3 and 13 Aug. 1584, had made an outright grant of this sum, to a certain William Ashbye, esq., 'our welbeloved servaunt', for unspecified services rendered to the Crown. Furthermore, after the passing of the Statute of 1586/7, the Exchequer was similarly informed, on 11 Oct. 1587, of an additional grant to the said Ashbye, of all future sums accruing to the Queen, at the rate of £260 a year, by reason of Draycott's continued recusancy, as from 22 Apr. 1587. On these grounds, Ashbye, in Trinity Term 1591, successfully petitioned the barons in the Court of Exchequer, for a formal judgement discharging Draycott (and himself) of all past and future debts to the Crown in this case, until the end of the reign.

67. No reference to John Draycott's recusancy appears in the RRs of James I's reign, until 1611, when two thirds of his lands are recorded as having been seized on 18 May of that year, and immediately leased by the Crown for 41 years to 'John Peersall esq.' for an annual rent of £27 – 4 – 5½ (Cf. E.377/19, under 'Res' Staff', post Bedfords'.) It is therefore clear that the Queen's scheme adopted for Draycott was not continued by her successor, who, from the above date, followed the normal system regarding the penalising of this recusant—without interference from William Ashbye.

DREWRYE, Drury, Henry, esq., of Lawshall, Suffolk. 10 mths recusancy from 1 Aug. 1581: conv. ? 18 July 1582,—II(56): and two later convictions, ending 10 July 1588.—III(66). VIII(73). Debts re-enrolled—III(65). IV(56). V(60). X(64).

DREWRYE, Drury, Henry, gent., of St. George's parish, Southwark, Surrey [prisoner][68]. 5 mths recusancy from 17 Feb. 1586/7: conv. 17 July 1587.—IX(54)

DREWRYE, John, gent., of Godwicke [Hall, Litcham], Norfolk. 3 mths recusancy from 13 Apr. 1587: conv. 1 Apr. 1588.—VIII(54). Record of land-seizure, 18 Oct. 1588—IX(45). Rental of lands seized 18 Oct. 1588.—IX(45).

DREWRYE, William, 'yoman', of Thrapston, Northants. 12 mths recusancy from 31 July 1587: conv. 4 Mar. 1588/9.—IX(47).

DRINKELL, Alice, of Wiersdale [Wyresdale], Lancs., wife of Michael Drinkell. 12 mths recusancy from 20 Sept. 1589: conv. 22 Mar. 1590/1.—X(39v).

DRYFFELD, Alice, wid., of Knottingley, W.R. Yorks. 2 mths recusancy from 4 Jan. 1585/6: conv. 14 Mar. 1585/6.—VI(20v).

DRYNGE, Thomas, 'yeoman', of Croulton [? Croughton], Northants. 12 mths recusancy from 31 July 1587: conv. 4 Mar. 1588/9.—IX(47).

DUBDEALE, Robert, 'yoman', of St. Margaret's parish, Westminster [prisoner][69]. (Pipe Roll entry under 'Oxfordshire') one month's recusancy from 18 May 1581: conv. 26 June 1581.—I(45v). Debt re-enrolled—III(73v). V(31v).

DUBDEALE, Dubdall, Robert, 'yoman', of Westminster, Middx [prisoner][70]. (Pipe Roll entry under 'London') 3 mths recusancy from 27 June 1581: conv. 16 Oct. 1581—II(32): and four later convictions, ending 16 Mar. 1581/2.—III(42)*. Debts re-enrolled—V(35)*.

DUCE, Thomas, 'yoman', of Cumberton [? Comberton], Worcs. 2 mths recusancy from 7 Apr. 1588: conv. 6 Mar. 1588/9.—IX(70v).

DUCKEWORTHE, Eliz., of Churche, Lancs., wife of Edward Duckworthe. 12 mths recusancy from 20 Sept. 1589: conv. 22 Mar. 1590/1.—X(40).

DUGDALE, Thomas, [   ], of Haslingdon [Haslingden], Whalley parish, Lancs. 13 mths recusancy from 14 Aug. 1586: conv. 25 Mar. 1588.—VIII(21v).

---

68. Henry Drewrye's description 'of St. George's parish, Southwark, Surrey', was a common way of describing the temporary abode of prisoners in the Marshalsea. He was described by Lord Burghley as, 'a young gentleman whose lands, being of the yearly value of £300, are lately come into his possession by the death of his father. He is a most obstinate recusant & receiver of priests and suspected persons, and refuseth to be conversant with any preacher, saying he will stop his ears'. (Cf. CRS II, p. 276.) See also CRS LVII, Introd., under 'Inherited debts', pp. xlii, and xliii, footnote 155. The subject of the last footnote is clearly identifiable with the same person, Henry Drury, whose domicile was at Lawshall Manor, Suffolk. He died a Jesuit lay-brother at Antwerp in 1593.

69. Robert Dibdale (Cf. Anstruther I, p. 101.)

70. See also CRS II, pp. 225, 230, 270.

DURHAM, Alice, wife of Richard Durham, 'haberdasher, barber', of the city of York. 4 mths recusancy from 28 Mar. 1581: conv. 17 July 1581.—I(8). Debt re-enrolled—III(10). V(8). VII(8). IX(8). Goods value 5s. seized from husband, 6 Feb. 1582/3.—II(8).

DURHAM, Richard, 'yoman', of Hemingbrough, E.R. Yorks. 4 mths recusancy from 28 Mar. 1581: conv. 17 July 1581.—I(21v). Debt re-enrolled—III(24). V(22).

DURRAM, William, gent., of Rusheton [Rushton], Dorset. 3 mths recusancy from 1 Apr. 1587: conv. 21 July 1587.—IX(16v). Debt re-enrolled—XII(78v).

DUTTON, Hugh, gent., of Acton Reynoldes [Reynold], Salop. 12 mths recusancy from 8 May 1581: convicted by informer's suit on 8 May 1582—II(13v)[71]. Debt re-enrolled—VI(13). VII(56). IX(60). XI(62v).

DYNES, John, 'yoman', of Horsham, Sussex. 3 mths recusancy from 1 Apr. 1588: conv. 3 Mar. 1588/9.—IX(53).

DYNLEY, Ellen, [   ], of Brammopp [Bramhope], W.R. Yorks. 6 mths recusancy from 3 July 1587: conv. 18 Mar. 1587/8.—VIII(27).

DYNNE, Katherine, 'spinster', of Racton, W. Sussex. 2 mths recusancy from 17 Apr. 1587: conv. 26 Feb. 1587/8.—VIII(63v).

EASTE, Edward, gent., of Bledlowe, Bucks. 3 mths recusancy from 27 Mar. 1587: conv. 18 Mar. 1587/8.—VIII(3). Goods value £2 – 11 – 8 seized 12 Oct. 1588—IX(70). Record of land-seizure in Bucks. 12 Oct. 1588—IX(70). Rental of lands seized in Bucks.—X(1). Seized lands in Bucks let by Crown to Thomas Sheffeild & Richard Brewster from 14 Feb. 1588/9—IX(2v). X(1). XI(2v). XII(2v). Record of land-seizure in Oxfords, 5 Oct. 1590—XI(35v). Lands seized in Oxfords let by Crown to John Hopkinson from 3 Nov. 1590—XI(35v). XII(53v).

EASTE, Cecily, his wife (same parish, recusancy period and conviction date).—VIII(3).

---

71. Hugh Dutton, 'a troublesome man', was committed to the Wood Street Counter, 20 June 1585, by warrant of the Earl of Leicester. (Cf. *CRS* II, p. 250.) He was described as a 'gentleman' but 'passing poor'. (Cf. *CRS* II, p. 259.) He was prosecuted by Hugh Cuffe—the outstanding personality among the informers of the period. Cuffe, together with the Queen, sued Dutton (and Sir John Southworth) on the *Qui Tam* system (Cf. *CRS* LVII, pp. xv – xxi, Recusancy and the Common Informer.) Dutton was held to forfeit £240: £160 for the Queen and the 'poor of Shawbury' and £80 for Cuffe. Summoned by the sheriffs of London/Middx., to attend the Court in the Octave of Michaelmas, Dutton failed to appear, nor did he attend in the Octave of Hilary, nor in the Octave of Trinity. Finally, on 20 June 1585, he appeared, with his required writ endorsed by the ex-sheriffs Henry Pranell and Anthony Radcliff, as a prisoner in Wood Street Counter, and, being brought to the bar, was asked by the barons there, if he had the money ready for payment. He replied no. Therefore, Dutton was sent back to the said prison, to remain there till he obtained it. Humphrey Mosely, one of the London secondaries, attending the Court for the current sheriff, was now given charge of Dutton to accept and guard him in the said prison. How long he remained at Wood Street Counter is not revealed, but his debt was repeatedly enrolled in the Pipe Rolls until 1590, when it ceases to reappear. (Cf. M.R., Q.R., 24 Eliz., Easter Term, E.159/382, mem. 94.)

EASTON, Ann, 'spinster', of Marten [? Merton], Surrey. 3 mths recusancy from 25 Mar. 1587: conv. 13 Feb. 1587/8.—VIII(63).

EATON, Henry, [ ], of Etwall, Derbys. 10 mths recusancy from 9 Sept. 1586: conv. 22 Mar. 1587/8.—VIII(21).

EATON, John, [ ] (same parish, recusancy period and conviction date)—VIII(21).

EATON, Ellen, wife of John Eaton (same parish, recusancy period and conviction date)—VIII(21).

EAVES, James, 'draper', of Preston, Lancs. 13 mths recusancy from 30 July 1587: conv. 17 Mar. 1588/9.—X(35).

ECCLES, Lancelot, 'taleor', of [? Thornley in Wheatley], Lancs. 12 mths recusancy from 20 Sept. 1589: conv. 22 Mar. 1590/1.—X(39).

ECCLES, Eliz., his wife (same parish, recusancy period and conviction date)—X(39).

ECCLES, William, 'laborer', of Wiswell, Lancs. (same recusancy period and conviction date)—X(40).

ECCLESTON, Eliz., 'spinster', of Thistleton, Lancs. 12 mths recusancy from 20 Sept. 1589: conv. 22 Mar. 1590/1.—X(39).

ECCLESTON, Eliz., 'spinster', of Whittle [-le-Woods, Leyland parish], Lancs. (same recusancy period and conviction date)—X(38v).

ECCLESTON, Eliz., of Thurneham [Thornham], Lancs., wife of William Eccleston, gent. (same recusancy period and conviction date)—X(39v).

ECCLESTON, John, 'yoman', of Thistleton, Lancs. (same recusancy period and conviction date)—X(39).

ECCLESTON, [ ], his wife. (same parish, recusancy period and conviction date)—X(39).

EDEN, George, gent., of Lambeth, Surrey. 3 mths recusancy from 25 Mar. 1588: conv. 6 Mar. 1588/9.—IX(53).

EDEN, Katherine, 'spinster', of Chedington [Cheddington], Bucks. 3 mths recusancy from 27 Mar. 1587: conv. 18 Mar. 1587/8.—VIII(3).

EDEN, Edon, William, gent. (same parish, recusancy period & conviction date)—VIII(3).

EDMONDES, Ambrose, gent., of St. Margaret's parish, Westminster, Middx. [prisoner][72]. (Pipe Roll entry under 'Oxfordshire'). 1 mth recusancy from 18 May 1581: conv. 26 June 1581.—I(45v). Debt re-enrolled—III(73v). V(31v).

EDMONDES, Frideswide, wid., of Staunton [Stanton] St. John, Oxfords. 12 mths recusancy from 26 Sept. 1586: conv. 7 Mar. 1587/8.—VIII(35).

---

72. Ambrose Edmundes was of Stanton St. John's, Oxfordshire (Cf. *CRS* XXII, p. iii.) In a Pipe Roll re-enrolment of his conviction for recusancy dated 1582/3, occurs in the margin, the note 'diem clausit extremum', indicating his death sometime within that year. He appears to have been moved from Newgate to the Westminster Gatehouse before his death. (Cf. *CRS* I, p. 60). His widow, Frideswide, appears in the next entry.

EDMUND, 'Crisillia' verch David, wife of John Edmund, [   ], of
  Llanthewy Rytherch, Mon. 5 mths recusancy from 24 Mar. 1586/7:
  conv. 13 Mar. 1587/8.—VIII(48).
EDWARD, 'Denissa' Jevan, wife of Philip Edward, [   ], of Llantilio
  Pertholey, Mon. (same recusancy period & conviction date).—
  VIII(48v).
EDWARD, Eliz., 'spinster', of Tredunnock, Mon. (same recusancy period &
  conviction date).—VIII(49).
EDWARD, Margaret John, wife of John Edward, [   ], of Llantilio
  Pertholey, Mon. (same recusancy period & conviction date).—
  VIII(48v).
EDWARD, William, 'yoman', of Llandenny, Mon. (same recusancy period
  & conviction date).—VIII(49v).
EDWARDES, Ann, wid., wife [sic] of John Edwardes, [   ], of Didlaston
  [Dudleston], Salop. 12 mths recusancy from 24 Feb. 1586/7: conv.
  18 July 1588.—VIII(16v).
EDWARDES, Francis, 'clericus', of Southwark, Surrey [prisoner][73]. 10
  mths recusancy ending 17 Feb. 1585/6, when convicted.—VI(49v).
EDWARDES, Francis, 'clericus', of St. George's parish, Southwark, Surrey
  [prisoner]. 5 mths recusancy from 17 Feb. 1586/7: conv. 17 July
  1587.—IX(54).
EDWARDES, Thomas, [   ], of St. Bride's parish, Farringdon Ward
  Without, London [? prisoner][74]. 1 mth recusancy from 6 Sept. 1581:
  conv. 6 Oct. 1581.—I(35)*: and one later conviction dated 20 Dec.
  1581.—I(35). Debts re-enrolled—III(38v)*. V(35)*.
EDWARDES, Thomas, gent., of Tottenham, Middx. 3 mths recusancy from
  18 June 1582: conv. 23 Sept. 1582.—IV(32v). Debt re-enrolled—
  VI(34).
EDWARDES, Thomas, 'yoman', of Westminster, Middx [? prisoner][75]. 1
  mth recusancy from 19 Nov. 1581: conv. 18 Dec. 1581—III(42)*: and
  three later convictions, ending 29 Jan. 1587/8—III(42)*. VIII(38v).
  Debts re-enrolled—V(35)*.
EDWARDES, Thomas, 'servingman', of Wye, Kent. 9 mths recusancy from
  18 Mar. 1580/1: conv. ? Dec. 1581.—II(28).
EDWARDES, Thomas, gent., of St. Dunstan's parish, Canterbury, Kent
  [? prisoner][76]. 4 mths recusancy ending 15 July 1583, when
  convicted.—III(28v). Debt re-enrolled—V(30).

---

73. Francis Edwards (Cf. Anstruther I, p. 108.)
74. Thomas Edwardes, a chandler of Reading, Berks., was sent into the Fleet in 1580 by the Bishop of London and the High Commissioners. (Cf. CRS II, p. 225.) He was then moved to the Westminster Gatehouse, and was still there on 29 Jan. 1587/8.
75. Thomas Edwardes, 'yoman', was a prisoner in the Westminster Gatehouse. He was still there on 30 Sept. 1588 (Cf. CRS II, p. 284.)
76. Thomas Edwardes of Canterbury, Kent., was convicted at Maidstone for 4 months recusancy, and was fined £80 on 15 July 1583 at the 'Gaol Delivery of the Castle of Canterbury'.

EGLAMBY, Alan, 'yeom'', of Coxewell Magna [Great Coxwell], Berks. 12 mths recusancy from 1 Sept. 1586: conv. 4 March 1587/8.—VIII(5).

ELDERSHAWE, Richard, 'medicus', of Awdlemere [? Audlem], Cheshire. 13 mths recusancy from 25 Sept. 1586: date of conviction omitted.—VIII(58v).

ELLERKER, Robert, gent., of Ellerker, E.R. Yorks. 6 mths recusancy from 3 July 1587: conv. 18 Mar. 1587/8.—VIII(25v). Goods value £2 – 10 – 8 seized 1588.—IX(22v).

ELLES, Mary, wife of John Elles, gent., of Kidhall [Kiddal], W.R. Yorks. 6 mths recusancy from 3 July 1587: conv. 18 Mar. 1587/8.—VIII(27).

ELLIOTT, Alice, 'spinster', of St. Owen's parish, Hereford city. 6 mths recusancy from 1 Sept. 1588: conv. 14 July 1589.—IX(25v). Debt re-enrolled—XI(29).

ELLIOTT, Elliote, John, gent., of the city of Hereford. 12 mths recusancy from 26 June 1581: conv. 30 May 1582—II(64); and thirteen later convictions, ending 22 July 1585—I(25). II(64)*. III(27). IV(64v)*. V(26), (26v)*.

ELLIOTT, Elliote, John, gent., of St. Peter's parish, Hereford city. 1 mth recusancy from 27 May 1583: conv. 15 July 1583—III(27): and four later convictions, ending 18 Mar. 1586/7—IV(64v). VI(25)*.

ELLIS, Edward, [   ], of St. Bride's parish, Farringdon Ward Without, London [? prisoner]. 3 mths recusancy from 18 Mar. 1580/1: conv. 28 July 1581.—I(32v). Debt re-enrolled—III(38v). V(35).

ELLIS, Henry, [   ], of parish of St. Martin before the gate of the bishop's palace ('ante port' pallac 'Episcopi Norwic''), Norwich city. 1 mth recusancy from 1 Nov. 1587: conv. ? Dec. 1587.—IX(10). Debt re-enrolled—XI(12).

ELLIS, William, [   ], of Westby, Lancs. 12 mths recusancy from 20 Sept. 1589: conv. 22 Mar. 1590/1.—X(39v).

ELTON, Alice, wife of Anthony Elton, gent., of Ledbury, Herefords. 12 mths recusancy from 1 Sept. 1586: conv. 18 Mar. 1587/8.—VIII(30).

ELWOOD, Geoffrey, gent., of Carlisle, Cumberland. 3 mths recusancy from 27 Apr. 1582: conv. ? July 1582.—II(7v).

ELWOOD, Geoffrey, 'yom'', of Grayrigge, Westmorland. 4 mths recusancy (period unspecified): conv. 31 July 1581.—V(66).

ENGLISHE, Eliz., wife of John Englishe, gent., of Aston Rowaunt, Oxfords. 12 mths recusancy from 26 Sept. 1586: conv. 7 Mar. 1587/8.—VIII(35).

ERDESWICK, Eardiswick, Erswick, Sampson, gent., of Sandon, Staffs. 4 mths recusancy from 31 Mar. 1582: conv. 23 July 1582—IV(62v); and six later convictions, ending 22 July 1588—IV(62v)*. V(66). VI(63v)*. VIII(58). Debts re-enrolled—VI(63)*.

ERDESWICK, Sampson, Esq. (of same place). 5 mths recusancy from 3 Apr. 1587: conv. 25 Mar. 1588.—VIII(78v).

ERDESWICK, Sampson, gent., of Leighton, Cheshire. 13 mths recusancy from 25 Sept. 1586: (date of conviction omitted).—VIII(58v).

ERRINGTON, George, 'yoman', of St. George's parish, Southwark, Surrey [prisoner]⁷⁷. 5 mths recusancy from 17 Feb. 1586/7: conv. 17 July 1587⁷⁸—IX(54).

ESDALL, Thomas, junior, 'husbandman', of St. Mary's parish, Reading, Berks. [? prisoner]. 7 mths recusancy from 20 Aug. 1586: conv. 6 Mar. 1586/7.—VI(48v).

ETHERIDGE, George, 'medicus', of Oxford. 3 mths recusancy from 25 Mar. 1581: conv. 29 June 1581.—I(45). Debt re-enrolled—III(73v).

ETHERIDGE, George, 'medicus', of St. Mary's parish, Oxford. 8 mths recusancy from 4 July 1583: conv. 27 Feb. 1583/4—IV(29); and five later convictions, ending 25 July 1586—IV(29). V(47)*. VI(47v)*. Debts re-enrolled—VI(30v)*.

EVANS, Hugh, [   ], of Llanvihangel Estonllewerne [Ystern Llewern], Mon. 5 mths recusancy from 24 Mar. 1586/7: conv. 13 Mar. 1587/8.—VIII(49).

EVANS, Ann, his wife (same parish, recusancy period & conviction date)—VIII(49v).

EVERARD, Ann, wife of Gawdy Everard, gent., of Linsted, Suffolk. 3 mths recusancy from 8 Apr. 1587: conv. 27 Mar. 1588.—VIII(73).

EVERARD, Henry, esq., of Magna Linsted [Linstead Magna], Suffolk. 12 mths recusancy from 3 July 1581: conv. 18 July 1582—II(56); and five later convictions, ending 5 Apr. 1587.—II(66). IV(57). V(60v). VI(58). VII(59). Debts re-enrolled—III(65). IV(56). V(60). VI(57). VII(59)*.

EVERARD, Everarde, Henry, gent., of Linstead, Suffolk. Record of land-seizure, 2 Nov. 1587—VIII(72). Rental of seized lands—IX(63). X(63). XI(65). XII(66). Arrearage of rent—X(80).

EVERARD, Henry, gent., of Linstead Parva [sic], Suffolk. Seized lands let by Crown to Laurence Hussey from Michaelmas 1590—X(80v). XI(65v). XII(66v).

EWBANCK, Christopher, 'yom'', of Gatherley [parish of Middleton Tyas], N.R. Yorks. 6 mths recusancy from 3 July 1587: conv. 18 Mar. 1587/8. —VIII(27).

EYRE, Francis, 'yoman', of Harmondesworthe [Harmondsworth], Middx. 3 mths recusancy from 10 Mar. 1588/9: conv. 4 Sept. 1589.—IX(37).

EYREMAN, Eyremane, Francis, [   ], or parish of St. Dunstan-in-the-West, Farringdon Ward Without, London. 3 mths recusancy prior to 20 Apr. 1588, when convicted.—VIII(38v).

EYREMAN, George, 'yom'', of Kirton, Suffolk. 9 mths recusancy from 3 July 1581: conv. 28 Mar. 1582.—II(56).

EYTON, Eaton, Eiton, Humphrey, 'yoman', of Westminster, Middx [prisoner]⁷⁹. 1 mth recusancy from 16 Oct. 1581: conv. 19 Nov.

---

77. George Errington (Cf. Ann M. C. Forster, 'The Venerable George Errington', in *RH*, vol. 3, no. 5, (1956), pp. 322–333.)
78. He was convicted at the Gaol Delivery of Guildford Castle.
79. Humphrey Eyton, a serving man, servant to Mr. Roper of Eltham, Kent., was confined in the Gatehouse from 1581 to 1584. (Cf. *CRS* II, pp. 225, 230, 235.)

1581—III(42); and three later convictions, ending 16 Mar. 1581/2.—
Debts re-enrolled—III(42)*. V(35)*.
EYTON, Humphrey, gent., of Westminster, Middx [prisoner][79a]. 3 mths recusancy from 15 Mar. 1581/2: conv. 17 June 1582—IV(32v); and three later convictions, ending 17 Nov. 1583.—IV(32v)*. VI(34)*.
EYVES, Jane, wid., of Fishwick, Preston parish Lancs. 13 mths recusancy from 14 Aug. 1586: conv. 25 Mar. 1588.—VIII(21v).

FALDRINGE, Alice, wid., of Leighe [Leigh], Staffs. 12 mths recusancy from 6 Sept. 1586: conv. 25 Mar. 1588.—VIII(78v).
FALDRINGE, Edward, 'husb'' (same parish, recusancy period and conviction date).—VIII(78v).
FALKENOR, Joan, 'spinster', of Alciston, Sussex. 5 mths recusancy from 20 Aug. 1587: conv. 5 July 1588.—VIII(63).
FAWKENOR, Faulkner, William, esq., of Laverstock, Wilts. 7 mths recusancy from 20 Aug. 1583: conv. Lent 1583/4—IV(25v); and two later convictions, ending Lent 1584/5.—IV(25v)*, (59v). Goods, value £46 – 19s., seized 8 Oct. 1588—IX(66). Debt re-enrolled—XI(68). Record of land-seizure in Wilts, 8 Oct. 1588—IX(66). Seized lands in Wilts (Laverstock & Tidworth) let by Crown to Sir James Marvin from Michaelmas 1588—IX(65v), (68). X(76), (76v). XI(67v), (68). XII(68v).
FAWKENOR, Fawkoner, William, gent., of Eastmeane [East Meon], Hants. 19 mths recusancy from 20 Feb. 1581/2: conv. 18 Aug. 1583.—IV(53)*. Debt re-enrolled—VI(54)*. VIII(68). Record of land-seizure in Hants., 22 Apr. 1588—VIII(67v). Rental of lands in Hants (Westbury manor) seized 22 Apr. 1588—VIII(66v), (68v). IX(57v). X(68v). Seized lands in Hants let by Crown to Sir James Marvin from Michaelmas 1588—IX(58). X(68v), XI(59v), (61v). XII(60v).
FAWKES, Nicholas, 'yom'',, of Ferneley, [? W.R.] Yorks. 5 mths recusancy from 1 Jan. 1582/3: conv. 17 May 1583.—IV(21). Debt re-enrolled—VI(22).
FECKINGHAM, Fekenham, *alias* WIBORNE, William, gent., of Westminster, Middx [? prisoner][80]. 3 mths recusancy from 27 June 1581: conv. 20 Dec. 1581.—II(49v). (An earlier conviction)[81]:—1 mth recusancy from 18 May 1581: conv. 27 June 1581.—V(52). Debt re-enrolled—VII(51). IX(55). XII(58).

79a. In his second series of prosecutions he is referred to in the Pipe Roll as 'gentleman'.
80. William Feckingham, formerly a monk of Westminster Abbey, was ordained priest by Bishop Bonner at the Abbey on 5 June 1558. (Cf. Justin McCann, *Ampleforth and its origins*, (1952), pp. 73, 77, 278.) Refused to take the oath of supremacy in 1559, and, therefore, committed to prison. Earliest recorded recusancy periods (Cf. Jeaffreson I, pp. 124, 126, 128) all in 1581.
81. In 1586, he was in the Fleet for conversing with and assisting seminary priests. (Cf. *CRS* II, pp. 264, 267, 269.) On 30 Oct. 1586, under the name of 'William Wibourne' he was removed by the Privy Council from Newgate to the Wood Street Counter. No further mention of him occurs after this date.

FEILDEN, Mary, 'spinster', of Blackborne [Blackburn], Lancs. 12 mths recusancy from 20 Sept. 1589: conv. 22 Mar. 1590/1.—X(40).
FELLES, Benjamin, gent., of the parish of St. Mary Steyning, Aldersgate Ward, London. 3 mths recusancy prior to 30 Apr. 1588, when convicted.—VIII(38v).
FELTON, Frances, gentlewoman ('generosa'), of Ayeworth [Eyworth], Beds. 3 mths recusancy from 29 Mar. 1597: conv. 20 Mar. 1587/8.—VIII(1).
FELTON, Frances, 'spinster', of Eyworth, Beds. 9 mths recusancy from 4 July 1587: conv. 3 July 1588.—VIII(lv).
FELTON, Joan, 'spinster', of Ashburnham, Sussex. 2 mths recusancy from 17 Apr. 1587: conv. 26 Feb. 1587/8.—VIII(63v).
FELTON, John, 'clericus', of Riple [Ripple], Worcs.[82]. 2 mths recusancy from 8 Jan. 1582/3: conv. 11 Mar. 1582/3.—II(61v). Debt re-enrolled—IV(61v). VI(62v).
FELTON, Thomas, gent., of Christ Church parish, Farringdon Ward Within, London [prisoner][83]. 13 mths recusancy from 13 Feb. 1586/7: conv. 14 April 1588.—VIII(38v).
FENNE, James, gent., of Southwark, Surrey [prisoner][84]. 10 mths recusancy ending 11 Mar. 1582/3, when convicted.—III(58v). Debt re-enrolled—V(52v).
FENNE, Robert, gent., of Southwark, Surrey [prisoner][85]. 4 mths recusancy ending 20 July 1584, when convicted.—V(50v).
FENNE, Robert, 'clericus', of Southwark, Surrey [prisoner][86]. 6 mths recusancy ending 18 Feb. 1584/5, when convicted.—V(52v).
FENNELL, Florence, [ ], of Ayshburneham [Ashburnham], Sussex. 5 mths recusancy from 20 Aug. 1587: conv. 5 July 1588.—VIII(63).
FENTON, Richard, gent., of [ ] in Hathersedge [Hathersage] parish, Derbys. 10 mths recusancy from 9 Sept. 1586: conv. 22 Mar. 1587/8.—VIII(21). Rental of lands in Yorks seized 28 Aug. 1591—XI(10v). XII(24). Seized lands in Yorks let by Crown to John Twiste & George Hill from Michaelmas 1591—XII(llv).
FERNE, Eliz., 'spinster', of Langford [Longford], Derbys. 10 mths recusancy from 9 Sept. 1586: conv. 22 Mar. 1587/8.—VIII(21).
FERRES, Ferrers, [Eliz.], wid., of Salford [Priors], Warwicks. 1 mth recusancy from 27 June 1588: conv. 5 Mar. 1588/9.—IX(llv).
FETTIPLACE, Dorothy, wife of Robert Fettiplace, gent., of Buckland, Berks. 12 mths recusancy from 1 Sept. 1586: conv. 4 Mar. 1587/8.—VIII(5).

---

82. John Felton was convicted at Worcester Assizes on 11 Mar. 1582/3 of 2 months recusancy, and of saying mass, but, is unidentified as a priest.
83. Thomas Felton (Cf. Challoner, pp. 138–140.)
84. James Fenn (Cf. Anstruther I, p. 114.)
85. Robert Fenn (Cf. Anstruther I, pp. 114, 115.)
86. Arrested and committed to the Marshalsea, 16 Feb. 1584/5, he remained there until he was banished, 19 Sept. 1585. (Cf. CRS II, pp. 233, 236, 240.)

FETTIPLACE, Humphrey, gent. (same parish, recusancy period and conviction date)—VIII(5).
FETTIPLACE, Margaret, wife of John Fettiplace, gent., of Uffington, Berks. (same recusancy period and conviction date).—VIII(5).
FIDLER, John, 'husb", of Preston, Lancs. 13 mths recusancy from 30 July 1587: conv. 17 Mar. 1588/9.—X(35).
FILBYE, George, 'carrier', of Southwark, Surrey [prisoner][87]. 9 mths recusancy ending 11 Mar. 1582/3, when convicted.—III(58v). Debt re-enrolled—V(52v).
FINCHE, Fynche, John, 'husbandman', of Bispam [Bispham], parish of Crofton [Croston], Lancs. 10 mths recusancy from 18 Mar. 1580/1: conv. 18 Jan. 1581/2.—II(38v). Debt re-enrolled—VIII(46).
FINCHE, Fynche, John, 'husband", of Salford, in parish of Manchester, Lancs [prisoner][88]. 3 mths recusancy from 17 Jan. 1581/2: conv. 2 May 1582; and 4 mths recusancy from 2 Sept. 1582: conv. 16 Jan. 1582/3—II(38v)*. Debts re-enrolled—VIII(46)*.
FINCHE, John, 'yoman' (of same place: prisoner)[88]. 12 mths recusancy from 20 Feb. 1582/3: conv. 22 Jan. 1583/4.—IV(37). Debt re-enrolled—IV(42v).
FISHEBORNE, Alice, wife of John Fisheborne, [   ], of St. Mary's parish, Nottingham town ('villa Nott"). 10 mths recusancy from 9 Sept. 1586: conv. 25 Mar. 1588—VIII(80).
FISHEBORNE, John, 'yeoman', of the same town, county and parish (same recusancy period and conviction date).—VIII(80).
FITTON, Fytton, William, gent., of Stoke Poges, Bucks. 3 mths recusancy from 27 Mar. 1587: conv. 18 Mar. 1587/8.—VIII(3). Goods, value (with those of Isabel Hampden, wid. [*q.v.*]) £17 – 9s., seized 12 Oct. 1588.—IX(70).
FITTON, Mary, his wife (of the same parish, recusancy period & conviction date).—VIII(3).
FITZHERBERT, Richard, gent., of Staffs., 'recusant and fugitive'. Goods, value £30 – 5 – 4, seized 4 Sept. 1589—X(14). Record of land-seizure, 4 Sept. 1589 (tenement called 'Hartesmere', in tenure of Edward Thorne, with lands in Bromley Hurst, Staffs.)—X(78v). Rental of seized lands—X(7v). XI(64v). XII(65v). Seized lands let by Crown to Edward Thorne from 22 Dec. 1591—XII(72v).
FITZHERBERT, Sir Thomas, knt. of Hamstall Ridware, Staffs. 12 mths recusancy ending 1 Apr. 1587, when convicted—IX(69v). 7 mths recusancy from 24 Mar. 1587/8 to 6 Oct. 1588. (Fine £140: paid 2 Dec. 1588. Quit.)—VIII(78). Recusancy for one year from 6 Oct. 1588. Annual fine (£260) paid. Quit.—IX(62v).
FITZHUGHES, [   ], wife of Richard Fitzhughes, gent., of Charlbury, Oxfords. 12 mths recusancy from 26 Sept. 1586: conv. 7 Mar. 1587/8.—VIII(35v).

---

87. George Filbye, an active recusant, was the father of two seminary priests—John and William Filbye—for whom (Cf. Anstruther I, pp. 115, 116.)
88. John Finch (Cf. Challoner, pp. 101 – 102, and *CRS* V, pp. 23 – 25, and 78 – 88.)

FLETCHER, Thomas, 'yoman', of Westminster, Middx [? prisoner]. 1 mth recusancy from 6 Oct. 1587: conv. 29 Jan. 1587/8.—VIII(38v).
FLOOD, 'Evanc'', gent., of Chippenham, Cambs. 10 mths recusancy from 1 Sept. 1586: conv. 24 Mar. 1587/8.—VIII(7v). See FLUDD.
FLORENCE, Anthony, 'yoman', of Alciston, Sussex. 2 mths recusancy from 17 Apr. 1587: conv. 26 Feb. 1587/8.—VIII(63v).
FLUDD, Jane, 'spinster', of West Wratting, Cambs. 10 mths recusancy from 1 Sept. 1586: conv. 24 Mar. 1587/8.—VIII(7v). See FLOOD.
FLUYTT, Humphrey, [   ], of Radford, Notts. 12 mths recusancy from 12 Mar. 1587/8: conv. 11 July 1589.—IX(48v).
FOLIAMBE, Katherine, 'spinster', of Carlebroughe [Barlborough], Derbys. 10 mths recusancy from 9 Sept. 1586: conv. 22 Mar. 1587/8.—VIII(21).
FOLIAMBE, Fuliambe, Lady Constance, wid., of [   ] in North Wingfeild parish, Derbys (same recusancy period & conviction date)—VIII(21). Goods, value £15 – 18 – 4, seized 27 Jan. 1588/9 – IX(17v). Record of land-seizure (in Tupton), 27 Jan. 1588/9—IX(17v). Rental of seized lands—IX(49v). X(18). XI(19). XII(19).
FOLLIOTT, Folliatt, Michael, gent., of Castlemoreton [Castlemorton], Worcs. 6 mths recusancy from 29 Sept. 1587: conv. 25 July 1588.—VIII(80v).
FOLLIOTT, Folliatt, Michael, gent., of Pirton, Worcs. 12 mths recusancy from 20 Sept. 1586: conv. 28 Mar. 1588.—VIII(77). Goods, value £3 – 3 – 3, seized 31 Sept. 1588—IX(68v).
FORD, *alias* of SYMS, William.
FORD, see FOURDE.
FORSHAWE, Alice, of Westby, Lancs., wife of Robert Forshawe, 'husb''. 12 mths recusancy from 20 Sept. 1589: conv. 22 Mar. 1590/1.—X(39v).
FORSHAWE, Ann, of Westby, Lancs., wife of Thomas Forshawe, 'taleor' (same parish, recusancy period and conviction date).—X(39v).
FORTESCUE, Anthony, gent., of Racton, Sussex. 3 mths recusancy from 1 Apr. 1588: conv. 3 Mar. 1588/9.—IX(53).
FORTESCUE, Eliz., of Ayworth [Eyworth], Beds., wife of John Fortescue, esq. 3 mths recusancy from 29 Mar. 1587: conv. 20 Mar. 1587/8.—VIII(1).
FORTESCUE, Rose, 'spinster', of Racton, Sussex. 2 mths recusancy from 17 Apr. 1587: conv. 26 Feb. 1587/8.—VIII(63v).
FOSTER, Christopher, gent., of Stanningfeild, Suffolk. 8 mths recusancy from 15 July 1588: conv. 2 July 1589—IX(64). Debt re-enrolled—XI(72v).
FOSTER, Humphrey, gent., of Drayton, Salop. 12 mths recusancy from 24 Feb. 1586/7: conv. 18 July 1588.—VIII(16v). Goods, value £18 – 10s., seized 9 Oct. 1589—IX(13v). Debt re-enrolled—X(58v). XI(63v). Record of land-seizure, 9 Oct. 1589—IX(13v). Rental of seized lands—IX(69v). X(59v). Seized lands let by Crown to William Jewett from 16 Apr. 1590.—X(58v). XI(62v).

FOSTER, Robert, 'mylner', of Woodhoose, West Kirkeby [Kirby] parish, Cheshire. 13 mths recusancy from 25 Sept. 1586: date of conviction omitted.—VIII(58v).

FOSTER, Thomas, gent., of Old Buckenham, Norfolk. 3 mths recusancy from 13 Apr. 1587: conv. 1 Apr. 1588.—VIII(54).

FOSTER, Joan, his wife (same parish, recusancy period & conviction date)—VIII(54).

FOSTER, Thomas, senior, gent., of Old Buckenham, Norfolk. 5 mths recusancy from 1 Feb. 1581/2: conv. 1 July 1582, and one later conviction dated 10 Mar. 1583/4—IV(44v)*.

FOURDE, Ford(e), Geoffrey, 'yom'', of Garsington, Oxfords. 3 mths recusancy from 24 Mar. 1580/1: conv. 18 June 1581—II(29v); and eleven later convictions, ending 25 July 1587—II(29v)*. III(4). IV(29)*. V(47)*. VI(11v), (47v)*. Debts re-enrolled—IV(29v). V(31v). VI(30v)*.

FOURDE, Peter, 'yeom'', of Somerton, Oxfords. 12 mths recusancy from 26 Sept. 1586: conv. 7 Mar. 1587/8.—VIII(35v).

FOWBERRY, George, gent., of [Newbald, E.R.] Yorks. Fined £50 by High Commissioners for 'contempt of court', 1585.[89]—V(23v).

FOWLER, Andrew, 'clericus', of Southwark, Surrey [prisoner][90]. 2 mths recusancy ending 11 Mar. 1582/3, when convicted—III(58v); and four later convictions, ending 18 Feb. 1584/5.—IV(49v)*. V(50v), (52v). Debts re-enrolled—V(52v). VI(51)*.

FOWLER, Brian, esq., of the 'manor upon Sowe', Staffs. 4 mths recusancy from 31 Mar. 1582: conv. 23 July 1582—IV(62v): and five later convictions, ending 15 Apr. 1587—IV(62v)*. VII(64). Debts re-enrolled—VI(63)*, (63v)*. VII(64)*.

FOWLER, Thomas, 'yoman', of Astley, Worcs. 2 mths recusancy from 7 Apr. 1588: conv. 6 Mar. 1588/9.—IX(70v).

FOXCROFT, William, senior, 'yom'', of Claughton, Lancs. 13 mths recusancy from 14 Aug. 1586: conv. 25 Mar. 1588.—VIII(21v).

FOXE, Ellen, wife of John Foxe, 'laborer', of [   ] in parish of North Wingfeild, Derbys. 10 mths recusancy from 9 Sept. 1586: conv. 22 Mar. 1587/8.—VIII(21).

FOXE, Ellen, 'spinster', of Hilton, in Marston parish, near Tutbury, Derbys. (same recusancy period and conviction date)—VIII(21).

FRAUNCIS, John, 'wever', of Toll Puddle [Tolpuddle], Dorset. 6 mths resucancy from 2 June 1588: conv. 10 Mar. 1588/9.—IX(16v). Debt re-enrolled—XII(78v).

FRISOR, Mary, wife of John Frisor, 'yom'', of Bilwine [? Dilwyn], Herefords. 12 mths recusancy from 1 Sept. 1586: conv. 18 Mar. 1587/8.—VIII(30).

---

89. A fine of £50 was imposed on George Fowberry by the High Commissioners, for the persistent recusancy of his wife. See footnote 6.

90. Andrew Fowler (Cf. Anstruther I, p. 123.)

FULLER, Margaret, wife of Michael Fuller, gent., of Mickfeild, Suffolk. 3 mths recusancy from 8 Apr. 1587: conv. 27 Mar. 1588.—VIII(73).
FULWELL, William, 'yeoman', of Linton, Cambs. 10 mths recusancy from 1 Sept. 1586: conv. 24 Mar. 1587/8.—VIII(7v). Record of land-seizure, 8 Oct. 1588—IX(5v). Rental of seized lands—IX(10v). X(6), (17). XI(6). Seized lands let by Crown to William Hartley from 14 Aug. 1590—X(17)[91]. Arrearage of rent (£1 – 10 – 6)—X(61v).
FYSHEWEEKE, James, 'yoman', of Harting, W. Sussex. 3 mths recusancy from 1 Apr. 1588: conv. 3 Mar. 1588/9.—IX(53).

GAGE, Eliz., 'spinster', of Alciston, E. Sussex. 2 mths recusancy from 17 Apr. 1587: conv. 26 Feb. 1587/8.—VIII(63v).
GAGE, Lady Eliz., wid., relict of Sir Edward Gage, knt., of Alciston, E. Sussex. 3 mths recusancy from 18 Mar. 1580/1: conv. 6 July 1581—V(49v): and nine later convictions, ending 3 Oct. 1583—V(50v)*. Debts re-enrolled—VI(51)*. VII(51v)*. IX(55v)*. Record of land-seizure, 20 Sept. 1587—VIII(63). Rental of seized lands—VIII(64). IX(52v). X(65v). XI(55v). Seized lands let by Crown to Edward Gage from 4 Aug. 1590—X(67). XI(55v). XII(56v).
GAGE, John, esq., of Westfirles [West Firle], E. Sussex. 3 mths recusancy from 18 Mar. 1580/1: conv. 6 July 1581—V(49v): and nine later convictions, ending 3 Oct. 1583—V(50v)*. Debts re-enrolled—VI(51)*. VII(51v)*. IX(55v)*. Summary of pre-1587 debts for recusancy (£1,140, remainder of £1,280, paid. Quit)—VII(48v). Annual fines for recusancy (£260) from 29 Oct. 1586: paid. Quit.—VII(48v). VIII(63). IX(52v). X(65v). XI(56v). XII(56v).
GAGE, Mary, gentlewoman, of Croydon, Surrey. 4 mths recusancy from 2 Oct. 1586: conv. 13 Feb. 1587/8.—VIII(63).
GAGE, Thomas, gent., of Alciston, E. Sussex. 2 mths recusancy from 17 Apr. 1587: conv. 26 Feb. 1587/8.—VIII(63v).
GAGE, Thomas, esq. [sic], (of same parish). Record of land-seizure, 17 Jan. 1588/9.—IX(54v). Rental of seized lands—X(65v). XI(55v).
GAGE, Thomas, gent. [sic], (of same parish). Lands seized 17 Jan. 1588/9 let by Crown to Richard Olive from 21 May 1590.—X(67). XI(55v). XII(56v).
GAINE, Richard John, 'yoman', of Groffinod [Grosmont], Mon. 5 mths recusancy from 24 Mar. 1586/7: conv. 13 Mar. 1587/8.—VIII(49v).
GAINE, 'Alsona' James, wife of the said Richard John Gaine (same parish, recusancy period and conviction date).—VIII(49v).
GARDENETT, John, 'yoman', of Thame, Oxfords. 6 mths recusancy from 1 Aug. 1588: conv. 3 July 1589.—IX(51).

---

91. William Fulwell's seized lands were let to William Hartley for £4 – 3 – 4 *per annum*. He was discharged (Cf. M.R., L.T.R., 33 Eliz., Hilary Term, 'Recorda' section, and Fulwell ceases to appear in the Rolls. Hartley's arrears amounted to £1 – 10 – 6.

GARDINER, Gardner, Francis, 'yom'', of Southwark, Surrey [prisoner][92]. 4 mths recusancy ending 11 Mar. 1582/3, when convicted—IV(49v): and three later convictions, ending 20 July 1584—IV(49v)*. V(50v). Debts re-enrolled—VI(51)*.

GARDINER, Gardener, John, esq., of Westminster, Middx. 3 mths recusancy from 28 June 1587: conv. 1 Dec. 1587.—VIII(38v).

GARDINER, Gardner, John, gent., of Fulmer, Bucks. 9 mths recusancy from 23 Sept. 1586: conv. 18 Mar. 1587/8—VIII(3): and one later conviction, dated 10 Mar. 1588/9—IX(lv). Record of land-seizure, 12 Oct. 1588—IX(70). Rental of seized lands—IX(70v). X(1). XI(2v). XII(2v).

GARDINER, Gardener, John, gent., of St. Mary Magdalen parish, Barmondsey [Bermondsey], Surrey. 3 mths recusancy from 5 Dec. 1587: conv. 6 Mar. 1588/9.—IX(53).

· GARLANDE, Thomas, 'yoman', of Watringbury [Wateringbury], Kent. 2 mths recusancy from 19 Dec. 1587: conv. 26 Feb. 1588/9.—IX(29).

GARNETT, Garnette, Ninian, 'yom'', of Startfurth [Startforth], N.R. Yorks. 5 mths recusancy from 16 Apr. 1587: conv. 4 Sept. 1587—VIII(25v).

GARNETT, Garnette, Richard, gent., of Brodwater [Broadwater], W. Sussex. 3 mths recusancy from 6 July 1581: conv. 2 Oct. 1581: and five later convictions, ending 17 July 1583—V(51v)*.

GASCOIGNE, Hanna, wife of Richard Gascoigne, esq., of Sedburie, parish of Gilling, N.R. Yorks. 13 mths recusancy from 3 Sept. 1586: conv. 4 Sept. 1587.—VIII(25v).

GASCOIGNE, Gascoyne, Francis, gent., of Shareston [? Sharleston], W.R. Yorks. 6 mths recusancy from 3 July 1587: conv. 18 Mar. 1587/8—VIII(27).

GASCON, Jane, wife of Richard Gascon, esq., of Setharghe [? Sedbury, N.R.], Yorks. 6 mths recusancy from 3 July 1587: conv. 18 Mar. 1587/8—VIII(27).

GATTACRE, Gatacre, Francis, esq., of Clareley [Claverley], Salop. 12 mths recusancy from 24 Feb. 1586/7: conv. 18 July 1588.—VIII(16v). Lands in Staffs and Salop seized by Crown 7 Feb. 1591/2, and let to Thomas Pigott from 22 July 1592—XII(16).

GATURD, Robert, 'yom'', of Diddersley Grange, parish of Melsonbye, N.R. Yorks. 13 mths recusancy from 3 Sept. 1586: conv. 4 Sept. 1587—VIII(25v).

GAWEN, Thomas, gent., of Fisherton Anger, near New Sarum, Wilts. 5 mths recusancy ending 30 Aug. 1581, when convicted—I(60v): and two later convictions, ending 28 Feb. 1582/3—I(60v)*. IV(25v). Debts re-enrolled—III(68)*. V(63)*. VI(59v)*. VII(60v)*. Lands seized and let to Hugh Cuffe from Ladyday 1583 (Pipe Roll entries under

---

92. Francis Gardiner was committed to the White Lion at Newington in Dec. 1582. He was one of the first ten sent into this small prison for 'Ecclesiastical causes'. (Cf. *CRS* II, pp. 234, 237.) The White Lion was the common gaol for the County of Surrey. Gardiner appears to have been released from prison on 8 Apr. 1584.

'Wilts')—IV(58v). VI(59). Lands seized and let to Hugh Cuffe from Ladyday 1583 (Pipe Roll entries under 'London/Middx')—VI(33v). VII(31v). VIII(36v). IX(32v). X(43v). XI(36v). Goods, value £2 – 16 – 2, seized Trinity term 1590—X(46).

GAWEN, Thomas, esq., of Fisherton, near New Sarum, Wilts. Record of land-seizure, 13 June 1588—VIII(74v). Rental of seized lands (Hurcote and Norrington)—VIII(74v). IX(65). X(76v). XI(67v). XII(68v). Rental of lands in Wilts seized 1 Sept. 1591—XI(73v). XII(68v). Lands seized 1 Sept. 1591 let by Crown to John Carpenter from 4 Feb. 1592—XII(69v).

GAWEN, Thomas, gent., of Babstock [Baverstock], Wilts. 3 mths recusancy from 2 Apr. 1587: conv. 1 Mar. 1587/8.—VIII(74v).

GAWEN, Thomas, gent., of Islington, Middx. 3 mths recusancy from 28 June 1587: conv. 1 Dec. 1587.—VIII(38v).

GELDARD, Gildard, Jane, wife of Percival Geldard of the city of York, 'butcher'. 4 mths recusancy from 26 Mar. 1582: conv. ? July 1582.—II(8). Debt re-enrolled—V(8). VII(8). IX(8).

GEORGE, Morgan, 'yoman', of Llanishen, Mon. 5 mths recusancy from 24 Mar. 1586/7: conv. 13 Mar. 1587/8.—VIII(49).

GEORGE, William, 'yoman', of Llanllowell, Mon. (same recusancy period and conviction date)—VIII(49v).

GERARD, John, gent., of Southwark, Surrey [prisoner][93]. 4 mths recusancy ending 20 July 1584, when convicted—V(50v): and one later conviction dated 17 Feb. 1584/5—V(52v).

GERRARD, Grace, of Ince, Lancs., wife of Miles Gerrard [   ]. 12 mths recusancy from 20 Sept. 1589: conv. 22 Mar. 1590/1.—X(38).

GERRARD, John, gent., of Hollynhey, Winwick parish, Lancs. 13 mths recusancy from 14 Aug. 1586: conv. 25 Mar. 1588.—VIII(21v).

GERRARD, Lionel, gent., of Aughton, Lancs. (same recusancy period and conviction date)—VIII(21v).

GERRARD, William, gent., of Clerkenwell, Middx. 12 mths recusancy from 6 Dec. 1588: conv. 2 Jan. 1590/1.—XI(75v). Rental of lands in Dorset seized 10 Aug. 1591 (Pipe Roll entry under 'Dorset')—XI(75v). XII(18a). Rental of lands in Somerset seized 21 Aug. 1591 (Pipe Roll entry under 'Somerset')—XI(75).

GIBBES, Thomas, 'yoman', of Llantilio Pertholey, Mon. 5 mths recusancy from 24 Mar. 1586/7: conv. 13 Mar. 1587/8.—VIII(48v).

GIBSON, Margaret, wid., of Exelbye [? Eppleby], N.R. Yorks. 13 mths recusancy from 3 Sept. 1586: conv. 4 Sept. 1587.—VIII(25v).

GIFFORD, Gyfford, John, esq., of Chillington, Staffs. 12 mths recusancy ending 1 Apr. 1587, when convicted—IX(69v): and one later conviction dated 25 Mar. 1588—VIII(78v). Record of land-seizure, 3 Apr. 1588—VIII(78v). X(14). Seized lands let by Crown to Ralph Husbond from 8 July 1588—VIII(78). IX(62v). X(62). XI(64v). XII(65).

---

93. John Gerard (Cf. Anstruther I, p. 130, and Philip Caraman, *John Gerard*, (1951).)

GILBERT, Ann, wid., of Orcopp [Orcop], Herefords. 6 mths recusancy from 1 Sept. 1588: conv. 14 July 1589.—IX(25v). Debt re-enrolled—XI(29).

GILDRIDGE, Alice, 'spinster', of Eastborne [Eastbourne], E. Sussex. 2 mths recusancy from 17 Apr. 1587: conv. 26 Feb. 1587/8.—VIII(63v). Record of land-seizure, 17 Jan. 1588/9—IX(54v). Rental of seized lands—X(65v). XI(55v). XII(56v). Seized lands let by Crown to John Salisbury from 3 Oct. 1590.—XI(57). XII(56v).

GILDRIDGE, Margaret, 'spinster', of Bedingham [Beddingham], E. Sussex. (same recusancy period and conviction date)—VIII(63v).

GILLES, Jane, 'spinster', of Llangibby, Mon. 5 mths recusancy from 24 Mar. 1586/7: conv. 13 Mar. 1587/8.—VIII(49v).

GILSON, Richard, 'tanner', of Meaddowes [? near Pemberton], Lancs. 12 mths recusancy from 20 Sept. 1589: conv. 22 Mar. 1590/1.—X(38).

GIRRY, Mary, wife of John Girry, gent., of All Saints parish, Hereford city. 12 mths recusancy from 1 Sept. 1586: conv. 18 Mar. 1587/8.—VIII(30).

GLASCOCKE, Ann, [   ], of St. Saviour's parish, Southwark, Surrey [? prisoner][94]. 5 mths recusancy from 8 Jan. 1587/8: conv. 30 June 1588.—IX(53).

GLOSSOPPE, Mary, 'spinster', of West Hallam, Derbys. 10 mths recusancy from 9 Sept. 1586: conv. 22 Mar. 1587/8.—VIII(21).

GODFREY, Simon, 'yoman', of Densworth in Funtington, Sussex.[95] 1 mth recusancy from 20 Dec. 1587: conv. 26 Feb. 1587/8.—VIII(63v).

GODSAFE, Godsaffe, George, gent., of Southwark, Surrey [prisoner][96]. 4 mths recusancy ending 20 July 1584, when convicted—V(50v): and one later conviction dated 18 Feb. 1584/5.—V(52v).

GOLDE, John, 'yoman', of Cramborne [Cranborne], Dorset. 6 mths recusancy from 1 Jan. 1586/7: conv. 21 July 1587.—IX(16v). Debt re-enrolled—XII(78v).

GOLDESBOROUGHE, Robert, [   ], of Knoyle Episcopi [East Knoyle], Wilts. 3 mths recusancy from 2 Apr. 1587: conv. 1 Mar. 1587/8[97].—VIII(74v).

GOMOND, John, gent., of St. Peter's parish, Hereford city. 1 mth recusancy from 27 May 1583: conv. 15 July 1583—III(27): and four later convictions, ending 27 Mar. 1587—IV(64v). VI(25)*. Debt re-enrolled—V(26).

---

94. Ann Glascocke, of St. Mary Overyes (Cf. *CRS* LVII, p. 180), was certainly in the Clink in Sept. 1594 (Cf. *CRS* II, p. 286.)

95. Simon Godfrey was committed to the Wood Street Counter between June and Nov. 1586, by the Lords of the Privy Council, and was discharged by Mr. Younge on 2 July 1586. (Cf. *CRS* II, p. 269.)

96. George Godsalf (Cf. Anstruther I, p. 133.) Prior to arriving at Douai, he had been a fellow of Trinity College, Cambridge, and Prebendary of Ferring in Chichester Cathedral.

97. Robert Goldsburgh A convicted Wiltshire recusant of this name is known to have been in the Kings Bench Gaol in Southwark between 1587 and 1595. (Cf. *CRS* II, p. 285.)

GOMOND, Goman, John, gent., of the city of Hereford. 8 mths recusancy from 13 July 1581: conv. 12 Mar. 1581/2—I(25): and seven later convictions, ending 22 July 1585—II(64)*. V(26v)*. Debts re-enrolled—III(27). V(26). VII(25)*. IX(25)*. Summary of pre-1587 debts for recusancy—XI(29)*. Record of land-seizure, 5 Sept. 1587.—VIII(30). Rental of seized lands—VIII(30v). IX(24). X(28). XI(28). XII(28). Lands seized 15 Sept. 1589 let by Crown to William Hunnis from 26 Mar. 1591—XII(25v).

GOODAKERS, William, 'yoman', of St. George's parish, Southwark, Surrey [prisoner][98]. 5 mths recusancy from 17 Feb. 1586/7: conv. 17 July 1587.—IX(54).

GOODLAKE, Alice, wife of Edward Goodlake, esq., of Letcombe Regis, Berks. 12 mths recusancy from 1 Sept. 1586: conv. 4 Mar. 1587/8.—VIII(5).

GOOSE, Lettice, of Thistleton, Lancs., wife of John Goose, 'husb''. 12 mths recusancy from 20 Sept. 1589: conv. 22 Mar. 1590/1.—X(39).

GOOSE, Roger, 'husb'', of Thestleton [Thistleton], Kirkham parish, Lancs. 13 mths recusancy from 14 Aug. 1586: conv. 25 Mar. 1588.—VIII(21v).

GORGE[99], John, gent., of Southwark, Surrey [prisoner]. 10 mths recusancy ending 11 Mar. 1582/3, when convicted—IV(49v). See GREY, John.

GOSTWICKE, Alice, wid., of St. Mary's parish, Bedford, Beds. 3 mths recusancy from 29 Mar. 1587: conv. 20 Mar. 1588.—VIII(1).

GOULDE, Joan, wid., of Chedulton [Cheddleton], Staffs. 12 mths recusancy from 6 Sept. 1586: conv. 25 Mar. 1588.—VIII(78v).

GOULDWIER, Goldwier, Jane, 'spinster', of Southwark, Surrey ['papist' prisoner][100]. 10 mths recusancy ending 11 Mar, 1582/3, when convicted—III(58v): and two later convictions, ending 15 Feb. 1583/4—IV(49v)*. Debts re-enrolled—V(52v). VI(51)*.

GOWER, Thomas, gent., of Clerkenwell, Middx. 3 mths recusancy from 10 Mar. 1588/9: conv. 4 Sept. 1589.—IX(37).

GRAUNGER, William, senior, 'yoman', of Bentham, W.R. Yorks. 13 mths recusancy from 3 Sept. 1586: conv. 4 Sept. 1587.—VIII(25v). Record of land-seizure, 8 Apr. 1589—IX(22v). Rental of seized lands—IX(21v). X(21v). XI(24v). XII(23v). Goods, value £3 – 7 – 4, seized 8 Apr. 1589 – IX(22v). Goods, value £1 – 19 – 8, owed to Graunger by George Battie of Westhouse, and seized for the Queen (same date)—IX(22v).

---

98. William Goodakers of the Marshalsea, was a barber of St. Andrew's, Holborn. He was convicted of recusancy in June 1599 (Cf. Jeaffreson I, p. 254.)

99. The same list of prisoners in the Marshalsea, repeated in the Pipe Rolls V(50v) and VI(51), gives GREY or De GRAYE instead of GORGE, as the true name of this person. Cf. *infra*, John GREY (footnote 105.) His home was at East Harling, Norfolk., and he came from a notable recusant family.

100. Jane Gouldwier was in the Clink, 8 Apr. 1584, 'for nott confirminge herselfe to her Majesty's Lawes'. (Cf. *CRS* II, p. 235.)

GRAUNTE, Edward, gent., of Idsall *alias* Shuffnall [Shifnal], Salop. 6 mths recusancy from 1 Aug. 1588: conv. 17 July 1589.—IX(13).

GRAVENOR, Margery, 'spinster', of Norton in Hales, Salop. 12 mths recusancy from 24 Feb. 1586/7: conv. 18 July 1588.—VIII(16v).

GRAVENOR, Richard, gent., of Brande, Salop. Fine of £20 imposed by High Commissioners at St. Paul's Cathedral, London, 15 June 1577 (offence unspecified: £5 – 13 – 4 paid)—V(58v). Debt re-enrolled—VI(13).

GRAVENOR, Richard, gent., of Norton in Hales, Salop. 12 mths recusancy from 24 Feb. 1586/7: conv. 18 July 1588.—VIII(16v). Goods, value £4, seized 9 Oct. 1589.—IX(13v). Debt re-enrolled—X(58v). XI(63v). Record of land-seizure, 9 Oct. 1589—IX(13v). Rental of seized lands—IX(69v). X(59v). XI(62v). XII(63v). Arrearage of rent—X(58v). Seized lands let by Crown to Isaac Burges and George Dickenson from 30 Nov. 1591.—XII (64v).

GRAY, William, gent., of Wokinge [Woking], Surrey. 3 mths recusancy (period undated): conv. 5 July 1588.—VIII(63). See GREY.

GREENE, Ann, wife of William Grene, gent., of Bungaie [Bungay], Suffolk. 3 mths recusancy from 8 Apr. 1587: conv. 27 Mar. 1588.—VIII(73).

GREENE, Grene, Anthony, 'yoman', of Wilbarston, Northants. 12 mths recusancy from 31 July 1587: conv. 4 Mar. 1588/9.—IX(47).

GREENE, Edmund, 'clotheworker', of Wigan, Lancs. 12 mths recusancy from 20 Sept. 1589: conv. 22 Mar. 1590/1.—X(38).

GREENE, Grene, Eliz., [   ], of Brotherton, W.R. Yorks. 6 mths recusancy from 3 July 1587: conv. 18 Mar. 1587/8.—VIII(27).

GREENE, John, 'joiner', of Quernedon [Quarndon], All Saints parish, Derby. 10 mths recusancy from 9 Sept. 1586: conv. 22 Mar. 1587/8.—VIII(21).

GREENE, Isabel, his wife (same place, recusancy period & conviction date)—VIII(21v).

GREENE, Isabel, 'spinster', (same place, recusancy period & conviction date)—VIII(21).

GREENE, Katherine, 'spinster', (same place, recusancy period and conviction date)—VIII(21).

GREENE, Mary, 'spinster', (same place, recusancy period and conviction date)—VIII(21).

GREENE, Grene, Norton, gent., of St. Saviour's parish, Southwark, Surrey [prisoner][101]. 5 mths recusancy from 17 Feb. 1586/7: conv. 17 July 1587.—IX(54). Record of land-seizure [Frognall, Teynham, Kent],

---

101. Norton Greene's original domicile, a manor farm called 'Frognall' in Teynham, Kent., still stands, a well preserved example of a small Elizabethan residence, bearing his initials, 'N.G.' carved on the lintel over the porch. Greene was committed to the Clink in June 1586 for receiving priests, and spent several months there, until he was delivered in Feb. 1586/7. He was convicted of 5 months recusancy and fined £100. (Cf. *CRS* II, pp. 258, 262, 263, 268.) His seized lands were let by the Crown to John Iden for a rent of £12 – 15 – 8 *per annum*. (Cf. *CRS* LVII, pp. 51 – 52.)

dated 8 Feb. 1590/1.—XI(9). [Pipe Roll entries under 'Kent']. Rental of seized lands.—XII(32v). Seized lands let by Crown to John Iden from 8 May 1591.—XII(33).

GREENE, Grene, Peter, gent., of Alveston [Alvediston], Wilts. 6 mths recusancy from 2 Jan. 1586/7: conv. 1 Mar 1587/8.—VIII(74v).

GREENE, Grene, Ralph, 'yoman', of Drayton, Salop. 12 mths recusancy from 24 Feb. 1586/7: conv. 18 July 1588.—VIII(16v).

GREENE, Grene, Roche ['Rocus'] or Richard ['Ricardus'], esq., of Little Sampford, Essex. 12 mths recusancy from 18 Mar. 1580/1: conv. 26 Apr. 1582.—II(19). Debt re-enrolled—VI(18v). IX(19). Record of land-seizure, 18 Oct. 1587—VIII(22v). Rental of seized lands [in Great Sampford and Canfield]—VIII(22v). Seized lands let by Crown to Thomas Gentt from 19 June 1589—IX(18v). X(25). XI(21). XII(20).

GREENE, Grene, Theobald, gent., of Southwark, Surrey [prisoner][102]. 10 mths recusancy ending 11 Mar. 1582/3, when convicted—IV(49v): and three later convictions, ending 20 July 1584—IV(49v)*. V(50v). Debts re-enrolled—VI(51)*.

GREENE, Grene, Thomas, gent., of St. Dunstan's parish, Canterbury, Kent [? prisoner]. 9 mths recusancy from 18 Mar. 1580/1: conv. ? Dec. 1581—II(28): and two later convictions, ending 22 Feb. 1583/4—III(28v). IV(12). Debts re-enrolled—V(30). VI(12).

GREENE, Grene, Thomas, 'yoman', of Tanworthe [sic], Warwicks. 1 mth recusancy from 27 June 1588: conv. 5 Mar. 1588/9.—IX(11v).

GREENE, Grene, William, 'scolemaister', of Southwark, Surrey [prisoner][103]. 10 mths recusancy ending 11 Mar. 1582/3, when convicted—IV(49v); and four later convictions, ending 17 Feb. 1585/6, when convicted—IV(49v)*. V(50v). VI(49v). Debts re-enrolled—VI(51)*.

GREENE, Grene, William, 'clericus' [prisoner: same place]. 6 mths recusancy ending 18 Feb. 1584/5, when convicted.—V(52v).

GREENE, Grene, William, 'yoman' [prisoner: same place]. 8 mths recusancy ending 16 Feb. 1586/7, when convicted.—VI(50).

GREENWOOD, John, 'clericus', of St. Sepulchre parish, Farringdon Ward Without, London [prisoner][104]. 13 mths recusancy from 18 Apr. 1587: conv. 30 Apr. 1588.—VIII(38v).

GREGSON, John, 'lynnen webster', of Whalley, Lancs. 12 mths recusancy from 20 Sept. 1589: conv. 22 Mar. 1590/1.—X(39v).

GREGSON, 'Jenetta', his wife (same parish, recusancy period and conviction date).—X(40).

---

102. Theobald Greene of Rutlandshire and Lincoln's Inn (Cf. *CRS* I, p. 70.) was committed to the Marshalsea by the Bishop of London, 15 May 1578 (Cf. *CRS* XXII, p. 102.), and remained there until 8 Apr. 1584. (Cf. *CRS* II, p. 236.)

103. William Greene was committed to the Marshalsea by the Bishop of London, 19 July 1572. Indicted for recusancy 5 times as a schoolmaster, once as a cleric, and finally as a 'yoman'—after being three times examined—he was still a prisoner in Sept. 1588, having remained in the Marshalsea for at least 16 years. (Cf. *CRS* II, pp. 231–284.)

104. John Greenwood was an 'independant divine'. (Cf. *DNB*, XXIII, p. 84.)

GRETTON, John, 'yeoman', of Gracedewe [Gracedieu], Leics. 10 mths recusancy from 9 Sept. 1586: conv. 19 Mar. 1587/8.—VIII(45v).
GRETTON, Thomas, 'supposed recusant and fugitive' of Staffs. Goods, value £2 – 18s., seized 4 Sept. 1589.—X(14).
GREVSNOR [? Grosvenor], Jane, wid., of Moleston [Mucklestone], Staffs. 6 mths recusancy from 6 Sept. 1587: conv. 22 July 1588.—VIII(58). See GRAVENOR.
GREY, Alice, wife of Anthony Grey, gent., of Carbrooke, Norfolk. 3 mths recusancy from 13 Apr. 1587: conv. 1 Apr. 1588.—VIII(54).
GREY, John, gent., of Melton Magna, Norfolk (same recusancy period and conviction date).—VIII(54).
GREY, Graye, John, gent., of Southwark, Surrey [prisoner][105]. 4 mths recusancy ending 22 July 1583, when convicted—VI(51); and two later convictions, ending 20 July 1584—V(50v). VI(51). See GORGE, John.
de GREY, Grey, Robert, esq., of Marten [Merton], Norfolk. 11 mths recusancy from 1 Aug. 1581: conv. 23 July 1582—II(40): and five later convictions, ending Lent 1586/7—IV(44v). V(41v), (46v)*. VI(25v). Debts re-enrolled—III(72v). IV(40), (44v). V(46v). VI(41v), (42). VII(41)*. Chattels-real in Norf., value £144 – 10s., seized in 1589 from Robert de Grey and Robert Downes—X(81v). Debt re-enrolled—XI(66). Record of land-seizure in Norf., 28 Sept. 1587—VIII(51). Record of further land-seizure in Norf., 1 Dec. 1590—X(81v). Rental of lands in Norf., seized 28 Sept. 1587—VIII(6v). IX(43v). X(52v)*. XI(46v). Rental of lands in Norf., seized 1 Dec. 1590—X(81v). XI(46v). XII(47v). Arrearage of rent—XII(48). Lands seized 1587 let by Crown to William Cordell from 20 Oct. 1589—X(53). XI(46v). XII(47v). Lands seized 1587 let by Crown to George Lee from 20 Oct. 1590—X(81). XI(46v). XII(47v). Lands seized 1590 let by Crown to William Huckerbye from 22 Dec. 1590—XII(48). Record of land-seizure in Suffolk, 20 Jan. 1589/90—X(80v). Lands seized in Suff. let by Crown to George Lee from 2 Mar. 1589/90—X(80v). XI(65v). XII(66v). George Lee's lease of lands in Suffolk: arrearage of rent—XI(72v).
GRIFFETH, Gryffithe, Ambrose, gent., of St. Bride's parish, Farringdon Ward Without, London [prisoner][106]. [Pipe Roll entry under 'Wales']. 1 mth recusancy from 7 Dec. 1581: conv. 19 Jan. 1581/2—IV(63v): and one later conviction dated 20 Mar. 1581/2—IV(63v). Debts re-enrolled—VI(64v).

---

105. John Graye (Cf. *supra*, John GORGE, footnote 99.) He was committed to the Marshalsea, 2 Jan. 1577/8; was still there July 1585,; but was absent June 1586. (Cf. *CRS* II, pp. 232, 235, 240.) His surname was misread by the Pipe Roll scribe, but correct name given twice in Pipe Roll VI(51).
106. Ambrose Griffieth, a member of Lincoln's Inn, was committed to the Fleet, 1581 – 1582 (Cf. *CRS* II, pp. 222, 229.) He was described in 1605 as, 'a half-Recusant and a dangerous man, said to be of Glamorganshire but dwelleth in Hereford'. (Cf. *CRS* II, p. 297.)

GRIFFETH, William, gent., ? recusant, of Llancarvan [Llancarfan], Glam., Wales. Seized lands [date of seizure omitted] let by Crown to John Cornewall from Ladyday 1589—X(74v).

GRIMESTON, Denise, wife of John Grimpston, gent., of Oxborough, Norfolk. 3 mths recusancy from 13 Apr. 1587: conv. 1 Apr. 1588.—VIII(54). See GRYMSTONE.

GROVE, John, gent., of Dunheed [Donhead St. Andrew], Wilts. 3 mths recusancy from 2 Apr. 1587: conv. 1 Mar. 1587/8.—VIII(74v). Record of land-seizure, 8 Oct. 1588—IX(66). Rental of seized lands—IX(66). X(76v)*. XI(67v). XII(68v).

GRUFF, David, 'yom', of Didlaston [Dudleston], Salop. 12 mths recusancy from 24 Feb 1586/7: conv. 18 July 1588.—VIII(16v).

GRYFFEN, Griffen, John, 'clericus', of Southwark, Surrey [prisoner][107]. 2 mths recusancy ending 20 July 1584, when convicted—V(52v); and one later conviction dated 18 Feb. 1584/5.—V(52v).

GRYFFYTH, Katherine, 'spinster', of Raglan, Mon. 5 mths recusancy from 24 Mar. 1586/7: conv. 13 Mar. 1587/8.—VIII(48).

verch GRYFFITH, Joan, 'spinster' (same parish, recusancy period and conviction date)—VIII(48).

verch GRIFFITH, Griffithe, Gryffith, Margaret, wid., (same parish, recusancy period and conviction date)—VIII(48).

GRYME, William, 'yeoman', of Hunston [Hunstanton], Norfolk. 3 mths recusancy from 13 Apr. 1587: conv. 1 Apr. 1588.—VIII(54).

GRYMSHAWE, Henry, 'husb', of Church, Lancs. 13 mths recusancy from 30 July 1587: conv. 17 Mar. 1588/9—X(35): and one later conviction dated 22 Mar. 1590/1.—X(40).

GRYMSHAWE, Ellen, his wife (of same parish). 12 mths recusancy from 20 Sept. 1589: conv. 22 Mar. 1590/1.—X(40).

GRYMSHAWE, John, 'laborer', his son (same parish, recusancy period and conviction date as preceding entry).—X(40).

GRYMSHAWE, Mary, 'spinster', his daughter (same parish, recusancy period and conviction date as preceding entry).—X(40).

GRYMSTONE, Ralph, 'yoman'[108], of Nidd, W.R. Yorks. 4 mths recusancy from 14 May 1587: conv. 14 Sept. 1587.—VIII(25v).

GUNTER, David, 'yoman', of Llanvihangel Crucorney, Mon. 5 mths recusancy from 24 Mar. 1586/7: conv. 13 Mar. 1587/8.—VIII(48v).

GUNTER, [ ], his wife (same parish, recusancy period and conviction date).—VIII(48v).

GUNTER, Jane, wid., of Llantilio Pertholey, Mon. (same recusancy period and conviction date).—VIII(48v).

---

107. John Gryffen (Cf. Anstruther I, p. 139 under Griffeth.)
108. Ralph Grimston (Cf. Challoner, p. 233.)

HADDEN, *alias* of SMITHE, Joan.
HADDOCK, Ralph, [   ], of Wasshingley [Washingley], Hunts. 12 mths recusancy from 31 Mar. 1587: conv. 5 July 1588.—VIII(7). See HAYDOCK.
HADNETT, William, 'yoman', of Tottenham, Middx. 6 mths recusancy from 1 Oct. 1587: conv. 19 Apr. 1588.—IX(37).
HAILE, Thomas. See HALE, Hales, Thomas.
HAKES, Hawkes, Christopher, 'sacerdos'/'clericus', of Salford in parish of Manchester, Lancs [prisoner][109]. 4 mths recusancy from 2 Sept. 1582: conv. 16 Jan. 1582/3—II(38v): and one later conviction dated 22 Jan. 1583/4—IV(37). Debt re-enrolled—IV(42v). VI(39). VIII(46).
HALE, Henry, 'mercer', of Treales, Lancs. 12 mths recusancy from 20 Sept. 1589: conv. 22 Mar. 1590/1.—X(39v).
HALE, [   ], his wife (same parish, recusancy period & conviction date)—X(39v).
HALE, Hales, Thomas, gent., of Southwark, Surrey [? prisoner][110]. 10 mths recusancy ending 17 Feb. 1585/6, when convicted—VI(49v).
HALE, Haile, Thomas, gent., of Walthamstowe, Essex[111]. Grant by Thomas Hale (by letters-patent dated Ladyday 1586) to William Whiskines of Grays Inn, Middx. esq., of £10 p.a. from Hale's lands & tenements in Walthamstow, in satisfaction of a debt of £100—IX(18). The same lands in Walthamstow seized by commissioner Francis Blythe, esq., in Sept. 1589 for the recusancy of Thomas Haile, and let by Crown to John Gerrard; the lease to begin upon the termination of the above grant to William Whiskines—X(26v). XI(21v). XII(20v).
HALL, Eliz., wid., of Somerton, Oxfords. 12 mths recusancy from 26 Sept. 1586: conv. 7 Mar. 1587/8.—VIII(35v).

---

109. Christopher Hawkes was a pre-Elizabethan priest. He was probably Rector of Bircholt, Kent from 1537, who held the livings of West Barming and Nettlestead in the Diocese of Rochester and St. Faith's in Old St. Paul's, London. After deprivation from all four livings, he was active in Lancashire, and was imprisoned in Salford Gaol, from 2 Sept. 1582. (Cf. Pipe Roll, E.372/427, under 'Lancaster'.)

110. Thomas Hale was committed to the Clink in Mar. 1584/5, under the name 'Thomas Hall'. (Cf. *CRS* II, p. 282.)

111. Thomas Hall's earliest financial penalty was imposed by the commissioner Francis Blythe in Sept. 1585, who debited him in the sum of £300 for his goods and chattels. His grant to William Whiskines, i.e. of £100, at the rate of £10 *per annum*, from the issue of his lands in Walthamstow, was completed in 1596. A marginal note in the 5th. RR. alongside this entry relating to the lessee John Gerrard, orders its termination. In the following RR. (E.377/6.), the Exchequer's further arrangements for the Walthamstow property are set out. Thomas, the father, is required to pay £20 *per annum*, from 'customary' lands there as from 6 Oct. 1596, the date of their seizure by the Crown, and his three recusant sons—William, Augustin and Richard, now have their part to play in the family's defence of their traditional faith. William and Augustin had each to pay, from the same date, £2 – 14s. *per annum*, for certain customary lands in Walthamstow, valued at £4 *per annum*. Richard, from the same date, for two thirds of certain other lands at Walthamstow in the tenure of —Mallory, gent., annually worth £40, was responsible for the payment of £26 – 13 – 4 *per annum*. This settlement worked smoothly until 1601, when a note of discharge appears in RR. 10, under the entry of their father, Thomas, indicating his death in that Easter Term, 1601 (Cf. M.R., L.T.R., 44 Eliz. Easter Term, 'Recorda' section.) The seized lands of William and Augustin Hale continue to appear in the RRs. at least up to 1611.

HALL, George, [ ], of the city of York. 4 mths recusancy from 28 Mar.
   1581: conv. ? July 1581—II(8).
HALL, Katherine, wid., of Lovington in the parish of Easton, Hants.
   18 mths recusancy from 18 Mar. 1580/1: conv. 16 Sept.
   1582—III(50v): and two later convictions, ending Sept. 1584—IV(53).
   V(56v). Debts re-enrolled—V(56)*. VI(54).
HALL, Robert, gent., of Steple [Steeple]Langford, Wilts. 3 mths recusancy
   from 2 Apr. 1587: conv. 1 Mar. 1587/8.—VIII(74v).
HALL, Thomas, 'yom', of Tottenham, Middx. 3 mths recusancy from
   5 Apr. 1587: conv. 1 Sept. 1587.—VIII(38v).
HALL, Ursula, 'spinster', of Astley, Worcs. 2 mths recusancy from 7 Apr.
   1588: conv. 6 Mar. 1588/9.—IX(70v).
HALL, William, 'yoman', of Berrington, Worcs. 6 mths recusancy from
   29 Sept. 1587: conv. 25 July 1588.—VIII(80v).
HALLIWELL, John, gent., of Wrightington, Eccleston parish, Lancs.
   13 mths recusancy from 30 July 1587: conv. 17 Mar. 1588/9.—X(35).
HALLIWELL, Margaret, 'spinster', of Standish, Lancs. 12 mths recusancy
   from 20 Sept. 1589: conv. 22 Mar. 1590/1.—X(38).
HALSEY, John, physician, of St. Brides's parish, Farringdon Ward
   Without, London [prisoner][112]. 4 mths recusancy from 18 Mar.
   1580/1: conv. 18 July 1581—I(32v): and five later indictments ending
   Jan. 1582/3—I(32v)*, (35)*. and—II(30v). Debts re-enrolled—
   III(38v)*. V(35)*.
HAMERTON, Paul, esq., of [ ], Yorks. 2 mths recusancy from 4 Jan.
   1585/6: conv. 14 Mar. 1585/6.—VI(20v).
HAMERTON, [ ], his wife (same recusancy period and conviction
   date)—VI(20v).
HAMERTON, Paul, esq., of Munrode [Monkroyd, in Featherstone parish],
   W.R. Yorks. 6 mths recusancy from 3 July 1587: conv. 18 Mar.
   1587/8—VIII(27). Record of land-seizure, 8 Apr. 1589—IX(22v).
   Rental of seized lands—IX(21v)[113]. XII(25).[113]
HAMOND, Robert, 'yoman', of Racton, Sussex. 2 mths recusancy from
   17 Apr. 1587: conv. 26 Feb. 1587/8.—VIII(63v).

---

112. John Halsey, physician of Tewkesbury, Gloucs., was committed to the Fleet in Feb. 1580/1. On 15 Feb. he was transferred to the Clink by Bishop Aylmer, because 'the said Halsey was a man thought to do much harm at the Fleet among the Papists there'. (Cf. *CRS* II, pp. 223, 227.)

113. Paul Hamerton of Monkroyd, and of various messuages, lands and tenements in Preston Jacklinge (Purston Jaglin), Yorks., WR., owed to the Crown, £140 for 6 months recusancy from 3 July 1587; rendering to the Treasury on 29 May 1590—for the next (Michaelmas) term—£6 – 13 – 4, and in every subsequent Michaelmas term, up to and including 1596, the same sum of £6 – 13 – 4. He, together with two sureties, namely, Thomas Ridlington, gent., of South Bramwith, Yorks. WR., and William Hamerton, gent., of the parish of St. Anthony in the Ward of Cheap, London, paid the said sum on the following dates: 23 Nov. 1591; 19 Nov. 1592; 5 Nov. 1593; 12 Feb. 1593/4; 31 Oct. 1594; 4 Nov. 1595; and 2 Dec. 1596. But, still owing £93 – 6 – 8 to cover his penalty for 6 months recusancy, Paul Hamerton was now surprisingly discharged, 'by consideration of the barons of the Exchequer'. The entry ends with a reference to the authority for the above decision (M.R., L.T.R., 39 Eliz., Michaelmas term, 'Recorda' section). The above extract is from the 5th. RR., under 'Ebor' (E.377/5).

HAMOND, Hammond, Hamon, Alexander, 'yom''', of Marten [Merton], Norfolk. 12 mths recusancy from 10 Mar. 1582/3: conv. 10 Mar. 1583/4—IV(44v): and one later conviction dated 1 Apr. 1588—VIII(54).

HAMPDEN, Isabel, wid., of Stoke Poges, Bucks. 3 mths recusancy from 27 Mar. 1587: conv. 18 Mar. 1587/8.—VIII(3). Goods, value (with those of William Fitton [q.v.]) £17 – 9s., seized 12 Oct. 1588—IX(70).

HANCOCKES, 'Elena', wid., of Draycot, Staffs. 4 mths recusancy (undated): conv. 21 July 1589.—IX(69v).

HAND, William, 'yom''', of St. Bride's parish, Farringdon Ward Without, London [? prisoner]. 3 mths recusancy from 25 Mar. 1587: conv. 10 July 1587.—VIII(38v).

HANKENSEN, Eliz., of Cifton [Clifton] in parish of Kirkham, Lancs., wife of Edmund Hankenson [   ][114a] 10 mths recusancy from 18 Mar. 1580/1: conviction date omitted—II(38v). Debt re-enrolled—VIII(46).

HANKENSEN, Eliz., 'spinster', of Salford in parish of Manchester, Lancs. [prisoner][114b]. 4 mths recusancy from 2 Sept. 1581: conv. 16 Jan. 1581/2.—II(38v). Debt re-enrolled—VIII(46).

HANKIN, Dorothy, 'spinster', of parish of St. Sepulchre, Bishopsgate Ward, London. 3 mths recusancy prior to 20 Apr. 1588, when convicted.—VIII(38v).

HANKYNE, John, 'yoman', of Iden, Sussex. 2 mths recusancy from 17 Apr. 1587: conv. 26 Feb. 1587/8.—VIII(63v).

HAPGOOD, Robert, 'yom''', of Dorchester, Dorset. 12 mths recusancy from 2 July 1587: conv. 15 July 1588.—VIII(19v).

HARDEMAN, Margery, 'spinster', of Milwich, Staffs. 4 mths recusancy prior to 21 July 1589, when convicted.—IX(69v).

HARDINGE, Jane, 'spinster', of Ashburnham, Sussex. 5 mths recusancy from 20 Aug. 1587: conv. 5 July 1588.—VIII(63).

HARDWICKE, Nicholas, [   ], of [   ] in Scarcliffe parish, Derbys. 10 mths recusancy from 9 Sept. 1586: conv. 22 Mar. 1587/8.—VIII(21).

HARE, Michael, esq., of Bruseyard [Bruisyard], Suffolk. 12 mths recusancy from 3 July 1581: conv. 18 July 1582—II(56): and three later convictions, ending 6 Nov. 1587—III(66). VI(58)*. VII(58v)*. Debts re-enrolled—V(61). VI(58)*. Summary of pre-1587 debts for recusancy (July 1582 to Nov. 1587). Total, £1,380, paid by 16 Nov. 1587. Quit.—VII(58v). Annual fines (£260) paid from 6 Nov. 1587.—VIII(73). IX(63v). X(63v). XI(66). XII(66v).

HARE, Michael, esq., of St. Nicholas' parish, Gippo [Ipswich], Suffolk. 7 mths recusancy from 12 Sept. 1586: conv. 5 Apr. 1587.—VI(58).

HARE, Mary, his wife (of same parish). 3 mths recusancy from 8 Apr. 1587: conv. 27 Mar. 1588.—VIII(73).

---

114. This and the next entry probably refer to the same person, Elizabeth Hankenson. The surname is spelt thus in both entries, and regularly in Exchequer lists. In (114b.) she is described as 'spinster'; in (114a.) as married. In CRS V, p. 25 footnote, she appears again as spinster, but her name is given as Elizabeth Hawkenson.

HARE, Richard, 'yeoman', of St. Mary's parish, Nottingham, Notts.
10 mths recusancy from 9 Sept. 1586: conv. 25 Mar. 1588.—VIII(80).

HARFORTHE, Hartforthe, Thomas, gent., of Norton nr. Faversham, Kent. 2 mths recusancy from 14 Jan. 1587/8: conv. 26 Feb. 1588/9—IX(29). Record of land-seizure, 10 June 1590[115].—X(33). Seized lands let by Crown to Richard Locksmyth from 31 Dec. 1590.—XII(33).

HARGREVES, Eliz., wid., of Burnley, Lancs. 12 mths recusancy from 20 Sept. 1589: conv. 22 Mar. 1590/1.—X(40).

HARGREVES, William, 'laborer' (same parish, recusancy period and conviction date).—X(40).

HARLEY, Matilda, wife of John Harley, esq., of Brampton Brian, Herefords. 3 mths recusancy from 24 Mar. 1580/1: conv. 29 June 1581—III(27), and four later convictions, ending 5 Mar. 1582/3—III(27)*.

HARLEY, Matilda, wid., of All Saints parish, Hereford city. 1 mth recusancy from 27 May 1583: conv. 15 July 1583[116].—III(27).

HARMAN, Juliana, gentlewoman/'spinster', of Lyford, Berks. 8 mths recusancy from 26 June 1581: conv. 26 Feb. 1581/2—I(11v); and one later conviction, ending 24 Feb. 1583/4—II(65v). IV(3v). Debts re-enrolled—III(33v). V(3v). VI(3v). VII(3v).

HARMAN, Juliana, gentlewoman/'spinster', of St. Mary's parish, Reading, Berks. [prisoner][117]. 8 mths recusancy from 30 June 1582: conv. 11 Feb. 1582/3—II(65v); and one later conviction, ending 20 July 1584—III(50v). IV(46). Debts re-enrolled—V(4v). VI(3v).

---

115. Upon conviction, two thirds of Thomas Hartfurthe's lands were seized by the commissioners, Sir Thomas Fludd and William Baineham, i.e. part of the site of the late monastery of Leedes (near Maidstone) Kent., with nearby lands; a brewhouse in Sittingbourne; the rectory house at Rainham; all in the tenure or occupation of John Norden (recusant *q.v.*) together with lands at Esthall and adjacent property at Tonge and Murston, leased by the Crown to Richard Locksmyth, gent., from 21 Dec. 1590 for £44 – 8 – 10 *per annum*. All these seized lands were quickly discharged, 'by consideration of the barons of the Exchequer', (Cf. M.R., L.T.R., 33 Eliz., Hilary Term, 'Recorda' section.) And both Hartfurth and Locksmyth are quit. See also 10th. RR., under 'Item Kanc'.

116. Matilda Harley moved, during widowhood, to All Saints parish, Hereford. The summary of her personal debts for recusancy is given in Pipe Roll III, under 'Hereford' in five dated indictments from 24 Mar. 1581/2 to 5 Mar. 1584/5: sum total of debts being £300. She was discharged in Hilary Term 1584/5, 'by consideration of the barons of the Exchequer'. (Cf. M.R., L.T.R., 27 Eliz., Hilary Term, 'Recorda' section.)

117. Juliana Harman was a Brigittine nun. Accompanied by Katherine Kingswell (*q.v.*) of the same Order, she was staying with six other nuns at Lyford, Berks., (the house of Edward Yate), who arrived at Lyford to find St. Edmund Campion there, ready to say mass. Campion was arrested (Cf. *VCH* Berks., II, p. 37.) Harman and Kingswell were closely associated in all local prosecutions for recusancy from 26 June 1581 till 20 July 1584, as follows:—
 (1) (8 months) 26 June 1581 to 26 Feb. 1581/2. Prisoner at Reading Castle
 (2) (5 months) Mar. 1581/2 to 31 July 1582. Prisoner at Lyford (Reading Assizes)
 (3) (4 months) Feb. 1582/3 to 4 June 1583. Prisoner at Reading Castle
 (4) (8 months) July 1583 to 15 Feb. 1583/4. Prisoner at Lyford (Reading Assizes)
 (5) (6 months) Feb. 1583/4 to 20 July 1584. Prisoner at Reading Castle
(Cf. *CRS* XXXII, p. 118.)

HARPER, [ ], wife of Thomas Harper, [ ], of Grosmont, Mon. 5 mths recusancy from 24 Mar. 1586/7: conv. 13 Mar. 1587/8—VIII(49v).

HARPER, Eliz., wife of John Harper, esq., of Chelston [? or Chilston] in parish of Madley, Herefords. 12 mths recusancy from 1 Sept. 1586: conv. 18 Mar. 1587/8.—VIII(30).

HARPER, William, [ ], (same place, recusancy period and conviction date).—VIII(30).

HARRIS, Joan, wife of Simon Harris, gent., of Haringflete [Herringfleet], Suffolk. 12 mths recusancy ending 27 Mar. 1588, when convicted— VIII(73).

HARRIS, Harries, Harrys, John, 'yeoman', of Southwark, Surrey [prisoner][118]. 10 mths recusancy ending 11 Mar. 1582/3, when convicted—III(58v); and one later conviction, dated 22 July 1583—IV(49v). Debts re-enrolled—V(52v). VI(51).

HARRY, George, 'yoman', of Llanishen, Mon. 5 mths recusancy from 24 Mar. 1586/7: conv. 13 Mar. 1587/8.—VIII(49).

HARRY, 'Gwenlia', 'spinster', of Llanthewy Skirrid, Mon. (same recusancy period and conviction date).—VIII(48v).

HARRYE, 'Gwenlliana' William, wife of William Harrye, [ ], of Llanishen, Mon. (same recusancy period and conviction date).— VIII(49).

HARRYE, John, [ ], of Llangoven, Mon. (same recusancy period and conviction date).—VIII(49v).

HARRYE, 'Gwenliana', his wife (same parish, recusancy period and conviction date).—VIII(49v).

HARRYSON, [ ], wid., of Weeton, Lancs. 12 mths recusancy from 20 Sept. 1589: conv. 22 Mar. 1590/1.—X(39).

HARRYSON, Jane, 'spinster', of Standish, Lancs. (same recusancy period and conviction date).—X(38v).

HARRYSON, *alias* of SAGER, Christopher (*q.v.*).

HARSAUNTE, Michael, gent., of Beccles, Suffolk. 6 mths recusancy from 20 Sept. 1588: conv. 2 July 1589.—IX(64). Debts re-enrolled— XI(72v).

HARTE, Richard, 'yeoman', of Wimborne Minster, Dorset. 6 mths recusancy from 15 Jan. 1586/7: conv. 21 July 1587.—IX(16v). Debt re-enrolled—XII(78v).

HARTELAND, William, 'yom'', of Collowe [Callow], Herefords. Two fines of £20 imposed for ignoring sheriff's summonses after excommunication, 4 Apr. and 27 May 1581.—III(28)*. Debts re-enrolled—V(26)*.

HARTFORTHE. See HARFORTHE, Thomas.

---

118. John Harris, a mercer by trade, was found with three other 'printers' at Stonor Park, Oxon., busily engaged in working the secret printing establishment there. (Cf. *CRS* II, p. 30 footnote.) Committed to the Tower, with the others, on 13 Aug. 1581, he was later moved to the Marshalsea, where he was caught serving mass for Fr. William Denton. (Cf. *CRS* II, p. 221.)

HARTLEY, Harteley, James, [   ], of St. Mary's parish, Nottingham, Notts. 3 mths recusancy from 1 Apr. 1588: conv. 17 Mar. 1588/9—IX(70). Debt re-enrolled—XII(75).

HARTLEY, William, 'yeoman', of Southwark, Surrey [prisoner][119]. 10 mths recusancy ending 11 Mar. 1582/3, when convicted.—III(58v). Debt re-enrolled—V(52v).

HARTON, Eliz., wid., of Wyckham [Wykeham], N.R. Yorks. 6 mths recusancy from 3 July 1587: conv. 18 Mar. 1587/8.—VIII(25v).

HARWARD, Alice, 'spinster', of Mickleton, Gloucs. 5 mths recusancy from 26 Mar. 1587: conv. 11 Mar. l587/8. —VIII(82).

HARWARD, Hareward, Harewood, Eleanor, wid., of Alborough, Norfolk. 3 mths recusancy from 13 Apr. 1587: conv. 1 Apr. 1588—VIII(54). Record of land-seizure, 18 Oct. 1588 (Two-thirds of the manor of Alborough and of hereditaments in Cramworth [Cranworth], Norf.)—IX(45). Rental of seized lands—IX(45). X(52v). XI(46v)[120]. Arrearage of rent at Michaelmas 1589—XII(48).

HARVYE, Harvie, John, 'printer'/'yoman', of Southwark, Surrey [prisoner][121]. 10 mths recusancy ending 11 Mar. 1582/3, when convicted—IV(49v); and one later conviction, dated 22 July 1583—IV(49v). Debts re-enrolled—VI(51)*.

HASELWOOD, Agnes, 'spinster', of All Saints parish, Oxford. 12 mths recusancy from 26 Sept. 1586: conv. 7 Mar. 1587/8.—VIII(35v).

HASKEN, 'Lisseta', wife of Edward William Hasken, [   ], of Llandenny, Mon. 5 mths recusancy from 24 Mar. 1586/7: conv. 13 Mar. 1587/8—VIII(49v).

HASSARD, John, [   ], of Stanley, Derbys. 10 mths recusancy from 9 Sept. 1586: conv. 22 Mar. 1587/8.—VIII(21).

HASTINGES, Joyce, wife of Walter Hastings, esq., of Kirkby [? Mallory], Leics. 10 mths recusancy from 9 Sept. 1586: conv. 19 Mar. 1587/8.—VIII(45v).

HATTON, Richard, 'clericus', of Salford in the parish of Manchester, Lancs. [prisoner][122]. 12 mths recusancy from 20 Feb. 1582/3: conv. 22 Jan. 1583/4.—IV(37). Debt re-enrolled—IV(42v). VI(39).

HATTON, Thomas, 'labourer', of Salford in the parish of Manchester, Lancs. [prisoner]. (same recusancy period and conviction date)—IV(37). Debt re-enrolled—IV(42v). VI(39).

---

119. William Hartlet (Cf. Anstruther I, p. 155, 156.)

120. Eleanor Harward owed the Queen a debt of £13 – 6 – 8, at Michaelmas 1589. She was then discharged (Cf. M.R., L.T.R., 31 Eliz., Michaelmas Term, 'Recorda' section.)

121. John Harvye was one of the workers of the secret printing press at Stonor Park, Oxon., who were committed to the Tower on 13 Aug. 1581, and thence moved to the Marshalsea on the following 23 Aug. He was discharged from there some time after 22 July. 1583. (Cf. footnote 118.)

122. Richard Hatton was born at Stockton Yate, near Malpas, Cheshire. (Cf. Wark, p. 175). He was a pre-Elizabethan priest, who had been incumbent of Shelley, Essex, from 1558. Arrested at Manchester, 17 Jan. 1583/4, he was condemned at Quarter Sessions, 'for extolling the Pope's authority'. (Cf. Foley II, pp. 135 *seq*.) His sentence was changed to life imprisonment. Convicted at Salford Gaol on 22 Jan. 1583/4 of 12 months recusancy.

HAUGHTON, Ellen, wife of Ralph Haughton, gent., of Kirkeleis [Kirkless] in Aspull, Lancs. 12 mths recusancy from 20 Sept. 1589: conv. 22 Mar. 1590/1.—X(38). See HOUGHTON.

HAWE [*sic*, for LAWE], Eliz., of Graunge [Grange-over-Sands], Lancs., wife of John Lawe, 'yoman'. 12 mths recusancy from 20 Sept. 1589: conv. 22 Mar. 1590/1.—X(40).

HAWKES, Christopher: see HAKES.

HAWKESWORTH, William, gent., [prisoner][123], of St. Bride's parish, Farringdon Ward Without, London. [Pipe Roll entry under 'Yorks'] 1 mth recusancy from 7 Dec. 1581: conv. 19 Jan. 1581/2—III(10v): and one later conviction, dated 20 Mar. 1581/2—III(10v). Debts re-enrolled—VI(8v). VII(8v).

HAWKINS, Hawins, Alice, 'spinster', of Pembridge, Herefords. 6 mths recusancy from 1 Sept. 1588: conv. 14 July 1589.—IX(25v). Debt re-enrolled—XI(29).

HAYDOCK, Haidock, Haddock, William, gent., of Cotton [Cottam] in parish of Preston, Lancs. 4 mths recusancy from 18 Mar. 1580/1: conv. 31 July 1581.—VI(40v). Goods, value £67, seized 24 Oct. 1587—X(40v). Record of land-seizure, 24 Oct. 1587—X(40v). Rental of lands seized 24 Oct. 1587—XII(44). Goods, value (with those of John Westbie) £53 – 13 – 4, seized 29 Mar. 1588—VIII(21v). Record of lands seized 29 Mar. 1588 for pre-1587 recusancy—VIII(21v). Rental of lands seized 29 Mar. 1588—VIII(60). X(37), (39). Seized lands let by Crown to John Chapman from 1 Aug. 1589—X(37). XII(44).

HEAPE, Robert, 'husb'', of Leighe, Staffs. 6 mths recusancy from 6 Sept. 1587: conv. 22 July 1588.—VIII(58).

HEATHE, Dorothy, wid., of Alchurch [Alvechurch], Worcs. 12 mths recusancy from 20 Sept. 1586: conv. 28 Mar. 1588—VIII(77): and one later conviction dated 25 July 1588—VIII(80v). Goods, value £8, seized 31 Sept. 1588—IX(68v). Record of land-seizure, 31 Sept. 1588—IX(68v). Lands seized from Dorothy Heathe and from William, junior [see below] let by Crown to James Wilcockes from 1 Mar. 1588/9—IX(68). X(75). XI(70). XII(71).

HEATHE, Jane, 'spinster' (of same parish). 6 mths recusancy from 29 Sept. 1587: conv. 25 July 1588.—VIII(80v).

HEATHE, Magdalen, of Westminster [prisoner][124], wife of Thomas Heathe of Fulham, Middx, gent. 3 mths recusancy from 26 June 1581: conv. 26 Sept. 1581.—III(42). Debt re-enrolled—V(35).

---

123. William Hawkesworth was released from the Fleet, 11 Nov. 1582, on bonds to return when required (Cf. *CRS* II, pp. 222, 229.) He was fined £20 for one months recusancy from 7 Dec. 1581; and again £40 for two months from 20 Jan. 1581/2 to 22 Mar. 1581/2. In the Treasury £20 was paid on 25 Oct. 1587. *Annotation:* But he ought not to be summoned for £40, because the Queen has already been answered by Brian Stapleton, esq., late sheriff of 1585, from issues of annual rents of £20 from lands and tenements in Hawksworth, Nassington and Mitton, Yorks. (Cf. RR., VII rotulet 8*v*., under 'Res Ebor'.)

124. Magdalen Heath was sent to the Gatehouse in 1581 by the Bishop of London and other commissioners. (Cf. *CRS* II, pp. 225, 230.)

HEATHE, William, junior, [ ], of Allchurche *alias* Alvechurch, Worcs. 12 mths recusancy from 1 Apr. 1587: conv. 28 Mar. 1588.—IX(68v). Record of land-seizure, 9 Jan. 1588/9—IX(68v). Lands seized from William Heathe, junior, and from Dorothy, widow [see above], let by Crown to James Wilcockes from 1 Mar. 1588/9—IX(68). X(75). XI(70). XII(71).

HELAIE, William, [ ], of Manton in Lindsey, Lincs. 10 mths recusancy from 9 Sept. 1586: conv. 28 Mar. 1588.—VIII(44v).

HELME, Joan, of Chipping, Lancs., wife of Edward Helme [ ]. 12 mths recusancy from 20 Sept. 1589: conv. 22 Mar. 1590/1.—X(39).

HEMSWORTH, Francis, 'yom'', of York Castle ('de Castro Ebor''), York [prisoner]. 5 mths recusancy from 1 Jan. 1582/3: conv. 17 May 1583.—IV(21). Debt re-enrolled—VI(22).

HENCOCKE, Thomas, 'tailer', of All Saints parish, Oxford city. 12 mths recusancy from 26 Sept. 1586: conv. 7 Mar. 1587/8.—VIII(35v).

HENDIE, Eliz., wid., of Chideock, Dorset. 10 mths recusancy from 1 May 1583: conv. Lent 1583/4.—IV(16v).

HENSLOWE, Katherine, wid., of West Burhant [Boarhunt], Hants. 6 mths recusancy from 1 Aug. 1587: conv. 8 July 1588.—VIII(68v).

HENSLOWE, Stephen, gent., of Southweeke [Southwick], Hants. 3 mths recusancy from 17 Dec. 1583: conv. Lent 1583/4.—IV(53). Debt re-enrolled—VI(54).

HERINGE, Agnes, 'spinster', of Wateringbury, Kent. 2 mths recusancy from 19 Dec. 1587: conv. 26 Feb. 1588/9.—IX(29).

HESKETH, Heskyth, Wilfred, gent. of Little Pulton [Poulton], Lancs. 13 mths recusancy from 14 Aug. 1586: conv. 25 Mar. 1588.—VIII(21v).

HESKETH, Heskethe, William, gent. (of same parish). 4 mths recusancy from 18 Mar. 1580/1: conv. 31 July 1581.—VI(40v).

HESKETH, William, gent., of St. Bride's parish Farringdon Ward Without, London [prisoner][125]. [2 convictions recorded under 'Lancs'. IV46v] 1 mth recusancy from 7 Dec. 1581: conv. 22 Jan. 1581/2—IV(46v): and one later conviction, dated 20 Mar. 1581/2—IV(46v). Debts re-enrolled—VI(39).

HESKETH, William, gent., of Little Poulton, Lancs. [Cuff's lease recorded under 'London Middx'] Seized lands let by Crown to Hugh Cuffe from Michaelmas 1585—VI(33v). VIII(16v) [Cuff's lease recorded under 'Staffs']. X(35v) [Cuff's lease recorded under 'Cheshire']. XII(9) [Cuff's lease recorded under 'Cheshire'].

---

125. William Hesketh, a prisoner in the Fleet (Cf. *CRS* II, p. 222.), was given a warrant of release by Walsingham on 11 Nov. 1582, under bond to return when required; and again on 15 Jan. 1582/3. Of the four Hesketh's here mentioned (all probably connected with the same family), the last three are clearly the same man. He was no longer in the Fleet on 22 Mar. 1583/4. (Cf. *CRS* II, p. 229.) His home was in Little Poulton, Lancs. Hugh Cuffe, the principal crown agent, had him in charge from Michaelmas 1585, for a rent of £5 – 13 – 4 *per annum*, from lands and tenements in Little Poulton, Kirkham and Croston.

HEVENINGHAM, Ann, wife of Walter Heveningham, esq., of Pipe [Ridware], Staffs. 6 mths recusancy from 6 Sept. 1587: conv. 22 July 1588—VIII(58).

HEVENINGHAM, Dorothy, wid., of Stone [? or Stoue], Staffs. 4 mths recusancy from 31 Mar. 1582: conv. 2 Aug. 1582.—II(14). Debt re-enrolled—IV(62). VI(63).

HEWES, Hughes, John, 'yom'', of Westminster, Middx. [prisoner][126]. 1 mth recusancy from 6 Oct. 1587: conv. 29 Jan. 1587/8.—VIII(38v).

HEWETT, George, 'yoman', of parish of St. Giles in the Fields, Middx. 2 mths recusancy from 2 July 1589: conv. 3 Dec. 1589.—IX(37).

HEYBORNE, John, gent., of Okeley [Oakley], Bucks. 12 mths recusancy from 12 Mar. 1587/8: conv. 23 June 1589.—IX(70).

HIBBERD, Alice, 'spinster', of Leckhampton, Gloucs. 5 mths recusancy from 26 Mar. 1587: conv. 11 Mar. 1587/8.—VIII(82).

HICKES, Ann, wife of Christopher Hicks, 'yom'', of Ipston [Ibstone], Bucks. 3 mths recusancy from 27 Mar. 1587: conv. 18 Mar. 1587/8—VIII(3).

HIDE, Brigit, wife of Hugh Hide, esq., of Letcombe Regis, Berks. 12 mths recusancy from 1 Sept. 1586: conv. 4 Mar. 1587/8.—VIII(5).

HIDE, Hyde, Dorothy, wife of Humphrey Hyde, gent., of Morecott [Norcott[127]], Berks. (same recusancy period and conviction date)—VIII(5).

HIDE, Eliz., wife of Richard Hide, gent., of Sutton Courtney, Berks. (same recusancy period and conviction date)—VIII(5).

HIDE, Valentine, 'yom'', of St. Bride's parish, Farringdon Ward Without, London [? prisoner][128]. 3 mths recusancy from 25 Mar. 1587: conv. 10 July 1587.—VIII(38v).

HIGGENSON, Hoggenson, Thomas, gent., of Barkeswell [Berkswell], Warwicks. 7 mths recusancy from 12 July 1586: conv. 15 Mar. 1587/8—VIII(76). Record of land-seizure, 2 Oct. 1588—IX(67v). Rental of seized lands—IX(67v). X(72). XI(69). XII(70).

HIGGES, Ann, wife of Christopher Higges, 'yeom'', of Chinnor, Oxfords. 12 mths recusancy from 26 Sept. 1586: conv. 7 Mar. 1587/8.—VIII(35v).

---

126. John Hewes, a Devonshire man, some time a clerk to one of the Secondaries of the Counter in London, was committed to the Gatehouse, 24 May 1582, being found conferring with a massing priest, and sent from the Council board in the Star Chamber. (Cf. *CRS* II, pp. 225, 230, 235, 253, 254, 271.) Possibly identifiable with 'John Hughes, gent.', a contemporary prisoner 'for eleven years in the Gatehouse', suspected of 'conveying money' to imprisoned priests and recusants. (Cf. *CRS* II, p. 253.)

127. Dorothy Hyde, on her marriage, became the Chatelaine of Norcott or Northcourt, the chief manor house of the Hyde family, purchased in 1547 by her grandfather, John Lyon. Northcourt lay in Abingdon. (Cf. *VCH* Berks IV, p. 419, and footnote 81.) With Dorothy, on 4 Mar. 1587/8, were also convicted of 12 months recusancy, Brigit, wife of Hugh Hide of Letcombe Regis and Elizabeth, wife of Richard Hide of Sutton Courtenay, both in Berks., and on the same date. (Cf. RR no. 8 E. 377/8, under 'Item Berks'.)

128. Valentine Hide An unidentified member of the Berkshire family abovementioned, she was probably a prisoner in the Fleet.

HIGGES, Richard, 'yoman', of St. George's parish, Southwark, Surrey [? prisoner][129]. 5 mths recusancy from 17 Feb. 1586/7: conv. 17 July 1587.—IX(54).

HIGGES, Robert, gent., of St. Saviour's parish, Southwark, Surrey [prisoner in the Clink] 5 mths recusancy ending 16 Feb. 1586/7, when convicted.—VI(50).

HIGGES, William, 'yom'', of Westhampsted, Berks. 8 mths recusancy from 3 July 1583: conv. 24 Feb. 1583/4.—IV(3v). Debt re-enrolled—VI(3v).

HIGGES, Higes, William, 'yom'', of St. Mary's parish, Reading, Berks. [prisoner][130]. 6 mths recusancy from 1 Feb. 1583/4: conv. 20 July 1584—IV(46): and two later convictions, ending 22 June 1585.—V(4v)*. Debts re-enrolled—VI(3v)*.

HIGGETT, Jane, [ ], of Etwall, Derbys. 10 mths recusancy from 9 Sept. 1586: conv. 22 Mar. 1587/8.—VIII(21).

HIGHAM, Joan, of Meaddowes [? near Pemberton], Lancs., wife of Ralph Higham, 'tanner'. 12 mths recusancy from 20 Sept. 1589: conv. 22 Mar. 1590/1.—X(38).

HIGHAM, William, gent., of the parish of St. Clement Danes, Without Temple Bar, Middx. Fine of 100 marks imposed for hearing Mass said on 30 Jan. 1585/6 by William Thompson in the house of Robert Bellamy (*q.v.*). Conv. at Old Bailey 18 Apr. 1586[131].—VI(34v).

HILDESLEY, Hillesley, Margaret, [ ], of Cromarshe [Crowmarsh Gifford], Oxfords. 12 mths recusancy from 26 Sept. 1586: conv. 7 Mar. 1587/8.—VIII(35).

HILDESLEY, Hillesley, Walter, gent., of [East Ilsley], Berks. Goods, value £8, seized 4 Oct. 1588.—IX(4v). Record of land-seizure, 4 Oct. 1588.—IX(4v). Rental of seized lands.—IX(4v). X(3v). XI(4). See ILLESLEY.

HILL, John, 'yoman', of Upton-on-Severn, Worcs. 2 mths recusancy from 7 Apr. 1588: conv. 6 Mar. 1588/9.—IX(70v).

HILL, Richard, 'yeoman', of Upton-on-Severn, Worcs. 12 mths recusancy from 20 Sept. 1586: conv. 28 Mar. 1588.—VIII(77). Goods, value £7 – 1s., seized 31 Sept. 1588.—IX(68v). Record of land-seizure, 31 Sept. 1588.—IX(68v). Rental of seized lands—IX(49v). X(75). XI(70). XII(71).

HILL, Alice, his wife (same parish, recusancy period and conviction date)—VIII(77).

---

129. Richard Higges of Westhampstead, Berks., was at first imprisoned in Reading Gaol (the Castle), thence he was transferred to the Marshalsea and attended the London Sessions in 1588—at which he was examined, tried and respited by Walsingham. He was thereupon recommitted to the Marshalea by the Lord Chamberlain. (Cf. *CRS* V, pp. 155, 156.)

130. William Higges was imprisoned in Reading Castle from 1 Feb. 1583/4 to 22 June 1585, and thereby convicted, on the latter date, of eleven months recusancy. (Cf. *CRS* XXXII, p. 118.)

131. William Higham was confined in the Wood Street Counter, 30 July 1585, and committed by Walsingham for hearing mass. Was still there, 7 Dec. 1586. (Cf. *CRS* II, pp. 249, 252, 255, 271.)

HILL, Thomas, 'yoman', of Podington, Beds. 12 mths recusancy from 6 July 1587: recusancy conv. 12 Mar. 1588/9.—IX(1v).

HILTON, Andrew, gent., of Carlisle, Cumberland. 3 mths recusancy from 27 Apr. 1582: conv. ? July 1582.—II(7v).

HILTON, Andrew, gent.,[132] of St. Mary's parish, Carlisle, Cumberland. 12 mths recusancy from 21 Aug. 1582: ? Aug. 1583—V(7v). Debt re-enrolled (under 'Westmorland')—VI(63). VIII(78). X(78). Record of land-seizure in Westmorland, 24 Apr. 1585—IX(7v). XII(72).

HILTON, Andrew, gent., of Burton [in Warcop], Westmorland. 1 mth recusancy from 1 June 1588: conv. 5 Aug. 1588.—IX(69).

HILTON, Mary, 'spinster', of Parke, in parish of Deane, Lancs. 2 mths recusancy from 2 June 1588: conv. 17 Mar. 1588/9.—X(35).

HINDE, Richard, 'yoman', of Preston, Lancs. 2 mths recusancy from 3 June 1588: conv. 17 Mar. 1588/9.—X(35).

HINDE, William, 'yoman', of Chedulton [Cheddleton], Staffs. 6 mths recusancy from 6 Sept. 1587: conv. 22 July 1588.—VIII(58).

HINTONE, Ann, 'spinster', of Fishbourne, Sussex. 2 mths recusancy from 17 Apr. 1587: conv. 26 Feb. 1587/8.—VIII(63v).

HINTONE, Briget, 'spinster' (same parish, recusancy period & conviction date)—VIII(63v).

HITCHE, Jane, wife of Thomas Hitche, 'yeom", of Wendlebury, Oxfords. 12 mths recusancy from 26 Sept. 1586: conv. 7 Mar. 1587/8.—VIII(35v).

HITCHMAN, John, gent., of Welford [Whelford], in parish of Kemsford [Kempsford], Gloucs. 10 mths recusancy from 30 Oct. 1586: conv. 11 Mar. 1587/8.—VIII(82). Record of land-seizure, 1 Oct. 1588—IX(23v). Rental of lands seized 1 Oct. 1588—IX(23v). Record of land-seizure, 14 Jan. 1588/9—X(27v). Lands seized 14 Jan. 1588/9 let by Crown to Francis Thynne from 7 Mar. 1588/9.—IX(23v). X(27). XI(27). XII(27).

HITCHMORE, Margaret, wid., of All Saints parish, Oxford city. 12 mths recusancy from 26 Sept. 1586: conv. 7 Mar. 1587/8.—VIII(35v).

HOBERT, Huberte, Hubarte, Henry, gent., of Dynnygnton [Dennington], Suffolk. 3 mths recusancy from 2 Apr. 1588: conv. 19 Mar. 1588/9—IX(64). Debt re-enrolled—XI(72v). Record of land-seizure, 20 Jan. 1589/90—X(80v). Seized lands let by Crown to Henry Marwood from 20 Mar. 1589/90—X(80v). XI(65v). XII(66v). Henry Marwood's lease: arrearage of rent (no payment recorded)—XI(72v).

HOBSON, Richard, [ ], of the Isle of Wight ['de Insula Vecta']. Fine of £40 imposed at Consistory Court of St. Paul's, London, by John [Aylmer] Bishop of London and other High Commissioners on

---

132. Andrew Hilton was confined to the 'Sheriff's ward' in St. Mary's Carlisle, Cumberland, from the end of 1592 to the second week of Advent 1593, when he and his wife were liberated. He was correspondent and assistant to Fr. John Boste. (Cf. *CRS* V, pp. 35–37, and 63–69; and Challoner, pp. 202–208, and Appendix III, pp. 597–600.)

25 Apr. 1576, for a 'contempt' against the Church[133]. [Pipe Roll entry under 'Hants']—III(62). Debt re-enrolled—VII(54). XI(60).
HOBSON, Thomas, gent. [place of origin omitted: Pipe Roll entry under 'Hants'] Similar fine of £40 imposed by High Commissioners at St. Paul's, London, on 7 Nov. [1576][134]. Fine payable by instalments of £8. £16 remaining debt. £8 paid.—IV(52).
HOCKENHULL, John, gent., of Prenton, Woodchurch parish, Cheshire. 13 mths recusancy from 25 Sept. 1586: date of conviction omitted.—VIII(58v).
HOCKNELL [Hockenhull], John, esq., of Salford, in parish of Manchester, Lancs [prisoner]. 4 mths recusancy from 2 Sept. 1582: conv. 16 Jan. 1582/3—II(38v): and three later convictions, ending 27 Dec. 1584—IV(42v). VI(39), (40v). Debts re-enrolled—IV(37). VI(39). VIII(46). Goods, value £4, seized Michaelmas 1587—VI(40v). Goods, value £69, seized 24 Oct. 1587—X(40v). Record of lands in Cheshire seized 24 Oct. 1587 [Recusant Roll entry under 'Lancs']—X(40v). Rental of lands in Cheshire seized 24 Oct. 1587 [Recusant Roll entry under 'Lancs']—XII(44).
HOCKNELL [Hockenhull], John, gent., of Salford, in parish of Manchester, Lancs. [prisoner]. 3 mths recusancy from 17 Jan. 1581/2: conv. 2 May 1582—II(38v): and three later convictions, ending 20 Apr. 1585—II(38v). VI(39), (40v). Debts re-enrolled—IV(46v). VIII(46)*. Seized lands in Prenton, Cheshire, let by Crown from Ladyday 1584 to John Hocknell, esq., of Hocknell [Hockenhull, in parish of Tarvin, Cheshire], his executors and assigns, for the use of Margaret, the present wife of the said John Hocknell, gent. and of her children ... for the satisfaction of a debt of £220. [Pipe Roll entries under 'Cheshire'] VI(63v). VIII(60v). X(37v). XII(9).
HODGES, Alice, 'spinster', of Irtlingburghe [Irthlingborough], Northants. 12 mths recusancy from 16 Apr. 1587: conv. 4 Mar. 1588/9.—IX(47v).
HODGSON, Hodgeson, Eliz., 'spinster', of Westby, Lancs. 12 mths recusancy from 20 Sept. 1589: conv. 22 Mar. 1590/1.—X(39v).
HODGSON, Ellen, of [ ], Lancs., wife of Richard Hodgson, 'husb''. (same recusancy period and conviction date)—X(39v).
HODGSON, Hodgesone, John, 'yom'', of Groman [Grosmont], N.R. Yorks. 6 mths recusancy from 3 July 1587: conv. 18 Mar. 1587/8.—VIII(25v).
HODGSON, Hodgeson, William, 'husb'', of Westby with Plumpton,[135], Lancs. 12 mths recusancy from 20 Sept. 1589: conv. 22 Mar. 1590/1.—X(39v).

---

133. Richard Hobson was committed to the Queen's Bench Prison, 8 May 1579, and was still there, 31 July 1580. (Cf. *CRS* I, p. 68.)
134. Thomas Hobson was committed to the Marshalsea, and thence discharged 31 July 1577. (Cf. *CRS* I, p. 70.) Sent to the King's Bench Prison in 1580. (Cf. *CRS* I, p. 61.)
135. William Hodgeson came from what is now 'Westby with Plympton', 3 miles w. of Kirkham, Lancs. (Cf. *CRS* XVIII, pp. 194, 195.)

HODGSON, Hodgeson, Katherine, his wife (same parish, recusancy period and conviction date)—X(39v).
HODGSON, Hodgeson, William, 'husb'', of Westby with Plumpton[135], Lancs. (same recusancy period and conviction date)—X(39v).
HODGSON, Hodgeson, Katherine, his wife (same parish, recusancy period and conviction date)—X(39v).
HOELL, David James, 'yoman', of Llangattock Vibon Avel, Mon. 5 mths recusancy from 24 Mar. 1586/7: conv. 13 Mar. 1587/8.—VIII(48v).
HOELL, Jane James, 'spinster' (same parish, recusancy period and conviction date)—VIII(48v).
HOELL, Joan, 'spinster', of Llandegaveth [Llandegveth], Mon. 5 mths recusancy from 24 Mar. 1586/7: conv. 13 Mar. 1587/8.—VIII(48).
HOELL, 'Jonetta', wid., of Skenfrith, Mon. (same recusancy period and conviction date)—VIII(48v).
HOELL, Katherine, wid., of Raglan, Mon. (same recusancy period and conviction date)—VIII(48).
HOELL, Matilda verch Jevan, wife of John Adam Hoell [ ], of Raglan, Mon. (same recusancy period and conviction date)—VIII(48).
HOELL, Howell, Thomas, 'yoman', of Raglan, Mon. (same recusancy period and conviction date)—VIII(48). Record of land-seizure, 24 Oct. 1588—IX(42v). Rental of lands seized 24 Oct. 1588—IX(42v). X(50). XI(45). See HOWELL.
HOLBORNE, William, gent., of Chelsey [Chelsea], Middx. 3 mths recusancy from 10 Mar. 1588/9: conv. 4 Sept. 1589.—IX(37).
HOLCOME, Juliana, 'spinster', of Stepney, Middx. 3 mths recusancy from 5 Apr. 1587: conv. 1 Sept. 1587.—VIII(38v).
HOLCROFT, 'Hamlettus', gent., of Woodende, Eccles parish, Lancs. 13 mths recusancy from 30 July 1587: conv. 17 Mar. 1588/9.—X(35).
HOLDEN, Margaret, wid., of Plesington [Pleasington], Lancs. 12 mths recusancy from 20 Sept. 1589: conv. 22 Mar. 1590/1.—X(40v).
HOLDGATE, Nicholas, 'webster', of Swynden [Swinden, nr Colne], Lancs. (same recusancy period and conviction date)—X(40).
HOLLAND, Ellen, [ ], of Clyfton, Eccles parish, Lancs. 13 mths recusancy from 30 July 1587: conv. 17 Mar. 1588/9.—X(35).
HOLLAND, Helen, wid., of Clifton, Eccles parish, Lancs. 13 mths recusancy from 14 Aug. 1586: conv. 25 Mar. 1588.—VIII(21v).
HOLLAND, Robert, gent., of Clyfton, Eccles parish, Lancs[136]. 4 mths recusancy from 2 May 1582: conv. 26 Aug. 1582.—II(38v).
HOLLAND, Robert, gent., of Salford, in parish of Manchester, Lancs. [prisoner] 12 mths recusancy from 20 Feb. 1582/3: conv. 22 Jan. 1583/4—IV(37): and two later convictions, ending 20 Apr. 1585—VI(40v)*. Debt re-enrolled—IV(42v). VI(39).

---

136. Robert Holland was imprisoned in Salford Gaol for 12 months recusancy from 20 Feb. 1582/3 to 22 Jan. 1583/4, and two later convictions ending on 20 Apr. 1585. (Cf. *CRS* V, p. 10.)

HOLLAND, Robert, gent., of Southwark, Surrey, [prisoner—in Marshalsea][137]. 7 mths recusancy ending 17 Feb. 1585/6—VI(49v).
HOLLINSHEDD, Eliz., wid., of Wigan, Lancs. 3 mths recusancy from 1 May 1588: conv. 17 Mar. 1588/9.—X(35).
HOLME, Joan, wid., of Barford [Barforth] Dykes, in Gilling parish, N.R. Yorks. 13 mths recusancy from 3 Sept. 1586: conv. 4 Sept. 1587—VIII(25v).
HOMES, Roger, 'yom'', of Drayton, Salop. 12 mths recusancy from 24 Feb. 1586/7: conv. 18 July 1588.—VIII(16v).
HOODE, Ralph, 'yeoman', of Everton, Cambs. [now Beds.]. 12 mths recusancy from 20 Mar. 1587/8: conv. 14 Mar. 1588/9.—IX(5).
HOOLE, George, 'blackesmythe', of Singleton Magna [Great Singleton], Lancs. 12 mths recusancy from 20 Sept. 1589: conv. 22 Mar. 1590/1.—X(39).
HOOLE, [   ], his wife (same parish, recusancy period and conviction date).—X(39).
HOOLE, Isabel, 'spinster' (same parish, recusancy period and conviction date).—X(39).
HOOLE, John, [   ], of Westby, Lancs. (same recusancy period and conviction date).—X(39v).
HOOLE, Margaret, [   ]. (same parish, recusancy period and conviction date).—X(39v).
HOORD, see HORDE.'
HOPER, Isabel, wife of Thomas Whoper, 'yoman', of Hanley Castle, Worcs. 6 mths recusancy from 29 Sept. 1587: conv. 25 July 1588.—VIII(80v). See WHOOPER.
HOPTON, William, 'clericus', of Buckland, Berks[138]. 12 mths recusancy from 1 Sept. 1586: conv. 4 Mar. 1587/8.—VIII(5).
HORDE, Hoord, William, gent., of the Soke of Winton [Winchester], Hants. 2 mths recusancy ending 16 May 1581, when convicted.—V(56). Debt re-enrolled—VII(54). IX(57v).

---

137. Robert Holland was then removed by the Earl of Derby 'out of Cheshire (*sic*) on 8 May 1585, to the Marshalsea, and, after examination by the High Commissioners at the Star Chamber (Cf. *CRS* II, p. 244.), began another two periods of close imprisonment in the Marshalsea itself. These two periods, each of four months duration, were dated 3 Sept. 1585 to 27 Dec. next following; the second period began on the next day, 28 Dec. 1585, and was planned to end on 20 Apr. 1586, but on 17 Feb. 1585/6 only his dead body was found. Morris III, p. 36, refers to Holland's death in prison as dated 'july 1586', but Exchequer records rectify this dating in the Exannual Roll (E. 363/9) where, under 'Surrey/Sussex'; 'Debita extrata de rotulo 27 Eliz.' it is plainly stated that Holland left a debt of £140 (at £20 a month) for recusancy during a period of 7 months immediately preceeding the 17th. day of February in the 28th. year of the reign of Queen Elizabeth (1585/6). A final summary of his character was 'neither wealthy nor wise, but very arrant'. His family now had to pay the fine, in addition to his previous convictions. He died, therefore, 'in bonds', in the 48th. year of his age. (Cf. Morris, and Foley III, p. 805.)

138. William Hopton was mentioned by a clerical writer, as 'supposed to be a priest'. (Cf. *CRS* V, pp. 64, 67.) But he is not mentioned in Anstruther, or known to have been a pre-Elizabethan priest. Fr. Pollen suggested his name was an alias, but he is officially named 'a cleric' and convicted of 12 months recusancy from 1 Sept. 1586.

HORDE, William, [   ], of the city of Winton, Hants. 5 mths recusancy from 6 May 1581: conv. ? Oct. 1581.—I(55). Debt re-enrolled—III(62). V(56). VII(54).

HORDE, William, [   ], of the parish of St. Maurice, Winchester, Hants. 3 mths recusancy from 1 Oct. 1581: conv. 9 Jan. 1581/2.—I(55). Debt re-enrolled—III(62). V(56). VII(54). Seized lands let by Crown to Hugh Cuffe from 2 Mar. 1583/4.—IV(52). V(55v). VI(53v). VII(53v). VIII(66v). IX(57v). X(68v). XI(59v). XII(60v).

HORDE, William, gent., of Preston Candiver [Candover], Hants.[139]. 6 mths recusancy from 1 Aug. 1587: conv. 8 July 1588—VIII(68v). Rental of lands seized 13 Nov. 1588—IX(59v). X(68v). XI(59v).

HORDE, Hoorde, William, gent., of the parish of St. Maurice, Winchester, Hants. Lands seized 13 Nov. 1588 let by Crown to John Peirson & Thomas Culleford from Michaelmas 1590—X(69). XI(59v). XII(60v).

HORNEBY, Grace, wid., of Wesham, Lancs. 12 mths recusancy from 20 Sept. 1589: conv. 22 Mar. 1590/1.—X(39).

HORNEBYE, Robert, senior, 'husb'' (same parish, recusancy period and conviction date)—X(39).

HORNEBYE, [   ], his wife (same parish, recusancy period and conviction date)—X(39).

HORNER, Nicholas, 'tailor', of Christ Church parish, Farringdon Ward Within, London [prisoner][140]. 12 mths recusancy from 13 Feb. 1586/7: conv. 16 Feb. 1587/8.—VIII(38v).

HORNOLD, Alice, wife of George Hornold, gent., of Breden [Bredon], Worcs. 6 mths recusancy from 29 Sept. 1587: conv. 25 July 1588—VIII(80v).

---

139. William Horde The three men bearing this name are obviously one and the same. He was imprisoned in the Wood Street Counter, 27 June 1586. (Cf. *CRS* II, p. 269.). Notes on the later history of his lands:—
   (a) lands seized for his recusancy and let by the Crown to Hugh Cuffe from 2 Mar. 1583/4 (Cf. *CRS* LVII, pp. 33, 34.)—rent charge, £24 – 13 – 4 *per annum*.
   (b) same lands let by Crown to John Pierson and Thomas Culleford from 13 Nov. 1590 (Cf. *CRS* LVII, p. 36.)—rent charge, £42 – 8 – 10 *per annum*.
All three farmers discharged in RR no. 6 (E. 377/6), 39 Eliz., under 'Hants', as follows: Cuffe's entry repeated; ends with Cuffe's debts, all unpaid—£344 – 15s.; Pierson and Culleford's entry repeated; ends with Pierson and Culleford's debts, all unpaid—£381 – 19 – 10½ . Total of debts £726 – 14 – 10½ . Formal discharge note: 'But they ought not to be summoned for the above debts, nor ought these separate farmers to be charged again by consideration of the barons of the Exchequer noted in the M.R., L.T.R., 40 Eliz., Michaelmas Term, 'Recorda' section, 'And they are quit'. The final entry in Horde's lands reads, 'the tenants of the two-thirds of the tenements lying in Preston Candover and Nutley in the same county owe to the Crown, £40 – 13 – 4, *viz.* for the rent of two-thirds of two tenements of the lands and tenements of William Hoorde, recusant, for one full year ending on the feast of St. Michael in the 31st. year of the reign of Queen Elizabeth (1588). But they (tenants) ought not to be summoned for this rent, for a reason given immediately above in the farms of Hugh Cuffe, gent., . . . And they are quit'.

140. Nicholas Horner of Grantley, W. Yorks., was imprisoned at Newgate, and martyred at Smithfield, 4 Mar. 1589/90. (Cf. *CRS* II, p. 238, *CRS* V, pp. 12, 178, 179, 291, and Challoner, pp. 160, 161.)

HORNOLD, Margaret, wife of Ralph Hornold, esq., of Hanley Castle, Worcs. 12 mths recusancy from 20 Sept. 1586: conv. 28 Mar. 1588—VIII(77).

HORNOLD, Horniold, Margaret, wife of Ralph Honiold, gent., of Hanley Castle, Worcs. 6 mths recusancy from 29 Sept. 1587: conv. 25 July 1588—VIII(80v).

HORSEMAN, Eleanor, wife of Abraham Horseman, gent., of Haseley, Oxfords. 12 mths recusancy from 26 Sept. 1586: conv. 7 Mar. 1587/8—VIII(35).

HORSEMAN, Thomas, gent., of Bury St. Edmunds, Suffolk. 8 mths recusancy from 3 July 1581: conv. 28 Mar. 1582—II(56).

HORSFALL, Horsfald, Ellen, of Bywreth [Byreworth, Garstang], Lancs., wife of Edward Horsfall [ ]. 12 mths recusancy from 20 Sept. 1589: conv. 22 Mar. 1590/1—X(39).

HOUGHE, William, esq., of Salford in the parish of Manchester, Lancs. [prisoner][141]. 4 mths recusancy from 17 Jan. 1581/2: conv. 2 May 1582—II(38v): and three later convictions ending 27 Dec. 1584—II(38v)*. IV(37). VI(40v). Debts re-enrolled—IV(42v). VI(39). VIII(46). Seized lands in Cheshire (Thorneton and Leighton) let by Crown to William Whitmore from 1 Mar. 1583/4 [Recusant Roll entry under 'Cheshire]—IV(62v). VI(39v). VIII(46v). X(35v). XII(9).

HOUGHE, William, gent., of Salford in the parish of Manchester, Lancs. [prisoner]. 3 mths recusancy from 22 Jan. 1583/4: conv. 15 Apr. 1584—IV(46v). Debt re-enrolled—VI(39).

HOUGHTON, Mary, of Charnock Richard, Lancs., wife of Richard Houghton, gent. 12 mths recusancy from 20 Sept. 1589: conv. 22 Mar. 1590/1—X(38).

HOUGHTON, Haughton, Thomas, priest ['sacerdos'/'clericus'], of Salford in the parish of Manchester, Lancs [prisoner][142]. 3 mths recusancy from 10 Oct. 1581: conv. 17 Jan. 1581/2—II(38v): and two later convictions, ending in Oct., 1582, when he probably died. IV(37). Debts re-enrolled—II(42v). VI(39). VIII(46). See HAUGHTON.

HOWELL, George John Thomas, 'yoman', of Raglan, Mon. 5 mths recusancy from 24 Mar. 1586/7: conv. 13 Mar. 1587/8—VIII(48).

HOWELL, Margaret, his wife (same parish, recusancy period and conviction date)—VIII(48). See HOELL.

HOWER, 'Jenetta', wid., of Whalley, Lancs. 12 mths recusancy from 20 Sept. 1589: conv. 22 Mar. 1590/1—X(40).

HOWER, John, 'wollen webster', of Wiswall [Wiswell], Lancs. (same recusancy period and conviction date)—X(40).

---

141. William Houghe was imprisoned in Salford Gaol, and, in 1581, was transferred to the Manchester Fleet. (Cf. CRS V, pp. 23 – 25.) The son of Alice, an illegitimate daughter of Thomas Cromwell, he was a determined recusant until his death in the new Fleet in June 1586. (Cf. Wark, pp. 36, 253.)

142. Thomas Houghton was a pre-Elizabethan priest, and had been incumbent of Wrenbury, Cheshire. Indicted at Quarter Sessions, he was imprisoned at Chester Castle, and Salford from 1581. (Cf. Wark, pp. 17, 31, 38, 67, 175.)

HOWER, William, 'wollen webster', of Graunge [Grange-over-Sands], Lancs. (same recusancy period and conviction date)—X(40).

HOWLETT, Ann, wife of Henry Howlett [ ] of Colney, Norfolk, 'inhabiting the parish of St. Peter Mancroft, Norwich' [Pipe Roll entry under 'Civitas Norwic'']. 1 mth recusancy from 20 Aug. 1586: conv. 26 Sept. 1586—VI(10).

HUBBARD, William, 'laborer', of Ashby Magna, Leics. 10 mths recusancy from 9 Sept. 1586: conv. 19 Mar. 1587/8—VIII(45v).

HUBBERSTYE, Isabel, wid., of Lancaster, Lancs. 12 mths recusancy from 20 Sept. 1589: conv. 22 Mar. 1590/1—X(39v).

HUETSON, Robert, 'husb'', of Torrisholme, Lancs. 12 mths recusancy from 20 Sept. 1589: conv. 22 Mar. 1590/1—X(39v).

HUETSON, Eliz., his wife (same parish, recusancy period and conviction date)—X(39v).

HUETT, Jane, wife of William Huett, esq., of Milbroke [Millbrook], Beds. 9 mths recusancy from 4 May 1587: conv. 3 July 1588—VIII(lv).

HUETT, Margery, wife of Philip Huett, 'yeoman', of St. Mary Magdalen parish, Oxford city. 12 mths recusancy from 26 Sept. 1586: conv. 7 Mar. 1587/8—VIII(35v).

HUETT, Roger, [ ], (same parish, recusancy period and conviction date)—VIII(35v).

HUGES, Margaret verch Richard, wife of William Huges, [ ], of Llanarth, Mon. 5 mths recusancy from 24 Mar. 1586/7: conv. 13 Mar. 1587/8—VIII(48).

ap HUGHE, Henry, gent., of Whitford, Flints. [Pipe Roll entry under 'Wales']. 5 mths recusancy from 1 Mar. 1580/1: conv. 25 Sept. 1581—IV(38v). Debt re-enrolled—VI(64v).

HUGHES, Hwe, Alice, 'spinster', of Skenfrith, Mon. 5 mths recusancy from 24 Mar. 1586/7: conv. 13 Mar. 1587/8—VIII(48). Record of land-seizure, 24 Oct. 1588—IX(42v). Rental of seized lands—IX(42v). X(50). XI(45). Seized lands let by Crown to Hugh Williams from 6 July 1590—XI(45). XII(46).

HUGHES, Katherine, 'spinster', of Llanthewy Skirrid, Mon. 5 mths recusancy from 24 Mar. 1586/7: conv. 13 Mar. 1587/8—VIII(48v).

HUGHES, Mary, wife of William Hughes, [ ], of Llantell Grissinginye [Llantilio Crossenny], Mon. (same recusancy period and conviction date)—VIII(49v).

HUGHES, Robert, 'yoman', of Llanthewy Skirrid, Mon. (same recusancy period and conviction date)—VIII(48v).

HUGHES, William, 'yoman', (same parish, recusancy period and conviction date)—VIII(48v).

HUGHES, Matilda, his wife (same parish, recusancy period and conviction date)—VIII(48v).

HULKER, Thomas, 'servingman', of Towneley [in Burnley], Lancs. 12 mths recusancy from 20 Sept. 1589: conv. 22 Mar. 1590/1—X(40).

HULSE, John, gent., of Sutton Courtney, Berks. 3 mths recusancy from 25 Mar. 1581: conv. 26 June 1581—I(llv): and three later convictions, ending 24 Feb. 1583/4—I(llv). II(65v). IV(3v). Debts re-enrolled—III(33v)*. V(3v)*. VI(3v). VII(3v)*.

HULSE, John, gent., of St. Mary's parish, Reading, Berks. [prisoner][143]. 4 mths recusancy from 11 Feb. 1582/3: conv. 4 June 1583—III(50v): and four later convictions, ending 22 June 1585—II(65v). IV(46). V(4v)*. Debt re-enrolled—VI(3v).

HULSE, John, esq., of Sutton Courtney, Berks. 12 mths recusancy from 1 Sept. 1586: conv. 4 Mar. 1587/8—VIII(5).

HULSE, Thomas, esq., of Sutton Courtney, Berks.[143] 3 mths recusancy from 24 Mar. 1580/1: conv. 18 June 1581—II(65v): and two later convictions, ending 4 Jan. 1581/2—II(65v)*. Debts re-enrolled—III(5). Record of land-seizure, 12 Sept. 1590—XI(4v). Seized lands in Berks and Oxon (Crowmarsh) let by Crown to Ralph Smythe from 27 Nov. 1590—XI(5v).

HULSE, Thomas, gent., of Sutton Courtney, Berks. 8 mths recusancy from 24 June 1582: conv. 1 July 1583—III(50v): and one later conviction dated 24 Feb. 1583/4—IV(3v). Debts re-enrolled—V(4v). VI(3v).

HULSE, Thomas, gent., of St. Mary's parish, Reading, Berks. [prisoner][143a]. 4 mths recusancy from 11 Feb. 1582/3: conv. 4 June 1583—III(50v): and one later conviction, dated 20 July 1584—IV(46). Debts re-enrolled—V(4v). VI(3v).

HUNTE, [ ], wife of 'Remigius' Hunte, [ ], of Lacebie [Lowesby][144], Leics. 10 mths recusancy from 9 Sept. 1586: conv. 19 Mar. 1587/8—VIII(45v).

Joan, servant of the same 'Remigius'. (same parish, recusancy period and conviction date)—VIII(45v).

---

143. Thomas Hulse was one of the most prominent catholic recusants of Berkshire. He and his brother John were the children of Andrew and Jane Hulse (nee Rythe) of Totford, Hants. (Cf. Harleian Society, *Visitations of Berkshire* LXI, pp. 33, 34.) Both brothers began a four month spell of imprisonment in Reading Castle on the same day—11 Feb. 1582/3. Thomas was set free in July 1584, but John was kept in prison a year longer, being enlarged in July 1585. Their 'capital messuage' or manor house, in which they both dwelt, was a fairly extensive tenement seized for the Crown on 12 Sept. 1590, by Thomas Parry, esq., and other Commissioners for a rent of £6 – 13 – 4 *per annum*, a very moderate figure. (Cf. *CRS* LVII, p. 2.) Twenty years later, in 1611, RR. (E.377/19) under 'Berks.' gives the current specification of the property. Ralph Smyth still held the lease of Sutton Courtnay, together with some property in Crowmarsh, Oxon. Particulars of Sutton Courtnay are given as follows:— £20 per annum to the Crown for the whole site; also seized were an apple orchard; a stable; 16 acres of meadow and pasture land in Sutton, yearly value £15, together with various other messuages, lands and tenements, with appurtenances specified in preceeding rolls as a parcel of the lands and possessions of Thomas Hulse of Sutton Courtnay, Berks., esq., recusant, taken and seized into the late Queen's hands on 10 Oct. 1598 by Sir Francis Knowles, and other Commissioners by reason of the recusancy of the same Thomas. To have and to hold the above property to the said Ralph Smithe, his executors and assigns from 15 Nov. 1608 till the end and term of 21 years next following; rendering yearly £20 at the Annunciation of the BVM and the feast of St. Michael the Archangel, to the receipt of the Exchequer in equal portions. Annotation:— In the Treasury, £10 was paid from the same farm. And he is quit! Eventually he married Dorothy, daughter of Thomas Yate of Lyford. (Cf. *Visitation of Berkshire* LVI, pp. 33, 34.)

144. Three people are indicted for recusancy in this entry—the husband, Remegius, his unamed wife, and Joan his servant.

HUNTE, Hunt, Henry, 'yom'', of Fareham, Hants. 7 mths recusancy from 19 Mar. 1580/1: conv. 1 Oct. 1581—I(55): and two later convictions, ending ? Mar. 1581/2—I(55). III(50v). Debts re-enrolled—III(62)*. V(56)*.

HUNTE, Katherine, 'spinster', of Clerkenwell, Middx. 6 mths recusancy from 1 Oct. 1587: conv. 19 Apr. 1588—IX(37).

HUNTER, Dorothy, wid., of Thorneton, W.R. Yorks. 6 mths recusancy from 3 July 1587: conv. 18 Mar. 1587/8—VIII(25v). Record of land-seizure, 10 Apr. 1589—IX(8v). Rental of seized lands—IX(21v). X(21v). XI(24v). XII(23v). Seized lands let by Crown to James Bellamy from 3 Aug. 1590.—X(13v). XI(24v). XII(23v).

HUNTON, Ann and Brigit (sisters) [of Fishbourne, Pipe Roll entry under 'Sussex']. £200, bequeathed to them by will of their father, John Hunton, deceased, from the issues of the manor of Motcombe, Dorset, seized by Crown from their brother Richard (son and heir of John), by reason of the recusancy of the said Ann and Brigit: ? Jan. 1588/9—IX(54)v. [See also Hinton.]

HUSSEY, Gilbert, esq., of Ownedell [Oundle], Northants. 12 mths recusancy ending 2 May 1587: conv. 12 Mar. 1587/8—VIII(52v).

HUTCHINS, Petronilla, wife of Thomas Hutchins, 'yeom'', of West Hendred, Berks. 12 mths recusancy from 1 Sept. 1586: conv. 4 Mar. 1587/8—VIII(5).

HUXLEY, Thomas, 'yoman', of Bunbury, Cheshire. 13 mths recusancy from 25 Sept. 1586: date of conviction omitted—VIII(58v).

HUYSHE, Silvester, gent., of St. Deacons [St. Decuman's], Somerset. 7 mths recusancy from 1 Jan. 1586/7: conv. 6 Mar. 1587/8—VIII(65). Record of land-seizure in Somerset, 2 Oct. 1590—XI(75).

HWE, see HUGHES, Alice.

HYTON, Richard, gent., of Abraham [Abram], Wigan parish, Lancs. 13 mths recusancy from 14 Aug. 1586: conv. 25 Mar. 1588—VIII(21v).

ICHEN, Katherine verch Jevan, wife of Thomas Ichen, [   ], of Llanthewy [Vach], Mon. 5 mths recusancy from 24 Mar. 1586/7: conv. 13 Mar. 1587/8—VIII(49).

ILDESLEY, see HILDESLEY, Walter.

ILLESLEY, Roger, 'yoman', of Yoxall, Staffs. 6 mths recusancy from 25 Mar. 1588: conv. 14 Mar. 1588/9—IX(69v): and one later conviction dated 21 July 1589—IX(69v).

ILLESLEY, Ildesley, Walter, gent., of East Illesley [Ilsley], Berks. 1 mth recusancy from 26 May 1585: conv. 24 June 1585—VI(48v): and three later convictions, ending 4 Mar. 1587/8—VI(48v)*. VIII(5). Seized lands of Walter Illesley and of Dorothy, his wife[145], let by Crown to Charles Pagett from 30 May 1589—IX(58). X(68v). XI(59v). XII(60v). See HILDESLEY.

IME, Alice, 'spinster', of Hanley Castle, Worcs. 6 mths recusancy from 29 Sept. 1587: conv. 25 July 1588—VIII(80v).

INCE, Alice, wife of John Ince, gent., of Ince, Lancs. 12 mths recusancy from 20 Sept. 1589: conv. 22 Mar. 1590/1—X(38).

INCE, Eliz., wife of Miles Ince, gent., of Ince, Lancs. (same recusancy period and conviction date)—X(38).

INGHAM, Eliz., of Graunge [Grange-over-Sands], Lancs., wife of Roger Ingham, 'laborer'. 12 mths recusancy from 20 Sept. 1589: conv. 22 Mar. 1590/1—X(40).

INGHAM, John, 'taleor', of Wiswell, Lancs., son of Laurence Ingham [ ]. (same recusancy period and conviction date)—X(40).

INGLEBY, Lady Ann, wid., of Ripley, W.R. Yorks. 2 mths recusancy from 4 Jan. 1585/6: conv. 14 Mar. 1585/6—VI(20v): and one later conviction, dated 4 Sept. 1587—VIII(25v).

INGLEBY, Inglebie, John, gent., of Ripley, W.R. Yorks. 13 mths recusancy from 3 Sept. 1586: conv. 4 Sept. 1587.—VIII(25v).

IRELAND, Irelande, John, 'tailor', of Pembridge, Herefords. 6 mths recusancy from 1 Sept. 1588: conv. 14 July 1589—IX(25v). Debt re-enrolled—XI(29).

IRELAND, Thomas, 'yoman', of Wigan, Lancs. 3 mths recusancy from 1 May 1588: conv. 17 Mar. 1588/9—X(35).

IRELAND, *alias* of KYDDE, Thomas.

ISAM, Edward, gent., of Clerkenwell, Middx. 6 mths recusancy from 29 Mar. 1587: conv. 1 Dec. 1587—VIII(38v).

ISAM, Mary, wid., of Stepney, Middx. 3 mths recusancy from 5 Apr. 1587: conv. 1 Sept. 1587—VIII(38v).

JACKSON, Edward, 'clericus'[146], of Eccles, nr. N. Walsham, Norfolk. 3 mths recusancy from 13 Apr. 1587: conv. 1 Apr. 1588—VIII(54). Goods, value £6, seized 18 Oct. 1588—IX(45). Record of land-seizure, 18 Oct. 1588—IX(45). Rental of seized lands—IX(45). X(52v). XI(46v).

---

145. The first lands in Berks. seized from Walter Illesley and Dorothy, his wife, included 'the farm of Illesley', which was let to Charles Pagett by the Crown from 30 May 1589, for a rent of 13s. 4d. *per annum*. These lands were discharged by the Crown in 1605 (E. 377/16) under ('Berks.' first entry) Other lands in Oxon., also owned by Walter Illesley and his mother, Margaret, a recusant, were now seized at Crowmarsh, Gifford and Newenham Moren (including the farm of 'howbery') and let by the Crown to Leonard Wilmot and John Simondes from Ladyday 1593, for a rent of £2 – 6 – 8 *per annum*. These lands in Oxon were still in the possession of Walter and his mother in 1611.

146. Edward Jackson An unidentified, but probably pre-Elizabethan priest of this name spent some time in the Marshalsea between 1582 and 1588 (Cf. *CRS* II, p. 231.)

JACKSON, Jacksone, Edward, 'husb'', of Wesham, Kirkham parish, Lancs. 13 mths recusancy from 14 Aug. 1586: conv. 25 Mar. 1588—VIII(21v): and one later conviction, dated 22 Mar. 1590/1—X(39).

JACKSON, [   ], his wife (of same parish). 12 mths recusancy from 20 Sept. 1589: conv. 22 Mar. 1590/1—X(39).

JACKSON, Francis, gent., of Sherreston [Sharleston], W.R. Yorks. 2 mths recusancy from 4 Jan. 1585/6: conv. 14 Mar. 1585/6—VI(20v). Goods, value £15, seized 8 Apr. 1589—IX(22v). Record of land-seizure, 8 Apr. 1589—IX(22v). Rental of seized lands—IX(21v). X(21v). XI(24v). XII(23v). Seized lands let by Crown to James Bellamy from 3 Aug. 1590—X(13v). XI(24v). XII(23v).

JACKSON, Henry, 'tailor', of Salford in parish of Manchester, Lancs. 12 mths recusancy from 20 Feb. 1582/3 [prisoner][147]: conv. 22 Jan. 1583/4—IV(37). Debt re-enrolled—IV(42v). VI(39).

JACKSON, Mary, 'spinster', of Wendlebury, Oxfords. 12 mths recusancy from 26 Sept. 1586: conv. 7 Mar. 1587/8—VIII(35v).

JACKSON, Jacksone, Richard, 'tallowchandler', of St. Swithin's parish, Walbroke Ward, London. 13 mths recusancy from 19 Jan. 1586/7: conv. 19 Jan. 1587/8—VIII(38v).

JACKSON, Jackeson, Richard, 'yom'', of York Castle, St. Mary's parish, York [? prisoner]. 1 mth recusancy from 31 Mar. 1583: conv. ? May 1583.—IV(21). Debt re-enrolled—VI(22).

JACKSON, Robert, 'yom'', of St. Saviour's parish, Southwark, Surrey [prisoner][148]. 5 mths recusancy ending 17 Feb. 1586/7, when convicted—VI(50).

JACKSON, Jacksone, Roger, 'yoman', of St. Bride's parish, Farringdon Ward Without, London [? prisoner]. 3 mths recusancy before 20 Apr. 1588, when convicted—VIII(38v).

JACKSON, Thomas, gent., of Sharleston, W.R. Yorks. 6 mths recusancy from 3 July 1587: conv. 18 Mar. 1587/8—VIII(25v).

JACKSON, Jacksone, William, gent., (same parish, recusancy period and conviction date)—VIII(25v).

JACKSON, William, 'husb'', of Wesham, Lancs. 12 mths recusancy from 20 Sept. 1589: conv. 22 Mar. 1590/1—X(39).

JACOBB, Jacobbe, John, 'yom''/gent., of Southwark, Surrey [prisoner][149]. 10 mths recusancy ending 11 Mar. 1582/3, when convicted—IV(49v): and two later convictions, ending 15 Feb. 1583/4—IV(49v)*. Debts re-enrolled—VI(51)*.

---

147. Henry Jackson was imprisoned in Salford Gaol from 20 Feb. 1583/4. (Cf. *CRS* V, p. 71.)
148. Robert Jackson was in the Clink for three months ending 17 Feb. 1586/7. (Cf. *CRS* II, p. 283.)
149. John Jacob was a prisoner in the Marshalsea between 16 Aug. 1581 and 8 Apr. 1584. (Cf. *CRS* II, pp. 221, 233, 235.)

JAMES, 'Alsona', wid., of Grosmont, Mon. 5 mths recusancy from 24 Mar. 1586/7: conv. 13 Mar. 1587/8—VIII(49v).

JAMES, Margaret, wid., of Burton Latymer, Northants. 12 mths recusancy from 16 Apr. 1587: conv. 4 Mar. 1588/9—IX(47v).

JAMES, Edward, 'clericus', see under Ralph Crocket[244b].

JAMES, Edward, 'clericus', of St. George's Parish, Southwark, Surrey. [prisoner] 5 mths recusancy from 17 Feb. 1586/7: conv. 17 July 1587—IX(54).

JAMES, William, 'yoman', of Llanthewy Skirrid, Mon. 5 mths recusancy from 24 Mar. 1586/7: conv. 13 Mar. 1587/8—VIII(48v).

JAMES, *alias* CHATHMAY[150], Philip, 'yoman', of Wanstowe [Wonastow], Mon. (same recusancy period and conviction date)—VIII(48v).

JEBBE, Jobbe, Robert, 'yoman', of Katridinge [Kate Ridding], Skelton parish, N.R. Yorks.[151] 12 mths recusancy from 1 June 1581: conv. Lent 1582/3—III(10v). Debt re-enrolled—V(20). VI(20v). VII(20v). IX(8v). XII(26).

JEFFERYE, Ellen, 'spinster', of Racton, Sussex. 2 mths recusancy from 17 Apr. 1587: conv. 26 Feb. 1587/8—VIII(63v).

JENKIN, Jenkine, 'Christiana', 'spinster', of Tredunnock, Mon. 5 mths recusancy from 24 Mar. 1586/7: conv. 13 Mar. 1587/8—VIII(49).

JENKIN, Jane, 'spinster', of Usk, Mon. (same recusancy period and conviction date)—VIII(49).

JENKIN, Katherine, 'spinster', of Skenfrith, Mon. (same recusancy period and conviction date)—VIII(49v).

JENKIN, Jenkyn, William Philip, of [ ], Mon. 5 mths recusancy from 4 Mar. 1585/6: conv. 22 July 1586—VI(40v).

JENKIN, Jenkyn, *alias* WELCHMAN, William, 'yom", of Abergavenny, Mon. 8 mths recusancy from 19 July 1585: conv. 1 Mar. 1585/6—VI(40v).

ap JENKIN, Jenkyn, Hoell, 'tailor', of Raglan, Mon. 3 mths recusancy from 25 Mar. 1581: conv. 29 June 1581—III(45): and one later conviction, dated 9 Mar. 1581/2—III(45). Debts re-enrolled—V(40v)*.

ap JENKIN, Jane John, 'spinster', of Skenfrith, Mon. 5 mths recusancy from 24 Mar. 1586/7: conv. 13 Mar. 1587/8—VIII(48).

ap JENKIN, Jenkyn, John, 'yoman', of Raglan, Mon. 8 mths recusancy from 10 July 1581: conv. 9 Mar. 1581/2—III(45). Debt re-enrolled—V(40v).

ap JENKIN, Philip John, 'yoman', of Skenfrith, Mon. 5 mths recusancy from 24 Mar. 1586/7: conv. 13 Mar. 1587/8—VIII(48). Record of land-seizure, 24 Oct. 1588—IX(42v). Rental of seized lands—IX(42v). X(50). XI(45).

ap JENKIN, Matilda, his wife (same parish, recusancy period and conviction date)—VIII(48).

---

150. Philip Jones's alias is spelt 'CATCHMAY' in the original RR
151. Robert Jebb died a prisoner in York Castle before 1590 (Cf. *CRS* V, p. 193.)

JENKINSON, Robert, [ ], of Ashby Magna, Leics. 9 mths recusancy before 10 Aug. 1587, when convicted—VIII(45v).

JENNYNGES, Eliz., 'spinster', of Lincolnes Inne grange, parish of St. Clement Danes, London. 3 mths recusancy from 10 Mar. 1588/9: conv. 4 Sept. 1589—IX(37).

JERMIN, Jermyne, Ambrose, esq., of Barnebye [Barnby], Suffolk. 6 mths recusancy from 1 July 1585: conv. 14 Jan. 1585/6—IX(64): and four later convictions, ending 27 Mar. 1588—IX(64)*. VIII(73). Debts re-enrolled—XI(72v)*. Record of land-seizure in Essex, 6 Feb. 1589/90 [Recusant Roll entry under 'Essex'][152]—X(26v). Seized lands in Essex let by Crown to Ralph Smythe from Michaelmas 1590—X(26v). XI(21v). XII(20v).

JERMIN, Ambrose, gent., of Lopham, Norfolk. 3 mths recusancy from 13 Apr. 1587: conv. 1 Apr. 1588—VIII(54).

JERRARD, Jerrett, Alice, wife of Richard Jerrard, 'yom'', of Dorchester, Dorset. 6 mths recusancy from 1 Jan. 1587/8: conv. 15 July 1588—VIII(19v).

JERRETT, Richard, 'yoman', of Wimborne Mynster [Minster], Dorset. 6 mths recusancy from 2 June 1588: conv. 10 Mar. 1588/9—IX(16v). Debt re-enrolled—XII(78v).

JESOPP, John, 'yom'', of Chickerell, Dorset. 6 mths recusancy from 1 Sept. 1583: conv. Lent 1583/4.—IV(16v).

JESOPP, John, 'yom'', of Dorchester, Dorset. 5 mths recusancy from 23 Mar. 1583/4: conv. 24 Aug. 1584—IV(16v).

JESOPP, Jessop, Robert, gent., of Southwark, Surrey [prisoner][153]. 10 mths recusancy ending 11 Mar. 1582/3, when convicted—IV(49v): and two later convictions, ending 15 Feb. 1583/4—IV(49v)*. Debts re-enrolled—VI(51)*.

JESOPP, Jessopp, Robert, 'yoman', of Southwark, Surrey [prisoner]. 4 mths recusancy ending 20 July 1584, when convicted—V(50v).

JETTOR, Ellen, 'spinster', of Flixton, Suffolk. 3 mths recusancy from 8 Apr. 1587: conv. 27 Mar. 1588—VIII(73).

JETTOR, Robert, gent., of Flixton, Suffolk. 12 mths recusancy from 3 July 1581: conv. 18 July 1582—II(56): and five later convictions, ending 5 Apr. 1587—III(66). IV(57). VII(59)*. VI(58). Debts re-enrolled—III(65). IV(56). V(60), (60v)*. Seized property in Lowestoft and Carlton Colville, Suffolk, let by Crown to Barnard Wakefeld from Ladyday 1585—IX(63v), (64). X(63v). XI(65v). Seized property in Lowestoft let by Crown to Walter Burde from Michaelmas 1585—IX(63). XI(65). Record of land-seizure, 2 Nov. 1587—VIII(72). Rental of lands seized 1585 and 1587—IX(63), (63v), (64). X(63), (63v). XI(65), (65v). XII(66v).

---

152. The Essex residence of the Jermin family, called 'the manor house of Bacons', seized by the Queen at Michaelmas 1590 for his recusancy, was at Dengie, near Southminster. (Cf. Philip Morant, *History and Antiquities of Essex*, (1768), pp. 368–369.)

153. Robert Jessopp was a prisoner in the White Lion, 23 Mar. 1583. He was still there 'for ecclesiastical matters' on 8 Apr. 1584. No later mention. (Cf. *CRS* II, pp. 234, 237.)

ap JEVAN, David, gent., of Morgan [? Morganstown], Glam., Wales. Lands seized for recusancy let by Crown to John Cornewall from Ladyday 1589—X(74v)[154].

ap JEVAN, Eliz. Hoell, wife of David ap Jevan, [ ], of Llanarth, Mon. 5 mths recusancy from 24 Mar. 1586/7: conv. 13 Mar. 1587/8—VIII(48).

ap JEVAN, Lewis ap John David, 'yoman' (same parish, recusancy period and conviction date)—VIII(48).

ap JEVAN, Hoell, 'tailor'/'yoman', of Raglan, Mon. 12 mths recusancy from 1 July 1581: conv. 23 July 1582—II(38): and six later convictions, ending 20 Mar. 1586/7—III(45). IV(38v)*. V(40v)*. VI(40). Debts re-enrolled—III(45). V(40v)*. VI(40).

ap JEVAN, Margaret, his wife (same parish, recusancy period and conviction date)—VIII(48).

ap JEVAN, William Lewis John David, 'yoman', of Llanarth, Mon. (same recusancy period and conviction date)—VIII(48).

JOBBE, see JEBBE, Robert.

JOHN, Andrew, 'yoman', of Llangattock Vibon Avel, Mon. 5 mths recusancy from 24 Mar. 1586/7: conv. 13 Mar. 1587/8—VIII(48v).

JOHN, Ann, wife of Thomas ap David John, [ ], of Llanarth, Mon. (same recusancy period and conviction date)—VIII(48).

JOHN, David Hoell, 'yoman', of Llantilio Pertholey, Mon. (same recusancy period & conviction date)—VIII(48v).

JOHN, Edward 'Dio', [ ], of Michaelston-on-Avon, Glam., Wales. Lands seized for recusancy let by Crown to John Griffin from 5 Sept. 1590—X(74v).

JOHN, James William, 'yoman', of Llanthewy Skirrid, Mon. 5 mths recusancy from 24 Mar. 1586/7: conv. 13 Mar. 1587/8—VIII(49).

JOHN, Jenkin, 'yoman', of Llanllowell, Mon. (same recusancy period & conviction date)—VIII(49v).

JOHN, Joan, 'spinster' (same parish, recusancy period and conviction date)—VIII(49v).

JOHN, John William, 'yoman', of Llanthewy Skirrid, Mon. (same recusancy period and conviction date)—VIII(49).

JOHN, Katherine, 'spinster', of Llangibby, Mon. (same recusancy period and conviction date)—VIII(49v).

JOHN, 'Llen'', of Haleston [Laleston?], Glam., Wales. Lands seized for recusancy let by Crown to John Griffin from 5 Sept. 1590—X(74v).

JOHN, Reginald, 'yoman', of Lenussen [Llanishen], Mon. 5 mths recusancy from 24 Mar. 1586/7: conv. 13 Mar. 1587/8—VIII(49).

JOHN, Thomas David, 'yom'', of Llanarth, Mon. 12 mths recusancy from 1 July 1581: conv. 23 July 1582—II(38). Debt re-enrolled—III(45). V(40v).

---

154. RR entries mostly illegible. See re-enrolments in *CRS* XVIII, pp. 375–376, or *CRS* LVII, p. 223.)

JOHN, William, 'yoman', of Llangoven, Mon. 5 mths recusancy from 24 Mar. 1586/7: conv. 13 Mar. 1587/8—VIII(49v).

JOHN, Ann, his wife (same parish, recusancy period and conviction date)—VIII(49v).

ap JOHN, James, 'yoman', of Llanthewy Rytherch, Mon. (same recusancy period and conviction date)—VIII(48).

ap JOHN, John, junior, 'yoman', of Llanvair Kilgedin, Mon. (same recusancy period and conviction date)—VIII(49).

ap JOHN, John, senior, 'yoman' (same parish, recusancy period & conviction date)—VIII(49).

ap JOHN, Jane David, wife of John, senior, (same parish, recusancy period & conviction date)—VIII(49).

ap JOHN, 'Llykia' Phillippe, wife of Phillippe ap John, [ ], of Llanarth, Mon. (same recusancy period & conviction date)—VIII(48).

ap JOHN, Margaret David, 'spinster', of Llanvair Kilgedin, Mon. (same recusancy period & conviction date)—VIII(49).

ap JOHN, Richard David, 'yoman' (same parish, recusancy period & conviction date)—VIII(49).

ap JOHN, Thomas, 'yoman', of Llandenny, Mon. (same recusancy period and conviction date)—VIII(49v).

ap JOHN, Thomas ap David, gent., of Llanarth, Mon. 12 mths recusancy from 3 July 1582: conv. 12 July 1583—III(45): and seven later convictions, ending 20 Mar. 1586/7—IV(38v)*. V(40v)*. VI(40v)*. VI(40).

ap JOHN, Thomas David, gent., of Llanarth, Mon. Seized lands let by Crown to Hugh Cuffe from Michaelmas 1585—VI(33v). VIII(16v). X(50v).

ap JOHN, *alias* SMITH, Smyth, John, [ ], of St. Moghan [St. Maughans], Mon. 5 mths recusancy from 24 Mar. 1586/7: conv. 13 Mar. 1587/8—VIII(49). Record of land-seizure, 24 Oct. 1588—IX(42v). Rental of seized lands in St. Maughans—IX(42v). X(50). XI(45).

verch JOHN, Ann, 'spinster', of Llanarth, Mon. 5 mths recusancy from 24 Mar. 1586/7: conv. 13 Mar. 1587/8—VIII(48).

verch JOHN, Ann, 'spinster', of Llanthewy Rytherch, Mon. (same recusancy period and conviction date)—VIII(48).

verch JOHN, Ann, 'spinster', of Llanthewy Skirrid, Mon. (same recusancy period and conviction date)—VIII(48v).

verch JOHN, Jane, 'spinster', of Llanthewy Rytherch, Mon. (same recusancy period and conviction date)—VIII(48).

verch JOHN, Jane, 'spinster', of Llanthewy Skirrid, Mon. (same recusancy period and conviction date)—VIII(48v).

verch JOHN, Joan, 'spinster', (same parish, recusancy period & conviction date)—VIII(48v).

verch JOHN, Joan, 'spinster', of Llanvair Kilgedin, Mon. (same recusancy period and conviction date)—VIII(49).

verch JOHN, 'Jonetta', wid., of Llantilio Pertholey, Mon. (same recusancy

period and conviction date)—VIII(48v).
verch JOHN, Katherine, 'spinster', of Llanthewy Skirrid, Mon. (same recusancy period and conviction date)—VIII(49).
verch JOHN, Katherine, wid., of Llanishen, Mon. (same recusancy period & conviction date)—VIII(49).
JOHNER, Jenkin, 'yoman', of Raglan, Mon. (same recusancy period and conviction date)—VIII(48).
JOHNSON, Ann, of Wesham, Lancs., wife of George Johnson, 'yoman'. 12 mths recusancy from 20 Sept. 1589: conv. 22 Mar. 1590/1—X(39).
JOHNSON, Eliz., wife of Francis Johnson, 'yoman', of [parish omitted], Yorks. 6 mths recusancy from 3 July 1587: conv. 18 Mar. 1587/8—VIII(25v).
JOHNSON, Ellen, of Elswick, Lancs., wife of Robert Johnson, [   ]. 10 mths recusancy from 18 Mar. 1580/1: conv. 25 Apr. 1582—II(38v). Debt re-enrolled—VIII(46).
JOHNSON, Ellen, wife of Thomas Johnson, 'husb'', of Great Crosby, Lancs. 12 mths recusancy from 20 Sept. 1589: conv. 22 Mar. 1590/1—X(38).
JOHNSON, Ellen, 'spinster', of Salford in parish of Manchester, Lancs. [prisoner][155]. 4 mths recusancy from 2 Sept. 1582: conv. 16 Jan. 1582/3—II(38v). Debt re-enrolled—VIII(46).
JOHNSON, Ellen, wid., of Standish, Lancs., relict of Richard Johnson, [   ]. 12 mths recusancy from 20 Sept. 1589: conv. 22 Mar. 1590/1—X(38).
JOHNSON, Joan, of Wesham, Lancs., wife of Henry Johnson, [   ]. (same recusancy period and conviction date)—X(39).
JOHNSON, John, 'milner' (same parish, recusancy period and conviction date)—X(39).
JOHNSON, Alice, his wife (same parish, recusancy period and conviction date)—X(39).
JOHNSON, Margaret, wife of John Johnson, 'yeoman', of All Saints parish, Oxford. 12 mths recusancy from 26 Sept. 1586: conv. 7 Mar. 1587/8—VIII(35v).
JOHNSON, Oliver, 'yoman', of Hillesden, Bucks. 3 mths recusancy from 27 Mar. 1587: conv. 18 Mar. 1587/8—VIII(3).
JOHNSON, Richard, 'yoman', of Westminster, Middx [prisoner][156]. 1 mth recusancy from 6 Oct. 1587: conv. 29 Jan. 1587/8—VIII(38v).
JOHNSON, Thomas, 'husb'', of Great Crosby, Lancs. 12 mths recusancy from 20 Sept. 1589: conv. 22 Mar. 1590/1—X(38).

---

155. Ellen Johnson was a prisoner in Salford Gaol from 2 Sept. 1582 to 16 Jan. 1582/3, when she was convicted of recusancy. (Cf. *CRS* V, p. 25 footnote.)
156. Richard Johnson, a pre-Elizabethan priest, was Prebendary of Sidlesham in Chichester Cathedral from 1558 until his resignation in 1562. He was 'brought to the Westminster Gatehouse by command of Sir Francis Walsingham on 8 Nov. 1583, for religion', being described as 'sometime a scolar at Oxford'. He was also 'sent in by the Privy Council on 19 Feb. 1583/4, for religion, and is a priest' (Cf. *CRS* II, pp. 232, 235, 245, 253, 255, 271.)

JOHNSON, Thomas, 'laborer', of Horesley [Horsley], Derbys. 10 mths recusancy from 9 Sept. 1586: conv. 22 Mar. 1587/8—VIII(21).

JOHNSON, William, gent., of St. Saviour's parish, Southwark, Surrey [prisoner][157]. 4 mths recusancy ending 17 July 1587, when convicted—IX(54).

JOINER, Grace, [ ], of Cromarshe [Crowmarsh], Oxfords. 12 mths recusancy from 26 Sept. 1586: conv. 7 Mar. 1587/8—VIII(35).

JOLLYBRAND, Joan, 'spinster', of Charnock Richard, Lancs. 12 mths recusancy from 20 Sept. 1589: conv. 22 Mar. 1590/1—X(38v).

JONES, Edmund, gent., of Stretford, Herefords. 19 mths recusancy from 24 Mar. 1580/1: conv. 8 Jan. 1582/3—II(64): and twelve later convictions, ending 27 Mar. 1587—II(64). IV(64v)*. V(26), (26v)*. VI(25)*. Debts re-enrolled—III(27). V(26). Seized property let by Crown to Hugh Cuffe from Michaelmas 1585—X(29). XI(28). XII(28).

JONES, Edward, gent., of All Saints parish, Hereford. 1 mth recusancy from 27 May 1583: conv. 15 July 1583—III(27). Debt re-enrolled—V(26). Seized property let by Crown to Hugh Cuffe from Michaelmas 1585—VI(33v).

JONES, John, 'yoman', of Hornsey, Middx. 2 mths recusancy from 2 July 1589: conv. 3 Dec. 1589—IX(37).

JOYE, Anthony, gent., of Eastmeane [East Meon], Hants. 6 mths recusancy from 1 Aug. 1587: conv. 8 July 1588—VIII(68v).

JOYE, Benedict, gent., (same parish, recusancy period & conviction date)—VIII(68v).

JOYE, Joie, Robert, gent., of East Meon, Hants. 6 mths recusancy from 1 Oct. 1581: conv. ? Mar. 1581/2—III(50v): and one later conviction, dated Apr. 1584—V(56v). Debt re-enrolled—V(56).

JOYE, Thomas, gent., of East Meon, Hants. 6 mths recusancy from 1 Aug. 1587: conv. 8 July 1588—VIII(68v).

JUSTICE, William, gent. [Pipe Roll entry under 'Yorks'] Fine of £40 imposed by High Commissioners, 1585 – 6.—VI(22). Debt re-enrolled —VIII(26). X(23).

KARVILE, see KERVILE, Henry.

KEINES, Katherine, wid., of Llantilio Pertholey, Mon. 5 mths recusancy from 24 Mar. 1586/7: conv. 13 Mar. 1587/8—VIII(48v). See KEYNES.

KELL, Leonard, 'yom'', of London. Fined 100 marks for hearing Mass 'in the mansion house of Lady Elizabeth Paulett, wid., in the parish of St.

---

157. William Johnson was committed for 4 months imprisonment in the Clink, ending with conviction on 17 July 1587, for counterfeiting the handwriting of their Lordships the High Commissioners (Cf. *CRS II*, p. 287.) See RR, (E. 377/9) rotulet 54, under 'Adhuc Item Sussex'.

Sepulchre, Farringdon Ward Without, London, on 12 Dec. 1585'
(convicted at Oyer and Terminer sessions, Old Bailey, 18 Apr.
1586)—VI(34v).

KELLAM, Laurence, 'yoman', of Westminster, Middx [? prisoner][158]. 1
mth recusancy from 6 Oct. 1587: conv. 29 Jan. 1587/8—VIII(38v).

KEMPE, David, 'clericus', of Southwark, Surrey [prisoner][159]. 1 mth
recusancy from 5 June 1588: conv. 5 July 1588—VIII(63).

KEMPE, Winifred, wife of John Kempe, gent., of Minver [St. Minver],
Cornwall. 13 mths recusancy from 20 July 1582: conv. Lent
1583/4—IV(6v). Debt re-enrolled—VI(6).

KERVER, Eliz., 'spinster', of Raglan, Mon. 5 mths recusancy from 24 Mar.
1586/7: conv. 13 Mar. 1587/8—VIII(48).

KERVER, William David, 'yoman'' (same parish, recusancy period &
conviction date)—VIII(48).

KERVILE, Kervyle, Karvile, Henry, gent., of Toftes [West Tofts], Norfolk.
3 mths recusancy from 13 Apr. 1587: conv. 1 Apr. 1588—VIII(54).
Goods, value £46 – 7s., seized 18 Oct. 1588—IX(45). Record of land-
seizure, 18 Oct. 1588—IX(45). Rental of seized lands—XI(48). Seized
lands let by Crown to Humphrey Sackford from 29 Mar.
1589—IX(44). X(52v). XI(46v). XII(47v).

KEYNES, Kaynes, Edward, gent., of Hampstead Norres [Norris], Berks. 8
mths recusancy from 3 July 1583: conv. 24 Feb. 1583/4—IV(3v).
Debt re-enrolled—VI(3v).

KEYNES, Edward, gent., of St. Mary's parish, Reading, Berks [prisoner][160].
6 mths recusancy from 1 Feb. 1583/4: conv. 20 July 1584—IV(46).
Debt re-enrolled—VI(3v).

KEYNES, Kaynes, Katherine, wife of Edward Keynes, gent., of Compton
Paunsford [Pauncefoot], Somerset. [Recusant Roll entry under
'Somerset'] 1 mth recusancy from 7 Dec. 1581: convicted at Old
Bailey, London, 9 Apr. 1582—I(68v).

KEYNES, Katherine, wife of Edward Keynes, gent., of Compton
Paunsfoot, Somerset. [Recusant Roll entry under 'Berks'] 5 mths
recusancy ending ult. July 1582 [sic]: convicted at Reading assizes,
9 July 1582: and one later conviction, dated 11 Feb. 1582/3 (also at
Reading)—II(65v)*.

---

158. Laurence Kellam received the tonsure at Douai College, 30 Mar. 1584, (Cf. Knox, p. 201.)
He assisted Dr. Matthew Kellison in publishing the latters controversial book, *A Survey of the New Religion*. (Cf. *CRS* XI, p. 53 footnote and Knox, p. 216.) Left Douai for England, 18 July 1587.
Was arrested at Westminster. Committed to the Gatehouse Prison from 6 Oct. 1587 to 29 Jan.
1587/8. The date of his discharge is unknown.

159. David Kemp (Cf. Anstruther I, pp. 194, 195.)

160. Edward Keynes of Compton Pauncefoot, Somerset; of Hampstead Norris, Berks.; and, as
a prisoner, of Reading Castle, was arrested with Edmund Campion at Lyford, Berks., in July 1581,
and sent, with several other prisoners, to the Tower of London. (Cf. Challoner, p. 30.) He was
discharged from thence on bonds after June 1582 (Cf. *CRS* II, p. 228.) He and his wife were
imprisoned at Reading Castle from 1 Feb. 1583/4 until 20 July 1584, when both were delivered on
bonds to appear before the Justices when required.

KEYNES, Katherine, wife of Edward Keynes, gent., of Hampstead Norres [Norris], Berks. 8 mths recusancy from 3 July 1583: conv. 24 Feb. 1583/4—IV(3v). Debt re-enrolled—VI(3v).

KEYNES, Katherine, wife of Edward Keynes, gent., of St. Mary's parish, Reading, Berks [prisoner][161]. 6 mths recusancy from 1 Feb. 1583/4: conv. 20 July 1584—IV(46). Debt re-enrolled—VI(3v).

KEYNES, Katherine, wid., of Llantilio Pertholey, Mon. Record of land-seizure, 24 Oct. 1588—IX(42v). Rental of seized lands—IX(42v). X(50). XI(45). See KEINES.

KEYTON, Kyton, Kyten, Philip, 'yoman', of Southwark, Surrey [prisoner]. 8 mths recusancy ending 16 Feb. 1586/7, when convicted—VI(50).

KIGHLEY, Kigley, Eliz., wid., of Lightshawe, Winwick parish, Lancs. 9 mths recusancy from 18 Mar. 1580/1: conv. 4 Aug. 1587 (*sic*)—X(36): and one later conviction, dated 25 Mar. 1588—VIII(21v). Lands seized 26 Mar. 1591 & let by Crown to John Parker from 1 July 1591—XII(44).

KINASTON, William, gent., of Welsh Hampton, in parish of Ellesmere, Salop[162]. 12 mths recusancy from 24 Feb. 1586/7: conv. 18 July 1588—VIII(16v).

KINGE, Dorothy, 'spinster', of Harrow, Middx. 3 mths recusancy from 6 June 1587: conv. 1 Dec. 1587—VIII(38v).

KINGESBURYE, John, 'husb"', of Evesham, Worcs. 6 mths recusancy from 29 Sept. 1587: conv. 25 July 1588—VIII(80v).

KINGESWOOD, David, 'yoman', of St. Saviour's parish, Southwark, Surrey [prisoner][163]. 5 mths recusancy ending 17 Feb. 1586/7, when convicted—VI(50).

KINGETON, John, gent., of Southwark, Surrey [? prisoner]. 4 mths recusancy ending 20 July 1584, when convicted—V(50v).

KINGSWELL, Kineswell, Katherine, gentlewoman, of Lyford, Berks. 8 mths recusancy from 26 June 1581: conv. 26 Feb. 1581/2—I(llv): and one later conviction dated 31 July 1582—II(65v). Debts re-enrolled—III(33v). V(3v). VII(3v).

KINGSWELL, Kinswell, Katherine, 'spinster', of Lyford, Berks. 8 mths recusancy from 3 July 1583: conv. 24 Feb. 1583/4—IV(3v). Debt re-enrolled—VI(3v).

---

161. Despite Katherine Keynes's conviction at the Old Bailey, there is no evidence that she accompanied her husband to the city. Their lands at Compton Pauncefoot, Somerset, including their 'capital messuage', were seized on 8 Oct. 1595, and let by the Crown to Matthew Ewens (a baron of the Exchequer) from 16 Dec. 1595 for a rent of £31 – 8 – $2\frac{3}{4}$ *per annum*. The specification of the property is remarkably full (Cf. *CRS* LXI, pp. 211 – 212.)

162. William Kinaston's earliest prosecution for recusancy began on 24 Feb. 1586/7 and ran on till 18 July 1588, when he was convicted of over 12 months absence from church. His name and parish are recorded in a Signification of Excommunication by William Overton, Bishop of Coventry and Lichfield, 20 Jan. 1600/1. (Cf. *CRS* LX, pp. 111 – 114.)

163. David Kingswood was committed to the Clink, 8 June 1586, where he was later joined by his wife. They were examined in 1592 and again in 1593 (Cf. *CRS* II, pp. 247, 268, 283, 285). The surname 'Kingeswood' at the head of this entry is very rarely found. 'Ringstead' is the name they commonly used—with variant spellings. (Cf. *CRS* LX, pp. 64, 65 etc.)

KINGSWELL, Katherine, gentlewoman ('generosa'), of St. Mary's parish, Reading, Berks [prisoner]¹⁶⁴. 8 mths recusancy from 30 June 1582: conv. 12 Feb. 1582/3—II(65v).

KINGSWELL, Katherine, 'spinster', of St. Mary's parish, Reading, Berks [prisoner]. 4 mths recusancy from 11 Feb. 1582/3: conv. 4 June 1583—III(50v): and one later conviction dated 20 July 1584—IV(46). Debts re-enrolled—V(4v). VI(3v).

KINNEBYE, Kynnebie, Francis, 'yom'', of East Walton, Norfolk. 2 mths recusancy from 1 May 1582: conv. 1 July 1582—IV(44v): and two later convictions, ending 1 Apr. 1588—IV(44v). VIII(54). Record of land-seizure, 18 Oct. 1588—IX(45). Rental of seized lands—IX(45). X(52v). XI(46v). Seized lands let by Crown to Richard Weston from 29 May 1590—X(81). XI(46v). XII(47v).

KIRKEHAM, Kirkham, Clemence, of Westby, Lancs., wife of George Kirkham, 'husb''. 12 mths recusancy from 20 Sept. 1589: conv. 22 Mar. 1590/1—X(39v).

KIRKEHAM, Isabel, of Thistleton, Lancs., wife of William Kirkeham, 'husb''. (same recusancy period and conviction date)—X(39).

KIRKEHAM, Kirkham, Richard, [ ], of Westby, Lancs. (same recusancy period and conviction date)—X(39v).

KIRKEMAN, Kirkmane, Katherine, [ ], of Addingham, W.R. Yorks. 6 mths recusancy from 3 July 1587: conv. 18 Mar. 1587/8—VIII(27). Goods, value £1 – 9s., seized 8 Apr. 1589—IX(22v).

KIRSHAWE, John, 'husb'', of Churche [Church Kirk?], Lancs. 12 mths recusancy from 20 Sept. 1589: conv. 22 Mar. 1590/1—X(40).

KIRSHAWE, 'Kirstabell', his wife (same parish, recusancy period & conviction date)—X(40).

KIRTON, Ralph, 'yoman', of Gunnerside, Grinton parish, N.R. Yorks. 13 mths recusancy from 3 Sept. 1586: conv. 4 Sept. 1587—VIII(25v).

KITCHEN, Kitchin, Joan, 'spinster', of [ ] in North Wingfeild parish, Derbys. 10 mths recusancy from 9 Sept. 1586: conv. 22 Mar. 1587/8—VIII(21).

KITCHEN, Joan, wife of John Kitchen, [ ], of [ ] in North Wingfeild parish, Derbys (same recusancy period & conviction date)—VIII(21).

KITCHEN, Mary, wife of John Kitchen, gent., of Cheddington, Bucks. 3 mths recusancy from 27 Mar. 1587: conv. 18 Mar. 1587/8—VIII(3).

KITCHIN, Richard, 'laborer', of [ ] in North Wingfeild parish, Derbys. 10 mths recusancy from 9 Sept. 1586: conv. 22 Mar. 1587/8—VIII(21).

---

164. Katherine Kingswell was a Brigettine nun, and a fellow prisoner with Juliana Harman (Cf. footnote 117), another nun of the same order, alternately at Lyford and at Reading Castle, Berks., at various periods between 26 June 1581 and 20 July 1584. She was described as owing a part of £4 – 13 – 4 *per annum* at Michaelmas 1600, being two-thirds of a messuage in Arborfield, Berks., annual value £7, seized into the Queen's hands by the said Commissioners by reason of her recusancy. This is the first entry of a seperate tenement, which takes the place of Lyford. It continues in her tenure until after 1611. Her debt had then reached £44 – 6 – 8.

KNAPPE, Edward, 'yeom", of Hawe Courte in Hampstead Norris, Berks. 12 mths recusancy from 1 Sept. 1586: conv. 4 Mar. 1587/8—VIII(5). Goods, value £16 – 6 – 8, seized 4 Oct. 1588—IX(4v). Debt re-enrolled—X(4v)[165].

KNARISBURGHE, Peter, gent., of Wallingham [Walkingham] Hill, W.R. Yorks. 13 mths recusancy from 3 Sept. 1586: conv. 4 Sept. 1587—VIII(25v).

KNIGHT, Alice, wid., of Itchin Abbattes [Itchen Abbas], Hants. 18 mths recusancy from 18 Mar. 1580/1: conv. ? Sept. 1582—III(50v): and three later convictions, ending Sept. 1584—IV(53). V(56v)*. Debts re-enrolled—V(56). VI(54). VII(54)*. VIII(68). IX(59)*. Seized lands let by Crown to Hugh Cuffe from 2 Mar. 1583/4—IV(52). V(55). Seized lands let by Crown to John Stockman from 25 Nov. 1584—V(56). VI(53v). VII(53v). VIII(66v). IX(57v). X(68v). XI(59v). XII(60v).

KNIGHT, Nicholas, 'clericus', of St. George's parish, Southwark, Surrey [prisoner][166]. 5 mths recusancy from 17 Feb. 1586/7: conv. 17 July 1587—IX(54).

KNIGHT, Robert, gent., of Godsfeild, Warrowton [Swarraton], Hants. 2 mths recusancy from 18 Mar. 1580/1: conv. 9 Sept. 1581—III(50v): and three later convictions, ending 1 Jan. 1583/4—III(50v). IV(53). V(56v). Debts re-enrolled—V(56)*. VI(54). VII(54)*. VIII(68). IX(59)*. Seized lands let by Crown to Hugh Cuffe from 2 Mar. 1583/4—IV(52). V(55). Seized lands let by Crown to John Stockman from 25 Nov. 1584—V(57). VI(53v). VII(53v). VIII(66v). IX(57v). X(68v). XI(59v).

KNIGHTES, Robert, gent., of Abbottes Ichen [Itchen Abbas], Hants. 6 mths recusancy from 1 Nov. 1586: conv. 26 Feb. 1587/8—VIII(67).

KNIVETT, Katherine, wife of Thomas Knivett, esq., of East Harling, Norfolk. 3 mths recusancy from 13 Apr. 1587: conv. 1 Apr. 1588—VIII(54).

KNOWLE, John, [   ], of Westby, Lancs. 12 mths recusancy from 20 Sept. 1589: conv. 22 Mar. 1590/1—X(39v).

KNOWLE, Jane, his wife (same parish, recusancy period and conviction date)—X(39v).

KNOWLES, Knolles, Agnes, wid., of [Hamstall] Ridware, Staffs. 4 mths recusancy from 13 Mar. 1585/6: conv. ? July 1586—X(78v). Goods, value £11 – 1s., seized 4 Sept. 1589—X(14). Record of land-seizure, 4 Sept. 1589—X(78v). Rental of seized land—X(7v). XI(64v). XII(65v). Seized lands let by Crown to Edward Thorne from 22 Dec. 1591—XII(72v).

---

165. Edward Knappe owed to the Queen £26 – 13 – 4 *per annum* for the farm of two-thirds of a certain lease of the farm of Hawe Courte in Hampstead Norris, Berks., of the annual value of £40, taken and seized into the hands of the said Queen by her Commissioners, Thomas Parry and John Doleman, esquires, by reason of his recusancy. And £26 – 13 – 4 for the preceeding year. Total debt, £53 – 6 – 8. By 1611, his unpaid debts to the Crown had increased to the sum of £266 – 13 – 4, and his goods, valued in Oct. 1588 at £16 – 6 – 8, were disregarded.

166. Nicholas Knight (Cf. Anstruther I, pp. 201, 202.)

KNOWLES, William, 'yoman', of Hamstall Ridware, Staffs. 8 mths recusancy from 1 Aug. 1585: conv. 13 Mar. 1585/6—VI(63v).
KNOWLES, Agnes, his wife (same parish, recusancy period and conviction date)—VI(63v): and one later conviction, dated 1 Aug. 1586—VI(63v).
KNOWLES, William, 'husb", of [Hamstall] Ridware, Staffs. 12 mths recusancy from 6 Sept. 1586: conv. 25 Mar. 1588—VIII(78v).
KYDDE, *alias* IRELAND, Ellen, wife of Thomas Kydde, *alias* Ireland, [   ], of Wigan, Lancs. 12 mths recusancy from 20 Sept. 1589: conv. 22 Mar. 1590/1—X(38).
KYDDE, *alias* IRELAND, Thomas, 'butcher', of Wigan, Lancs. (same recusancy period and conviction date)—X(38).

LABIER, Robert, 'laborer', of Llanthewy Skirrid, Mon. 5 mths recusancy from 24 Mar. 1586/7: conv. 13 Mar. 1587/8—VIII(49).
LABIER, [   ], his wife (same parish, recusancy period & conviction date)—VIII(49).
LABORER, 'Moricius', 'laborer', of Llantilio Pertholey, Mon. 5 mths recusancy from 24 Mar. 1586/7: conv. 13 Mar. 1587/8—VIII(48v).
LABORER, Roger, 'laborer' (same parish, recusancy period and conviction date)—VIII(48v).
LABORER, Thomas, 'laborer', of Llanvetherine, Mon. (same recusancy period and conviction date)—VIII(49).
LABORNE, James, gent., of the city of Carlisle, Cumberland [prisoner]. 3 mths recusancy from 27 Apr. 1582: conv. ? July 1582—II(7v).
LABORNE, James, esq., of Salford in the parish of Manchester, Lancs. [prisoner][167]. 4 mths recusancy from 2 Sept. 1582: convicted on 16 Jan. 1582/3—II(38v). Debt re-enrolled—VIII(46).
LACYE, William, gent., of Sherborne [Sherburn-in-Elmet], E. Yorks. Fined £50 by ? High Commissioners on 29 Mar. 1582 for recusancy, period undated[168]—XI(25).
LACY, William, gent., of Dripoole [Drypool Ward], parish of Swyne [Swine], Kingston-upon-Hull, E.R. Yorks. [Recusant Roll entry under 'Kingston-upon-Hull] [prisoner][169] 12 mths recusancy from 6 Aug. 1581: conv. 6 Aug. 1582—II(29). Debt re-enrolled—VI(22).
LAITHWAIT, Laythwaitt, Henry, 'yoman', of Meaddowes, Lancs. 12 mths recusancy from 20 Sept. 1589: conv. 22 Mar. 1590/1—X(38).
LAITHWAIT, Henry, 'yoman', of Pemberton, Wigan parish, Lancs. 12 mths recusancy from 1 Aug. 1587: conv. 17 Mar. 1588/9—X(35).

---

167. James Laborne (Cf. Pollen, pp. 217–221.)
168. William Lacy produced a recognisance of £50 for 'not coming to church' by a composition of 3 Commissioners, *viz.* Thomas Lucie of Beverley, gent., John Spence of Yedingham and Thomas Wilberforce of Beverley, gent., taken before the barons of the Exchequer on 29 Mar. 1582. (Cf. M.R., Q.R., 31 and 32 Eliz., Michaelmas Term, 'Recorda' section.) Annotation: £50 paid into the Treasury on 15 May 1590; and they are quit. (Cf. RR. (E.377/11,) under 'Item Ebor'.)
169. William Lacey (Cf. Challoner, pp. 66–68.)

Lands seized 26 Mar. 1591 let by Crown to John Parker from 1 July 1591—XII(44).

LAMBARTE, Robert, gent., of Stanwicke [St. John], N.R. Yorks. 13 mths recusancy from 3 Sept. 1586: conv. 4 Sept. 1587—VIII(25v).

LAMPE, William, 'yom'', son of Roger Loupe of Rusheton [Rushton], Dorset. 6 mths recusancy from 1 Jan. 1587/8: conv. 15 July 1588—VIII(19v). See LOPE, LOUPE.

LANE, Ellen, 'spinster', of Fishbourne, Sussex. 2 mths recusancy from 17 Apr. 1587: conv. 26 Feb. 1587/8—VIII(63v).

LANE, Felicia, wife of David Lane of Cotten [Coton] in St. Mary's parish, Stafford, 'yoman'. 8 mths recusancy from 1 Aug. 1585: conv. 13 Mar. 1585/6—VI(63v): and one later conviction, dated 1 Aug. 1586—VI(63v).

LANE, Humphrey, 'husb'', of Tenbury, Worcs. Two fines of £20 imposed for ignoring sheriff's summonses after excommunication, 4 Oct. 1580 and 24 May 1581—III(70). (Debts discharged by virtue of his inclusion in the Queen's general free pardon at the Parliament of 26 Nov. 1584. And he is quit.)

LANE, Alice, his wife, of Tenbury, Worcs. Two fines of £20 imposed... (Similar offences, same dates. Discharged as above)—III(70).

LANE, Katherine, 'spinster', of Fishbourne, Sussex. 2 mths recusancy from 17 Apr. 1587: conv. 26 Feb. 1587/8—VIII(63v).

LANE, Mary, wife of Thomas Lane, gent., of Fishbourne, Sussex (same recusancy period and conviction date)—VIII(63v).

LANGDALE, Thomas, gent., of Masseham [Masham], N.R. Yorks. 6 mths recusancy from 3 July 1587: conv. 18 Mar. 1587/8—VIII(25v).

LANGFORD, Lankford, Nicholas, esq., of Langford [Longford], Derbys. 9 mths recusancy ending 12 Jan. 1581/2: convicted by informer's suit (Hugh Cuffe)[170]—IV(17). Debt re-enrolled—VII(17v). IX(17v). Chattels-real, value £180, seized 1585—VI(17v).

10 mths recusancy from 9 Sept. 1586: convicted by indictment 22 Mar. 1587/8—VIII(21). Record of land-seizure, 13 Apr. 1591—Rental of seized lands, 13 Apr. 1591—XII(19).

LANGLEY, Robert, 'yoman', of Alciston, Sussex. 2 mths recusancy from 17 Apr. 1587: conv. 26 Feb. 1587/8—VIII(63v).

LANKFORD, Langford, Nicholas, gent.,[171] of Fulham, Middx. 3 mths recusancy from 5 Apr. 1587: conv. 1 Sept. 1587—VIII(38v).

---

170. Nicholas Langford's first prosecution for recusancy was by the informer Nicholas Cuffe, of which Langford was discharged. (Cf. CRS XVIII, p. 28.) His second prosecution (by indictment) ended likewise by discharge on 13 Apr. 1591 by the barons in the Easter Term of that year.

171. Nicholas Langford's third prosecution refers to a Lancashire property he held at Withington, near Manchester, for which the Crown expected to receive a rent of £144 – 2 – 8 *per annum*. This manor was seized by the Queen in Trinity Term 1600. The Langfords (or Lankfords) Nicholas and Martha, his wife, moved from Derbyshire to Fulham, Middx., in June 1585. He was imprisoned in the Marshalsea from 14 June 1585, for an unspecified period. (Cf. *CRS* II, p. 240.) He is missing from the list in the following year, and does not appear again. For the similarity of treatment of Langford and Sir John Southworth. (Cf. *CRS* LVII, Introd. pp. xx and lxxxiii, footnote 331.)

LANKFORD, Martha, his wife[171] (same parish, recusancy period and conviction date)—VIII(38v).
LATHOM, Lathome, Henry, gent., of Mosboroe [Mosborough], Prescott parish, Lancs. 13 mths recusancy from 6 May 1587: conv. 17 Mar. 1588/9—X(35). Debt re-enrolled? —X(36). Lands, seized 26 Mar. 1591, let by Crown to John Parker from 1 July 1591—XII(44).
LAUGHTON, James, gent., of Intwood, Norfolk. 3 mths recusancy from 13 Apr. 1587: conv. 1 Apr. 1588—VIII(54).
LAUNDER, Agnes, 'spinster', of Southwark, Surrey [prisoner][172]. 8 mths recusancy ending 16 Feb. 1586/7, when convicted—VI(50).
LAUNDER, Laundry, John, gent., of Southwark, Surrey [prisoner][173]. 6 mths recusancy ending 18 Feb. 1584/5, when convicted—V(52v): and two later convictions, ending 16 Feb. 1586/7—VI(49v), (50).
LAWE, Eliz., wife of John Lawe, 'yom''', of Graunge [Grange-over-Sands], Whalley parish, Lancs. 13 mths recusancy from 14 Aug. 1586: conv. 25 Mar. 1588—VIII(21v). See HAWE.
LAWE, Thomas, gent., of Ownedell [Oundle], Northants. 12 mths recusancy ending 2 May 1587: conv. 12 Mar. 1587/8—VIII(52v). Record of land-seizure, 22 June 1588—IX(47). Seized lands let by Crown to Edward Batley from 10 July 1588—IX(47), (71v). XI(49v). XII(49v).
LAWE, [ ], his wife (same parish, recusancy period & conviction date)—VIII(52v).
LAWES, Dorothy, 'spinster', wife of John Lawes, 'yoman', of Blicklinge, Norfolk. 11 mths recusancy from 1 Aug. 1582: conv. 8 July 1583—III(72v). Debt re-enrolled—V(46v).
LAWES, Lowes, Henry, 'yeoman', of Beckhamwell [Beechamwell], Norfolk. 3 mths recusancy from 13 Apr. 1587: conv. 1 Apr. 1588—VIII(54). Goods, value £1 – 10s., seized 18 Oct. 1588—IX(45).
LAWRENSON, Laurenson, John, 'blackesmythe', of Wesham, Lancs. 12 mths recusancy from 20 Sept. 1589: conv. 22 Mar. 1590/1—X(39).
LAWRENSON, [ ], his wife (same parish, recusancy period and conviction date)—X(39).
LAWSON, Eliz., wife of Ralph Lawson, esq., of Burghe [Brough], Catterick parish, N.R. Yorks. 13 mths recusancy from 3 Sept. 1586: conv. 4 Sept. 1587—VIII(25v): and one later conviction, dated 18 Mar. 1587/8—VIII(27).

---

172. The Prison Lists (Cf. *CRS* II) definitely state that the recusants John and Agnes Launder (Lander, Lawnder, Landry) were man and wife. and that she (given that christian name in the original RR.), after some imprisonment at Hull, was sent to join him in the Clink at Southwark on 22 Mar. 1585/6. (Cf. *CRS* II, pp. 246, 252, 271.), where she is invariably referred to as 'Anne'. Actually, she died in the latter prison towards the end of 1589.
173. John Launder had been committed to the Clink on 18 June 1584 by Fleetwood, Recorder of London, after a number of indictments for recusancy. He did not outlive his wife for long, dying in the Clink on 26 Jan. 1590/1. (Cf. Morris III, p. 36.)

LAWSON, Peter, 'yom"/'generos", of Southwark, Surrey [prisoner][174]. 4 mths recusancy ending 22 July 1583, when convicted—IV(49v): and three later convictions, ending 17 Feb. 1585/6,—V(50v), (52v). VI(49v). Debt re-enrolled—VI(51).

LAWTON, Mary, wife of William Lawton, esq., of Church Lawton, Cheshire. 13 mths recusancy from 26 Sept. 1586: conviction date not stated—VIII(58v).

LAWTY, Alice, of Blumpton [Plumpton], Kirkham parish, Lancs., wife of George Lawty, gent. 12 mths recusancy from 20 Sept. 1589: conv. 22 Mar. 1590/1—X(39v).

LAWTY, Thomas, 'tailor' (same parish, recusancy period and conviction date)—X(39v).

LAYTON, Isabel, 'spinster', of Southwark, Surrey [prisoner][175]. 5 mths imprisonment for recusancy ending 15 Feb. 1583/4, when convicted—IV(49v). Debt re-enrolled—VI(51).

LEAKE, Helen, 'spinster', of Edmonton, Middx. 6 mths recusancy from 1 Oct. 1587: conv. 19 Apr. 1588—IX(37).

LEAKE, Henry, gent., of Edmonton, Middx. 3 mths recusancy from 1 July 1588: conv. 2 Dec. 1588—IX(37).[176]

LEAKE, Henry, gent., of East Smithfield, Middx. 2 mths recusancy from 2 July 1589: conv. 3 Dec. 1589—IX(37).

LEAKE, Jane, 'spinster', of Edmonton, Middx. 6 mths recusancy from 1 Oct. 1587: conv. 19 Apr. 1588—IX(37).

LECHWORTHE, Charles, 'yoman', of Clerkenwell, Middx. (same recusancy period and conviction date as preceding entry)—IX(37).

LEDDES, see LEEDES, Thomas.

LEE, Isabel, of Great Marsden, Lancs., wife of Thomas Lee [ ]. 12 mths recusancy from 20 Sept. 1589: conv. 22 Mar. 1590/1—X(40).

LEE, John, 'yeom", of [ ] in Reighton [? Beighton] parish, Derbys. 10 mths recusancy from 9 Sept. 1586: conv. 22 Mar. 1587/8—VIII(21).

LEE, Nathaniel, 'yoman', of Salbury [Salesbury], Blackburn parish, Lancs. 6 mths recusancy from 4 Feb. 1587/8: conv. 17 Mar. 1588/9—X(35).

LEE, Nicholas, gent., of Clarkenwell [Clerkenwell], Middx. 3 mths recusancy from 20 Mar. 1587/8: conv. 28 June 1588—IX(37).

LEE, Thomas, 'yoman', of Leigh, Staffs. 6 mths recusancy from 6 Sept. 1587: conv. 22 July 1588—VIII(58). See LEIGHE.

---

174. Peter Lawson was arrested at Dunwing (?Dunwich), Suffolk, and, at first, thought to be a priest. (Cf. CRS II, p. 231.) Examined by Walsingham and committed, as a layman, to the Marshalsea on 1 Feb. 1581/2, he died a prisoner there in Sept. 1586, aged 48. (Cf. Morris III, p. 36.)

175. Isabel Layton was committed to the Marshalsea for 5 months recusancy ending 15 Feb. 1583/4. She, with Jane Gouldwire, spinster, were the only women prisoners in the gaol between Aug. 1583 and 15 Feb. 1583/4. The 29 others were all males.

176. Henry Leake had been imprisoned in the Marshalsea by the Council on 22 May 1586, for an unspecified time. (Cf. CRS II, p. 245.) Two other members of the Edmonton family had been imprisoned in the Marshalsea for six months at this time, viz. Helen and Jane Leake (both described as 'spinsters') who were due to be discharged on 19 Apr. 1588. They are not mentioned in CRS II, but see the list given in RR., (E. 377/9) under 'Item adhuc Res 'London' '.

RECUSANTS 1581 – 1592   109

LEEDES, John, gent., of Steyning, Sussex. 3 mths recusancy from 1 Apr. 1588: conv. 3 Mar. 1588/9—IX(53).

LEEDES, Leeds, Lionel, 'yoman', of Southwark, Surrey [? prisoner]. 8 mths recusancy ending 16 Feb. 1586/7, when convicted—VI(50).

LEEDES, Leeds, Thomas, esq., of Dripole [Drypool Ward], Swine parish, Kingston-upon-Hull, E.R. Yorks. [? prisoner] (Pipe Roll entry under 'Kingston-upon-Hull') 12 mths recusancy from 6 Aug. 1581: conv. 6 Aug. 1582—II(29). Debt re-enrolled—VI(22).

LEEDES, Leddes, Thomas, gent., of North Milfurth [Milford], W.R. Yorks. 6 mths recusancy from 3 July 1587: conv. 18 Mar. 1587/8—VIII(25v). Record of land-seizure, 8 Apr. 1589—IX(22v). Rental of seized lands—IX(21v). X(21v). XI(24v). XII(23v).

LEIGHE, Ann, wife of Richard Leighe, 'yeoman', of Hanley Castle, Worcs. 12 mths recusancy from 1 Apr. 1587: conv. 28 Mar. 1588—VIII(80).

LEIGHE, Edward, esq., of Bagule [Baguley], Cheshire. Forfeiture of Bond (£200) taken on 10 Mar. 1571/2 before Edmund [Grindal], Archbp. of York, and other High Commissioners—II(37v). Debt re-enrolled—VI(39v). VIII(46v). X(36v).

LEIGHE, Lee, John, gent., of Salford in parish of Manchester, Lancs [prisoner][177]. 12 mths recusancy from 20 Feb. 1582/3: conv. 22 Jan. 1583/4—IV(37): and three later convictions, ending 20 Apr. 1585—IV(46v). VI(40v)*. Debts re-enrolled—IV(42v). VI(39)*.

LEIGHTON, Thomas, gent., of St. Saviour's parish, Southwark, Surrey [prisoner][178]. 5 mths recusancy ending 17 Feb. 1586/7, when convicted—VI(50).

LENTHALL, Ann, wife of William Lenthall, gent., of Haseley, Oxfords. 12 mths recusancy from 26 Sept. 1586: conv. 7 Mar. 1587/8—VIII(35).

LENTHALL, Frances, 'spinster' (same parish, recusancy period & conviction date)—VIII(35v).

LEONARD, Thomas, 'yoman', of Westminster, Middx [prisoner][179]. 1 mth recusancy from 6 Oct. 1587: conv. 29 Jan. 1587/8—VIII(38v).

LESEMAN, James, 'clericus', of Webley [Weobley], Herefords[180]. 2 mths recusancy from 6 Jan. 1582/3: conv. 4 Mar. 1582/3—II(64).

---

177. John Leighe was probably the notable recusant, John Leigh of Barlowe Hall, Lancs., who, with his wife Mary, was imprisoned in Salford Gaol between Feb. 1582/3 and Apr. 1585. (Cf. *CRS* V, p. 70.)

178. Thomas Leighton was first committed to the Tower of London, 27 May 1585 to 18 June 1586, charged with conveying Godfrey Folgeham into Scotland; and conveying intelligence between Mary, Queen of Scots, and Francis Throgmorton. He was removed by the Lords to the Clink, 20 Aug. 1586. (Cf. *CRS* II, pp. 238, 251, 268.) Was still in the Clink, 30 Sept. 1588.

179. Thomas Leonard was committed to the Westminster Gatehouse by Sir Francis Walsingham between 29 Sept. and 19 Oct. 1586, 'Suspected to be a priest, but denieth the same'. (Cf. *CRS* II, p. 268.)

180. James Leseman, a pre-Elizabethan priest, was a Franciscan friar, who had once held the living of Tardebigge, Worcs. The rolls have at least 4 entries against him for recusancy, all except Weobley, being for recusancy in various parishes within Hereford City, and dating from 6 Jan. 1582/3 to 27 Mar. 1587.

LESEMAN, James, 'clericus', of the city of Hereford. 3 mths recusancy from 24 June 1583: conv. 16 Sept. 1583—V(26v).

LESEMAN, James, 'clericus', of St. Owen's parish, Hereford. 1 mth recusancy from 27 May 1583: conv. 15 July 1583—III(27). Debt re-enrolled—V(26).

LESEMAN, James, 'clericus', of St. Peter's parish, Hereford. 3 mths recusancy from 16 Sept. 1583: conv. 6 Jan. 1583/4—V(26v): and six later convictions, ending 27 Mar. 1587—IV(64v)*. V(26v)*. VI(25)*.

LETCHMORE, Ann, wife of Edmund Letchmore, gent., of Hanley Castle, Worcs. 12 mths recusancy from 1 Apr. 1587: conv. 28 Mar. 1588—VIII(80).

LETCHMORE, Lechemore, Ann, wife of Edmund Lechemore, gent., of Ribbesford, Worcs. 6 mths recusancy from 29 Sept. 1587: conv. 25 July 1588—VIII(80v).

LEWIS, Lewes, David, 'husb'', of Ewiasharold [Ewyas Harold], Herefords. 6 mths recusancy from 1 Sept. 1588: conv. 14 July 1589—IX(25v). Debt re-enrolled—XI(29).

LEWIS, Henry, 'yoman', of Llanthewy Skyre [Skirrid], Mon. 5 mths recusancy from 24 Mar. 1586/7: conv. 13 Mar. 1587/8—VIII(48v).

LEWIS, Jane Thomas, 'spinster' (same parish, recusancy period & conviction date)—VIII(48v).

LEWIS, John, 'yoman', of Llanthewy Rytherch, Mon. (same recusancy period and conviction date)—VIII(48).

LEWIS, John Harris, 'yoman', of Llanthewy Skirrid, Mon. (same recusancy period and conviction date)—VIII(48v).

LEWIS, Lewes, Katherine, wid., of Raglan, Mon. (same recusancy period & conviction date)—VIII(48). Record of land-seizure, 24 Oct. 1588—IX(42v). Rental of seized lands—IX(42v). X(50). XI(45).

LEWIS, 'Lissoda', wife of Henry Lewis, 'yoman', of Llanthewy Skirrid, Mon. (same recusancy period and conviction date)—VIII(48v).

LEWIS, Margaret, 'spinster', of Llanthewy Rytherch, Mon. (same recusancy period and conviction date)—VIII(48).

LEWIS, Matilda, wife of John William Lewis, 'yoman', of Llanthewy Skirrid, Mon. (same recusancy period and conviction date)—VIII(49).

LEWIS, Nesta, wife of William Lewis, [   ], of Llangattock-nigh-Usk, Mon. (same recusancy period and conviction date)—VIII(49).

LEWIS, Lewes, Richard, [   ], of Christ Church parish, Farringdon Ward Within London [? prisoner] 3 mths recusancy from 18 Mar. 1580/1: conv. 28 July 1581—I(32v). Debt re-enrolled—III(38v). V(35).

LEWIS, Richard, 'yoman', of Llanover, Mon. 5 mths recusancy from 24 Mar. 1586/7: conv. 13 Mar. 1587/8—VIII(48v).

LEWIS, Richard, junior, 'yoman', of Llanarth, Mon. (same recusancy period and conviction date)—VIII(48).

LEWIS, Richard, senior, 'yoman' (same parish, recusancy period & conviction date)—VIII(48).

LEWIS, Thomas Morgan, 'yoman', of Llanchenock [Llanhennock], Mon. (same recusancy period and conviction date)—VIII(49).

LEWIS, Lewes, William, 'yom'', of Llangattock-nigh-Usk, Mon. 12 mths recusancy from 1 July 1581: conv. 23 July 1582—II(38): and five later convictions, ending ? Mar. 1586/7—IV(38v)*. V(40v)*. VI(40), (40v)*. Seized property let by Crown to Hugh Cuffe from Michaelmas 1585—VI(33v)*. VIII(16v)*. X(50v). XI(45). XII(46).

verch LEWIS, 'Crislia', wid., of Llangattock vibon Avel, Mon. 5 mths recusancy from 24 Mar. 1586/7: conv. 13 Mar. 1587/8—VIII(48v).

LIGON, Lion, Lygon, Hugh, gent., of Hanley Castle, Worcs. 12 mths recusancy from 1 Apr. 1587: conv. 28 Mar. 1588—VIII(80). Goods, value £2 – 13 – 4, seized 31 Sept. 1588—IX(68v). Record of land-seizure, 30 Sept. 1588—IX(49v). Rental of seized lands—IX(68v). X(75). XI(70). XII(71).

LINCOLN, Benedict, 'clericus', of Northdighton [North Deighton Manor], W.R. Yorks[181]. 4 mths recusancy from 28 Mar. 1580/1: conv. 17 July 1581—I(21v). Debt re-enrolled—III(24). V(22).

LINCOLN, Robert, 'yoman', of Twyford, Hants. 7 mths recusancy from 16 Sept. 1583: conv. ? Mar. 1583/4—V(56v).

LINGEN, Lyngen, Richard, esq., of Dormington, Herefords[182] 8 mths recusancy from 13 July 1581: conv. 12 Mar. 1581/2—I(25): and three later convictions, ending 7 Mar. 1583/4—II(64)*. IV(64v).

LINGEN, Richard, esq., of the city of Hereford. 3 mths recusancy from 24 June 1583: conv. 16 Sept. 1583—V(26v).

LINGEN, Richard, [   ], of All Saints parish, Hereford. 1 mth recusancy from 27 May 1583: conv. 15 July 1583—III(27): and three later convictions, ending 10 Feb. 1585/6—IV(64v). V(26v). VI(25). Debts re-enrolled—V(26)*. Goods, value £6 – 13 – 4, seized 1584 by sheriff Richard Walwyn—X(28v). Chattels real, value £4, seized in 1585 by Hugh Cuffe, commissioner—X(29v).

LINGEN, Ann, his wife, of All Saints parish, Hereford. 2 mths recusancy from 6 Jan. 1583/4: conv. 9 Mar. 1583/4—IV(64v).

LINGEN, William, gent. junior, of Davies [Thavie's] Inne, London[182a]. 12 mths recusancy from 2 Jan. 1582/3: conv. 22 Jan. 1583/4—IV(32v). Debt re-enrolled—VI(34).

---

181. Benedict Lincoln, a pre-Elizabethan priest, had been harboured by Mrs. Watson of Brimham Hall, Ripon and later at North Deighton with Henry Suttle, gent., with whom he was convicted of four months imprisonment for recusancy from 28 Mar. 1581. 'Benet Lincoln' was the alias used by him for Edmund Hartburne while he was at Brimham Hall. (Cf. CRS V, p. 194, and J.C. Aveling, *Catholic Recusants of the West Riding of Yorkshire*, (1963), pp. 200, 201.)

182. Richard Lingen was never moved to London. He moved from Dormington to Hereford about Mar. 1583 with his wife, Anne, and there suffered his second prosecution on 24 June 1583, followed by three further indictments in the close confinement of Hereford Gaol. His goods were seized after 10 Feb. 1585/6, to the value of £6 – 13 – 4, with the assistance of Hugh Cuffe.

182A. William Lingen was indicted for 12 months recusancy from 2 Jan. 1582/3, convicted on 22 Jan. 1583/4, and put into Newgate for a whole year. He was removed from thence to the Westminster Gatehouse. Although discharged in 1586, he was still in prison in Sept. 1588, when he appears finally to have been delivered. (Cf. CRS II, pp. 237, 258, 260, 267, 282.)

LION, Margaret, 'spinster', of Hanley Castle, Worcs. 12 mths recusancy from 20 Sept. 1586: conv. 28 Mar. 1588—VIII(77). See LIGON, Hugh.
LISTARD, John, 'clericus', of Southwark, Surrey [prisoner][183]. 10 mths recusancy ending 17 Feb. 1585/6, when convicted—VI(49v). See LYSTER, John.
LISTER, Alice, wife of Laurence Lister, of [ ], Yorks. 2 mths recusancy from 4 Jan. 1585/6: conv. 14 Mar. 1585/6—VI(20v).
LISTER, Alice, wife of Thomas Lister, gent., of [ ], Yorks. (same recusancy period & conviction date)—VI(20v). See LYSTER.
LITLEBURY, Andrew, gent., of Asheby [Ashby in Bottesford], Lincs. 12 mths recusancy from 1 Mar. 1587/8: conv. 7 July 1589—IX(9). Debt re-enrolled—XI(ll).
LLEWELYN, Ann, 'spinster', of Raglan, Mon. 5 mths recusancy from 24 Mar. 1586/7: conv. 13 Mar. 1587/8—VIII(48).
LLEWELYN, Eliz., 'spinster', of Wonastow, Mon. (same recusancy period and conviction date)—VIII(48v).
LLEWELYN, 'Jonetta', wid., of Tredunnock, Mon. (same recusancy period and conviction date)—VIII(49).
LLEWELYN, Katherine, 'spinster', of Raglan, Mon. (same recusancy period & conviction date)—VIII(48).
LLOYD, Lloyde, Loid, 'Alsona' verch Rees, wife of William Lloyde, [ ], of Aburgavenny [Abergavenny], Mon. 5 mths recusancy from 24 Mar. 1586/7: conv. 13 Mar. 1587/8—VIII(48).
LLOYD, Evans, 'spinster' [sic], of Bettws Newydd, Mon. (same recusancy period and conviction date)—VIII(49v).
LLOYD, Jenkin, 'yoman', of Tredunnock, Mon. (same recusancy period and conviction date)—VIII(49).
LLOYD, John, gent., of Llanvarda [Llanforda, nr. Oswestry], Salop.[184] 12 mths recusancy from 24 Feb. 1586/7: conv. 18 July 1588—VIII(16v). Record of land-seizure [two-thirds of lands at Llanforda @ £13 – 6 – 8 p.a. in rent], seized 8 Apr. 1589—IX(13v). Rental of lands seized 8 Apr. 1589—IX(71). X(59). Seized lands [the whole capital messuage of Plas Ucha in Salop] let by Crown to John Lloyd, junior, from 12 Dec. 1588 (31 Eliz.), for a rent of £20 p.a.[185]—IX(13v). X(59). XI(62). XII(63).
LLOYD, Margaret, 'spinster', of Tredunnock, Mon. 5 mths recusancy from 24 Mar. 1586/7: conv. 13 Mar. 1587/8—VIII(49).

---

183. John Lister (Listard) (Cf. Anstruther I, pp. 210, 211.)
184. John Lloyd had been outlawed ('utlagatus') prior to 12 Dec. 1588. This outlawry was now no longer enforced in his case, and the present lease to 'John Lloyd, Junior' continues in the Exchequer Roll until 3 James I, when the entry is cancelled with a note of final discharge. (Cf. M.R., L.T.R., 4 James I, Easter Term, 'Recorda' section.) It then disappears from the Rolls.
185. The whole capital messuage of Plas Ucha in Salop was now let by the Crown to John Lloyd, junior, from 12 Dec. 1588, for a rent of £20 *per annum*.

LLOYD, Richard, gent., of Lloynymaen [Llwnymaen], Salop.[186] 12 mths recusancy from 24 Feb. 1586/7: conv. 18 July 1588—VIII(16v). Record of land-seizure, 8 Apr. 1589—IX(13v). Rental of [two-thirds of the capital messuage called 'Loynneman', at £6 – 13 – 4 p.a.] lands seized 8 Apr. 1589—IX(71). X(59). XI(62). Lands seized 8 Apr. 1589 let by Crown to Edward Lloid from 17 May 1589—X(15). XI(62v). XII(63v). Goods, value £23, seized 9 Oct. 1589—IX(13v). Debt re-enrolled—X(58v). XI(63v). Record of land-seizure, 9 Oct. 1589—IX(13v). Rental of demesne lands of Llwnymaen, Salop, [at £13 – 6 – 8 p.a.], seized 9 Oct. 1589—IX(69v). X(59v).

LLOYD, Thomas, of [ ], Salop, recusant. Goods, value £12, seized 9 Oct. 1589—IX(13v)[187]. Debt re-enrolled—X(58v). XI(63v).

LOCKYER, Richard, 'yom", of Kingeston [Kingston], Dorset. 6 mths recusancy from 1 Jan. 1587/8: conv. 15 July 1588—VIII(19v).

LONGLEY, Ann, [ ], of Grymthorpe [Grimthorpe], E.R. Yorks. 6 mths recusancy from 3 July 1587: conv. 18 Mar. 1587/8—VIII(27).

LONGLEY, Katherine, [ ], (same parish, recusancy period and conviction date)—VIII(27).

LONGLEY, Margaret, [ ], (same parish, recusancy period and conviction date)—VIII(27).

LONGWORTH, Longeworthe, Peter, 'scolem[aster]', of Ballam, Kirkham parish, Lancs. 13 mths recusancy from 30 July 1587: conv. 17 Mar. 1588/9—X(35).

LONGWORTH, [ ], his wife, of Westby, Lancs. 12 mths recusancy from 20 Sept. 1589: conv. 22 Mar. 1590/1—X(39v).

LONGWORTH, Peter, 'scholem[aster]', of Westby, Lancs. (same recusancy period and conviction date)—X(39v).

LOPE, Loupe, Loope, Roger, 'surgeon', of Rusheton [Rushton], Dorset. 4 mths recusancy from 20 Apr. 1583: conv. (?) 24 Aug. 1584—IV(16v). See LAMPE, William.

LOPE, Roger, 'surgeon', of Dorchester, Dorset. 5 mths recusancy from 1 Sept. 1585: conv. Lent 1586—VI(16).

LOPE, Roger, 'yom", of Dorchester, Dorset. 6 mths recusancy from 1 Jan. 1587/8: conv. 15 July 1588—VIII(19v).

LOVATT, *alias* of TAILOR, Giles.

LOVEDEN, Dorothy, wid., of Lamborne [Lambourn], Berks.[188] 3 mths

---

186. Richard Lloyd's property included the lands of John Lloyd, junior, at Llanvarda, which were let by the Crown to Edward Lloid from 17 May 1589. The above lease continues in the RRs until RR (E.377/11) the last Elizabethan roll, when it, too, ceases, with the annotation—(Cf. M.R., L.T.R., 44 Eliz, Easter Term, 'Recorda' section.)

187. Thomas Lloyd's conviction for recusancy cannot be traced in the RRs. Nevertheless, the Commissioners Jerome Corbett and Edward Davies on 9 Oct. 1589, produced £12 from the goods and chattels of Thomas Lloid and £23 from similar resources of Richard Lloyd. This money was owed and paid to the sheriff.

188. Dorothy Lovedon was the widow of Walter Lovedon, who died in 1580. (Cf. *VCH Berks.*, *IV*, p. 514.) She was imprisoned for recusancy in Reading Castle for 4 months from 11 Feb. 1582/53. Bailed from the Castle by warrant of Sir Francis Walsingham, she was discharged on 4 June 1583. (Cf. *CRS* XXXII, p. 118.)

recusancy from 24 Mar. 1580/1: conv. 26 June 1581—II(65v): and five later convictions, ending 7 Feb. 1582/3—II(65v)*. III(50v). V(4v). Debts re-enrolled—III(5)*.

LOVEDEN, Dorothy, wid., of St. Mary's parish, Reading, Berks [prisoner]. 4 mths recusancy from 11 Feb. 1582/3: conv. 4 June 1583—III(50v). Debt re-enrolled—V(4v).

LOVELL, Alice, wife of Thomas Lovell, esq., of East Harling, Norfolk. 3 mths recusancy from 13 Apr. 1587: conv. 1 Apr. 1588—VIII(54).

LOVELL, Eleanor, wife of Philip Lovell, gent., of Garboldisham, Norfolk. (same recusancy period and conviction date)—VIII(54).

LOVELL, Eliz., wid., of Marten [Merton], Norfolk. (same recusancy period and conviction date)—VIII(54).

LOVELL, Francis, junior, gent., of East Harling, Norfolk. (same recusancy period and conviction date)—VIII(54).

LOVELL, Robert, esq., of Bychamwell [Beechamwell], Norfolk. 11 mths recusancy from 1 Aug. 1581: conv. 23 July 1582—II(40): and six later convictions, ending Lent 1587—III(72v). IV(44v)*. V(46v)*. VI(25v). Goods, value £6, seized Michaelmas 1587—VII(41). Seized lands let by Crown to Barnard Guilpin at £33 – 6 – 8 p.a. from Ladyday 1584—V(41v). VII(40). VIII(50). IX(43), (43v). X(52). XI(46). XII(47). Rental (£86 – 8 – 10 p.a.) of lands seized 26 Sept. 1587 for pre-1587 arrears—VIII(6v). X(52v). XI(46v). XII(47).

LOWE, Agnes, 'spinster', of Wiswell, Lancs. 12 mths recusancy from 20 Sept. 1589: conv. 22 Mar. 1590/1—X(40).

LOWE, John, 'goldsmythe' (same parish, recusancy period and conviction date)—X(40).

LOWE, Robert, 'husb'' (same parish, recusancy period and conviction date)—X(40).

LOWE, Alice, his wife (same parish, recusancy period and conviction date)—X(40).

LOWE, Sibyl, wife of John Lowe, 'laborer' (same parish, recusancy period and conviction date)—X(40).

LOWNEM, Thomas, 'husb'', of [ ] in Norton parish, Derbys. 10 mths recusancy from 9 Sept. 1586: conv. 22 Mar. 1587/8—VIII(21).

LUDLOWE, John, gent., of Cames Eysell, Fareham parish, Hants.[189] 12 mths recusancy from 1 Oct. 1581: conv. ? Oct. 1582—III(50v): and

---

189. John Ludlowe's house is called 'Cams' (Cames, Cambes) 'Hall', (near Fareham). He was committed to the White Lion Gaol in Southwark by the Bishop of Winchester in Oct. 1581 (Cf. *CRS* I, pp. 61, 69.) The final entry in RR. (E.377/4) runs as follows:— 'the tenants of two thirds of the lands and tenements of John Lydlowe of Cambes owes £53 – 6 – 8 *per annum*, for the farm of various lands and tenements in Fareham of the clear annual value of £80, taken and seized into the hands of the King by the said commissioners for the recusancy of the same John. And the sum of £106 – 13 – 4 owed by Sir Daniel Norton, Kt., Sheriff of the preceeding year, as is contained in the preceeding roll, and its arrears, under 'Southt'. Sum total £160. *Discharge*. But he (Ludlowe) ought not to be summoned for this money, nor to be charged in the future for the same, by consideration of the barons of the Exchequer. (Cf. M.R., L.T.R., 4 James I, Michaelmas Term, 'Recorda, section) And he is quit'.

one later conviction, dated 7 Jan. 1583/4—IV(53). Debts re-enrolled—V(56). VI(54).

LUSSHER, Richard, 'scryvener', of the parish of SS. Simon and Jude, city of Norwich, Norfolk[190]. 8 mths recusancy from 20 Dec. 1586: conv. 18 Dec. 1587—VIII(13). Debt re-enrolled—X(17).

LUTYE, Lutys, Margaret, 'spinster', of the city of York [for not attending the parish church of St. John at the end of the Ouse bridge ('ad fin' pontis de Owse in comitat' civitat'')] [? prisoner]. 1 mth recusancy from 22 June 1582: conv. ? July 1582—II(8). Debt re-enrolled—V(8). VII(8). IX(8).

LYGON, see LIGON, Lion, Hugh.

LYMPLYE, Cicily, wid., of Stepney, Middx. 3 mths recusancy from 28 June 1587: conv. 1 Dec. 1587—VIII(38v).

LYNE, John, gent., of Westminster, Middx [? prisoner]. 1 mth recusancy from 6 Oct. 1587: conv. 29 Jan. 1587/8—VIII(38v).

LYNE, Roger, gent., of St. Botolph's parish, Bishopsgate Ward Without, London. Fine of 100 marks imposed for hearing Mass said on 30 Jan. 1585/6 by William Thomson, *alias* Blackborne, in the house of Robert Bellamy (*q.v.*); Thomson convicted at Old Bailey, 18 Apr. 1586[191]—VI(34v).[192]

LYNGEN, see LINGEN, Richard.

LYSTER, Alice, wife of Thomas Lyster, gent., of Westbie [Westby Hall, nr. Gisburn], W.R. Yorks. 6 mths recusancy from 3 July 1587: conv. 18 Mar. 1587/8—VIII(27).

LYSTER, 'Avarilla', wife of Laurence Lyster, gent., of Thorneton [? Bishop Thornton], W.R. Yorks. (same recusancy period and conviction date)—VIII(25v). See LISTER.

LYSTER, John, 'clericus', of St. George's parish, Southwark, Surrey [prisoner][193]. 5 mths recusancy from 17 Feb. 1586/7: conv. 17 July 1587—IX(54). See LISTARD.

MACCLESFEILD, Maclefeld, Andrew, gent., of Mere [Maer], Staffs. 4 mths recusancy from 31 Mar. 1582: conv. 2 Aug. 1582—II(14): and one later conviction, dated 25 July 1583—III(64v). Debts re-enrolled—IV(62). V(66). VI(63). VII(64). See MAXFEILD.

MACCLESFEILD, Maclefeld, William, esq., of Meare [Maer], Staffs. 8 mths recusancy from 3 Aug. 1582: conv. 8 Mar. 1582/3—VI(63v):

---

190. Richard Lusher was committed to the Clink with a total debt of £240, by the Archbishop of Canterbury, 16 Oct. 1586. (Cf. *CRS* II, p. 268.)

191. Roger Line (Lyne) was committed to the Wood Street Counter by Sir Francis Walsingham on 3 Feb. 1583/4, accompanied by William Higham. (Cf. *CRS* II, pp. 249, 252, 255, 271.)

192. William Thomson, *alias* Blackborne, a seminary priest, was executed at Tyburn on 20 Apr. 1586 for this offence. (Cf. Morris II, pp. 50, 51.)

193. John Lyster See footnotes 12 and 183.

and three later convictions, ending 19 July 1585—VI(63v). VII(64)*.
See MAXFEILD.

MACCLESFEILD, Maclefeld, William, gent., of Meare [Maer], Staffs. 4 mths recusancy from 18 Mar. 1582/3: conv. 9 July 1583—IV(62v): and eight later convictions, ending 1 Aug. 1586—IV(62v). V(66)*. VI(63), (63v)*. Record of land-seizure, 9 Sept. 1587—VIII(70v). Rental of lands seized 9 Sept. 1587—IX(62)*. X(62). Record of increased land-seizure in Milwich, Staffs., Mar. 1590/1—XI(20v). Lands, seized March 1590/1, let by Crown to Hugh Worthe from 14 June 1591, at £8 – 11 – 11¾ p.a.—XI(64v). XI(71v). XII(65v).

MACESCEN, Margery, wid., of Malpas, Cheshire. 13 mths recusancy from 25 Sept. 1586: conviction date omitted—VIII(58v).

MACHELL, Barnabas, 'tanner', of Kirkbythure [Kirkby Thore], Westmld. 1 mth recusancy from 1 June 1588: conv. 5 Aug. 1588.—IX(69).

MACKEWORTH, George, esq., of Harnesey [Hornsey], Middx. 2 mths recusancy from 2 July 1589: conv. 3 Dec. 1589—IX(37).

MADDOCK, John, 'yoman', of Malpas, Cheshire. 12 mths recusancy from 26 Sept. 1586: conv. 25 Sept. 1587—VIII(58v).

MADDOCK, Matilda, his wife (same parish, recusancy period and conviction date)—VIII(58v).

MADDOCK, Thomas, 'laborer', of St. Mary's parish, Chester city [? prisoner]. 13 mths recusancy from 21 Sept. 1583: conv. Sept. 1584—VI(48v).

MADDOCK, Thomas, 'yoman', of Chester Castle, Cheshire [prisoner]. 13 mths recusancy from 14 Sept. 1585: conv. 3 Oct. 1586—X(35v): and one later conviction, dated 24 Apr. 1587—VIII(58v).

MADISSHAM, Jane, of Crosby, Lancs., wife of Ralph Madissham, gent. 12 mths recusancy from 20 Sept. 1589: conv. 22 Mar. 1590/1—X(38).

MAGHULL, alias MALE, Mary, wife of Anthony Maghull, alias Male, 'yoman', of Ayntree [Aintree], Lancs. (same recusancy period and conviction date)—X(38).

MALLAGE, Thomas, 'yoman', of St. Clement's parish, Winchester, Hants. 6 mths recusancy from 1 Dec. 1588: conv. 23 June 1589—IX(59v).

MALLAM, Ann, wid., of Grange, parish of West Kirkeby [West Kirby], Cheshire. 13 mths recusancy from 25 Sept. 1586: conviction date omitted—VIII(58v).

MALLETT, Arthur, gent., of Feryfryston [Ferry Frystone], W.R. Yorks. 6 mths recusancy from 3 July 1587: conv. 18 Mar. 1587/8—VIII(25v).

MALLETT, John, [   ], of Normanton, W.R. Yorks. Fine of £50 imposed by High Commissioners, 1582 – 3.—III(25). Debt re-enrolled— V(23v). IX(22). XII(25v).

MANFEILD, Mansfeld, Henry, gent./esq., of Hamerden [Amerden], parish of Taplowe, Bucks. 6 mths recusancy from 25 Sept. 1586: conv. Lent 1587—VI(2v). Record of land-seizure, 16 Oct. 1587—VIII(2v). Goods, value £24 – 0 – 8, seized ? 16 Oct. 1587—X(2). Seized lands let by Crown to Robert Balthroppe from 24 Feb. 1587/8—VIII(3). IX(2). X(1). XI(2v). XII(2).

MANFEILD, Hester, wife of Henry Manfeild of Amerden in Taplowe, Bucks., gent. 3 mths recusancy from 27 Mar. 1587: conv. 18 Mar. 1587/8—VIII(3).

MANNINGE, Mary, wife of Edmund Manninge, gent., of Dedington [Deddington], Oxfords. 12 mths recusancy from 26 Sept. 1586: conv. 7 Mar. 1587/8—VIII(35).

MANNOCKE, Ann, wife of Francis Mannocke, esq., of Stoke by Nayland, Suffolk. 3 mths recusancy from 23 Mar. 1588/9: conv. 18 Mar. 1589/90—XI(22v). Record of land-seizure in Cambs. and Essex, 1 Apr. 1590—XI(22v). XII(20v). [Pipe Roll entries under 'Essex']. Seized lands in Cambs. and Essex let by Crown to William Twitty from 1 May 1591—XI(52v). XII(6). [Pipe Roll entries under 'Cambs'].

MANNOCKE, Giles, gent., of Stoke [by Nayland], Suffolk. 3 mths recusancy from 8 Apr. 1587: conv. 27 Mar. 1588—VIII(73).

MANNOCKE, Katherine, wife of Edmund Mannocke, gent., of Halton [? Holton], Suffolk (same recusancy period and conviction date)—VIII(73).

MANNOCKE, William, junior, gent., of Stoke by Mailond [Nayland], Suffolk. 6 mths recusancy from 20 Sept. 1588: conv. 2 July 1589—IX(64). Debt re-enrolled—XI(72v). Record of land-seizure in Essex and Suffolk, 1 Apr. 1591—XI(22v). Rental of seized lands-XII(20v).

MARKEHAM, Alice, 'spinster', of Passenham, Northants. 12 mths recusancy from 31 July 1587: conv. 4 Mar. 1588/9—IX(47).

MARRALL, Thomas, 'husb'', of Sephton [Sefton], Lancs. 12 mths recusancy from 20 Sept. 1589: conv. 22 Mar. 1590/1—X(38).

MARRIATT, Marriett, Humphrey, gent., of Arthingworth, Northants. 12 mths recusancy from 30 May 1587: conv. 17 Mar. 1589/90—X(55). Record of land-seizure, 6 Oct. 1590—X(55). Goods, value £40, seized 6 Oct. 1590—X(55). Rental of seized lands—XI(50v). XII(49v). Seized lands let by Crown to John Checkley from 12 Feb. 1590/1—XII(50v).

MARSDEN, Alice, of [? Thornley in Wheatley], Lancs., wife of William Marsden. 12 mths recusancy from 20 Sept. 1589: conv. 22 Mar. 1590/1—X(39).

MARSHE, John, 'clericus', of Southwark, Surrey [prisoner][194]. 1 mth recusancy from 5 June 1588: conv. 5 July 1588—VIII(63).

MARSHE, Katherine, 'spinster', wife of Humfrey Marshe, [ ], of Wigan, Lancs. 3 mths recusancy from 10 Oct. 1581: conv. 18 Jan. 1581/2—II(38v). Debt re-enrolled—VIII(46). See MERSHE, Katherine.

MARTEN, Martine, Martyn, Richard, gent., of Melford [Long Melford], Suffolk. 3 mths recusancy from 8 Apr. 1587: conv. 27 Mar. 1588—VIII(73). Record of land-seizure in Essex, 4 Mar.

---

194. John Marsh (Cf. Anstruther I, p. 219.)

1589/90—X(26v). Seized lands in Essex let by Crown to Francis Mannock from [?] Mar. 1589/90—X(26v). XI(21v). XII(20v). [Pipe Roll entries under 'Essex'].

MARTEN, Martyn, Roger, esq., of Melford [Long Melford], Suffolk. 10 mths recusancy from 1 Aug. 1581: conv. 18 July 1582—II(56): and two later convictions, ending 5 Apr. 1587—III(66). VI(58). Record of land-seizure, 2 Nov. 1587—VIII(72). Rental of seized lands—IX(63). X(63). XI(65). Seized lands let by Crown to Thomas Keys and Thomas Stowe from Michaelmas 1589—X(64). XI(65v). XII(66), (67). [Pipe Roll entries under 'Suffolk'].

MARTYNE, Marten, Marton, Alice, wid., of Martyn [Martin], W.R. Yorks. 6 mths recusancy from 3 July 1587: conv. 18 Mar. 1587/8—VIII(27). Record of land-seizure, 8 Apr. 1589—IX(22v). Rental of seized lands—IX(21v). X(21v). XI(24v). XII(23v). Seized lands let to William Hunnis by Crown, 26 Mar. 1591—XII(25v).

MASON, Mayson, Alice, 'spinster', of the city of York. 4 mths recusancy from 26 Mar. 1582: conv. ? July 1582—II(8). Debt re-enrolled—V(8). VII(8). IX(8).

MASON, Ann, wid., of Wessham [Wesham], parish of Kirkham, Lancs. 4 mths recusancy from 6 Apr. 1588: conv. 17 Mar. 1588/9—X(35).

MASON, Margaret, wid., of Sutton, Cheshire. 12 mths recusancy from 26 Sept. 1586: conv. 25 Sept. 1587—VIII(58v).

MASON, Mayson, Richard, 'taylor', of East Hendred, Berks.[195a] 8 mths recusancy from 3 July 1583: conv. 24 Feb. 1583/4—IV(3v).

MASON, Richard, 'taillor', of St. Mary's parish, Reading, Berks. [prisoner][195b]. 8 mths recusancy ending 31 June 1582, when convicted—II(65v): and five later convictions, ending 6 Mar. 1586/7—V(4v)*. VI(4v)*, (48v).

MASON, Richard, 'yom'', of St. Mary's parish, Reading, Berks. [prisoner][195c]. 4 mths recusancy from 11 Feb. 1582/3: conv. 1 July 1583—III(50v): and one later conviction, dated 20 July 1584—IV(46). Debt re-enrolled—V(4v).

MASSIE, Massey, Ann, wid., of Rixton, Warrington parish, Lancs[196]. 6 mths recusancy from 1 Feb. 1587/8: conv. 17 Mar. 1588/9.—X(35). Lands seized 26 Mar. 1591 and let by Crown to John Parker from 1 July 1591.—XII(44).

MASSIE, Richard, gent., of St. Mary's parish, Chester [Chester Castle]. 8 mths recusancy from 1 Sept. 1584: conv. 26 Apr. 1585.—VI(48v).

MASSIE, Richard, gent., of Chester Castle, Cheshire [prisoner]. 13 mths recusancy from 14 Sept. 1585: conv. 3 Oct. 1586.—X(35v): and one later conviction, dated 24 April 1587.—VIII(58v).

---

195. Richard Mason, who lived at East Hendred, Berks., was convicted of recusancy from 3 July 1583, and moved, by the sheriff, to the prison in Reading Castle. (Cf. CRS XXIII, p. 118.) He was released on 6 Mar. 1586/7.

196. Ann Massie was brought before the Ecclesiastical Commissioners for Cheshire and her conformity proved. (Cf. CRS V, p. 70.)

MASSIE, Margaret, his wife, of Chester Castle, Cheshire [prisoner]. 7 mths recusancy from 26 Sept. 1586: conv. 24 Apr. 1587.—VIII(58v).
MATHEWE, John, gent., of Silley, parish of Llanner Waterdyne [Llanvair Waterdine], Salop. 6 mths recusancy from 1 Aug. 1588: conv. 17 July 1589.—IX(13).
MATHEWE, Matthew, 'yeoman', of Irtlingburghe [Irthlingborough], Northants. 12 mths recusancy ending 2 May 1587, when convicted—.VIII(52v).
MATHEWES, Joan, 'spinster', of Birrington [Berrington], Salop. 1 mth recusancy from 9 June 1588: conv. 10 Mar. 1588/9.—IX(13).
MAWDESLEY, Hugh, 'yoman', of Standish, Lancs. 12 mths recusancy from 20 Sept. 1589: conv. 22 Mar. 1590/1.—X(38v).
MAWDESLEY, 'Jenetta', 'spinster', of Litherland, Lancs. (same recusancy period and conviction date).—X(38).
MAXFEILD, Maxfeld, Andrew, gent., of Meare [Maer], Staffs. 12 mths recusancy from 6 Sept. 1586: conv. 25 Mar. 1588.—VIII(78v).
MAXFEILD, Ellen, wid., of Meare [Maer], Staffs. 6 mths recusancy from 6 Sept. 1587: conv. 22 July 1588.—VIII(58).
MAXFEILD, Humphrey, gent., of Southwark, Surrey [prisoner][197]. 6 mths recusancy ending 18 Feb. 1584/5, when convicted.—V(52v).
MAXFEILD, John, gent., of Meare [Maer], Staffs. 12 mths recusancy from 6 Sept. 1586: conv. 25 Mar. 1588.—VIII(78v).
MAXFEILD, William, esq., of Meere [Maer], Staffs. 12 mths recusancy; convicted Easter term 1581 – 2 by informer's suit—II(54v). Debt re-enrolled.—III(64v). V(66). VII(64). IX(69). XI(71v). See MACCLESFEILD.
MAYNE, Jane, wife of Benedict Mayne of Hoggeston, Bucks., gent. 3 mths recusancy from 27 Mar. 1587: conv. 18 Mar. 1587/8.—VIII(3).
MAYNERD, Margaret, wid., of St. Bride's parish, Farringdon Ward Without, London. 13 mths recusancy from 19 Jan. 1586/7: conv. 19 Jan. 1587/8.—VIII(38v).
MAYNEY, Ann, wid., of Highley Carr, Winwick parish, Lancs., relict of Walter Mayney [ ] of Staplehurst, Kent., deceased. [Pipe Roll entry under 'Kent']. Rental of lands in Kent seized 21 Aug. 1591 for her recusancy.—XI(14v). XII(32v). See MEYNEY, Ann.
MEADE, Mary, wife of Christopher Meade, gent., of Hitcham, Suffolk. 3 mths recusancy from 8 Apr. 1587: conv. 27 Mar. 1588.—VIII(73).
MEASIE, Mary, wife of Simon Measie, 'yeom'', of Somerton, Oxfords. 12 mths recusancy from 26 Sept. 1586: conv. 7 Mar. 1587/8.—VIII(35v).
MELLEN, Richard, 'clericus', of Dorchester, Dorset[198]. 5 mths recusancy from 1 Sept. 1585: conv. Lent 1586.—VI(16).
MELLING, Jane, wid., of Great Crosby, Lancs. 12 mths recusancy from 20 Sept. 1589: conv. 22 Mar. 1590/1.—X(38).

---

197. Humphrey Maxfield was committed to the Marshalsea for six months recusancy.
198. Richard Mellen an unidentified priest.

MELLYN, Richard, 'clericus', of Farneham [Farnham], Dorset[199]. 5 mths recusancy from 20 Jan. 1583/4: conv. ? Summer 1584.—V(70). See MELLEN, Richard.

MERCER, Agnes, wife of George Mercer, 'husb"', of Hardwick, Oxfords. 12 mths recusancy from 26 Sept. 1586: conv. 7 Marc. 1587/8.—VIII(35v).

MERCER, Eliz., of Brynenge [Bryning with Kellamergh], Lancs., wife of William Mercer [ ]. 12 mths recusancy from 20 Sept. 1589: conv. 22 Mar. 1590/1.—X(39v).

MERCER, Mary, wife of William Mercer of East Cleidon [Claydon], Bucks., 'yoman'. 3 mths recusancy from 27 Mar. 1587: conv. 18 Mar. 1587/8.—VIII(3).

MERCER, Thomas, [ ], of Westby, Lancs. 12 mths recusancy from 20 Sept. 1589: conv. 22 Mar. 1590/1.—X(39v).

MERCER, Jane, his wife (same parish, recusancy period and conviction date).—X(39v).

MERCER, William, junior, of East Cleidon [Claydon], Bucks. 3 mths recusancy from 27 Mar. 1587: conv. 18 Mar. 1587/8.—VIII(3).

MERFEILD, John, 'laborer', of Staveley, Derbys. 10 mths recusancy from 9 Sept. 1586: conv. 22 Mar. 1587/8.—VIII(21).

MERRICK, Lucy, 'spinster', of Llandenny, Mon. 5 mths recusancy from 24 Mar. 1586/7: conv. 13 Mar. 1587/8.—VIII(49v).

MERSHE, Katherine, 'spinster', of Salford in the parish of Manchester, Lancs. [prisoner], wife of Humfrey Mershe [ ]. 3 mths recusancy from 17 Jan. 1581/2: conv. 2 May 1582.—II(38v): and one later conviction, dated 16 Jan. 1582/3.—II(38v). Debts re-enrolled—VIII(46)*. See MARSHE, Katherine.

METCALF, John, gent., of Heminge, in Askarth [Aysgarth] parish, N.R. Yorks. 4 mths recusancy from 14 May 1587: conv. 4 Sept. 1587.—VIII(25v).

METCALF, Roger, gent., of Berryparke, [Aysgarth parish], N.R. Yorks. (same recusancy period and conviction date).—VIII(25v).

METHAM, Katherine, wife of Thomas Metham, esq., of Kyrkebyesletham [Kirkby Fleetham], N.R. Yorks. 4 mths recusancy from 14 May 1587: conv. 4 Sept. 1587.—VIII(25v).

MEYNEY, Ann, wid., of Higlecare [Highley Carr], Winwick parish, Lancs. 13 mths recusancy from 14 Aug. 1586: conv. 25 Mar. 1588.—VIII(21v). See MAYNEY, Ann.

MIDDLETON, Midleton, John, 'yoman', of Burton-upon-Trent, Staffs. 6 mths recusancy from 6 Sept. 1587: conv. 22 July 1588.—VIII(58).

MIDDLETON, Midleton, Margaret, of Leighton [Layton], Lancs., wife of George Midleton, esq.[200]. 12 mths recusancy from 20 Sept. 1589: conv. 22 Mar. 1590/1.—X(39v).

---

199. Same as above.
200. Margaret Middleton, wife of George Middleton of Poulton, Lancs., was bound over by the Ecclesiastical Commissioners for Cheshire for her continued appearance (endorsed '15 Feb. 1583'). (Cf. *CRS* V, p. 71.)

MIDDLETON, Richard, gent., of Spofforth, W.R. Yorks. 6 mths recusancy from 3 July 1587: conv. 18 Mar. 1587/8.—VIII(27).

MIDDLEMORE, John, esq., of Kingesnorton [Kings Norton], Worcs. 6 mths recusancy from 29 Sept. 1587: conv. 25 July 1588.—VIII(80v). Seized lands let by Crown to Henry Middlemore from 22 June 1588.—IX(68v). X(75). XI(70). XII(71).

MIDDLEMORE, 'Amphilis', his wife (same parish, recusancy period & conviction date).—VIII(80v).

MIDFURTHE, Oswin, gent., of Riall [Ryal], Northumberland. 12 mths recusancy from 1 Aug. 1582: conviction date unspecified.—III(52). Debt re-enrolled.—VIII(57v).

MILMAN, alias WILLIAMS, Eliz., 'spinster', of Hanley Castle, Worcs. 12 mths recusancy from 20 Sept. 1586: conv. 28 Mar. 1588.—VIII(77).

MILMAN, alias WILLIAMS, Joan, 'spinster' (same parish, recusancy period & conviction date).—VIII(77).

MILTON, Katherine, 'spinster', of Lopham, Norfolk. 3 mths recusancy from 13 Apr. 1587: conv. 1 Apr. 1588.—VIII(54).

MILWARD, Alice, 'spinster', of Hanley Castle, Worcs. 12 mths recusancy from 1 Apr. 1587: conv. 28 Mar. 1588.—VIII(80).

MINNERS, Jane, wife of Roger Minners, gent., of Sellack, Herefords. 12 mths recusancy from 1 Sept. 1586: conv. 18 Mar. 1587/8.—VIII(30).

MINORS, Mynors, Mynners, William, gent., of Garwey [Garway], Herefords[201]. 12 mths recusancy from 1 Sept. 1586: conv. 18 Mar. 1587/8.—VIII(30). Record of land-seizure, 23 Aug. 1588.—IX(25v). Rental of seized lands.—IX(25v). X(28). XII(28). Arrearage of rent.—XI(28v).

MOLYNEUX, Molynex, Cecily, wid., of Inskippe, parish of Michaelles [St. Michael-on-Wyre], Lancs. 13 mths recusancy from 14 Aug. 1586: conv. 25 Mar. 1588.—VIII(21v).

MOLYNEUX, Thomas, gent., of Pemberton, Wigan parish, Lancs. 3 mths recusancy from 1 May 1588: conv. 17 Mar. 1588/9.—X(35).

MONNINGTON, Katherine, wid., of Sarnesfeild, Herefords. 12 mths recusancy from 1 Sept. 1586: conv. 18 Mar. 1587/8.—VIII(30).

MONNINGTON, Richard, gent. (same parish, recusancy period and conviction date).—VIII(30).

MONNINGTON, Richard, [   ], of Sernefeld [Sarnesfeild], Herefords. Two fines of £20 imposed for ignoring sheriff's summonses after excommunication, 4 Apr. and 27 May 1581.—III(28)*. Debts re-enrolled.—V(26), (26v).

MOORE, Ann, [   ], of Barnebroughe [Barnbrough], W.R. Yorks. 6 mths recusancy from 3 July 1587: conv. 18 Mar. 1587/8.—VIII(27).

---

201. William Minors and Katherine, his wife, were among the principal and most dangerous recusants in Hereford Diocese in 1603. (Cf. CRS II, p. 296.)

MOORE, More, Edward, gent., of Southwark, Surrey [prisoner]²⁰². 10 mths recusancy ending 11 Mar. 1582/3, when convicted.—IV(49v); and three later convictions, ending 20 July 1584.—IV(49v)*. V(50v). Debts re-enrolled.—VI(51)*.

MOORE, More, Edward, 'yeoman', of Islington [Tilney with Islington], Norfolk. 9 mths recusancy from 18 July 1587: conv. 15 July 1588.—VIII(54v). Debt re-enrolled.—X(53).

MOORE, More, John, gent., of Launceston, Cornwall. 2 mths recusancy from 13 Oct. 1587: conv. 18 Mar. 1587/8.—VIII(8). Debt re-enrolled.—X(8v).

MOORE, John, gent., of Westminster, Middx [prisoner]²⁰³. [Pipe Roll entries under 'Oxfords'] 3 mths recusancy from 27 June 1581, conv. 20 Dec. 1581.—II(29v): and eleven later convictions, ending 17 Nov. 1583.—II(29v)*,(44)*. Debts re-enrolled.—IV(29)*,(29v)*. VI(30v)*.

MOORE, Katherine, 'spinster', of Hampton, Oxfords. 12 mths recusancy from 26 Sept. 1586: conv. 7 Mar. 1587/8.—VIII(35v).

MOORE, Robert, 'yom'', of Breckelles Magna, Norfolk. 12 mths recusancy from 10 Mar. 1582/3: conv. 10 Mar. 1583/4.—IV(44v): and one later conviction, dated 1 Apr. 1588.—VIII(54).

MOORE, Thomas, gent., of Southwark, Surrey [prisoner]²⁰⁴. 80 days recusancy ending 22 July 1583, when convicted.—IV(49v): and one later conviction, dated 20 July 1584.—V(52v). Debts re-enrolled.—VI(51).

MOORE, Thomas, gent., of Layton [Leyton], Essex²⁰⁴⁽ᵃ⁾. 3 mths recusancy

---

202. Edward More (Moore) was born at Whaddon, Cambs., 4m. north of Royston. (Cf. *CRS* II, p. 231.) The grandson of St. Thomas More, he was arrested at Dover on arrival from overseas on 2 Aug. 1581, and committed with John, his nephew, to the Westminster Gatehouse before June 1583. (Cf. *CRS* II, pp. 230, 231.) He was moved from the Gatehouse to the Marshalsea before the last day of June, disappearing after 8 Apr. 1584.

203. John More (Moore) of Westminster, Middx., was the great grandson of St. Thomas More. He was committed to Newgate on 1 Jan. 1585/6 'for the Romish Religion' and was twice examined by Justice Young and other commissioners. (Cf. *CRS* II, pp. 248, 252.) Was still there in June 1586. Was busily engaged with the authorities over recusancy penalties. (Cf. *CRS* II, p. 235.) (Cf. D. Shanahan, 'The Descendants of St. Thomas More. John More, 1557–1599', in *Essex Recusant*. vol. 19, (1977), pp. 2–4). From Exannual Roll ex Pipe Roll of 23 Eliz. (E.372/427) under 'Oxon', John More was fined £20 for recusancy from 19 Nov. 1581 to his conviction on 18 Dec., when his debts due to the Crown amounted to:—

£60 from 15 Mar. 1581 to 17 June	(3 months recusancy)
£60 from 18 June 1581 to 23 Sept.	(3 months recusancy)
£60 from 25 Sept. 1581 to 1 Jan.	(3 months recusancy)
£40 from 3 Jan. 1580/1 to 17 Mar.	(2 months recusancy)
£40 from 18 Mar. 1580/1 to 17 May	(2 months recusancy)
£60 from 18 May 1580 to 18 Aug.	(3 months recusancy)
£40 from 22 Sept. 1580 to 17 Nov.	(2 months recusancy)

204. Thomas More (Moore) of Chelsea, Middx., was the grandson of St. Thomas More. He was committed to the Marshalsea, 28 Apr. 1582. (Cf. *CRS* II, pp. 231, 233, 235, 240.) He was recommitted as 'Thomas Moore, Gent.' by Mr. Justice Young on 1 Jan. 1585/6, and 'since not examined'. (Cf. *CRS* II, pp. 242, 244, 251.) He was still in the Marshalsea on 18 June 1586.

204A. Thomas Moore had two-thirds of his lands at Barnburgh Manor and Moseley Tilte, Yorks. W.R., seized for his recusancy on 9 Dec. 1590. These were then let by th Crown to John Southerne, gent., for the same rent (£10–0–4 *per annum*) from Ladyday 1591.

from 25 Mar. 1588: conv. 13 Mar. 1588/9—XI(10v) [Pipe Roll entries under 'Yorks']. Record of land-seizure in Yorks, 9 Dec. 1590.—XI(10v). Rental of seized lands in Yorks.—XII(24). Seized lands in Yorks let by Crown to John Southerne from Ladyday 1591.—XII(25v).

MOORE, More, Thomas, 'yoman', of Riple [Ripple], Worcs. 6 mths recusancy from 29 Sept. 1587: conv. 25 July 1588.—VIII(80v).

MOORE, *alias* of TALBOTT, Elizabeth.

MORDANTE, Agnes, wife of William Mordante, esq., of Okeley [Oakley], Beds. 3 mths recusancy from 29 Mar. 1587: conv. 20 Mar. 1587/8.—VIII(1).

MORE, see MOORE.

MORECOCK, William, 'yom'', of Dorchester, Dorset. 12 mths recusancy from 2 July 1587: conv. 15 July 1588.—VIII(19v).

MOREY, Margery, wife of Richard Morey, [ ], of St. Mary's parish, Nottingham. 10 mths recusancy from 9 Sept. 1586: conv. 25 Mar. 1588. [Pipe Roll entry under 'Nottingham Town' ('Villa Not").]

MORGAN, Ann, 'spinster', of Llantilio Pertholey, Mon. 5 mths recusancy from 24 Mar. 1586/7: conv. 13 Mar. 1587/8.—VIII(48v).

MORGAN, Ann, wife of Philip Morgan, [ ], of Skenfrith, Mon. (same recusancy period and conviction date).—VIII(48v).

MORGAN, Christopher, gent., of St. Dunstan's parish, Canterbury, Kent [? prisoner]. 7 mths recusancy ending 22 Feb. 1583/4, when convicted—IV(12). Debt re-enrolled.—VI(12).

MORGAN, Christopher, gent., of Gowdeherst [Goudhurst], Kent. 9 mths recusancy from 18 Mar. 1580/1: conv. ? 9 Jan. 1581/2.—II(28).

MORGAN, Eliz., 'spinster', of Llantilio Pertholey, Mon. 5 mths recusancy from 24 Mar. 1586/7: conv. 13 Mar. 1587/8.—VIII(48v).

MORGAN, George, gent. (same parish, recusancy period & conviction date).—VIII(48v).

MORGAN, Jane, 'spinster' (same parish, recusancy period & conviction date).—VIII(48v).

MORGAN, Jane James, 'spinster', wife of John ap John Morgan, [ ], of Llangattock nigh Usk, Mon. (same recusancy period and conviction date).—VIII(49).

MORGAN, Joan, 'spinster', of Llantilio Pertholey, Mon. (same recusancy period and conviction date).—VIII(48v).

MORGAN, John, gent. (same parish, recusancy period and conviction date).—VIII(48v).

MORGAN, Jane, his wife (same parish, recusancy period & conviction date).—VIII(48v).

MORGAN, John Watkin, 'yoman', of Llanarth, Mon. (same recusancy period & conviction date).—VIII(48).

MORGAN, Lady, wife of Sir Richard Morgan, knt., of Llanthewy Skirrid, Mon. (same recusancy period and conviction date).—VIII(49).

MORGAN, Margaret, 'spinster', wife of [ ] Morgan, [ ], of Aburgavenny [Abergavenny], Mon. 8 mths recusancy from 19 July

1585: conv. 4 Mar. 1585/6.—VI(40v).

MORGAN, Margaret, wife of Roger Morgan, [ ], of Usk, Mon. 5 mths recusancy from 24 Mar. 1586/7: conv. 13 Mar. 1587/8.—VIII(49).

MORGAN, Margaret verch John, wife of Walter Morgan, 'yoman', of Llanthewy Skirrid, Mon. (same recusancy period & conviction date).—VIII(49).

MORGAN, Mary, wid., wife [sic] of Richard Morgan, esq., of Llanvihangel Crucorney, Mon. (same recusancy period and conviction date).—VIII(48v).

MORGAN, Matilda, 'spinster', of Llanthewy Skirrid, Mon. (same recusancy period and conviction date).—VIII(48v).

MORGAN, 'Polidorus', gent., of Westminster, Middx [prisoner][205]. [Pipe Roll entries under 'Monmouth'] 3 mths recusancy from 27 June 1581: conv. 26 Sept. 1581.—II(38): and four later convictions, ending 16 Mar. 1581/2.—II(38)*.

MORGAN, Richard, 'clericus recusans' of Salop[206]. Goods, value £8, seized Jan. 1590/1; paid May 1591.—IX(69v).

MORGAN, Roger, gent., of Tredennocke [Tredunnock], Mon. 5 mths recusancy from 24 Mar. 1586/7: conv. 13 Mar. 1587/8.—VIII(49). Record of land-seizure, 24 Oct. 1588—IX(42v). Rental of seized lands.—IX(42v). X(50). XI(45).

MORGAN, Eleanor, his wife (same parish, recusancy period & conviction date).—VIII(49).

MORGAN, Thomas, gent., of parish of St. Dubricius [St. Devereux?], Herefords. Two fines of £20 imposed for ignoring sheriff's summonses after excommunication, 4 Apr. and 27 May 1581.—III(28)*. Debts re-enrolled.—V(26),(26v).

MORGAN, Thomas, esq., of Arkeston, parish of Kingstone, Herefords. 2 mths recusancy from 2 Jan. 1584/5: conv. ult. Feb. 1584/5.—V(26v): and five later convictions, ending 18 Mar. 1587/8.—V(26v). VI(25)*. VIII(30).

MORGAN, William, gent., of Llantilio Pertholey, Mon. 5 mths recusancy from 24 Mar. 1586/7: conv. 13 Mar. 1587/8.—VIII(48v).

MORLEY, Morreley, John, 'yeom'', of Newton by Tofte, Lindsey, Lincs. 10 mths recusancy from 9 Sept. 1586: conv. 28 Mar. 1588.—VIII(44v). Debt re-enrolled.—X(16v). Goods, value £4, seized 12 Aug. 1588.—IX(40v). Record of lands seized 12 Aug. 1588.—IX(40v). Rental of seized lands.—IX(9). X(42). XI(42). XII(41).

MORLEY, Richard, 'husb'', of Alciston, Sussex. 5 mths recusancy from 20 Aug. 1587: conv. 5 July 1588.—VIII(63).

MORRIS, Ann, 'spinster', of Hanley, Worcs. 6 mths recusancy from 29 Sept. 1587: conv. 25 July 1588.—VIII(80v).

---

205. Polidor Morgan was a prisoner in the Westminster Gatehouse. He was discharged by Walsingham, 18 Aug. 1582. (Cf. CRS II, pp. 219, 225, 230).

206. Richard Morgan an unidentified priest.

MORRIS, Ann, 'spinster', of Longdon, Worcs. 2 mths recusancy from 7 April 1588: conv. 6 Mar. 1588/9.—IX(70v).

MORRIS, Ann, 'spinster', of Raglan, Mon. 5 mths recusancy from 24 Mar. 1586/7: conv. 13 Mar. 1587/8.—VIII(48).

MORRIS, David, 'laborer', of Newton, Salop. 12 mths recusancy from 24 Feb. 1586/7: conv. 18 July 1588.—VIII(16v).

MORRIS, David, 'yoman', of Llandenny, Mon. 5 mths recusancy from 24 Mar. 1586/7: conv. 13 Mar. 1587/8.—VIII(49v).

MORRIS, Mores, Morres, Morrys, Edmund, gent., of Great Coxwell, Berks. 3 mths recusancy from 23 Mar. 1580/1: conv. 18 June 1581.— II(65v): and seven later convictions, ending 4 Mar. 1587/8.—II(65v). III(50v). IV(3v). V(4v). VIII(5). Debts re-enrolled.—VI(3v).

MORRIS, Morres, Edmund, gent., of St. Mary's parish, Reading, Berks [prisoner][207]. 80 days recusancy from 11 Feb. 1582/3: conv. 4 June 1593.—III(50v): and one later conviction, dated 20 July 1584—IV(46). Debt re-enrolled.—V(4v). VI(3v).

MORRIS, Morres, Morrys, Francis, esq., of St. Bride's parish, Farringdon Ward Without, London [prisoner][208]. [Pipe Roll entries under 'Berks']. 1 mth recusancy from 7 Dec. 1581: conv. 19 Jan. 1581/2.— I(3v): and two later convictions, ending 27 Dec. 1582.—I(3v). II(65v). Debts re-enrolled.—III(33v). V(3v). VII(3v).

MORRIS, Moris, George, 'clericus', of Usk, Mon.[209] 5 mths recusancy from 24 Mar. 1586/7: conv. 13 Mar. 1587/8.—VIII(49).

MORRIS, Moris, 'Jenetta', wid., lately wife of William Moris, [   ], of Usk, Mon. (same recusancy period and conviction date).—VIII(49).

MORRIS, Joan, 'spinster', of Raglan, Mon. (same recusancy period & conviction date).—VIII(48).

MORRIS, 'Jonetta', 'spinster' (same parish, recusancy period & conviction date).—VIII(48).

MORRIS, Moris, Lewis, 'yoman', of Llanvetherine, Mon. (same recusancy period and conviction date).—VIII(49).

MORRIS, 'Llykua', 'spinster', of Raglan, Mon. (same recusancy period and conviction date).—VIII(48).

MORSE, Ann, wife of Lionel Morse, gent., of Westhorpe, Suffolk. 3 mths recusancy from 8 Apr. 1587: conv. 27 Mar. 1588.—VIII(73).

MOUNDINGE, William, 'webster', of Livesey, Blackeborne [Blackburn] parish, Lancs. 13 mths recusancy from 30 July 1587: conv. 17 Mar. 1588/9.—X(35).

---

207. Edmund Morries was imprisoned in Reading Castle; bailed by warrant of the Privy Council. (Cf. *CRS* XXXII, p. 118.); date of discharge unrecorded.

208. Francis Morris, of Great Coxwell Manor, Berks., was imprisoned in the Fleet, and bailed by warrant of the Privy Council on 12 Feb. 1582/3. (Cf. *CRS* II, pp. 223, 229.) He died in 1584.

209. George Morris, a pre-Elizabethan priest, was an Oxford MA., and held the living of Yate in the Diocese of Gloucester from King Edward VI's reign. He was deprived 'on account of not reading the Articles' of 1571, and went to Rheimes in 1581. He had the reputation of being a 'catholic recusant'. (Cf. Knox, p. 82.)

MOUNSEY, Samuel, of Southwark, Surrey [prisoner][210]. 80 days recusancy ending 20 July 1584, when convicted.—V(52v).

MOUNTFORD, Ann, [ ], of Colshull [Coleshill], Warwicks. 6 mths recusancy from 1 Sept. 1588: conv. 21 July 1589.—IX(11v).

MOUNTFORD, Ann, wife of William Mountford, gent., of Kingeshurst, Colshall [Coleshill] parish, Warwicks. 7 mths recusancy from 12 July 1586: conv. 15 Mar. 1586/7.—VIII(76).

MUNCKTON, Christopher, esq., of Londesbrough [Londesborough], E.R. Yorks. Fine of 100 marks for recusancy imposed by High Commissioners, 25 Mar. 1583. Payments by instalments completed 22 Oct. 1589.—VIII(27).

MUNCKTON, Christopher, esq., (of same parish). 6 mths recusancy from 3 July 1587: conv. 18 Mar. 1587/8.—VIII(27).

MURRYN, MORWEN, John, 'clericus', of Salford in the parish of Manchester, Lancs. [prisoner][211]. 12 mths recusancy from 20 Feb. 1582/3: convicted 22 Jan. 1583/4 [*sic*].—IV(37). Debt re-enrolled.—IV(42v). VI(39).

MURYELL, James, 'yoman', of Harleston, parish of Rednall [Redenhall], Norfolk. 12 mths recusancy from 12 July 1588: conv. 7 July 1589.—IX(45v). Debt re-enrolled.—XI(48).

MYNNERS, see MINORS.

NANFAN, Giles, esq., of London, *alias* of Brints Mooreton [Birtsmorton], Worcs. 1 mth recusancy from 2 Apr. 1592: conviction date not stated [Pipe Roll entry under 'London'][212].—XII(40v).

NARWOOD, Eliz., wife of William Narwood, esq., of Lekehampton [Leckhampton], Gloucs. 5 mths recusancy from 26 Mar. 1587: conv. 11 Mar. 1587/8.—VIII(82).

NASHE, Nayshe, Alice, [widow], of St. Sepulchre's parish, Farringdon Ward Without, London. 3 mths recusancy from 25 Mar. 1587: conv. 10 July 1587.—VIII(38v). Goods, value £8 – 11 – 10, seized Trinity term, 1590.—X(46).

NASHE, John, 'yeoman', of Southwark, Surrey [prisoner][213]. 10 mths recusancy ending 11 Mar. 1582/3, when convicted.—III(58v). Debt re-enrolled.—V(52v).

NEEDHAM, Nedeham, Nedham, Brian, 'clericus', of Hamstall Ridware, Staffs. 4 mths recusancy from 31 Mar. 1582: conv. 2 Aug. 1582.—II(14). Debt re-enrolled.—IV(62). VI(63).

---

210. Samuel Mounsey, a Brownist prisoner in the Clink, was convicted on 20 July 1584, for nonconformity in religion. (Cf. *CRS* II, p. 235.)

211. John Murren's life as a pre-Elizabethan priest is outlined until 1561 in *DNB* XXXIX, p. 170. His career as a fugitive recusant priest is described in Wark, pp. 176, 177.)

212. Giles Nanfan (Cf. *CRS* XVIII, pp. 146, 363.)

213. John Nash, a 'precisian', was a prisoner in the Marshalsea in 1583, and was moved to Newgate on 19 Mar. 1583/4. (Cf. *CRS* II, pp. 226, 229.)

NEEDHAM, Nedeham, Nedham, Brian, 'clericus', of Southwark, Surrey [prisoner][214]. 5 mths recusancy ending 11 Mar. 1582/3, when convicted.—III(58v). Debt re-enrolled.—V(52v).

NEEDHAM, Thomas, 'yoman', of Envild [Enville], Staffs. 6 mths recusancy from 6 Sept. 1587: conv. 22 July 1588.—VIII(58).

NEWCOMBE, Joan, wid., of Barford [? Barforth] Dykes, in Gillinge parish, N.R. Yorks. 13 mths recusancy from 3 Sept. 1586: conv. 4 Sept. 1587.—VIII(25v).

NEWETHE, Thomas, 'tailor', of Hemingbrough, E.R. Yorks. 4 mths recusancy from 28 Mar. 1581: conv. 17 July 1581.—I(21v). Debt re-enrolled.—III(24). V(22).

NEWLAND, Gregory, 'yeoman', of Scoruston [South Rushton], Norfolk. 3 mths recusancy from 13 Apr. 1587: conv. 1 Apr. 1588—VIII(54).

NEWPORTE, Geoffrey ['Galfridus'], 'yoman', of Patsill [Patshull], Staffs. 6 mths recusancy from 25 Mar. 1588: conv. 14 Mar. 1588/9.—IX(69v).

NEWPORTE, John, gent., of Hanley Castle, Worcs. 12 mths recusancy from 20 Sept. 1586: conv. 28 Mar. 1588.—VIII(77). Goods, value £5 – 13 – 4, seized 31 Sept. 1588.—IX(68v).

NEWPORTE, Margaret, his wife (same parish, recusancy period and conviction date).—VIII(77).

NEWSAM, Bridget, 'spinster', of Weton [Weeton], Lancs. 12 mths recusancy from 20 Sept. 1589: conv. 22 Mar. 1590/1.—X(39).

NICOLLS, Thomas, 'tanner', of Rosse [Ross-on-Wye], Herefords. Fine of £20 imposed 27 May 1581 for ignoring sheriff's summons after excommunication.—III(28).

NICOLLS, Thomas, 'yoman', of the parish of St. John Baptist, Hereford. 6 mths recusancy from 1 Sept. 1588: conv. 14 July 1589.—IX(25v). Debt re-enrolled.—XI(29).

NOBLE, John, gent., of the parish of St. Mary in Wolchurch, Brodestreate [Broadstreet] Ward, London. 3 mths recusancy prior to 20 Apr. 1588, when convicted.—VIII(38v).[215]

NORDEN, John, gent., of Norton, Kent. 2 mths recusancy from 17 Dec. 1587: conv. 26 Feb. 1588/9.—IX(29). Record of land-seizure, 10 June 1590.—X(33).[216]

---

214. Brian Needham, an unidentified priest probably connected with the Staffordshire Fitzherbert's had been committed to the Marshalsea since June 1582, and still remained there in Mar. 1583/4. (Cf. *CRS* II, p. 231.)

215. John Noble a person of this name was imprisoned in the Westminster Gatehouse on 8 Apr. 1584, 'for matters of religion'. (Cf. *CRS* II, p. 235.)

216. John Norden's lands seized, 10 June 1590, for a rent of £73 – 6 – 8 *per annum*, was two-thirds of the site of the late monastery of Leeds, near Maidstone, with lands in Leeds, Bromfield and Sutton Valence in Kent, in the tenure or occupation of John Norden, William Reynold, Robert Lambe, gent., Walter Taylor, gent., Thomas Wyatt, and John Rouse; two-thirds of a brewhouse in Sittingbourne and Milton, Kent; and two-thirds of the Rectory house in Rainham, Kent. These lands now discharged. (Cf. M.R., L.T.R., 33 Eliz., Hilary Term, 'Recorda' section.)

NORRIS, Norrys, Richard, 'clericus', of Southwark, Surrey [prisoner][217]. 10 mths recusancy ending 11 Mar. 1582/3, when convicted.—III(58v). Debt re-enrolled.—V(52v).

NORTHE, Agnes, wid., of [ ] in Edleston [Edlaston] parish, Derbys. 10 mths recusancy from 9 Sept. 1586: conv. 22 Mar. 1587/8.—VIII(21).

NORTON, Anthony, [ ], of St. Clement's parish, Winchester, Hants. 6 mths recusancy from 1 Dec. 1588: conv. 23 June 1589.—IX(59v).

NORTON, Henry, 'yoman', of Westham, Sussex. 2 mths recusancy from 17 Apr. 1587: conv. 26 Feb. 1587/8.—VIII(63v). Record of land-seizure, 17 Jan. 1589.—IX(54v). Rental of seized lands.—X(65v). XI(55v). XII(56v).

NORTON, Richard, gent., of Cheston [Chediston], Suffolk. 3 mths recusancy from 8 Apr. 1587: conv. 27 Mar. 1588.—VIII(73).

NORTON, Walter, esq., of Cheston [Chediston], Suffolk. 9 mths recusancy from 29 Sept. 1581: conv. 18 July 1582.—VI(58): and two later convictions, ending 12 Sept. 1586.—VI(58)*. Lands seized & let by Crown to John Forrest from Ladyday 1589.—IX(64). X(63v). XII(66). John Forrest's lease: arrearage of rent (£30 debt).—XI(72v).

NORTON, Walter, gent., of Wereham, Norfolk. 6 mths recusancy from 6 Sept. 1585: conv. 21 Mar. 1585/6.—VI(25v).

NORTON, Walter, esq., of Wereham, Norfolk. 3 mths recusancy from 6 Jan. 1586/7: conv. 6 Apr. 1587.—VI(25v).

NORWOOD, Thomas, gent., of Great Stanmore, Middx. 3 mths recusancy from 1 July 1588: convicted 2 Dec. 1588.—IX(37).[218]

NUTTALL, Margaret, 'spinster', of York Castle, Yorks [prisoner]. 5 mths recusancy from 1 Jan. 1582/3: conv. 17 May 1583.—IV(21). Debt re-enrolled.—VI(22).

NUTTER, Robert, 'clericus', of St. George's parish, Southwark, Surrey [prisoner][219]. 5 mths recusancy from 17 Feb. 1586/7: conv. 17 July 1587.—IX(54).

NUTTNALL, Grace, [ ], of Swillond [Swilland], Suffolk. 9 mths recusancy from 13 July 1587: conv. 10 July 1588.—VIII(73). Debt re-enrolled.—X(64).

NYTINGALE, Ellen, 'spinster', of Charsfeild, Suffolk. 3 mths recusancy from 8 Apr. 1587: conv. 27 Mar. 1588.—VIII(73).

OGLES, Edward, 'yoman', of Duxbury, Lancs. 12 mths recusancy from 20 Sept. 1589: conv. 22 Mar. 1590/1.—X(38v).

OGLESTROPE, George, gent., of Gisley [? Guiseley], W.R. Yorks. 6 mths recusancy from 3 July 1587: conv. 18 Mar. 1588.—VIII(27).

---

217. Richard Norris (Cf. Anstruther I, pp. 254, 255.)
218. Thomas Norwood was three times convicted of recusancy between 18 Mar. and 24 Dec. 1582, (Cf. Jeaffreson I, pp. 122, 127, 129.) the first time being the earliest indictment issued in Middlesex in 1581 for this offence. These earlier convictions do not seem to have been certified to the Exchequer.
219. Robert Nutter (Cf. Anstruther I, pp. 259, 260.)

OGLETHORPE, Henry, gent., of Beal [or Beaghall], W.R. Yorks. Fine of 100 marks imposed by High Commissioners, 1582 – 3.—III(25). Debt re-enrolled.—V(23v). IX(22). XII(25v).

OGLETHORPE, Henry, gent., of Dripoole [Drypool Ward], parish of Swyne [Swine], Kingston-upon-Hull, E.R. Yorks. [prisoner]. [Pipe Roll entry under 'Kingston-upon-Hull']. 12 mths recusancy from 6 Aug. 1581: conv. 6 Aug. 1582.—II(29). Debt re-enrolled.—VI(22).

OKES, Emma, 'spinster', wife of Henry Okes, 'yoman', of Aylesham, Norfolk. 11 mths recusancy from 1 Aug. 1582: conv. 8 July 1583.— III(72v). Debt re-enrolled.—V(46v).

OLIVER, *alias* STONE, Thomas.

ONSLOWE, Katherine, wid., of Castleton [Chastleton], Oxfords., recusant. Lands seized 17 Apr. 1591 and let by Crown to Richard Ferris from 27 July 1591.—XII(54). See ANSLOWE, Katherine.

ORME, Richard, 'yoman', of Alchurche [Alvechurch], Worcs. 2 mths recusancy from 7 Apr. 1588: conv. 6 Mar. 1588/9.—IX(70v).

OVEINGTON, Joan, wid., of Exelbye [? Eppleby], N.R. Yorks. 13 mths recusancy from 3 Sept. 1586: conv. 4 Sept. 1587.—VIII(25v).

OWEN, Juliana, 'spinster', of Llantilio Pertholey, Mon. 5 mths recusancy from 24 Mar. 1586/7: conv. 13 Mar. 1587/8.—VIII(48v).

OWEN, Richard, esq., of Godstowe, Oxfords. Fine of £40 imposed 28 June 1577 by High Commissioners at consistory of St. Paul's Cathedral, London.—IV(29v).[220].

OWEN, Richard, esq., [of Godstowe, Oxfords]. 1 mth recusancy from 6 Sept. 1581: conv. at Old Bailey, London, 6 Oct. 1581.—I(45): and three later convictions ending 9 Apr. 1582.—I(45)*. Debts re-enrolled.—III(73v)*. VI(30)*. [Pipe Roll entries under 'Oxfords'].

OWEN, Richard, gent., of St. Bride's parish, Farringdon Ward Without, London. 3 mths recusancy from 18 Mar. 1580/1: conv. 28 July 1581[221]. [Pipe Roll entry under 'London'].—I(32v). Debt re-enrolled.—III(38v). V(35). VII(30v).

OWEN, Richard, gent., of Oxfordshire. Record of land-seizure, 21 Feb. 1587.—VIII(59v). Rental of lands seized in Oxfordshire (Wolvercote manor and Godstowe messuage).—VIII(14v). IX(50). X(57). XI(53). XII(53).

OWEN, Owene, Richard, 'yoman', of Llanllowell, Mon. 5 mths recusancy from 24 Mar. 1586/7: conv. 13 Mar. 1587/8.—VIII(49v).

OWEN, Owene, Margaret, his wife (same parish, recusancy period and conviction date).—VIII(49v).

OWEN, Owyn, Thomas, gent., of Elsfeild [Ellisfield], Hants.[222] 12 mths

---

220. Richard Owen answered the fine in rotulo 2 James I.

221. Richard Owen was a prisoner in the Fleet for 'matters of relgion'. He was discharged on 11 Nov. 1582. (Cf. CRS II, p. 229.)

222. Thomas Owen was committed to the Wood Street Counter in June 1586, until he gave surety for payment of his fines for hearing mass. He was still there in Nov. 1586, desiring to have his debt stalled in the Exchequer. (Cf. CRS II, pp. 252, 262, 265, 269.). Owen's lands at Ellisfield, near Basingstoke, Hants., were let by the Crown to William Style from Michaelmas 1588, but he held the lease only until Easter term 1589. (Cf. M.R., L.T.R., 31 Eliz., Easter Term, 'Recorda' section.)

recusancy from 16 Sept. 1582: conv. 7 Jan. 1583/4.—IV(53): and three later convictions, ending 29 Oct. 1586.—V(57)*. VII(53v), (54). Debts re-enrolled.—VI(54). VIII(68). Record of land-seizure, 22 Apr. 1588.—VIII(67v). Seized lands in Ellisfield let by Crown to William Style from Michaelmas 1588, @ £6 – 13 – 4 p.a.—VIII(68v).

PACKINGTON, Humphrey, gent., of London, *alias* of Chaddesley [Corbett], Worcs., recusant[223]. Crown Lease. Lands in Salop (*viz.* the manor and rectory of Dutton *alias* Ditton [Ditton Priors] and all lands pertaining to them in Dutton, Middleton, Dorrington, Pokesmore and Huddwick, in the tenure of John Markes, and a pasture called 'Powehede' in the parish of Hopton, Salop): also lands in Worcs. (*viz.* the manor or capital messuage of Harvington in the parish of Chaddesley Corbett). Seized for recusancy 2 Oct. 1591 and let by Crown to William Sebright, esq., from 25 Nov. 1591, for an annual rent of £26 – 13 – 4.—XII(64v).

PAGE, Jane, 'spinster', of St. John's parish 'at the end of Owse bridge', city of York [? prisoner][224]. 3 mths recusancy from 12 Apr. 1582: conv. ? July 1582.—II(8). Debt re-enrolled.—V(8). VII(8). IX(8).

PALMER, John, gent., of Shawe village, 1½ m. N. of Newbury, Berks. 3 mths from 25 Mar. 1580/1: conv. 26 June 1581.—I(11v). Debt re-enrolled.—III(33v). V(3v). VII(3v).

PALMER, John, gent., of Spene, village, 1½ m. N.W. of Newbury, Spyne [Speen], Berks[225]. 8 mths recusancy from 26 June 1581: conv. 26 Feb. 1581/2.—I(11v): and two later convictions, ending 24 Feb. 1583/4.—II(65v). IV(3v). Debts re-enrolled.—III(33v). V(3v). VI(3v). VII(3v)[225(a)] Palmer of Shawe had left prison by this date: Palmer of Speen was nearby free by Feb. 1583/4.

PALMER, Paulmer, John, gent., of St. Mary's parish, Reading, Berks. [prisoner][226] 8 mths in prison from 30 June 1582: convicted ? Feb. 1582/3.—II(65v): and six later convictions, ending ? Aug. 1586.—III(50v). IV(46). V(4v)*. VI(4v)*.

PALMER, John, gent., of Edmonton, Middx. 3 mths recusancy from 3 Oct. 1588: conv. 14 Feb. 1588/9.—IX(36v).

PALMER, Richard, 'yoman', of Edmonton, Middx. 3 mths recusancy from 20 Mar. 1587/8: conv. 28 June 1588.—IX(37).

PALMER, Simon, 'clericus', of the city of Winchester, Hants. [? prisoner][227]. 5 mths in prison from 6 May 1581: convicted ? Nov.

---

223. Humphrey Pakington (Cf. L. and V.A. Webster, 'The Pakingtons of Harvington', in *RH*, vol. 12, (1974), pp. 203 – 215, and Michael Hodgetts, 'Elizabethan Priest Holes IV—Harvington', in *RH*, vol. 13. (1975), pp. 18 – 55.)

224. Jane Page was a prisoner in York Castle. (Cf. CRS V, p. 194.)

225. John Palmer was a prisoner in Reading Castle. (Cf. CRS XXXII, p. 118.)

226. John Palmer's personal address is apparently omitted in this entry, and he is described as 'of Reading Castle'.

227. Simon Palmer an unidentified priest, also called 'Simon Parker' in the Pipe Rolls.

1581.—I(55). Debt re-enrolled.—III(62). 2 mths in prison ending 4 October 1581, when convicted.—V(56).

PALMER, Thomas, gent., of Halton, Bucks. 12 mths recusancy from 1 Apr. 1582: conv. 24 June 1583.—III(3): and one later conviction dated 18 Mar. 1587/8.—VIII(3). Debt re-enrolled.—V(2). VII(2v). Record of land-seizure in Herefords, 8 Apr. 1591 [Pipe Roll entry under 'Bucks'].—XI(3).

PALMER, William, 'yeoman', of Irtlingburghe [Irthlingborough], Northants. 12 mths recusancy ending 2 May 1587: conv. 12 Mar. 1587/8.—VIII(52v).

PALMES, John, esq., of Naburn, E.R. Yorks[228]. Fine of £100 imposed in his absence for 'contempt' towards the Archbishop of York and other High Commissioners, 2 Nov. 1585.—V(23v).

PALMES, Joan, wife of John Palmes, gent., of Nayborne [Naburn][229], E.R. Yorks. 2 mths recusancy from 4 Jan. 1585/6: conv. 14 Mar. 1585/6.—VI(20v).

PARKE, George, 'husb''', of Cople [Coppull], Lancs. 12 mths recusancy from 20 Sept. 1589: conv. 22 Mar. 1590/1.—X(38).

PARKER, Ann, 'spinster', of Stepney, Middx. 3 mths recusancy from 28 June 1587: conv. 1 Dec. 1587.—VIII(38v).

PARKER, Barbara, wife of James Parker, gent., of Drayton, Salop. 12 mths recusancy from 24 Feb. 1586/7: conv. 18 July 1588.—VIII(16v).

PARKER, Charles John, 'yoman', of Raglan, Mon. 5 mths recusancy from 24 Mar. 1586/7: conv. 13 Mar. 1587/8.—VIII(48).

PARKER, 'Christiana', 'spinster', of Llantilio Pertholey, Mon. (same recusancy period and conviction date).—VIII(48v).

PARKER, Jane, 'spinster', of Bettesneweth [Bettws Newydd], Mon. (same recusancy period and conviction date).—VIII(49v).

PARKER, Joan, lately of Marham, Norfolk, wife of Gawin Paris [sic] of same, 'yeoman'. 3 mths recusancy from 13 Apr. 1587: conv. 1 Apr. 1588.—VIII(54). See PARIS, Joan.

PARKER, Parkar, Roger, 'yom''', of Ferneley [? W.R.] Yorks. 5 mths recusancy from 1 Jan. 1582/3: conv. 17 May 1583.—IV(21). Debt re-enrolled.—VI(22).

PARKER, Roger, 'yom''',[230] of Yeatmister [Yetminster], Dorset. 6 mths recusancy from 1 Jan. 1587/8: conv. 15 July 1588.—VIII(19v).

PARKER, Simon, 'clericus', of the city of Winchester, Hants. [? prisoner]. 2 mths recusancy ending 16 May 1581, when convicted.—III(50).

PARKER, Parkar, William, 'miller', of Linton, Cambs. 10 mths recusancy from 1 Sept. 1586: conv. 24 Mar. 1587/8.—VIII(7v).

---

228. See footnote 6.
229. Joan Palmes was fined £40 on her belated appearance.
230. Roger Parker was a prisoner in the Wood Street Counter in 1586. His wife and family lived at Lisbon. He was regarded as a spy, and a carrier of letters beyond the seas; between Sept. 1586 and July 1587, at the time of the Babington Plot, it was noted how he frequented the company of priests and papists about London. (Cf. CRS II, pp. 260, 262, 264, 269.)

PARKINS, Ann, wife of Henry Parkins, gent., of East Illesley, Berks. 12 mths recusancy from 1 Sept. 1586: conv. 4 Mar. 1588.—VIII(5).

PARKINS, Perkins, Francis, gent., of Longford [Hanging Langford], Wilts. 3 mths recusancy from 2 Apr. 1587: conv. 1 Mar. 1587/8.—VIII(74v). Record of lands in Berks (capital messuage of Ufton, and lands in Padworth etc) seized 1 Sept. 1590.—X(10v). Rental of same lands.—XI(4). XII(4). Above seized lands in Berks (including Sulhampstead, Snowswick & Buscot), and in Wilts (including capital messuage of Bathampton) let by Crown to Thomas Purcell from 15 Dec. 1590.—XI(5v). XII(4).

PARKINSON, Margaret, 'spinster', of Whalley, Lancs. 12 mths recusancy from 20 Sept. 1589: conv. 22 Mar. 1590/1.—X(40).

PARKINSON, Richard, gent., of Aldburgh, Stanwick [St. John] parish, N.R. Yorks. 13 mths recusancy from 3 Sept. 1586: conv. 4 Sept. 1587.—VIII(25v).

PARKINSON, Robert, of Whalley, Lancs., son of Richard Parkinson, 'glover'. 12 mths recusancy from 20 Sept. 1589: conv. 22 Mar. 1590/1.—X(40).

PARRIS, Paris, Parrys, Eliz., 'spinster', of Marten [Merton], Norfolk. 3 mths recusancy from 13 Apr. 1587: conv. 1 Apr. 1588.—VIII(54).

PARRIS, Paris, Parrys, Ferdinand, esq., of Pudding Norton, Norfolk. 11 mths recusancy from 1 Aug. 1581: conv. 23 July 1582.—II(40): and two later convictions, ending 8 July 1583.—III(72v). V(41v). Summary of pre-1587 debts for recusancy (£833 – 6 – 8, remainder of £1,100, paid. Quit).—VII(40v). Annual fines for recusancy (£260) from 15 Oct. 1586: paid. Quit.—VII(40v). VIII(51). IX(43v). X(52v). XI(48). XII(47v).

PARRIS, Frances, wife of Ferdinand Parris, esq., of Linton, Cambs. 10 mths recusancy from 1 Sept. 1586: conv. 24 Mar. 1587/8.—VIII(7v).

PARRIS, Paris, Joan, wife of Gawin Paris, 'yeoman', of Marham, Norfolk. 3 mths recusancy from 13 Apr. 1587: conv. 1 Apr. 1588.—VIII(54). See PARKER, Joan.

PARTON, Robert, 'clericus', of Tamworthe [Tamworth], Staffs.[231] 8 mths recusancy from 22 July 1588: conv. 21 July 1589.—IX(69v).

PARTRIDGE, Partriche, Henry, [   ], of Sernefeld [Sarnesfield], Herefords. Two fines of £20 imposed for ignoring sheriff's summonses after excommunication, 4 Apr. and 27 May 1581.—III(28)*. Debts re-enrolled.—V(26), (26v).

PATYE, Robert, 'yom'', of Berryparke, parish of Ayskarth [Aysgarth], N.R. Yorks. 13 mths recusancy from 3 Sept. 1586: conv. 4 Sept. 1587.—VIII(25v).

---

231. Robert Parton an unidentified Staffordshire priest, possibly connected with the Fitzherbert family.

PAULETT, Pawlett, [Elizabeth], Lady, wid., of Crondall, Hants. Record of property-seizure, 8 Nov. 1588 (rents in Ellisfield & Preston Candover, Hants.)—IX(58). Rental of seized property.—IX(59v). X(68v). XI(59v). XII(60v). Chattels real, value £3 – 6 – 8, seized 1589.X(70v). See SCROOPE, Elizabeth, for conviction as recusant.

PAUNSFOOTE, Ann, wife of Richard Paunsfote, esq., of Hafeilde [? Hasfield], Gloucs. 5 mths recusancy from 26 Mar. 1587: conv. 11 Mar. 1587/8.—VIII(82).

PAVER, Ann, wid. [relict of Barnard Paver of Branton Grange, Yorks (? W.R.)]. 6 mths recusancy from 3 July 1587: conv. 18 Mar. 1587/8.—VIII(27). Record of annuity-seizure, 8 Apr. 1589 (issuing from three granges in W.R. Yorks., *viz.* Branton, Barrowby and Micklethwaite).—IX(22v). Rental of seized property (£8 – 17 – 10 p.a., payable by Thomas Tankard, esq., of Boroughbridge and Richard Beilbie, gent., of Micklethwaite).—IX(21v). X(21v). XI(24v). XII(23v). Seized property let by Crown to William Hunnis from 26 Mar. 1591.—XII(25v).

PAXETON, Emma, wife of Thomas Paxeton, 'husb'', of Wendlebury, Oxfords. 12 mths recusancy from 26 Sept. 1586: conv. 7 Mar. 1587/8.—VIII(35v).

PEACOCKE, Pecock, Joan, wife of William Peacocke, [   ], of Worminghurst, W. Sussex. 2 mths recusancy from 17 Apr. 1587: conv. 26 Feb. 1587/8.—VIII(63v).

PEARSON, William, 'yeoman', of Cottesford [Cottisford], Oxfords. 12 mths recusancy from 26 Sept. 1586: conv. 7 Mar. 1587/8.—VIII(35v).

PEASE, Isabel, wid., of Kippax, W.R. Yorks. 6 mths recusancy from 3 July 1587: conv. 18 Mar. 1587/8.—VIII(27).

PECKHAM, Sir George, knt, of St. Saviour's parish, Southwark, Surrey [prisoner][232]. 3 mths recusancy from 28 Jan. 1586/7: conv. 13 Feb. 1587/8.—VIII(63).

PEERS, John, gent., of Norwold [Northwold], Norfolk. 3 mths recusancy from 13 Apr. 1587: conv. 1 Apr. 1588.—VIII(54).

PENINGTON, Robert, junior, 'yoman', of Wigan, Lancs. 3 mths recusancy from 1 May 1588: conv. 17 Mar. 1588/9.—X(35).

PENKEVILL, Thomas, 'yom'', of London [prisoner][233]. 12 mths recusancy from 2 Jan. 1582: conv. 20 Jan. 1583/4.—IV(32v). Debt re-enrolled.—VI(34).

PENKEWELL, Mary, 'spinster', of St. Saviour's parish, Southwark, Surrey [prisoner][234]. 5 mths recusancy from 17 Feb. 1586/7: conv. 17 July 1587.—IX(54).

---

232. Sir George Peckham of Denham, Bucks., and his son, were imprisoned in the Clink in Sept. 1586. (Cf. CRS II, p. 257.)
233. Thomas Penkevill was imprisoned in the Poultry Counter in Apr. 1584; was removed to Newgate for hearing mass, 4 Oct. 1584; and was still there in 1588. (Cf. *CRS* II, pp. 238, 248, 252, 256, 270, 283).
234. Mary Penkewell was probably a prisoner in the Clink at Southwark.

PENN, Thomas, gent., of Penne [Penn], Bucks. 3 mths recusancy from 27 Mar. 1587: conv. 18 Mar. 1587/8.—VIII(3).

PENTES, Ellen, 'spinster', of Langford [Longford], Derbys. 10 mths recusancy from 9 Sept. 1586: conv. 22 Mar. 1587/8.—VIII(21).

PERKINS. See Parkins, Francis.

PERSALL, Charles, gent., of Hillesden, Bucks. 3 mths recusancy from 27 Mar. 1587: conv. 18 Mar. 1587/8.—VIII(3).

PETTIE, *alias* TAILER, Agnes, 'spinster', of Munckton [Monckton], Dorset. 6 mths recusancy from 2 Jan. 1587/8: conv. 15 July 1588.—VIII(19v).

PETTIT, Margaret, 'spinster', wife of Thomas Pettit, 'husb'', of West Wickham, Cambs. 10 mths recusancy from 1 Sept. 1586: conv. 24 Mar. 1587/8.—VIII(7v).

PHELIPPE, John, 'yom'', of Garwey [Garway], Herefords. Fine of 100 marks imposed for hearing Mass. Convicted at Hereford assizes 8 Aug. 1586.—VI(25).

PHELLIPPES, Alice, 'spinster', of St. Saviour's parish, Southwark, Surrey [? prisoner]. 5 mths recusancy from 17 Feb. 1586/7: conv. 17 July 1587.—IX(54).

PHILBE, Alice, wid., of St. Mary Magdalen parish, Oxford city. 12 mths recusancy from 26 Sept. 1586: conv. 7 Mar. 1587/8.—VIII(35v).

PHILLIPPE, Agnes, 'spinster', of St. Saviour's parish, Southwark, Surrey [? prisoner]. 5 mths recusancy from 17 Feb. 1586/7: conv. 17 July 1587.—IX(54).

PHILLIPPE, 'Alsona', 'spinster', of Llangattock vibon Avel, Mon. 5 mths recusancy from 24 Mar. 1586/7: conv. 13 Mar. 1587/8.—VIII(49v).

PHILLIPPE, Cicilia John, wife of Thomas Phillippe, [ ], of Tredunnock, Mon. (same recusancy period and conviction date).—VIII(49).

PHILLIPPE, Eliz., wid., of Skenfrith, Mon. (same recusancy period & conviction date).—VIII(48).

PHILLIPPE, Hoell David, 'yoman', of Llangattock vibon Avel, Mon. (same recusancy period and conviction date).—VIII(48v).

PHILLIPPE, Hugh, 'yoman', of Skenfrith, Mon. (same recusancy period and conviction date).—VIII(48v).

PHILLIPPE, James, 'yoman', of Usk, Mon. (same recusancy period and conviction date).—VIII(49).

PHILLIPPE, John David, 'yoman', of Llangattock vibon Avel, Mon. (same recusancy period and conviction date).—VIII(48v).

PHILLIPPE, John Richard, 'yoman', of Raglan, Mon. (same recusancy period and conviction date).—VIII(48).

PHILLIPPE, Margaret, 'spinster', of Bettws Newydd, Mon. (same recusancy period and conviction date).—VIII(49v).

PHILLIPPE, Margaret, 'spinster', of Raglan, Mon. (same recusancy period and conviction date).—VIII(48).

PHILLIPPE, Walter David, 'yoman', of Llanarth, Mon. (same recusancy period and conviction date).—VIII(48). Rental of lands seized

(? 24 Oct. 1588).—IX(42v). X(50). XI(45).

PHILLIPPE, 'Jonetta' Reignoldes, his wife (same parish, recusancy period and conviction date).—VIII(48).

PHILLIPPE, William, 'yoman', of Usk, Mon. (same recusancy period & conviction date).—VIII(49).

PHILLIPPE, William, 'yom''', of Danby in le forest, E.R. Yorks. 6 mths recusancy from 3 July 1587: conv. 18 Mar. 1587/8.—VIII(27).

PHILLIPPS, Richard, 'yoman', of Milwich, Staffs. 4 mths recusancy prior to 21 July 1589, when convicted.—IX(69v).

PHILLIPPS, Richard, 'yoman', of Newton, Salop. 12 mths recusancy from 24 Feb. 1586/7: conv. 18 July 1588.—VIII(16v).

PHILLIPPS, Robert [from Lincs.: Pipe Roll entry under 'London']. (?) of St. Bride's parish, Farringdon Ward Without, London [? prisoner]. 1 mth recusancy from 6 Sept. 1581: conv. [at Old Bailey, London]6 Oct. 1581.—I(35): and one later conviction dated 20 Dec. 1581.—I(35). Debts re-enrolled.—III(38v)*. V(35)*.

PHILLIPPS, Thomas, 'yom''', of Romsey, Hants. Fine of 100 marks imposed for hearing Mass. Convicted at Winchester Sessions of the Peace, 7 Jan. 1583/4.—IV(53). Debt re-enrolled.—VI(54).

PHILLIPS, William, 'yoman''', of Milwich, Staffs. 4 mths recusancy prior to 21 July 1589, when convicted.—IX(69v).

PHILLIPPS, William, gent., of Southwark, Surrey [prisoner][238]. 10 mths recusancy ending 11 Mar. 1582/3, when convicted.—IV(49v): and two later convictions, ending 15 Feb. 1583/4.—IV(49v)*. Debts re-enrolled.—VI(51)*.

PICKERINGE, Thomas, gent., of Crosthwaite, Westmorland. 1 mth recusancy from 3 May 1588: conv. 8 Aug. 1588.—IX(7v). Debt re-enrolled.—XI(71).

PIGOTT, Margaret, wife of Nicholas Pigott, gent., of Stokenchurch, Oxfords. 12 mths recusancy from 26 Sept. 1586: conv. 7 Mar. 1587/8.—VIII(35).

PIKE, George, 'yoman', of Islington, Middx. 3 mths recusancy from 3 Oct. 1588: conv. 14 Feb. 1588/9.—IX(36v).

PILCHER, Pylcher, Agnes, [   ], of Hooe, Sussex. 2 mths recusancy from 17 Apr. 1587: conv. 26 Feb. 1587/8.—IX(54v). Record of land-seizure, 17 Jan. 1589/90 (two-thirds of lands in Hooe recently belonging to David Pilcher, deceased).—IX(54v). Rental of seized lands.—X(65v). XI(55v). XII(56v).

PITTES, Pyttes, Margaret, wid., of Yestley [Iffley], Oxfords. 3 mths recusancy from 24 Mar. 1580/1: conv. 18 June 1581.—II(29v): and ten later convictions, ending 7 Mar. 1587/8.—II(29v)*. III(4). IV(29)*. V(47)*. VI(47v). VIII(35). Debts re-enrolled.—IV(29v). V(31v). VI(30v)*. VII(30v)*. Summary of three unpaid debts for recusancy,

---

238. William Phillipps was sent into the Marshalsea, 6 Nov. 1578, by the Privy Council, for 'papistry', and he was still there on 8 Apr. 1584. (Cf. *CRS* I, p. 70, and *CRS* II, pp. 231, 233, 235.)

dated 25 Feb. 1582/3 to 26 June 1585. Total £320.—IX(51). Debt re-enrolled.—XII(54v).

PLATER. See Playter.

PLATT, Oliver, 'smith', of Wigan, Lancs.[239] 3 mths recusancy from 10 Oct. 1581: conv. 18 Jan. 1581/2.—II(38v). Debt re-enrolled.—VIII(46).

PLATT, Oliver, 'blacksmith', of Salford in the parish of Manchester, Lancs. [prisoner][239]. 3 mths recusancy from 17 Jan. 1581/2: conv. 2 May 1582.—II(38v): and one later conviction, dated 22 Jan. 1583/4.—IV(37). Debts re-enrolled.—IV(42v). VI(39). VIII(46)*.

PLATT, Oliver, 'laborer', of Salford in the parish of Manchester, Lancs. [prisoner]. 4 mths recusancy from 2 Sept. 1582: conv. 16 Jan. 1582/3.—II(38v). Debt re-enrolled.—VIII(46).

PLAYTER, Plater, William, esq., of Saterley [Sotterley], Suffolk[240]. Four debts, covering 23 mths of recusancy:
(1) 9 mths recusancy from 3 July 1581. £182 – 9 – 6 paid into Treasury on 27 June 1584, by Robert Barney.
(2) 3 mths recusancy from 29 Mar. 1582. £103 paid into Treasury on 20 Nov. 1584, by Robert Barney.
(3) 3 mths recusancy from 1 Apr. 1583. £87 – 5 – 3 paid into Treasury on 23 June 1585, by Robert Barney.
(4) 8 mths recusancy from 7 July 1583. £87 – 5 – 3 paid into Treasury on 4 Feb. 1585/6, by Robert Barney.
The sum of these four debts amounted to £460. The final conviction was recorded on 9 Mar. 1585/6 at the Assizes held at Bury St. Edmunds. 'And he (William Playter) is quit'.—IV(57).

PLESINGTON, Ellen, wid., of Wesham, Lancs. 12 mths recusancy from 20 Sept. 1589: conv. 22 Mar. 1590/1.—X(39).

POKER, William, 'supposed recusant and fugitive', Staffs. Goods, value £22 – 10s, seized 4 Sept. 1589.—X(14).

POLE, John, 'yoman', of Alchurche [Alvechurch], Worcs. 2 mths recusancy from 7 Apr. 1588: conv. 6 Mar. 1588/9.—IX(70v). See POOLE, Edward.

POLLARD, Gregory, 'slaytmaker', parish of St. George, Colgate, Norwich city. 1 mth recusancy from 1 Nov. 1587: conv. ? Dec. 1587.—IX(10). Debt re-enrolled.—XI(12).

PONDE, John, 'clericus', of Southwark, Surrey [prisoner][241]. 1 mth recusancy ending 20 July 1584, when convicted.—V(52v): and one later conviction, dated 18 Feb. 1584/5.—V(52v). See POUNDE, Thomas, gent., (brother).

---

239. Oliver Platt was imprisoned in Wigan for three months from 10 Oct. 1581 to 18 Jan. 1582/3. He was then moved to Salford Gaol till 22 Mch. 1582/3, when he was given two periods of twelve months in gaol. (Cf. *CRS* V, pp. 23, 24.)

240. William Playter's relative, Robert Barney, between 27 June 1584 and 4 Feb. 1585/6, paid into the Treasury at the Assizes at Bury St. Edmunds, all four debts, totalling £460. For William Playter, (Cf. Alfred Suckling, *History and Antiquities of the County of Suffolk*, I, p. 86.)

241. John Pound (Cf. Anstruther I, p. 281.)

RECUSANTS 1581 – 1592   137

POOLE, Pole, Polle, Pooley, Poule, Powle, Powell, Edward, 'yom''', of Westminster, Middx [prisoner][242]. [Pipe Roll entry under 'Suffolk']. 3 mths recusancy from 27 June 1581: conv. 26 Sept. 1581.—II(55v): and four later convictions, ending 16 Mar. 1581/2.—II(55v)*. [Record of debts continued] 3 mths recusancy from 15 Mar. 1581/2: conv. 17 June 1582.—IV(57): and six later convictions, ending 17 Nov. 1583.—IV(57)*. Total, twelve debts. Final conviction at Old Bailey (gaol-delivery of Newgate) 20 Jan. 1583/4. Debts relegated to the Exchequer Exannual Roll.

POOLE, Ellen, 'spinster', of Spinkhill in parish of Gokington [Eckington], Derbys. 10 mths recusancy from 9 Sept. 1586: conv. 22 Mar. 1587/8.—VIII(21).

POOLE, Katherine, 'spinster', of Racton, Sussex. 2 mths recusancy from 17 Apr. 1587: conv. 26 Feb. 1587/8.—VIII(63v).

POOLEY, Philip, gent., of Boughton, Norfolk. 3 mths recusancy from 13 Apr. 1587: conv. 1 Apr. 1588.—VIII(54). See POOLE, Edward.

POORE, Prudence, wife of Francis Poore, esq., of Bechington [? Bletchington], Oxfords. 12 mths recusancy from 26 Sept. 1586: conv. 7 Mar. 1587/8.—VIII(35).

PORTER, Thomas, gent., of Mickleton, Gloucs. 5 mths imprisonment from 26 Mar. 1587: conv. 11 Mar. 1587/8.—VIII(82). Record of land-seizure in Mickleton, 14 Jan. 1588/9.—X(27v). Seized lands let by Crown to Thomas Keyes from 15 Feb. 1588/9.—IX(23). X(27).

PORTER, [   ], his wife (same parish, recusancy period and conviction date).—VIII(82).

PORTER, Thomas, gent., of Warbarrow [Warborough], Oxfords. 5 mths recusancy from 27 Feb. 1583/4: conv. 23 July 1584.—IV(29): and one later conviction, dated 5 Feb. 1584/5.—V(47). Debt re-enrolled.— VI(30v).

POTTER, George, 'clericus', of St. George's parish, Southwark, Surrey [prisoner][243]. 5 mths recusancy from 17 Feb. 1586/7: conv. 17 July 1587.—IX(54). [The Pipe Office Clerk confused George Potter with Ralph CROCKET[244] and Edward JAMES[245].]

POULE, see POOLE, Edward (priest); cf. Footnote[242].

POUNDE, Poundes, Pownde(s), Thomas, gent., of Farlington, Hants. 12 mths imprisonment from 3 Mar. 1588/9: convicted 17 Aug. 1590.

---

242. Edward Pole (Cf. Anstruther I, p. 279.)
243. George Potter (Cf. Anstruther I, pp. 337 – 339, under George Stransham).
244. Ralph Crockett (Cf. Anstruther I, pp. 93 – 94, and Richard Simpson, 'The Chichester Martyrs' in *The Rambler*, vol. 7, (1857), pp. 269 – 284.)
245. Edward James was martyred with Ralph Crockett. The payment of their escort still survives:— 'To John Puttrell, one of the messangers of H.M. Chamber, upon Warrant of 8 Nov. 1588, for charges in escorting four prisoners—two from the Clink (John Owen and Edward James) and two from the Marshalsea (Ralph Crockett and Francis Edwards)—to the sheriff of Surrey and Sussex at his house at Cranley (Cranleigh), Surrey, and from thence to Chichester, and there delivered two of the prisoners and returned with the other two to Horsham and there delivered them'. (Cf. Treasurer of the Chamber Accounts, E. 351/542, mem. 127v.) John Owen and Francis Edwards recanted.

Record of land-seizure in Hants, 29 Dec. 1590.—XI(61). Rental of lands seized in Sussex, 14 Jan. 1591/2.—XI(57). Rental of lands seized in Hants, 29 Dec. 1590.—XI(61). XII(60v). Seized lands in Hants, let by Crown to Francis Cotton from 20 Feb. 1590/1.—XII(62).

POWELL, 'Alsona', wife of Thomas Powell, [ ], of Llanthewy Skirrid, Mon. 5 mths recusancy from 24 Mar. 1586/7: convicted 13 Mar. 1587/8.—VIII(49).

POWELL, Edward, 'yom'', of St. Margaret's parish, Westminster [prisoner]. [Pipe Roll entry under 'Warwicks']. 1 mth in prison from 18 May 1581: conv. 26 June 1581.—I(62v). Debt re-enrolled.—III(69v). V(64v). See POOLE, Edward, and Footnote[242].

POWELL, George, 'yoman', of Tredunnock, Mon. 5 mths in prison from 24 March 1586/7: conv. 13 Mar. 1587/8.—VIII(49).

POWELL, Joan, wife of Watkin Powell, [ ], of Llanthewy Skirrid, Mon. (same recusancy period and conviction date).—VIII(49).

POWLE, see POOLE, Edward, and footnote[242].

POWLTHRELL, Cassandra, of West Hallam, Derbys., wife of Walter Powlthrell, esq. 10 mths imprisonment from 9 Sept. 1586: conv. 22 Mar. 1587/8.—VIII(21).

PRATT, Agnes, 'spinster', of Harrowden, Northants. 12 mths in prison ending 2 May 1587: conv. 12 Mar. 1587/8.—VIII(52v).

PREESTE, [ ], wid., of Filloughley [? Fillongley], Warwicks. 6 mths recusancy from 1 Sept. 1588: conv. 21 July 1589.—IX(11v).

PRESCOTTE, Ann, wid., of Shevington, Lancs. 12 mths imprisonment from 20 Sept. 1589: conv. 22 Mar. 1590/1.—X(38v).

PRESTON, John, gent., of Dreyton [Drayton], Salop. 12 mths recusancy from 24 Feb. 1586/7: conv. 18 July 1588.—VIII(16v). Record of land-seizure in Salop, 8 Apr. 1589.—IX(13v). Record of land-seizure in Salop & Staffs, 1 Apr. 1591.—XI(54v). Rental of lands seized 8 Apr. 1589.—IX(69v). X(59v). XI(62). XII(63). Rental of lands seized 1 Apr. 1591.—XI(54v). XII(63v). Chattels, value £13 – 6 – 8, seized 1 Apr. 1591.—XI(54v). Lands seized 8 Apr. 1589 let by Crown to Thomas Palgrave & John Murfyne from 2 Dec. 1590.—X(67). Lands seized 1 Apr. 1591 let by Crown to Griffin Price from 25 June 1591.—XII(64v).

PRICE, 'Aloicia' verch Watkin, wife of Thomas Powell Price, [ ], of Llanvetherine, Mon. 5 mths recusancy from 24 Mar. 1586/7: conv. 13 Mar. 1587/8.—VIII(49).

PRICE, Jane Harbert, wife of David Price, [ ], of Llanvihangel Kilcornell [Crucorney], Mon. (same recusancy period & conviction date).—VIII(48v).

PRICE, John, 'joyner', of Cholmondeley [nr. Malpas], Cheshire. 13 mths recusancy from 25 Sept. 1586: conviction date unstated.—VIII(58v).

PRICE, Margery, 'spinster', of Skenfrith, Mon. 5 mths recusancy from 24 Mar. 1586/7: conv. 13 Mar. 1587/8.—VIII(48v).

PRICE, Pryse, William, gent., of Southwark, Surrey [prisoner]. 4 mths recusancy ending 17 Feb. 1585/6, when convicted.—VI(49v).

PRICE *alias* DAVIE, Alice, wife of Richard Price *alias* Davie, 'yeom'', of Windlebury [Wendlebury], Oxfords. 12 mths recusancy from 26 Sept. 1586: conv. 7 Mar. 1587/8.—VIII(35v). See APRICE *alias* DAVIE, Richard.

PROBERT, Ann Somersett, wife of William Probert, [   ], of Tralleye [Trelleck], Mon. 5 mths recusancy from 24 Mar. 1586/7: conv. 13 Mar. 1587/8.—VIII(49).

PROBINE, Edward, 'yoman', of [Guilden] Sutton, Cheshire. 12 mths recusancy from 26 Sept. 1586: conv. 25 Sept. 1587.—VIII(58v).

PROBINE, Joan, Edward's wife[246] (same parish, —malpas—same recusancy period and conviction date).—VIII(58v).

PROBINE, Probyne, Edward, 'husb'', of Whichalgh [Malpas parish], Cheshire[247]. 13 mths recusancy from 25 Sept. 1586: conviction date unstated.—VIII(58v).

PROBINE, 'Ranus' [? Randle], 'yoman', of Malpas, Cheshire[248]. 12 mths recusancy from 26 Sept. 1586: conv. 25 Sept. 1587.—VIII(58v). See ROBYN, 'Gwenna'.

PROCTER, Alice, wid., of Gargrave, W.R. Yorks. 6 mths recusancy from 3 July 1587: conv. 18 Mar. 1587/8.—VIII(27). Record of land-seizure, 8 Apr. 1589.—IX(22v). Rental of seized lands (£8 – 17 – 10 p.a.).—IX(21v). X(21v). XI(24v). XII(23v).

PROCTER, Eliz., wid., of Winterborne [Winterburn], W.R. Yorks. 6 mths recusancy from 3 July 1587: conv. 18 Mar. 1587/8.—VIII(27).

PROCTER, Katherine, of Toresholme [Torrisholme, nr. Lancaster], Lancs., wife of Richard Procter, 'husb''. 12 mths recusancy from 20 Sept. 1589: conv. 22 Mar. 1590/1.—X(39v).

PROCTER, Mary, wid., of Winterborne, W.R. Yorks. 6 mths recusancy from 3 July 1587: conv. 18 Mar. 1587/8.—VIII(27).

PROGER, Prosser, John William John, [   ], of Aburgavenny, Mon. 5 mths recusancy from 24 Mar. 1586/7: conv. 13 Mar. 1587/8.—VIII(48). Record of land-seizure, 24 Oct. 1588.—IX(42v). Rental of seized lands (13s.4d. p.a.).—IX(42v). X(50). XI(45).

PROGER, Margaret Lawrens, his wife (same parish, recusancy period & conviction date).—VIII(48).

PROSSER, David Thomas, 'yoman', of Llantilio Pertholey, Mon. (same recusancy period and conviction date).—VIII(48v).

PROUDE, Eliz., 'spinster', of Marten [Merton], Norfolk. 12 mths recusancy from 10 July 1587: conv. ? July 1588.—IX(45): and one later conviction dated 7 July 1589.—IX(45v). Debts re-enrolled—XI(48)*.

---

246. Joan Probin was indicated for hearing mass in May 1582, and was imprisoned in Chester Castle, c. 1587. She had a series of convictions for recusancy until 1613. (Cf. Wark, pp.41, 45, 56, 67, 134, 162.)

247. Edward Probin, like his wife, was regularly indicted for hearing mass and recusancy after 1582. He was imprisoned in Chester Castle between 1592 and 1594, and again in 1598. (Cf. Wark, pp. 41, 45, 56, 65, 67, 82, 120, 134, 161.)

248. Randle Probin was imprisoned in Chester Castle in 1587. Mass had been said in his house, c.1580. (Cf. Wark, pp. 161 – 162.)

PUDSEY, Eliz., wid., of Barford [? Barforth] Dikes, in Gillinge parish, N.R. Yorks. 13 mths recusancy from 3 Sept. 1586: conv. 4 Sept. 1587—VIII(25v). Record of land-seizure, 10 Apr. 1589.—IX(8v). Rental of seized lands (£40 p.a.).—IX(21v). X(21v). XI(24v). XII(23v). Seized lands let by Crown to William Steare from 11 Oct. 1589.—X(13v). XI(24v). XII(23v).

PUDSEY, Frances, wife of Ambrose Pudsey, gent., of Arneforth (?), Yorks. 6 mths recusancy from 3 July 1587: conv. 18 Mar. 1587/8.—VIII(27).

PUDSEY, Helen, [   ], (of same place, same recusancy period and conviction date).—VIII(27).

PUDSEY, Katherine, [   ], (same place, recusancy period & conviction date).—VIII(27).

PULLAND, Isabel, wid., of Kippax, W.R. Yorks. 6 mths recusancy from 3 July 1587: conv. 18 Mar. 1587/8.—VIII(27).

PULLEYN, Samuel, [   ], of Killinghall, Ripley parish, W.R. Yorks. 13 mths recusancy from 3 Sept. 1586: conv. 4 Sept. 1587.—VIII(25v).

PURDEY, John, 'yoman', of St. Olave's parish, Southwark, Surrey. 3 mths recusancy from 25 Mar. 1588: conv. 6 Mar. 1588/9.—IX(53).

PURVEY, Mary, 'alias Okeley in comitatu predict' [Oakley], Beds., 'spinster'. 3 mths recusancy from 29 Mar. 1587: conv. 20 Mar. 1587/8.—VIII(1).

PYE, Pie, Matilda, 'spinster', of St. Peter's parish, Hereford city. 9 mths recusancy from 24 June 1583: conv. 2 Mar. 1583/4.—V(26v): and six later convictions, ending 27 Mar. 1587.—IV(64v)*. VI(25)*.

PYMOCK, Lettice, 'spinster', of Hanley Castle, Worcs. 6 mths recusancy from 29 Sept. 1587: conv. 25 July 1588.—VIII(80v).

PYNE, Katherine, 'spinster', of Whitechappell, Middx. 2 mths recusancy from 2 July 1589: conv. 3 Dec. 1589.—IX(37).

PYTTES, see PITTES, Margaret.

RABY, Alice, of Wesham, Lancs., wife of John Raby, 'husb''. 12 mths recusancy from 20 Sept. 1589: conv. 22 Mar. 1590/1.—X(39).

RADCLYFFE, Lady Ann, wid., of Crosthwaite, Cumberland. 1 mth recusancy from 3 May 1588: conv. 8 Aug. 1588.—IX(7v).

RAVENSCROFT, William, 'husb''', of Wetnal [Wettenhall] in parish of Over, Cheshire[249]. 13 mths recusancy from 25 Sept. 1586: conviction date unstated.—VIII(58v).

RAND, Rande, Joan, wid., of Somerton, Oxfords. 12 mths recusancy from 26 Sept. 1586: conv. 7 Mar. 1587/8.—VIII(35v).

RAND, Nicholas, 'yeom''', of Somerton, Oxfords (same recusancy period and conviction date).—VIII(35).

---

249. Wlilliam Ravenscroft was indicted for recusancy at the Chester Assizes 20 Sept. 1587. (Cf. Wark, pp. 67 footnote, 163.)

RAND, Katherine, his wife (same parish, recusancy period & conviction date).—VIII(35v).
RATLEY, Richard, gent., of Clarkenwell [Clerkenwell], Middx. 6 mths recusancy from 1 Oct. 1587: conv. 19 Apr. 1588.—IX(37).
RAWDEN, William, 'yom''', of Bransbye [Brandsby], N.R. Yorks. 6 mths recusancy from 3 July 1587: conv. 18 Mar. 1587/8.—VIII(25v).
RAWLEY, Margery, wid., of Wichnor [Wichenor], Staffs. 4 mths recusancy prior to 21 July 1589, when convicted.—IX(69v).
RAYLY, James, [ ], of Westby, Lancs. 12 mths recusancy from 20 Sept. 1589: conv. 22 Mar. 1590/1.—X(39v).
REASON, John, 'yom''', of Harlington, Middx[250]. 3 mths recusancy from 18 June 1582: conv. ? 23 Sept. 1582.—IV(32v). Debt re-enrolled.—VI(34).
REASON, John, 'yoman', of Westminster, Middx [prisoner][250]. 1 mth recusancy from 6 Oct. 1587: conv. 29 Jan. 1587/8.—VIII(38v).
REES, Lewis John, 'yoman', of Llantilio Pertholey, Mon. 5 mths recusancy from 24 Mar. 1586/7: conv. 13 Mar. 1587/8.—VIII(48v). Record of land-seizure, 24 Oct. 1588.—IX(42v). Rental of seized-lands (6s. 8d. p.a.).—IX(42v). X(50). XI(45).
REES, Matilda John, 'spinster' (same parish, recusancy period and conviction date).—VIII(48v).
REIGNOLDES, Edward Thomas, 'yoman', of Llanllowell, Mon. 5 mths recusancy from 24 Mar. 1586/7: conv. 13 Mar. 1587/8.—VIII(49v).
REIGNOLDES, Eliz., 'spinster' (same parish, recusancy period and conviction date).—VIII(49v).
REIGNOLDES, George, 'yoman', of Llanllowell, Mon. (same recusancy period and conviction date).—VIII(49v).
REIGNOLDES, James Thomas, 'yoman', of Llanllowell, Mon. 5 mths recusancy from 24 Mar. 1586/7: conv. 13 Mar. 1587/8.—VIII(49v). Record of land-seizure, 24 Oct. 1588.—IX(42). Rental of seized land (£1 – 6 – 8 p.a.).—IX(42v). X(50). XI(45). Seized lands let by Crown to Hugh Williams from 6 July 1590.—XI(45). XII(46).
REIGNOLDES, Elizabeth Kemes, his wife (same parish, recusancy period and conviction date).—VIII(49v).
REIGNOLDES, Jane, 'spinster' (same parish, recusancy period & conviction date).—VIII(49v).
REIGNOLDES, Morgan, 'yoman' (same parish, recusancy period & conviction date).—VIII(49v).
REIGNOLDES, Roger Thomas, 'yoman' (same parish, recusancy period & conviction date).—VIII(49v).
REIGNOLDES, William, 'yoman' (same parish, recusancy period & conviction date).—VIII(49v).

---

250. John Reason was a singing man and musical assistant to William Byrd, the composer, and Juliana, his wife, living near their house at Harlington, from 20 May 1581 to 1 Jan. 1586/7, when he and Mrs. Byrd were indicated on 13 occasions (twice together with William Byrd) for recusancy. (Cf. Jeaffreson I, pp. 123, 125, 128, 129, 143, 150, 156, 158, 163, 167.) He was committed to the Clink in Jan. 1583/4 for an unknown time. (Cf. *CRS* II, pp. 226 – 230.)

REVELL, Thomas, 'clericus', of Southwark, Surrey [prisoner][251]. 6 mths imprisonment ending 18 Feb. 1584/5, when convicted.—V(52v).

REYNES, Reignes, Andrew, [   ], of Barrowe-on-Sore [—Soar], Leics. 7 mths recusancy ending 10 Aug. 1587, when convicted.—VIII(45v). Goods, value £31 – 17 – 4, seized 26 Feb. 1588.—IX(41v). Rental of lands seized in Barrow, 26 Feb. 1588 (13s.4d. p.a.).—IX(41v).

REYNES, Margaret, his wife (same parish, recusancy period & conviction date).—VIII(45v).

REYNES, Nicholas, [   ], of Stanford [-upon-Soar], Notts. 3 mths recusancy from 10 Dec. 1589: conv. 30 Mar. 1590.—XI(51v). Goods, value £3 – 6 – 8, seized 4 Dec. 1590.—XI(51v). Record of land-seizure, 4 Dec. 1590.—XI(51v). Rental of seized lands (£6 – 13 – 4 p.a.).—XII(51).

REYNOLDES, Richard, 'yeoman', of Southwark, Surrey [prisoner][252]. 10 mths recusancy ending 11 Mar. 1582/3, when convicted.—III(58v): and four later convictions, ending 18 Feb. 1584/5.—IV(49v)*. V(50v), (52v). Debts re-enrolled.—V(52v)*. VI(51)*.

REYNOLDES, Reighnoldes, Richard, gent., of St. Botolph's parish, Bishopsgate Ward Without, London. Fine of 100 marks imposed for hearing Mass said on 30 Jan. 1585/6 by William Thompson in the house of Robert Bellamy (*q.v.*). Conv. at Old Bailey, 18 Apr. 1586.— VI(34v).

RICE, Alice, wife of Owen Rice, [   ], of Wonastow, Mon. 5 mths recusancy from 24 Mar. 1586/7: conv. 13 Mar. 1587/8.—VIII(48v).

ap RICE, Joan, 'spinster', of Lugwarden [Lugwardine], Herefords. 6 mths recusancy from 1 Sept. 1588: conv. 14 July 1589.—IX(25v). Debt re-enrolled.—XI(29). See APRICE. APPRICE.

RICHARD, Elinor Harry, wife of Philip John Richard, [   ], of Llanthewy Skirrid, Mon. 5 mths recusancy from 24 Mar. 1586/7: conv. 13 Mar. 1587/8.—VIII(49).

ap RICHARD, John, 'yom'', of Didlaston [Dudleston], Salop. 12 mths recusancy from 24 Feb. 1586/7: conv. 18 July 1588.—VIII(16v).

ap RICHARD, Thomas, 'yom'' (same parish, recusancy period and conviction date).—VIII(16v). Record of land-seizure, 8 Apr. 1589.— IX(13v). Rental of seized lands (6s.8d. p.a.).—IX(69v). X(59v). XI(62). XII(63). Seized lands let by Crown to Thomas Palgrave & John Murfyne from 2 Dec. 1590.—X(67).

verch RICHARD, Eleanor, 'spinster' (same parish, recusancy period & conviction date).—VIII(16v).

---

251. Thomas Revell's earlier career is sketched in Knox, pp. 9, 141, 145. He is listed in Anstruther I, p. 56, under his real name, 'Thomas Brown'. He was arrested at Islington and sent to the Clink in July 1585, the episode being described, and the 37 persons present being listed on the Exannual Roll (E. 363/9, under Surrey/Sussex V, 52*v*, 27 Eliz.)

252. Richard Reynoldes was imprisoned in the Marshalsea, 18 Feb. 1580/1, and was still there on 8 Apr. 1584. (Cf. *CRS* II, pp. 231, 233, 235.)

[surname omitted] Matilda, 'spinster', servant of Ellen verch Richard of Didlaston [Dudleston], Salop (same recusancy period and conviction date).—VIII(16v).

verch RICHARD, Eliz., 'spinster', of Llanvihangel Pontymoile, Mon. 5 mths recusancy from 24 Mar. 1586/7: conv. 13 Mar. 1587/8.—VIII(49).

verch RICHARD, Jennett, 'spinster' (same parish, recusancy period & conviction date).—VIII(49).

RICHARDES, Mary, 'spinster', of Newporte, Mon. (same recusancy period and conviction date).—VIII(49v).

RICHARDSON, Peter, 'yoman', of Clapham, Sussex. 3 mths recusancy from 1 Apr. 1588: conv. 3 Mar. 1588/9.—IX(53).

RIDGE, Rydge, John, 'yom'', of Southwark, Surrey [prisoner][253]. 4 mths (£80) recusancy ending 22 July 1583, when convicted.—IV(49v). Debt re-enrolled.—VI(51).

RIGBY, Rigbye, Edward, 'yoman', of Standish [nr. Wigan], Lancs. 12 mths recusancy from 20 Sept. 1589: conv. 22 Mar. 1590/1.—X(38v).

RIGBY, Jenetta, 'spinster', of Westby, Lancs. (same recusancy period and conviction date).—X(39v).

RIGMADEN, Regmaden, Ann, of Weddecar [Wedacre], Lancs., wife of Walter Rigmaden, esq. 12 mths recusancy from 20 Sept. 1589: conv. 22 Mar. 1590/1.—X(39).

RIGMADEN, John, esq., of Wedaker manor [nr. Garstang], Lancs. 4 mths recusancy from 18 Mar. 1580/1: conv. Summer 1581.—VI(40v). Debt re-enrolled.—VIII(21v). Record of land-seizure in Wedaker and Garstang, 24 Oct. 1587.—X(36). Rental of seized lands (£137 – 8 – 10 p.a.).—X(40v). XIII(44). [Discharge reference—[254]]. Seized property (a mill in Garstang) let by Crown to John Sankey, gent., from 1 May 1588.—X(35), (36) [Discharged as above]. Goods, value £254, seized 24 Oct. 1587.—X(36), (40v). Goods, value £49 – 6 – 8, seized and paid 10 June 1589 [In this entry Rigmaden is described as 'defunct''].—VIII(21v).

RIPINGALL, Agnes, wife of John Ripingall, 'yeoman', of Rigboroughe [Ryburgh] Magna, Norfolk. 3 mths recusancy from 13 Apr. 1587: conv. 1 Apr. 1588.—VIII(54).

RISSHETON, Ryssheton, Agnes, of Churche, Lancs., wife of John Rissheton, 'husb''. 12 mths recusancy from 20 Sept. 1589: conv. 22 Mar. 1590/1.—X(40).

RISSHETON, Eliz., 'spinster', daughter of John Rissheton, 'husb'' (same parish, recusancy period and conviction date).—X(40).

RISSHETON, Ryssheton, Eliz., of Burnley, Lancs., wife of Geoffrey Rissheton, gent. (same recusancy period and conviction date).—X(40).

---

253. John Ridge was imprisoned in the Marshalsea from 9 Dec. 1580, and was still there on 8 Apr. 1584. (Cf. CRS II, pp. 231, 233, 235.)

254. John Rigmarden was discharged in 1588. (Cf. M.R., L.T.R., 30 Eliz., Hilary Term, 'Recorda' section.)

RISSHETON, Ryssheton, John, 'husb'', of Churche [nr. Accrington],
   Lancs. (two convictions)[1] 13 mths recusancy from 30 July 1587:
   conv. 17 Mar. 1588/9. [2] 12 mths recusancy from 20 Sept. 1589: conv.
   22 Mar. 1590/1.—X(35), (40). See RUSHTON.
ROBENETT, Jasper, 'yoman', of Racton, Sussex. 2 mths recusancy from
   17 Apr. 1587: conv. 26 Feb. 1587/8.—VIII(63v).
ROBERT, Thomas, 'laborer', of Raglan, Mon. 5 mths recusancy from
   24 Mar. 1586/7: conv. 13 Mar. 1587/8.—VIII(48).
ROBERTES, Edward, 'yoman', of Cumberton [Comberton], Worcs. 2 mths
   recusancy from 7 Apr. 1588: conv. 6 Mar. 1588/9.—IX(70v).
ROBERTES, William, 'yoman' of Didlaston [Dudleston], Salop. 12 mths
   recusancy from 24 Feb. 1586/7: conv. 18 July 1588.—VIII(16v).
ROBERTES, *alias* DOUGHTIE, Jane, 'spinster', of Benham [Bentham],
   W.R. Yorks. 13 mths recusancy from 3 Sept. 1586: conv. 4 Sept.
   1587.—VIII(25v).
ROBINSON, Ellen, wid., of Bunbury, Cheshire[255]. 12 mths recusancy from
   26 Sept. 1586: conv. 25 Sept. 1587.—VIII(58v).
ROBINSON, John, 'yom'', of Addington, W.R. Yorks. 6 mths recusancy
   from 3 July 1587: conv. 18 Mar. 1587/8.—VIII(27).
ROBINSON, Robynson, Ralph, 'yoman', of Gonnerside [Gunnerside],
   Grinton parish, N.R. Yorks. 13 mths recusancy from 3 Sept. 1586:
   conv. 4 Sept. 1587.—VIII(25v).
ROBINSON, Richard, 'yoman', of Westby, Lancs. 12 mths recusancy from
   20 Sept. 1589: conv. 22 Mar. 1590/1.—X(39v).
ROBINSON, William, 'taleor', (same parish, recusancy period and
   conviction date).—X(39v).
ROBINSON, Robynson, [   ], wid., of Magna Marseden [Great Marsden,
   Whalley parish], Lancs., relict of Robert Robynson, [   ] (same
   recusancy period and conviction date).—X(40).
ROBYN, 'Gwenna', wid., of Wichalgh, Malpas parish, Cheshire[256]. 13 mths
   recusancy from 25 Sept. 1586: conviction date unstated.—VIII(58v).
   See PROBINE.
ROCK, Henry, gent., of St. Mary's parish, Reading, Berks [? prisoner]. 2
   mths recusancy from 28 Apr. 1585: conv. 24 June 1585.—V(4v).
ROCKES, Henry, gent., of Swyncombe, Oxfords. 5 mths recusancy from 24
   Feb. 1585/6: conv. 25 July 1586.—VI(47v). See ROOKES, Henry.
ROCKBY, see ROOKBY, John.
ROFFE, Alice, wid., of St. Bride's parish, Farringdon Ward Without,
   London. 13 mths recusancy from 19 Jan. 1586/7: conv. 19 Jan.
   1587/8.—VIII(38v).

---

255. Ellen Robinson was indicted for recusancy at the Quarter Sessions at Chester in May 1582 and May 1584. She appeared to conform in Oct. 1585, but was imprisoned in Chester Castle, c. 1587. (Cf. Wark, pp. 56, 67, 163.)

256. Gwen Probin (Robyn) was indicated for recusancy at the Assizes at Chester in Sept. 1587. (Cf. Wark, pp. 67, 162.)

ROGERLEY, Margaret, of Preese [nr. Kirkham], Lancs., wife of George Rogerley, gent. 12 mths recusancy from 20 Sept. 1589: conv. 22 Mar. 1590/1.—X(39).

ROGERLEY, Margaret, wife of Roger Rogerley, gent., of Weeton, Kirkham parish, Lancs. 13 mths recusancy from 14 Aug. 1586: conv. 25 Mar. 1588.—VIII(21v): and one later conviction, dated 22 Mar. 1590/1.—X(39).

ROGERS, Edward, gent., and Alice, his wife [Pipe Roll entry under 'London'] owe 100 marks for hearing Mass said on 7 Jan. 1581/2 by Edward Osborne[257] in the Fleet Prison, parish of St. Bride, Farringdon Ward Without, London.—I(32v). II(30v)[258].

ROOKBY, Rockby, Roobie, John, esq., of Moreton [Mortham], Rokebie [Rokeby] parish, N.R. Yorks. 13 mths recusancy from 3 Sept. 1586: conv. 4 Sept. 1587.—VIII(25v). Record of land-seizure, 10 Apr. 1589.—IX(8v). Rental of seized lands (£4 – 8 – 10 p.a.).—IX(21v). X(21v). XI(24v). Seized lands in Mortham let by Crown to Laurence Dutton from 4 Apr. 1590.—XI(24). XII(23v).

ROOKES, Henry, gent., of [   ], Oxfords. 8 mths recusancy from 25 July 1586: conv. 17 Mar. 1586/7.—VI(11v). See ROCKES, Henry.

ROOKWOOD, Rookewood, Edward, esq., of Besthorpe, Norfolk. 6 mths recusancy from 1 Jan. 1581/2: conv. (?) July 1582[259].—IV(44v).

ROOKWOOD, Rookewood, Edward, esq., of Ewston [Euston], Suffolk. Summary of pre-1587 debts for recusancy (Jan. 1581/2 to Oct. 1586). Total £940. Paid by 28 Nov. 1589.—VII(58v). Annual fines for recusancy (£260): first payment covering the period 7 Oct. 1586 to 6 Oct. 1587.—VII(58v). VIII(73). IX(63v). X(63v). XI(66). XII(66v).

ROOKWOOD, Rookewood, Robert, esq., of Stannyngfeld [Stanningfield], Suffolk. 7 mths recusancy from 12 Sept. 1586: conv. 5 Apr. 1587.—VI(58). Record of land-seizure, 2 Nov. 1587.—VIII(72). Rental of seized lands (£76 – 1 – 2 p.a.).—IX(63). X(63). XI(65). Arrearage of rent.—XII(67). Seized lands let by Crown to Thomas Keys and Thomas Stowe from Michaelmas 1589.—X(64). XI(65v). XII(66).

ROOKWOOD, Rookewood, Dorothy, his wife (of same parish). 3 mths recusancy from 8 Apr. 1587: conv. 27 Mar. 1588.—VIII(73).

ROOKWOOD, Rookewood, Thomas, gent., of Great Shelford, Cambs. 10 mths recusancy from 1 Sept. 1586: conv. 24 Mar. 1587/8.—VIII(7v).

ROSKOWE, Margaret, 'spinster', of Charnock Richard, Lancs. 12 mths recusancy from 20 Sept. 1589: conv. 22 Mar. 1590/1.—X(38v).

ROSKOWE, Margery, 'spinster', (same parish, recusancy period and conviction date).—X(38).

---

257. Edward Osborne (Cf. Anstruther I, pp. 261, 262.)
258. Edward Rogers and Alice, his wife, were prosecuted for hearing mass said by Edward Osborne in the Fleet Prison, on the information of Osborne himself. He also reported three other prisoners. (Cf. Godfrey Anstruther, *Vaux of Harrowden*, (1953), pp. 141 – 143.)
259. The sum (£120) discharged by fine and payment under 'Euston, Suff'., Cf. VII(58v)

ROSSE, Roose, Richard, 'clericus', of St. Margaret's parish, Westminster [prisoner][260]. [Pipe Roll entry under 'Cumberland'] 1 mth recusancy from 18 May 1581: conv. 26 June 1581—I(7v). Debt re-enrolled—IX(7v).

ROSSE, Roose, Richard, 'clericus', of St. Margaret's parish, Westminster [Pipe Roll entries under 'London']. 3 mths recusancy from 26 June 1581: conv. 26 Sept. 1581—III(42): and nine later convictions, ending 23 Sept. 1583—III(42)*. IV(32v)*. V(35)*. VI(34)*.

ROSSECARROCK, Trevenor, gent., of 'Newe Inne', Middx. 12 mths recusancy from 2 Jan. 1582/3: conv. 20 Jan. 1583/4—IV(32v). Debt re-enrolled—VI(34). Fine of 100 marks imposed for hearing Mass on 1 Dec. 1583 in St. Bride's parish, Farringdon Ward Without, London. Convicted at Old Bailey, 20 Jan. 1583/4[261]—IV(32v). Debt re-enrolled—VI(34).

ROSSER, Ann verch David, wife of Thomas William Rosser, [ ], of Raglan, Mon. 5 mths recusancy from 24 Mar. 1586/7: conv. 13 Mar. 1587/8—VIII(48).

ROSSER, Matilda, wife of Morgan Rosser, [ ], of Llanvihangel Ystern Llewern, Mon. (same recusancy period & conviction date)—VIII(49v).

ROWLAND, Ann, 'spinster', of Cottesford, Oxfords. 12 mths recusancy from 26 Sept. 1586: conv. 7 Mar. 1587/8—VIII(35v).

ROWSE, Ann, wid., of Dinnington [Dennington], Suffolk. 3 mths recusancy from 8 Apr. 1587: conv. 27 Mar. 1588—VIII(73). Goods, value £15 – 15s., seized 7 Oct. 1588—IX(64). Rental of lands seized 7 Oct. 1588 (£20 p.a.)—IX(64). Seized lands let by Crown to Edward Androwes from 28 Jan. 1588/9—IX(64). X(63v). XI(65v). XII(66).

ROWSE, Anthony, gent., of Dennington, Suffolk. 3 mths recusancy from 1 Jan. 1587/8: conv. 10 July 1588—VIII(73). Debt re-enrolled—X(64).

ROWSHAM, Stephen, 'clericus', of Southwark, Surrey [prisoner][262]. 6 mths recusancy ending 18 Feb. 1584/5, when convicted—V(52v). See RUSSHAM, Stephen.

ROYDON, Edward [*sic*, for Edmund], gent., of Gretton, Northants. 12 mths recusancy from 16 Apr. 1587: conv. 4 Mar. 1588/9—IX(47v).

ROYDON, [ ], 'father of the said Edmund', of Gretton, Northants (same recusancy period and conviction date)—IX(47v).

ROYDON, Edmund, recusant [Pipe Roll entry under 'Northants']. Goods, value £2, seized 6 Oct. 1590—X(55).

---

260. Richard Rosse, 'an ould massing priest' was a prisoner in the Gatehouse, sent there by the Bishop of London and the High Commissioners. He was still there on 8 Apr. 1584. (Cf. *CRS* II, pp. 225, 230, 235.)
261. Trevenor Rossecarrock was a prisoner in the Tower of London in 1581, and in Newgate from Jan. 1583/4. (Cf. *CRS* II, pp. 220, 229, 237.)
262. Stephen Rownsham (Cf. Anstruther I, pp. 296, 297.)

ROYLEY, Alice, 'spinster', of Leigh, Staffs. 4 mths recusancy prior to 21 July 1589, when convicted—IX(69v).

ROYSTON, Edward, gent., recusant, of Kridlinge [Cridling] Stubbs, W.R. Yorks. [Recusancy period and conviction date omitted in the Pipe Rolls[263]]. Record of land-seizure (in Pontefract and Hamphall Stubbs, W.R. Yorks)—for pre-1587 recusancy of eight months—at a rent of £6 – 16 – 8 p.a.—XII(24).

RUDBYE, see RUGBY, John.

RUDD, Dorothy, wife of Edward Rudd, gent., of Killinghall, Ripley parish, W.R. Yorks. 13 mths recusancy from 3 Sept. 1586: conv. 4 Sept. 1587—VIII(25v).

RUDSTONE, Martin, gent., of Heyton [Hayton], E.R. Yorks. 6 mths recusancy from 3 July 1587: conv. 18 Mar. 1587/8—VIII(25v).

RUGBY, Rudbye, John, gent. [Pipe Roll entry under 'Yorks'][264]. 1 mth recusancy from 20 Jan. 1581/2: conv. 20 Mar. 1581/2—I(21v). Debt re-enrolled—III(24). V(22). VII(22v). IX(22). XII(26).

RUGBY, Rudbye, John, gent., of St. Bride's parish, Farringdon Ward Without, London [prisoner]. 7 mths recusancy from 13 June 1582: conv. 18 Jan. 1582/3—II(22v). Debt re-enrolled—VI(22).

RUSHTON, Edward, 'clericus', of St. Margaret's parish, Westminster, Middx [prisoner][265]. [Pipe Roll entry under 'Northants'] 1 mth recusancy from 18 May 1581: conv. 26 June 1581—I(42v). Debt re-enrolled—III(48v). V(43v). VII(43v).

RUSHTON, Ellen, wid., of Parkehill, Whalley parish, Lancs. 12 mths recusancy from 20 Sept. 1589: conv. 22 Mar. 1590/1—X(38v). See RISSHETON.

RUSSELL, Eliz., wife of John Russell, gent., of Welland, Worcs. 6 mths recusancy from 29 Sept. 1587: conv. 25 July 1588—VIII(80v).

RUSSELL, Jane, wife of Richard Russell, 'yoman', of Harting, Sussex. 2 mths recusancy from 17 Apr. 1587: conv. 26 Feb. 1587/8—VIII(63v).

RUSSHAM, Stephen, gent., [Priest: Martyr], of Southwark, Surrey [prisoner]. 4 mths recusancy ending 20 July 1584, when convicted—V(50v). See ROWSHAM, Stephen, 'clericus'.

RUTLAND, Joan, 'spinster', of St. Saviour's parish, Southwark, Surrey. 3 mths recusancy (period undated): conv. 5 July 1588—VIII(63).

RUTTERFEILD, John, 'scolemaster', of Sutton, Prescott parish, Lancs. 13 mths recusancy from 30 July 1587: conv. 17 Mar. 1588/9—X(35).

SADLER, John, 'yom'', of Thorolbye [Thoralby], parish of Askarth [Aysgarth], N.R. Yorks. 13 mths recusancy from 3 Sept. 1586: conv. 4 Sept. 1587—VIII(25v).

---

263. A most exceptional omission.
264. John Rugby of Danby, Yorks., was a prisoner in the Fleet in 1582. (Cf. *CRS* II, pp. 223, 229.)
265. Edward Rushton (Cf. Anstruther I, pp. 290–292, under Rishton.)

SADLER, Margaret verch Morgan, wife of Robert Sadler, [   ], of Aburgavenny, Mon. 5 mths recusancy from 24 Mar. 1586/7: conv. 13 Mar. 1587/8—VIII(48).

SAGER, Edward, 'scolemaster', of Dinckeley, Lancs. 12 mths recusancy from 20 Sept. 1589: conv. 22 Mar. 1590/1—X(40v).

SAGER, Stephen, 'goldsmythe', of Wiswell, Lancs. (same recusancy period & conviction date)—X(40).

SAGER, *alias* HARRYSON, Christopher, 'husb'', of Whalley, Lancs. (same recusancy period & conviction date)—X(40).

ST. JOHN, Frances, wife of Henry St. John, gent., of Hockering, Norfolk. 3 mths recusancy from 13 Apr. 1587: conv. 1 Apr. 1588—VIII(54).

SALE, John, gent., of Worsall, N.R. Yorks. 6 mths recusancy from 3 July 1587: conv. 18 Mar. 1587/8—VIII(25v). See SAYER, John.

SALISTEN, George, 'clericus', of Newington, Surrey [prisoner][266]. 11 mths recusancy ending 17 Feb. 1585/6, when convicted—VI(49v).

SAMPSON, Richard, 'yoman', of Newington, Surrey [prisoner][267]. 6 mths recusancy ending 18 Feb. 1584/5, when convicted—V(52v). See SIMPSON, Richard, gent.

SAMPSON, Richard, 'yoman'/gent., of Southwark, Surrey [prisoner][268]. 4 mths recusancy ending 11 Mar. 1582/3, when convicted—IV(49v): and four later convictions ending 16 Feb. 1586/7, when convicted—IV(49v)*. V(50v). VI(50). Debts re-enrolled—VI(51)*.

SAMPSON, Thomas, 'clericus', of St. George's parish, Southwark, Surrey [prisoner][269]. 5 mths recusancy from 17 Feb. 1586/7: conv. 17 July 1587—IX(54).

SANDALL, Robert, gent., of Sheringham, Norfolk. 3 mths recusancy from 13 Apr. 1587: conv. 1 Apr. 1588—VIII(54).

SANDELAND, Isabel, wife of William Sandeland, 'yeoman', of 'the county of Worcester' [? Hanley Castle]. 12 mths recusancy from 20 Sept. 1586: conv. 28 Mar. 1588—VIII(77).

SANDELL, Anthony, 'yoman', of Cumberton [Comberton], Worcs. 2 mths recusancy from 7 Apr. 1588: conv. 6 Mar. 1588/9—IX(70v).

SANGWYN, Eleanor, wife of John Sangwyn, 'husb'', of Inglefeild [Englefield], Berks. 4 mths recusancy from 1 Nov. 1587: conv. 1 July 1588—VIII(5).

SAUNDER(S), Erasmus, gent., of St. Bride's parish, Farringdon Ward Without, London [prisoner][270]. [Pipe Roll entry under 'London'] 3 mths recusancy from 18 Mar. 1580/1: conv. (Old Bailey) 28 July 1581—I(32v). Debt re-enrolled—III(38v). V(35).

---

266. George Salisten (Cf. Anstruther I, p. 85, under Collinson.)
267. Richard Sampson was committed to the White Lion by the Bishop of London in July 1580. (Cf. *CRS* I, p. 69.) He was still there in Mar. 1583/4, on 8 Apr. 1584, and in 1598 after 19 years in gaol. (Cf. *CRS* II, pp. 234, 237, 255, 271, 283, 287.)
268. Probably the same man as in the previous note, but the description, 'of Southwark, Surrey' usually refers to the Marshalsea, and the Prison Lists never connect him with that prison.
269. Thomas Sampson (Cf. Anstruther I, pp. 317–318, under Simpson.)
270. Erasmus Saunders was born in 1575 and lived, until Apr. 1592, at Revingham in Norfolk. (Cf. Anstruther I, p. 300.)

SAUNDER(S), Erasmus, esq., (of same London parish: prisoner) [Pipe Roll entry under 'Wales'] 1 mth recusancy from 7 Dec. 1581—IV(63v): and two later convictions, ending Jan. 1582/3—IV(63v), (38v). Debt re-enrolled—VI(64v)*.[270]

SAUNDER(S), Erasmus, gent., of Clarkenwell [Clerkenwell], Middx. 3 mths recusancy from 3 Oct. 1588: conv. 14 Feb. 1588/9—IX(36v).

SAUNDERS, Eliz., 'spinster', of Alton, Hants. 2 mths recusancy ending 16 May 1581, when convicted—V(56).[271]

SAUNDERS, Eliz., 'spinster', of St. Clement's parish, Winchester, Hants.[271] [prisoner]. 5 mths recusancy ending 30 Sept. 1581, when convicted—I(55)*: and two later convictions, ending 9 Jan. 1581/2 and 24 Apr. 1582—III(50v). Debts re-enrolled—III(62)*.

SAVELL, Savile, Mary, [ ], of Dalton [? Darton], W.R. Yorks. 6 mths recusancy from 3 July 1587: conv. 18 Mar. 1587/8—VIII(25v). Goods, value £6, seized 8 Apr. 1589—IX(22v). Record of land-seizure, 8 Apr. 1589 (property in Kikesborough [Kexbrough], with the Spring Wood)—IX(22v). Rental of seized lands (£28 – 17 – 9 p.a.)—IX(21v). X(21v). XI(24v). XII(23v).

SAXTON, see SEXTON.

SAYER, John, esq., of Worsall, N.R. Yorks. 6 mths recusancy from 3 July 1587: conv. (at York Castle) 18 Mar. 1587/8 [£120 paid, 28 Nov. 1588. Quit]; and one later month of recusancy from 9 Aug. 1588 to 10 Sept. next [£20 paid, 2 Dec. 1588. Quit]—VIII(11v)*. Annual fines for recusancy (£260). First payment, covering the period 16 Sept. 1588 to 15 Sept. 1589—IX(20v). Paid. (refs to succeeding years:) X(21v). XI(25v). XII(11v).

SCLATER, Agnes, 'spinster', of Burnley, Lancs. 12 mths recusancy from 20 Sept. 1589: conv. 22 Mar. 1590/1—X(40).

SCOTT, Edward, gent., of Iden, Sussex[272]. 2 mths recusancy from 17 Apr. 1587: conv. 26 Feb. 1587/8—VIII(63v).

SCOTT, Scotte, Eliz., 'spinster', of Iden, Sussex (same recusancy period and conviction date)—VIII(63v).

SCOTTE, Ralph, 'clericus'/priest ('sacerdos'), of Salford, in the parish of Manchester, Lancs [prisoner][273]. 3 mths imprisonment from 10 Oct. 1581: convicted 18 Jan. 1581/2—II(38v): and three later convictions, ending 22 Feb. 1583/4[274]—II(38v)*. IV(37)[275]. Debt re-enrolled—IV(42v). VI(39). VIII(46)*.

---

271. Elizabeth Saunders, a nun of Sion, sister of Dr. Nicholas Sanders, visited England in 1580 from her convent in Rouen. She was arrested at Alton, Hants., the home of William Pitts, in Nov. 1580, and imprisoned in Winchester Gaol. She remained there until May 1587, when she returned home. (Cf. Foley III, p. 65.)

272. Edward Scott was imprisoned in the Gatehouse, 14 Sept. 1586. (Cf. *CRS* II, p. 259.)

273. Ralph Scott was a prisoner in Salford Gaol, 28 Feb. 1582/3. (Cf. *CRS* V, pp. 23, 24.)

274. The Exannual Rolls of the Exchequer, (E. 363/9) beginning in 1581 until 1634/5, give details of all Lancashire convictions.

275. Ralph Scott was convicted with seven other recusants, three of them women, on 18 Jan. 1581/2, and with nine, nineteen and twenty three respectively, in his four convictions.

SCOTTE, William, gent., of Southwark, Surrey [prisoner][276]. 4 mths recusancy ending 11 Mar. 1582/3, when convicted—IV(49v). Debt re-enrolled—VI(51). Goods, value £19 – 16 – 8, seized by Walter Covert, sheriff of Surrey/Sussex: Michaelmas 1584—X(67).

SCROGGES, Eliz., wife of Oliver Scrogges, gent., of Reignold [Renhold], Beds. 3 mths recusancy from 29 Mar. 1587: conv. 20 Mar. 1588—VIII(1).

SCROGGES, Eliz., wife of Richard Scrogges, gent., (same parish, recusancy period and conviction date)—VIII(1).

SCROOPE, Scrope, Eliz. ('lately called Elizabeth Paulett'), wid., of Crondall, Hants. 10 mths recusancy from 12 Sept. 1586: conv. 25 Feb. 1586/7—VIII(67). See Paulett, Lady.

SCROOPE, Katherine, wid., of Litlehorton, parish of Gilling, N.R. Yorks. 4 mths recusancy from 14 May 1587: conv. 4 Sept. 1587—VIII(25v).

SCROOPE, Scrope, Nicholas, gent., of Itchen Stoke, Hants. 18 mths recusancy from 18 Mar. 1580/1: conv. 24 Apr. 1582—III(50v): and four later convictions, ending 8 July 1588—IV(53). V(56), (56v). VIII(68v). Debts re-enrolled—V(56)*, (56v)*. VI(54).

SCUDAMORE, Alice, 'spinster', of St. Devereux, Herefords. 6 mths recusancy from 1 Sept. 1588: conv. 14 July 1589—IX(25v). Debt re-enrolled—XI(29).

SCUDAMORE, John, esq., of Kenchurch [? Kentchurch], Herefords. 1 mth recusancy from 27 May 1583: conv. 15 July 1583—III(27): and eight later convictions, ending 27 Mar. 1587—IV(64v). V(26v)*. VI(25)*. Summary of pre-1587 debts for recusancy—VIII(30). X(29). XI(29). Debts re-enrolled—V(26). Lands seized for recusancy 16 Apr. 1582, and let by Crown to Thomas Braban from Michaelmas 1588—IX(24). X(28). XI(28). XII(28).

SCUDAMORE, John, esq., of the city of Hereford [? prisoner]. 12 mths recusancy from 26 June 1581: conv. 26 June 1582—II(64): and one later conviction, dated 7 Mar. 1582/3—II(64). Debts re-enrolled—III(27). V(26). VII(25). IX(25). Summary of pre-1587 debts for recusancy—XI(29).

SCUDAMORE, John, gent., of the city of Hereford [? prisoner]. 2 mths recusancy from 6 Jan. 1582/3: conv. ? Mar. 1582/3—II(64): and three later convictions, ending 3 Aug. 1584—IV(64v)*.

SCUDAMORE, Thomas, esq., of Kenchurch [Kentchurch], Herefords. 3 mths recusancy from 22 Sept. 1582: conv. ? Dec. 1582—III(27): and six later convictions, ending 22 July 1585—III(27). V(26v)*. Debts re-enrolled—V(26). VII(25). Summary of pre-1587 debts—V(26v). XI(29).

SCUDAMORE, Thomas, esq., of Kendelchurch [? Kenderchurch], Herefords. 3 mths recusancy from 22 Sept. 1582: conv. 9 Apr. 1583—IV(64v): and six later convictions, ending 27 Mar.

---

276. William Scott, (? of Iden, Sussex), was a prisoner in the White Lion on 8 Apr. 1584. (Cf. *CRS II*, p. 237.)

1587—IV(64v)*. VI(25)*. Summary of pre-1587 debts—VIII(30). X(29).
SCUDAMORE, Thomas, gent., of Kenderchurch, Herefords. 8 mths recusancy from 8 Feb. 1581/2: conv. 20 Sept. 1582—II(64).
SCUDAMORE, Thomas, gent., of Kenchurch [? Kentchurch], Herefords. 3 mths recusancy from 22 Sept. 1582: conv. 5 Jan. 1582/3—II(64): and one later conviction, dated ? Mar. 1582/3—II(64).
SCUDAMORE, Thomas, 'son of Thomas'. Goods, value £4, seized for the Crown by sheriff, Richard Walwyn esq., 1584.—X(28v).
SEABORNE, Seborne, John, gent., [Pipe Roll entry under 'Herefords'] 19 mths recusancy from 24 Mar. 1580/1: conv. 8 Jan. 1582/3—II(64). Debts re-enrolled—III(27). V(26).
SEABORNE, John, esq., of Sutton [St. Michael], Herefords. 12 mths recusancy from 1 Sept. 1586: conv. 18 Mar. 1587/8—VIII(30).
SEABORNE, John, gent. Record of land-seizure, 23 Aug. 1588—IX(25v). Rental of seized lands, manor of Allensmore & property in Peterchurch (£16 – 13 – 4 p.a.)—IX(25v). X(28). XI(28). XII(28). Seized lands let by Crown to William Wellington from Ladyday 1589—X(29). XI(28). XII(28).
SEARSON, Sherson, Martin, 'clericus', of St. George's parish, Southwark, Surrey [prisoner][277]. 5 mths recusancy from 17 Feb 1586/7: conv. 17 July 1587—IX(54).
SEMOR, Seimor, Jane, 'spinster', wife of Anthony Seimor, [ ], of Hartshorne, Derbys. 10 mths recusancy from 9 Sept. 1586: conv. 22 Mar. 1587/8—VIII(21).
SEWALL, Edward, 'laborer', of Querndon in All Saints parish, Derby, Derbys. 10 mths recusancy from 9 Sept. 1586: conv. 22 Mar. 1587/8—VIII(21v).
SEWALL, Thomas, 'laborer' (same place, recusancy period and conviction date)—VIII(21v).
SEWALL, William, 'laborer' (same place, recusancy period and conviction date)—VIII(21v).
SEWALL, Agnes, wife of William (same place, recusancy period and conviction date)—VIII(21v).
SEXTON, Shaxton, Edmund, gent., of Southwark, Surrey [prisoner][278]. 4 mths recusancy ending 11 Mar. 1582/3, when convicted—IV(49v)*: and four later convictions, ending 17 Feb 1585/6, when convicted—V(50v), (52v). VI(49v), (51). Debt re-enrolled—VI(51).
SEXTON, Edmund, recusant [Pipe Roll entry under 'Sussex']. Goods, value £40, seized 1585 (12 May)—V(52v). £40 paid 2 Mar. 1585/6: Quit—VII(51v).
SHAKERLEY, Henry, gent., of 'Sowthnewton', Oxfords. 12 mths recusancy from 26 Sept. 1586: conv. 7 Mar. 1587/8—VIII(35).

---

277. Martin Sherson (Cf. Anstruther I, p. 310.)
278. Edmund Sexton was a prisoner in the Marshalsea from June 1582 to July 1586. (Cf. CRS II, pp. 231, 233, 235, 240, 242, 244, 251, 254.)

SHARPULLS, James, 'husb''', of Ribby, Lancs. 12 mths recusancy from 20 Sept. 1589: conv. 22 Mar. 1590/1—X(39v).
SHARPULLS, William, 'milner' (same parish, recusancy period and conviction date)—X(39v).
SHATTERTONE, Henry, gent., of Erneley [Earnley], Sussex. 2 mths recusancy from 17 Apr. 1587: conv. 26 Feb 1587/8—VIII(63v). See CHADERTON.
SHAWE, Barnabas, gent., of Ribby [Kirkham], Lancs. 12 mths recusancy from 20 Sept. 1589: conv. 22 Mar. 1590/1—X(39v).
SHAWE, Francis, 'clericus', of Southwark, Surrey [prisoner][279]. 4 mths recusancy ending 20 July 1584, when convicted—V(52v): and one later conviction, dated 18 Feb 1584/5—V(52v).
SHAWE, William, 'yom''', of St. Bride's parish, Farringdon Ward Without, London [? prisoner]. 3 mths recusancy from 25 Mar. 1587: conv. 10 July 1587—VIII(38v).
SHAXTON, see SEXTON, Edmund.
SHELDON, Jane, wid., of Alchurch [Alvechurch], Worcs. 2 mths recusancy from 7 Apr. 1588: conv. 6 Mar. 1588/9—IX(70v).
SHELDON, Ralph, esq., of Beeley [Beoley], Worcs[280]. 12 mths recusancy ending 10 Sept. 1587 (£240 debt): and 1 mth recusancy from 11 Sept. 1587 ending 9 Oct. next (£20 debt). Annual fine (£260) paid 28 Nov. 1587, in two tallies. Quit.—VII(63v). Refs to succeeding yearly payments—VIII(77v). IX(68). X(75) [£260 due—unpaid].
SHELLEY, Edward, gent., of Southwark, Surrey [prisoner][281]. 10 mths recusancy ending 11 Mar. 1582/3, when convicted at Guildford Assizes—III(58v): and three later periods of recusancy, viz. 4 mths ending 22 July 1583; 6 mths ending 15 Feb. 1583/4, & 5 mths ending 20 July 1584, when convicted—IV(49v)*. V(50v). Debts re-enrolled—V(52v). VI(51).
SHELLEY, Henry, gent., of Southwark, Surrey [prisoner][282]. 4 mths recusancy ending 11 Mar. 1582/3, when convicted at Guildford Assizes—IV(49v): and one later period of recusancy, viz. 4 mths ending 22 July 1583, when convicted. Debts re-enrolled—VI(51).
SHELLEY, Richard, esq., of Southwark, Surrey [prisoner][283]. 10 mths recusancy ending 11 Mar. 1582/3, when convicted at Guildford Assizes—III(58v). Debt re-enrolled—V(52v).

---

279. Francis Shaw (Cf. Anstruther I, p. 396.)
280. Ralph Sheldon (Cf. Alan Davidson, 'The Recusancy of Ralph Sheldon', in *Worcestershire Recusant*, no. 12, (1968), pp. 1–7.)
281. Edward Shelley of Worminghurst in Sussex was imprisoned in the Clink, 8 Feb. 1584/5. (Cf. *CRS* II, p. 235.) He was martyred at Tyburn, 30 Aug. 1588, for 'receiving, aiding and comforting one William Deane', (Cf. footnote 56), a seminary priest. (Cf. E.H. Burton and J.H. Pollen, *Lives of the English Martyrs* I, (1914), pp. 416–421.)
282. Henry Shelley, elder brother of Edward Shelley of Worminghurst, was imprisoned in the White Lion, 23 Mar. 1583/4, and was still there, 8 Apr. 1584. (Cf. *CRS* II, pp. 234, 237.)
283. Richard Shelley of Worminghurst was imprisoned in the Marshalsea, where mass was said in his chamber by the future martyr William Hartley. Shelley disappears from the Prison Lists after July 1585. (Cf. *CRS* II, pp. 221, 231, 233, 235, 240.) See also Roger B. Manning, 'Richard Shelley of Worminghurst and the Catholic Petition for Toleration', in *RH*, vol. 6, (1962), pp. 265–274.)

SHELLEY, Richard, gent., of Southwark, Surrey [prisoner][283]. 4 mths recusancy ending 22 July 1583, when convicted—IV(49v): and one later period of recusancy, viz. 6 mths ending 15 Feb. 1583/4, when convicted—IV(49v). Debts re-enrolled—VI(51).

SHELLEY, Shellye, John, gent., of Clapham, W. Sussex[284]. 7 mths recusancy from 18 Mar. 1580/1: conv. 2 Oct. 1581—VI(49v): and nine later convictions ending 1 Oct. 1584—VI(49v)*; and a final period of recusancy viz. 2 mths from 17 Apr. 1587, for which he was convicted 26 Feb. 1587/8—VIII(63v). Goods, value £24 – 13 – 4, seized Mich. 1591 (paid 28 Jan. 1591/2. Quit)—IX(54v). Chattels real (21 year lease, to John Baker esq., of woodland at Clapham, Arundel, Patching etc), value £30, seized Mich. 1591 (paid 23 Nov. 1591. Quit.)—IX(54v). Rental of lands in Wilts (Two-thirds of the manor of Eston [Easton] *alias* Eston Bassett in the parishes of Donhead [St. Andrew] & Barwick [Berwick] St. John, Wilts; and of the grange or manor called 'Lucies' in the said parishes) seized by Crown for recusancy on 1 Sept. 1591: (rent, £11 – 7 – 6 p.a.) [Pipe Roll entry under 'Wilts']—XI(73v). XII(68v). Seized lands in Wilts (see above) and in Sussex ($\frac{2}{3}$ of the reversion of a moiety of the manor of Kingsham House W. Sussex, with lands in Kingsham, Oving, and the parish of St. Pancras [Chichester]; and of 'les Downes' with appurtenances called 'Bartholmews' in Storrington, W. Sussex: being a parcel of the possessions of the Almshouse of the Holy Trinity in Arundel) seized 1 Sept. and 2 Oct. 1591, and let by Crown to Edward Stone from 12 Nov. 1591 for a total rent of £16 – 5 – 4 p.a. [Pipe Roll entry under 'Wilts'—XII(69v).

SHELLEY, John, 'yoman', of West Firle, E. Sussex.[285] 2 mths recusancy from 17 Apr. 1587: conv. 26 Feb. 1587/8—VIII(63v).

SHEMAN, John, 'yeoman', of Tanworthe [Tamworth], Staffs. 12 mths recusancy from 6 Sept. 1586: conv. 25 Mar. 1588—VIII(78v).

SHEPLEY, Hugh, 'yoman', of Cronton, parish of Farneworth [Farnworth], Lancs. 13 mths recusancy from 30 July 1587: conv. 17 Mar. 1588/9—X(35).

SHEPPARD, Agnes, 'spinster', of Ashby Magna, Leics. 10 mths recusancy from 9 Sept. 1586: conv. 19 Mar. 1587/8—VIII(45v).

SHEPPARD, Joan, 'spinster', of Harrow, Middx. 3 mths recusancy from 6 June 1587: conv. 1 Dec. 1587—VIII(38v).

SHEREWIN, John, senior, 'husb''', of Rodesley [Rodsley], parish of Langeford [Longford], Derbys. 10 mths recusancy from 9 Sept. 1586: conv. 22 Mar. 1587/8—VIII(21).

SHEREWIN, Constance, his wife[286]. (same parish, recusancy period and conviction date)—VIII(21).

---

284. This detailed specification of John Shelley's seized property in Sussex and Wilts. is not repeated in the next, i.e. the first RR. (Cf. *CRS* XVIII, p. 355.)

285. Despite the different description, John Shelley of Firle is probably identical with John Shelley of Clapham above.

286. Constance and John Sherwin must be relatives of Ralph Sherwin, priest and Martyr.

SHEREWOOD, Sherwood, Henry, 'draper'/'yoman', of Southwark, Surrey [prisoner][287]. 4 mths recusancy ending 22 July 1583, when convicted—IV(49v); and two later periods ending 18 Feb. 1584/5, when convicted—V(50v), (52v). Earliest debt re-enrolled—VI(51).

SHERINGTON, Eliz., of Wigan, Lancs., wife of James Sherington [   ]. 12 mths recusancy from 20 Sept. 1589: conv. 22 Mar. 1590/1—X(38).

SHERRATT, Isabel, wid., of Leigh, Staffs. 8 mths recusancy from 1 Aug. 1585: conv. 13 Mar. 1585/6—VI(63v).

SHERRATT, Isabel, 'spinster', of Leigh, Staffs. 4 mths recusancy from 13 Mar. 1585/6: conv. 1 Aug. 1586—VI(63v).

SHERWOOD, William, gent., 'recusant', of Walkington, E.R. Yorks[288]. [Crown Lease] Thomas Sherwood, gent., owes to the Queen £9 p.a. for the farm of the whole tenement or messuage, with all appurtenances, situated in Walkington in the aforesaid county, and of all the 18 oxgangs [270 acres] of arable land in Walkington aforesaid in the tenure or occupation of a certain WILLIAM SHERWOOD, gent., or his assigns, and afterwards ('postea') in the tenure or occupation of Thomas Fairefax, of which said 18 oxgangs of arable, 3 oxgangs & 2 closes, called 'Howsemes land', are a parcel of the said 18 oxgangs of land and were lately in the separate tenures of John Sherwood, senior, Gabriel Cowper & Anthony Faray, and their assigns; and one oxgang & a half of arable, being likewise a portion of the said 18 oxgangs, was lately in the tenure of George Petas, and afterwards in the tenure or occupation of Francis Nawton, cleric & Rector of Walkington aforesaid, with all appurtenances being a parcel of the possessions of WILLIAM SHERWOOD, gent., recusant (always excepting all woodlands, underwood, mines & quarries reserved for the Queen, her heirs & successors). To have and to hold the aforesaid tenement or messuage and other premisses, with all their appurtenances, to the fore-named Thomas Sherwood and his assigns from Ladyday, 22 Eliz. [1580], for as long as they shall remain in the Queen's hands for the satisfaction of the said debt, rendering to the Queen and her successors £9 p.a. of lawful English money to the Receipt of the Exchequer or the current sheriff of the county at Michaelmas & Ladyday, in equal portions; as is contained in the Roll of the Enrolment of Leases of the twenty-second year of the reign of Queen Elizabeth, under 'Yorks'. And £76 – 10s. from preceding years. Total debt (as at Ladyday, 1580) = £85 – 10s. Cf. IX(8v). X(21v). XI(24v). XII(11v), The entry appears for the last time in Recusant Roll No. I (*C.R.S.* XVIII, p. 49).

---

287. Henry Sherwood was a prisoner in the Marshalsea from 11 Feb. 1581/2 to July 1586. (Cf. *CRS* II, pp. 231, 233, 236, 240.)

288. William Sherwood, as a boy, was arrested on board a boat which had crossed over to Dover sometime after 1577. He was committed to the Gatehouse under 'Prisoners in Queen's Bench', for 'certen trespaces and contempts', and, on 23 Jan. 1578/9, he was sentenced to perpetual imprisonment. (Cf. *CRS* I, pp. 62, 67.) The document is a full translation of the earliest Pipe Roll enrollment of the Crown's seizures of William Sherwood's lands in Walkington, Yorks., and of their lease to Thomas Sherwood. The lease had been achieved nine years earlier on Ladyday 1580. (Cf. IX(8v.))

SHIPMAN, Chipman, Thomas, gent., of Webley [Weobley], Herefords. Two fines of £20 imposed for ignoring the sheriff's summonses after excommunication, 4 Apr. and 27 May 1581—III(28)*. Debts re-enrolled—V(26), (26v).

SHIPPBOTHAM, Robert, 'yoman', of Leecke [Leek], Staffs. 4 mths recusancy (undated): convicted 21 July 1589—IX(69v).

SHORROCK, Cicily, 'spinster', of Salisbury [Salesbury; Blackburn], Lancs. 12 mths recusancy from 20 Sept. 1589: conv. 22 Mar. 1590/1—X(40).

SHOULDHAM, Jane, 'spinster', of Oxborough, Norfolk. 2 mths recusancy from 24 Jan. 1588/9: conv. 7 July 1589—IX(45v). Debt re-enrolled—XI(48).

SILVESTER, Sylvester, Margaret, wid., of the city of York. 4 mths recusancy from 28 Mar. 1581: conv. 17 July 1581—I(8). Debt re-enrolled—III(10). V(8). VII(8). IX(8). Goods, value 9s., seized 6 Feb. 1582/3—II(8).

SIMPSON, Richard, gent., of Newington, Surrey [prisoner][289]. 11 mths recusancy ending 17 Feb. 1585/6, when convicted—VI(49v). See SAMPSON, Richard.

SINGLER, Alice, 'spinster', of Hanley Castle, Worcs. 2 mths recusancy from 7 Apr. 1588: conv. 6 Mar. 1588/9—IX(70v).

SINGLETON, Eliz., of Chipping, Lancs., wife of Thomas Singleton, gent. 12 mths recusancy from 20 Sept. 1589: conv. 22 Mar. 1590/1—X(39).

SINGLETON, George, 'husb'', of Wessham [Wesham], parish of Kirkham, Lancs. 13 mths recusancy from 30 July 1587: conv. 17 Mar. 1588/9—X(35).

SINGLETON, George, 'yoman', (of same parish). 12 mths recusancy from 20 Sept. 1589: conv. 22 Mar. 1590/1—X(39).

SINGLETON, [ ], his wife (same parish, recusancy period & conviction date)—X(39).

SINGLETON, Henry, gent., of Fintham [Fincham], Norfolk. 1 mth recusancy from 10 June 1582: conv. 10 July 1582—VI(25v).

SINGLETON, Henry, gent., of Thorndon (All Saints), Suffolk. 3 mths recusancy from 8 Apr. 1587: conv. 27 Mar. 1588—VIII(73).

SINGLETON, Richard, gent., of Chippen [Chipping], Lancs. 13 mths recusancy from 14 Aug. 1586: conv. 25 Mar. 1588—VIII(21v): and two later convictions, ending 22 Mar. 1590/1—X(35), (39).

SINGLETON, Alice, his wife (same parish, recusancy period & conviction date)—X(39).

SKAN, Eliz., 'spinster', of Ashby Magna, Leics. 9 mths recusancy ending 10 Aug. 1587, when convicted—VIII(45v).

SKERNE, Ann, 'spinster', of Oxborough, Norfolk. 3 mths recusancy from 13 Apr. 1587: conv. 1 Apr. 1588—VIII(54).

SKILLICORNE, Jane, of Preese [nr. Kirkham], Lancs., wife of William Skillycorne, esq. 12 mths recusancy from 20 Sept. 1589: conv. 22 Mar. 1590/1—X(39).

---

289. Richard Simpson See footnote 267, Richard SAMPSON.

SKILLICORNE, Richard, gent., of Presthall [Preesall], Kirkham parish, Lancs. 13 mths recusancy from July 30th 1587: conv. 17 Mar. 1588/9—X(35).

SKYNNER, Ann, wife of John Skynner, [   ], of Weathers, Ledbury parish, Herefords. 12 mths recusancy from 1 Sept. 1586: conv. 18 Mar. 1587/8—VIII(30).

SLEIGH, Thomas, 'husb', of Stowe, Staffs. 6 mths recusancy from 6 Sept. 1587: conv. 22 July 1588—VIII(58).

SMALL, Smale, Christopher, 'clericus', of Southwark, Surrey [prisoner][290]. 9 mths recusancy ending 11 Mar. 1582/3, when convicted—III(58v); and four later convictions, ending 18 Feb. 1584/5—IV(49v)*. V(50v), (52v). Debt re-enrolled—V(52v). VI(51).

SMITHE, Alice, 'spinster', of Blackborne [Blackburn], Lancs. 12 mths recusancy from 20 Sept. 1589: conv. 22 Mar. 1590/1—X(40v).

SMITHE, Ann, gentlewoman, wife of George Smithe, gent., of Brontingbie [Brentingby], Leics. 10 mths recusancy from 9 Sept. 1586: conv. 19 Mar. 1587/8—VIII(45v).

SMITHE, Ann, 'spinster', of Ashby Magna, Leics. 9 mths recusancy ending 10 Aug. 1587, when convicted—VIII(45v).

SMITHE, Ann, wife of Roger Smithe, 'husb''', of Hardwick, Oxfords. 12 mths recusancy from 26 Sept. 1586: conv. 7 Mar. 1587/8—VIII(35v).

SMITHE, Eliz., wife of Francis Smithe, esq., of Ashebie Flavile [? Ashby Folville], Leics. 10 mths recusancy from 9 Sept. 1586: conv. 19 Mar. 1587/8—VIII(45v).

SMITHE, Eliz., wife of James Smithe, gent., of Somerton, Oxfords. 12 mths recusancy from 26 Sept. 1586: conv. 7 Mar. 1587/8—VIII(35).

SMITHE, Smyth, George, 'clothier', of Leeds, W.R. Yorks. 6 mths recusancy from 3 July 1587: conv. 18 Mar. 1587/8—VIII(27).

SMITHE, Humphrey, [   ], of Ashebie Magna, Leics. 7 mths recusancy ending 10 Aug. 1587, when convicted—VIII(45v).

SMITHE, Katherine, 'spinster', of Passenham, Northants. 12 mths recusancy ending 2 May 1587: conv. 12 Mar. 1587/8—VIII(52v).

SMITHE, William, gent., of the Middle Temple, London [prisoner][291]. 12 mths recusancy from 2 Jan. 1582/3: conv. 22 Jan. 1583/4—IV(32v). Debt re-enrolled—VI(34).

SMITHE, Smyth, William, gent., of Newington, Surrey [prisoner][292]. 6 mths recusancy ending 18 Feb. 1584/5, when convicted—V(52v); and one later conviction, ending 17 Feb. 1585/6—VI(49v).

SMITHE, Smyth, William, 'clericus', of Southwark, Surrey [prisoner][293]. 4 mths recusancy ending 20 July 1584, when convicted—V(52v).

---

290. Christopher Small (Cf. Anstruther I, p. 319.)
291. William Smith was a prisoner in the White Lion, 8 Apr. 1584. (Cf. CRS II, p. 237.)
292. William Smith of Newington, Surrey, is identical with the above.
293. William Smith (Cf. Anstruther I, p. 323.)

SMITHE, Smyth, William, 'yom'', of Southwark, Surrey [? prisoner]. 4 mths recusancy ending 11 Mar. 1582/3, when convicted—IV(49v); and two later convictions, ending 15 Feb. 1583/4—IV(49v)*. Debt re-enrolled—VI(51)*.

SMITHE, *alias* HADDEN, Joan, wid., of Wendlebury, Oxfords. 12 mths recusancy from 26 Sept. 1586: conv. 7 Mar. 1587/8—VIII(35v).

SMYTHE, Ann, 'spinster', of Wateringbury, Kent. 2 mths recusancy from 19 Dec. 1587: conv. 26 Feb. 1588/9—IX(29).

SMYTHE, 'Felicia', 'spinster', of St. Devereux, Herefords. 6 mths recusancy from 1 Sept. 1588: conv. 14 July 1589—IX(25v). Debt re-enrolled—XI(29).

SMYTHE, Francis, 'yoman', of Cockfeild [Cockfield], Suffolk. 7 mths recusancy from 15 July 1588: conv. 2 July 1589—IX(64). Debt re-enrolled—XI(72v).

SMYTH, John, 'clericus', of St. George's parish, Southwark, Surrey [prisoner][294]. 5 mths recusancy from 17 Feb. 1586/7: conv. 17 July 1587—IX(54).

SMYTHE, John, 'laborer', of St. John Baptist parish, Hereford city. 6 mths recusancy from 1 Sept. 1588: conv. 14 July 1589—IX(25v). Debt re-enrolled—XI(29).

SMYTHE, Katherine, wid., of St. Devereux, Herefords (same recusancy period & conviction date)—IX(25v). Debt re-enrolled—XI(29).

SMYTHE, Margaret, 'spinster' (same parish, recusancy period & conviction date)—IX(25v). Debt re-enrolled—XI(29).

SMYTH, Margaret, wife of Henry Smyth, [ ], of Raglan, Mon. 5 mths recusancy from 24 Mar. 1586/7: conv. 13 Mar. 1587/8—VIII(48).

SMYTHE, 'Quintus', 'yoman', of St. Olave's parish, Southwark, Surrey. 3 mths recusancy from 25 Mar. 1588: conv. 6 Mar. 1588/9—IX(53).

SMYTH, Richard, 'yom'', of Harrow, Middx. 3 mths recusancy from 6 June 1587: conv. 1 Dec. 1587—VIII(38v).

SMYTHSON, Smythsone, Brian, [ ], of Cowton Grange, parish of Middleton Tyas, N.R. Yorks. 13 mths recusancy from 3 Sept. 1586: conv. 4 Sept. 1587—VIII(25v).

SMYTHSON, 'Jenetta', wid., of Burroubridge [Boroughbridge], W.R. Yorks. 5 mths recusancy from 16 Apr.. 1587: conv. 4 Sept. 1587—VIII(25v).

SMYTHSON, John, 'yom'', of Melsenbye [Melsonby], N.R. Yorks. 13 mths recusancy from 3 Sept. 1586: conv. 4 Sept. 1587—VIII(25v). Goods, value £20, seized 10 Apr. 1589—IX(8v). Record of land-seizure, 10 Apr. 1589—IX(8v). Rental of seized lands at Stokley [Stokesley, N.R.], at £1 – 6 – 8 p.a.—IX(21v). X(21v). XI(24v). XII(23v). Seized lands let by Crown to James Bellamy from 3 Aug. 1590—X(13v). XI(24v).

---

294. John Smith (Cf. Anstruther I, p 263, under John Owen.)

SMYTHSON, William, 'yom''', of Newsham, parish of Kirkby
Ravensworth, N.R. Yorks. 13 mths recusancy from 3 Sept. 1586:
conv. 4 Sept. 1587—VIII(25v).
SNAPPE, Anthony, 'yoman', of Westminster, Middx [prisoner][295]. 1 mth
recusancy from 6 Oct. 1587: conv. 29 Jan. 1587/8—VIII(38v).
SNAPPE, Grace, wid., of Charlesburie [Charlbury], Oxfords. 12 mths
recusancy from 26 Sept. 1586: conv. 7 Mar. 1587/8—VIII(35).
SOMERSETT, Thomas, esq., of St. Bride's parish, Farringdon Ward
Without, London [prisoner][296]. [Pipe Roll entry under 'Gloucs'] 13
mths recusancy from 18 Mar. 1580/1: conv. (Old Bailey, London)
27 Apr. 1582—IV(23v). Debts re-enrolled—VI(23v). Wollaston
Grange & Tedenham farm, Gloucs, seized at Michaelmas 1585 and let
by Crown to Hugh Cuffe for a rent of £20 p.a.—VI(33v). VIII(16v).
X(50v), (82). XI(27). XII(27), (46).
SONKEY, Ann, wid., of Sonkey [Great Sankey], Warrington parish, Lancs.
6 mths recusancy from 1 Feb. 1587/8: conv. 17 Mar. 1588/9—X(35).
Lands & water-mill at Sonkey Hall seized 26 Mar. 1591 and let by
Crown to John Parker from 1 July 1591—XII(44).
SOTHERNE, Simon, 'clericus', of the city of Worcester[297]. 2 mths recusancy
from 8 Jan. 1582/3: conv. 11 Mar. 1582/3—II(61v). Debt re-
enrolled—IV(61v). VI(62v).
SOUTHWORTH, Ann, [   ], of Samlesbury, Blackborne [Blackburn]
parish, Lancs. 3 mths recusancy from 21 May 1587: conv. 25 Mar.
1588—VIII(21v).
SOUTHWORTH, Dorothy, 'spinster', of Barton, Broughton parish, Lancs.
(same recusancy period and conviction date)—VIII(21v).
SOUTHWORTHE, Jane, 'spinster', of Westby, Lancs. 12 mths recusancy
from 20 Sept. 1589: conv. 22 Mar. 1590/1—X(39v).
SOUTHWORTH, Sir John, knt, of Blakborne [Blackburn], Lancs. 9 mths
recusancy from 19 Mar. 1580/1 (convicted upon informer's
suit)[298]—VI(39). Debt re-enrolled—VIII(78v). X(38).
SOUTHWORTH, Sotheworth, Sir John, knt, of Salford in the parish of
Manchester, Lancs [prisoner][299]. 1 mth recusancy from 29 Mar. 1582:
conv. 2 May 1582—II(38v): and five later convictions, ending
? 1 Sept. 1584—II(38v)*. IV(37), (46v). VI(40v). Debts re-enrolled—
IV(42v). VI(39v). VIII(46).

---

295. Anthony Snappe was a serving man of William Shelley of Clapham, Sussex. He was imprisoned in the Westminster Gatehouse from 1 Apr. 1585, and was still there in 1588, suspected of complicity in the escape of Charles Paget. (Cf. CRS II, pp. 245, 253 – 255, 271, 283.)
296. Thomas Somersett, brother of the Earl of Worcester, was committed to the Fleet on 10 Jun. 1562. (Cf. CRS I, p. 49.)
297. Simon Sotherne was a pre-Elizabethan priest, who had held the living of Hinton on the Green, near Evesham, Worcs., until his deprivation in 1541.
298. John Southworth was convicted under the procedure described in CRS LVII, introd., pp. xvii – xix.
299. Sir John Southworth was committed to Salford Gaol on 29 Mar. 1582/3. (Cf. CRS V, p. 24.)

SOUTHWORTH, Sotheworth, Sir John, knt, of St. Mary's parish, Chester ('inhabitans apud Castrum Cestr") [prisoner]. 8 mths recusancy from 1 Sept. 1584: conv. 26 Apr. 1585—VI(48v).
SOUTHWORTH, Sir Richard [*sic* for 'John'], knt, of Chester Castle [prisoner]. 13 mths recusancy from 14 Sept. 1585: conv. 3 Oct. 1586—X(35v). Summary of debts for pre-1587 recusancy (47 months): £1,060—VIII(78v). Goods, value £388, seized 24 Oct. 1587—X(40v). Record of lands seized 24 Oct. 1587 (rent charged by Crown, £280 – 16 – 8 p.a.: seizures specified—⅔ of lands in Samlesbury, Mellor & Stanley Hurst, rents in Pleasington, Wrightington & Goosnargh; 2 mills in Samlesbury & a free fishery there; ⅔ of 240 acres called 'the demesne of Southworth'; rents in Southworth with Croft, Middleton, Houghton, Arbury, Newton, Lawton, Golborne, Woolston, Poulton with Fernhead, Holme, Warrington, Orford, Ribchester, Oswaldtwistle & Brockholes: all in Lancs)—X(40v). Rental of seized lands—XII(44). All debts discharged by 2 royal pardons, dated 1 Dec. 1587 and 1 July 1592[300].
SOUTHWORTH, John, 'son of Sir John, knt,', of Samlesbury, Blackborne parish, Lancs. 3 mths recusancy from 21 May 1587: conv. 25 Mar. 1588—VIII(21v).
SOUTHWORTH, Thomas, gent., of Middleton, Winwick parish, Lancs. 13 mths recusancy from 14 Aug. 1586: conv. 25 Mar. 1588—VIII(21v).
SOUTHWORTH, Sotheworth, William, 'yoman', of Westby, Lancs. 12 mths recusancy from 20 Sept. 1589: conv. 22 Mar. 1590/1—X(39v).
SOUTHWORTH, Eliz., his wife (same parish, recusancy period and conviction date)—X(39v).
SOWERBYE, 'Jenetta', wid., of Stavley [Staveley], W.R. Yorks. 6 mths recusancy from 3 July 1587: conv. 18 Mar. 1588—VIII(27).
SPARKES, Roger, gent., of Bedhampton, Hants. 2 mths recusancy from 25 Feb. 1586/7: conv. 26 Feb. 1587/8—VIII(67).
SPENCE, Paul, 'clericus', of Southwark, Surrey [prisoner][301]. 4 mths recusancy ending 20 July 1584, when convicted—V(52v): and one later conviction, dated 18 Feb. 1584/5—V(52v).
SPENCE, Paul, 'clericus', of Worcester city [? prisoner]. 12 mths recusancy from 5 Mar. 1587/8: conv. 14 July 1589—IX(68v).
SPENCER, Agnes, 'spinster', of 'St. Maries Westoute in Lewes', Sussex. 3 mths recusancy from 1 Nov. 1588: conv. 27 June 1589—IX(53).
SPENCER, Andrew, 'yeoman', of Romsey, Hants. 6 mths recusancy from 1 Nov. 1586: conv. 26 Feb. 1587/8—VIII(67).
SPENCER, Francis, 'draper', of New Sarum, Wilts. 5 mths recusancy from 20 Mar. 1583/4: conv. 20 Aug. 1584—IV(59v). Debt re-enrolled—VI(59v). 100 marks fine imposed for hearing Mass: convicted 7 Jan.

---

300. Sir John Southworth's debts were discharged. (Cf. M.R., L.T.R., 35 Eliz., Easter Term, 'Recorda' section. See *CRS* LVII, introd., p. xxxi and note.) Southworth died on 3 Nov. 1595. (Cf. *CRS* XXII, p. 309.)
301. Paul Spence (Cf. Anstruther I, p. 328.)

1583/4 at Winchester Sessions of the Peace. Debt re-enrolled—VI(59v).

SPENCER, John, junior, 'taylor', of Totbaldon [Baldon, Toot], Oxfords. 7 mths recusancy from 23 July 1584: conv. 5 Feb. 1584/5—V(47): and two later convictions, dated 26 June 1585 & 24 Feb. 1585/6—V(47). VI(47v).

SPENCER, John, junior, 'husb'' [of same parish & county]. 3 mths recusancy from 24 Mar. 1580/1: conv. 29 June 1581—IV(29v): and four later convictions ending 23 July 1584—II(29v). III(4). IV(29)*. Debt re-enrolled—V(31v). VI(30v).

SPENCER, John, junior, 'yom'' [of same parish & county]. 8 mths recusancy from 25 July 1586: conv. 17 Mar. 1586/7—VI(11v).

SPENCER, John, senior, 'taylor', of Totbaldon [Baldon, Toot], Oxfords. 3 mths recusancy from 24 Mar. 1580/1: conv. 29 June 1581—IV(29v): and five later convictions, ending 17 Mar. 1586/7—II(29v). III(4). IV(29)*. VI(11v). Debts re-enrolled—V(31v). VI(30v).

SPENCER, John, senior, 'husb'' [of same parish & county]. 7 mths recusancy from 23 July 1584: conv. 5 Feb. 1584/5—V(47): and two later convictions, ending 24 Feb. 1585/6—V(47). VI(47v). Lands seized 17 Apr. 1591 & let by Crown to Richard Ferris from 27 July 1591—XII(54).

SPENCER, William, 'yom'', of Rumsey [Romsey], Hants. 6 mths recusancy from 1 Nov. 1586: conv. 26 Feb. 1587/8—IV(53). Debt re-enrolled—VI(54). VIII(67).

SPENCER, Joan, his wife, of Romsey, Hants. Fine of 100 marks imposed for hearing Mass: convicted at Winchester, Jan. 1583/4.—IV(53). Debt re-enrolled—VI(54).

SPICER, Laurence, 'husb'', of Goosey, Berks. 3 mths recusancy from 24 Mar. 1580/1: conv. 26 June 1581—II(65v): and four later convictions, ending 1 July 1583—II(65v)*. III(50v). Debts re-enrolled—III(5). V(4v).

SPICER, Laurence, 'taylor', of Goosey, Berks. 8 mths recusancy from 3 July 1583: conv. 24 Feb. 1583/4—IV(3v).

SPICER, Laurence, 'yom'', of St. Mary's parish, Reading, Berks [prisoner][302]. 4 mths recusancy from 11 Feb. 1582/3: conv. ? June 1583—III(50v): and four later convictions, ending 21 Feb. 1585/6—IV(46). V(4v)*. VI(3v), (4v).

SPICER, Spycer, Laurence, 'husbondman', of St. Mary's parish, Reading, Berks. 6 mths recusancy from 21 Feb. 1585/6: conv. 9 Aug. 1586—VI(4v): and one later conviction, ending 6 Mar. 1586/7—VI(48v).

SPINSTER, Ann, 'spinster', of Llantilio Pertholey, Mon. 5 mths recusancy from 24 Mar. 1586/7: conv. 13 Mar. 1587/8—VIII(48v).

SPINSTER, Blanch, 'spinster', of St. Maughans, Mon. (same recusancy period and conviction date)—VIII(49).

---

302. Laurence Spicer, husbandman, was listed as a prisoner in Berkshire Gaol (Reading Castle) in 1582. (Cf. *CRS* XXII, p. 118.)

SPINSTER, Edith, 'spinster', of Llanvetherine, Mon. (same recusancy period and conviction date)—VIII(49).
SPINSTER, 'Elnora', 'spinster', (same parish, recusancy period and conviction date)—VIII(49).
SPINSTER, Elizabeth, 'spinster', of Usk, Mon. (same recusancy period and conviction date)—VIII(49).
SPINSTER, 'Gwenliana', [   ], of Llanllowell, Mon. (same recusancy period and conviction date)—VIII(49v).
SPINSTER, Jane, 'spinster', of Llanvihangel Ystern Llewern, Mon. (same recusancy period and conviction date)—VIII(49v).
SPINSTER, Joan, 'spinster', of Llanthewy Skirrid, Mon. (same recusancy period and conviction date)—VIII(48v).
STAMPE, Bridget, wife of John Stampe, gent., of Halton [Holton], Oxfords. 12 mths recusancy from 26 Sept. 1586: conv. 7 Mar. 1587/8—VIII(35).
STANBORNE, James, 'yeoman', of Denham, Bucks. 3 mths recusancy from 20 Mar. 1587/8: conv. 10 Mar. 1588/9—IX(1v).
STANDISHE, Eliz., of Standish, Lancs., wife of Alexander Standishe, gent. 12 mths recusancy from 20 Sept. 1589: conv. 22 Mar. 1590/1—X(38v).
STANLEY, Ann, wid., of Westley [West Leigh], parish of Leigh, Lancs. 13 mths recusancy from 14 Aug. 1586: conv. 25 Mar. 1588—VIII(21v).
STANLEY, 'Harbert', gent., of Islington, Middx. 3 mths recusancy from 28 June 1587: conv. 1 Oct. 1587—VIII(38v).
STANLEY, Lady Lucy, his wife (same parish, recusancy period and conviction date)—VIII(38v).
STAPLETON, John, 'yoman', of Bradley, Staffs. 6 mths recusancy from 6 Sept. 1587: conv. 22 July 1588—VIII(58).
STAPLETON, Stepleton, Joyce, 'spinster', of Bradley, Staffs. 4 mths recusancy from 31 Mar. 1582: conv. 2 Aug. 1582—II(14): and five later convictions, ending 13 Mar. 1585/6—III(64v). IV(62v). V(66)*. VI(63v). Debts re-enrolled—IV(62). VI(63), (63v).
STAPLETON, William, gent., of Southwark, Surrey [prisoner][303]. 10 mths recusancy ending 11 Mar. 1582/3, when convicted—IV(49v): and three later convictions, ending 18 Feb. 1584/5—IV(49v). V(52v)*. Debts re-enrolled—V(52v). VI(51). A moiety of the farm of Litlewood at Bradley, Staffs., seized and let by Crown to Hugh Cuffe from Michalemas 1585, for a rent of £16 – 3 – 10 p.a.—VI(33v). VIII(16v). X(78v). XI(64v). XII(72v).
STARKEY, Margaret, 'spinster', of Crosbie, Sephton [Sefton] parish, Lancs. 13 mths recusancy from 30 July 1587: conv. 17 Mar. 1588/9—X(35): and one later conviction, ending 22 Mar. 1590/1—X(38).
STAVELEY, William, 'laborer', of West Hallam, Derbys. 10 mths recusancy from 9 Sept. 1586: conv. 22 Mar. 1587/8—VIII(21).

---

303. William Stapleton was committed to the Clink for recusancy on 17 June 1582, and was still there on 8 Apr. 1584. (Cf. *CRS* II, pp. 227, 235.)

Goods, value (with goods of Oliver Wright) £18 – 4 – 2, seized 27 Jan. 1589—IX(17v).

STEPHENSON, Robert, gent., recusant, of Gowle [Goole] in parish of Snaith, W.R. Yorks. [date of earliest conviction for recusancy missing] Lands in Goole seized 2 Nov. 1591—XI(10v). XII(24). Seized lands let by Crown to Richard Mussendine from 29 Nov. 1591: rent charged, £4 – 8 – 11 p.a.—XII(11v).

STEPHENSON, William, gent., recusant, of Swinefleet, parish of Whitgift, W.R. Yorks. [date of earliest conviction for recusancy missing]. Seized lands [moiety of a messuage or tenement in Swinefleet & Reednes (in parish of Whitgift) called 'Westholding'; and lands in Patrington (E.R.) & Ottringham (E.R.)]. Date of seizure 2 Nov. 1591—XI(10v). XII(24). Leased by Crown to Richard Mussendine from 29 Nov. 1591 for a combined total rent of £7 – 15 – 9 p.a. from Robert and William Stephenson—XII(11v).

STERNE, George, 'yeoman', of Albie [Alby], Norfolk. 3 mths recusancy from 13 Apr. 1587: conv. 1 Apr. 1588—VIII(54).

STIDDOLFE, John, gent., of Chertsey, Surrey. 3 mths recusancy from 25 Mar. 1588: conv. 6 Mar. 1588/9—IX(53).

STIDDOLFE, Margery, 'spinster' (same parish, recusancy period and conviction date)—IX(53).

STOCKE, Joan, wife of William Stocke, 'yeoman', of Hanley Castle, Worcs. 12 mths recusancy from 20 Sept. 1586: conv. 28 Mar. 1588—VIII(77).

STOCKER, George, gent., of Westminster [prisoner][304]. 3 mths recusancy from 20 Mar. 1587/8: conv. 28 June 1588—IX(37).

STOCKWITHE, Benjamin, gent., of parish of St. Clement Danes, without Temple Bar, Middx. Fine of 100 marks imposed for hearing Mass said on 30 Jan. 1585/6 by William Thompson in the house of Robert Bellamy (q.v.) Conv. at Old Bailey, 18 Apr. 1586[305]—VI(34v).

STOCKWITHE, Benjamin, gent., of Southwark, Surrey [prisoner]. 8 mths recusancy ending 16 Feb. 1586/7, when convicted—VI(50).

STOCKWITHE, Thomas, gent., of Limington [Lymington], Hants. 7 mths recusancy from 12 Sept. 1586: conv. 26 Feb. 1587/8—VIII(67).

STOKES, Walter, 'clericus', of Southwark, Surrey [prisoner][306]. 4 mths recusancy ending 20 July 1584, when convicted—V(52v): and one later conviction, dated 18 Feb. 1584/5—V(52v).

---

304. George Stocker had been a prisoner in the Tower for six months in 1588. He had lived in France for 20 years, and came over to England to fetch the Earl of Westmoreland's daughter. (Cf. CRS II, p. 282.) He was committed to the Marshalsea. He was listed, 30 Sept. 1588, as refusing the Oath and being determined to take the part of the Pope's army. (Cf. CRS II, p. 267.) Absent thereafter.

305. Robert Bellamy of Harrow on the Hill was committed to Newgate, 30 Jan. 1585/6, and convicted for hearing mass, 18 Apr. 1586. He was still there on 7 Dec. 1586, but there is no later mention of him. (Cf. CRS II, pp. 248, 252, 256, 271, 283.)

306. Walter Stokes (Cf. Anstruther I, p. 356.)

STONE, *alias* OLIVER, Thomas, 'yoman', of Bury St. Edmunds, Suffolk. 7 mths recusancy from 12 Sept. 1586: conv. ? Feb. 1587/8—VI(58)*: and one later conviction. Record of land-seizure in Bury St. Edmunds, 2 Nov. 1587 [⅔ of a tenement in a place called 'Cockrowe' in Old Baxters Street, and of an orchard in High Street]—VIII(72). Rental of seized land, £8 – 17 – 9 p.a.—IX(63). X(63). XI(65). XII(66).

STONE, Joan, wife of Thomas Stone *alias* Oliver (of same parish). 3 mths recusancy from 8 Apr. 1587: conv. 27 Mar. 1588—VIII(73).

STONOR, Stoner, Lady Cicily, wid., of Pirton [Pyrton], Oxfords[307]. 5 mths recusancy from 15 Feb. 1581/2: conv. 23 July 1582—V(47): and one later conviction, dated 5 Feb. 1584/5—V(47). Goods, value £13 – 6 – 8, seized by sheriff Owen Oglethorpe, 21 Feb. 1587/8—VIII(59). Debt re-enrolled—XI(53v): £13 – 6 – 8 paid 4 Nov. 1591. Quit. Summary of pre-1587 debts for recusancy [total £440]—VII(30v). Record of land-seizure, 21 Feb. 1587/8—VIII(59v). Seized lands let by Crown to Francis Stonard from Michaelmas 1585 [*sic*], for a rent of £30 p.a. [seizures specified: the manor of Stonor or Pishill, with Warmodescombe, and the farms of Hollandridge & Broundesden, Oxfords]—VIII(35v). IX(50). X(57). XI(53). XII(53). Crown lease to Francis Stoner, dated 29 Dec. 1591, of the residue of Lady Stoner's lands, seized 7 Oct. 1591. Rent charged, £18 – 4 – 10 p.a. [allowing for the retention by the recusant of the 'third part' of the lands, in accordance with the Statute of 1586 – 7, § iv][308].—XII(54).

STRANGWISHE, Margaret, wife of [   ] Strangwishe, esq., of Sugton?, Yorks. 6 mths recusancy from 3 July 1587: conv. 18 Mar. 1587/8—VIII(27).

STRATCHE, Thomas, 'yoman', of Tansor, Northants. 12 mths recusancy from 31 July 1587: conv. 4 Mar. 1588/9—IX(47).

STREETE, Eliz., 'spinster', of Hampton Lovett, Worcs. 2 mths recusancy from 7 Apr. 1588: conv. 6 Mar. 1588/9—IX(70v).

STUDLEY, Daniel, 'yoman', of St. Bride's parish, Farringdon Ward Without, London [? prisoner][309]. 3 mths recusancy prior to 20 Apr. 1588, when convicted—VIII(38v).

STUTTESBURY, John, gent., of Souldron [Souldern], Oxfords. 3 mths recusancy from 24 Mar. 1580/1: conv. 29 June 1581—IV(29v); and eleven later convictions, ending 7 Mar. 1587/8—II(29v)*. III(4). IV(29)*. V(47)*. VI(11v), (47v). VIII(35). Debts re-enrolled—V(31v). VI(30v)*.

SUFFEILD, Susanna, wife of William Suffeild, [   ], of Hanley Castle, Worcs. 6 mths recusancy from 29 Sept. 1587: conv. 25 July 1588—VIII(80v).

---

307. Lady Cecily Stonor (Cf. 'The Memoires of Fr. Robert Parsons'—*CRS* II, pp. 29, 182.)
308. Cf. RR no. 4 (*CRS* LXI, p. 201, and 203 footnote 2.)
309. Daniel Studley was a Calvinistic sectary. He was committed to Newgate in 1595, and was probably moved to the Fleet shortly afterwards. (Cf. *CRS* II, pp. 284, 287.)

SULLIARD, Sullyard, Edward, esq., of Wetherden, Suffolk[310]. 12 mths recusancy from 3 July 1581: conv. 18 July 1582—II(56): and four later convictions, ending 22 Oct. 1587—III(66). V(60v). VI(58). VII(58v)*, (59). Debt re-enrolled—III(65). Summary of pre-1587 debts for recusancy (July 1581 to Oct. 1586. Total £1,380: paid by 27 Nov. 1587. Quit)—VII(58v). Annual fines for recusancy (£260): first payment covering period 23 Oct. 1586 to 22 Oct. 1587—VII(58v). VIII(73). IX(63v). X(63v). XI(66). XII(66v).

SULLIARD, Frances, wife of Edward Sulliard, gent., of Wetherden, Suffolk. 3 mths recusancy from 8 Apr. 1587: conv. 27 Mar. 1588—VIII(73).

SULLIARD, Sullyard, Thomas, gent., of Wetherden, Suffolk. 12 mths recusancy from 3 July 1581: conv. 18 July 1582—II(56): and two later convictions, ending 5 Apr. 1587—III(66). VI(58). Debts re-enrolled—III(65). IV(56). V(60). (60v). Summary of pre-1587 debts for recusancy: total (by Act of 28 Eliz., cap. 6) £1,500. Unpaid. [Debt cancelled. Sir Nicholas Bacon and other commissioners charged for issues of $\frac{2}{3}$ of Thomas Sulliard's lands, in a sum of £1,500]—VI(57), (58). VII(59). Record of land-seizure, 2 Nov. 1587 ($\frac{2}{3}$ of a messuage and 180 acres of land in Norton, Hunston and Stowe Langtoft, Suffolk. Rent charged, £32 – 1s. p.a.)—VIII(72).

SULLIARD, Thomas, gent., of Wetherdemain [sic], Suffolk. Rental of seized lands (no payment)—X(64). Annotation (Michaelmas term 1588. Thomas Sulliard discharged by Barons of Exchequer; lands restored)[311].

SUTTLE, Henry, gent., of Northdighton [North Deighton Manor], W.R. Yorks. 4 mths recusancy from 28 Mar. 1581: conv. 17 July 1581—I(21v). Debt re-enrolled—III(24). V(22). VII(22v). IX(22). XII(26).

SUTTON, Eliz., wife of John Sutton, 'yoman', of Upton on Severn, Worcs. 2 mths recusancy from 7 Apr. 1588: conv. 6 Mar. 1588/9—IX(70v).

SUTTON, Ralph, [   ], of St. Saviour's parish, Southwark, Surrey [? prisoner]. 2 mths recusancy from 22 Oct. 1588: conv. 30 June 1589—IX(53).

SUTTON, Robert, 'yoman', of Westminster, Middx [prisoner][312]. 1 mth recusancy from 6 Oct. 1587: conv. 29 Jan. 1587/8—VIII(38v).

SWALLOWE, Rose, 'spinster', of Bidford [on Avon], Warwicks. 1 mth recusancy from 27 June 1588: conv. 5 Mar. 1588/9—IX(11v).

---

310. Edward Sulliard and his brother Thomas were noted recusants in Suffolk. (Cf. *CRS* V, p. 73, and *CRS* XXII, p. 121.)

311. Thomas Sulliard's lands were discharged by the barons of the Exchequer. (Cf. M.R., L.T.R., 30 Eliz., Michaelmas Term, 'Recorda' section.) On 11 Nov. the lands of Thomas Sulliard were ascertained to be held by copy of the Court Rolls of the Manor of Norton, Suffolk, and consequently unseizable as a penalty for recusancy. The barons therefore decided that the 'Queen's hands' be removed therefrom, and the lands be restored to their rightful owners. (Cf. Hugh Bowler, 'Some notes on the Recusant Rolls of the Exchequer', in *RH*, vol. 4, no. 5, (1958), p. 194.)

312. Robert Sutton was listed as a prisoner in Sept. 1588, for being reconciled. (Cf. *CRS* II, p. 282.)

SWYNNEY, Alice, 'spinster', of Leigh, Staffs. 4 mths recusancy (undated): convicted 21 July 1589—IX(69v).
SWYNNEY, 'Elena', 'spinster' (same parish, recusancy period and conviction date)—IX(69v).
SWYNNEY, Thomas, 'yoman' (same parish, recusancy period and conviction date)—IX(69v).
SYLER, John, 'yom''', of Wimborne Minster, Dorset. 1 mth recusancy from 1 Jan. 1587/8: conv. 15 July 1588—VIII(19v).
SYMKINSON, Isabel, of Wyresdale, Lancs., wife of Robert Symkinson [ ]. 12 mths recusancy from 20 Sept. 1589: conv. 22 Mar. 1590/1—X(39v).
SYMONS, Joan, wife of Andrew Symons, 'yoman', of Winterborne [St.] Martin, Dorset. 6 mths recusancy from 10 Jan. 1586/7: conv. 21 July 1587—IX(16v). Debt re-enrolled—XII(78v).
SYMPSON, Alice, 'spinster', of the city of York. 4 mths recusancy from 28 Mar. 1581: conv. 17 July 1581—I(8). Debt re-enrolled—III(10). V(8). VII(8). IX(8).
SYMS, *alias* FORD, William, 'yeom''', of Netherbury, Dorset. 6 mths recusancy from 1 Jan. 1587/8: conv. 15 July 1588—VIII(19v).

TAILER, *alias* of PETTIE, Agnes.
TAILOR, Edmund, 'yeom''', of Draiton [Drayton], Oxfords. 12 mths recusancy from 26 Sept. 1586: conv. 7 Mar. 1587/8—VIII(35v).
TAILOR, Margaret, wife of Robert Tailor, 'yoman', of St. Saviour's parish, Southwark, Surrey. 3 mths recusancy from 25 Mar. 1587: conv. 5 July 1588—VIII(63).
TAILOR, Philip, [ ], of St. Peter's parish, Hereford. 6 mths recusancy from 1 Sept. 1588: conv. 14 July 1589—IX(25v). Debt re-enrolled—XI(29).
TAILOR, William, 'yeoman', of Ormesbie, Norfolk. 3 mths recusancy from 13 Apr. 1587: conv. 1 Apr. 1588—VIII(54). See TALEOR; TAYLOR.
TAILOR, *alias* LOVATT, Giles, 'husb''', of Kempley, Gloucs. 5 mths recusancy from 26 Mar. 1587: conv. 11 Mar. 1587/8—VIII(82).
TALBOTT, Talbote, Ann, of Carre [Carr Hall], Lancs., wife of George Talbott, gent. 12 mths recusancy from 20 Sept. 1589: conv. 22 Mar. 1590/1—X(40v).
TALBOTT, Talbote, John, esq., of Salebury [Salesbury], Blackburn parish, Lancs. 13 mths recusancy from 14 Aug. 1586: conv. 25 Mar. 1588—VIII(21v).
TALBOTT, John, esq., of Grafton [Manor], Worcs.[313] 12 mths recusancy ending 10 Sept. 1587 (£240 paid). 1 mth recusancy from 11 Sept. 1587

---

313. John Talbot was said to have lands worth £1,000, and goods worth £3,000 a year at least, in 1577. (Cf. *CRS* XXII, p. 65.)

to 9 Oct. (£20). Total: £260 paid.—VII(63), (63v). Annual fines for recusancy (£260): first serial payment covering period 9 Oct. 1587 to 9 Oct. 1588—VIII(77v). IX(68). X(75v). XI(70v). XII(71v).

TALBOTT, Talbotte, John, gent., of Otteringham [South Otterington], N.R. Yorks.[314]. 6 mths recusancy from 3 July 1587: conv. 18 Mar. 1587/8—VIII(27).

TALBOTT, Talbotte, Eliz., (same parish, recusancy period and conviction date)—VIII(27).

TALBOTT, *alias* MOORE, Eliz., of Dinckley, Lancs., wife of Robert Talbott, *alias* Moore, gent. 12 mths recusancy from 20 Sept. 1589: conv. 22 Mar. 1590/1—X(40v).

TALEOR, John, [   ], of Westby, Lancs. 12 mths recusancy from 20 Sept. 1589: conv. 22 Mar. 1590/1—X(39v).

TALEOR, Richard, [   ], of Heath Charnock, Lancs. 12 mths recusancy from 20 Sept. 1589: conv. 22 Mar. 1590/1—X(38v).

TALEOR, Constance, wife of Richard Taleor of Heath Charnock, Lancs. (same recusancy period and conviction date)—X(38v). See TAILOR: TAYLOR.

TALKE, *alias* TAWKE, John, gent., of St. Bride's parish, Farringdon Ward Without, London [prisoner][315]. 3 mths recusancy from 18 Mar. 1580/1: conv. 28 July 1581—I(32): and three later convictions ending 27 Dec. 1582—I(32), (35). II(30v). Debts re-enrolled—III(38v)*. V(35)*. VII(34v)*.

TALKE, Taulke, Tawke, John, 'yeoman', of Southwark, Surrey [prisoner][316]. 4 mths recusancy ending 20 July 1584, when convicted—V(50v).

TALKE, Taulke, John, 'yoman', of Newington, Surrey [? prisoner][317]. 6 mths recusancy ending 18 Feb. 1584/5, when convicted—VII(51v).

TALYARD, Ann, 'spinster', of Washingley, Hunts. 5 mths recusancy from 20 Oct. 1587: conv. 5 July 1588—VIII(7).

TASKER, Katherine, [   ], of Drayton, Salop. 12 mths recusancy from 24 Feb. 1586/7: conv. 18 July 1588—VIII(16v).

TATAM, Leonard, 'yoman', of Burye [Bury], Lancs. 4 mths recusancy from 1 Apr. 1588: conv. 17 Mar. 1588/9—X(35).

TAWKE, see Talke, John.

TAYLOR, Philip, 'yom'', of Marden, Herefords. 9 mths recusancy from 24 June 1583: conv. 2 Mar. 1583/4—V(26v).

TAYLOR, Walter, gent., of Southwark, Surrey [prisoner][318]. 4 mths recusancy ending 20 July 1584, when convicted—V(50v).

---

314. John Talbot was martyred at Durham on 9 Aug. 1600. (Cf. Hugh Bowler, 'Exchequer Dossiers I: The Recusancy of Ven. John Talbot', in *RH*, vol. 2, (1953). pp. 4–22.)

315. John Talke of Chichester, Sussex, was a prisoner in the Fleet from 1581, and was moved to the Marshalsea on 18 Dec. 1583. (Cf. *CRS* II, pp. 223, 229, 240.)

316. John Talke was wrongly described as a seminary priest in 1583. (Cf. *CRS* II, pp. 233, 236.)

317. John Talke was moved to the White Lion until Feb. 1584/5, when he ceases to reappear.

318. Walter Taylor, who was born in Dublin, was imprisoned in the Marshalsea before June 1582. (Cf. *CRS* II, p.231.)

TAYLOR, Walter, 'yom'', of Southwark, Surrey [prisoner]. 10 mths recusancy ending 11 Mar. 1582/3, when convicted—IV(49v): and two later convictions, ending 22 July 1583 and 18 Feb. 1584/5—IV(49v). V(52v). Debt re-enrolled—VI(51). See TAILOR; TALEOR.

TEASDELL, Francis, 'yeoman', of Ascome [Askham], Westmorland. 1 mth recusancy from 1 June 1588: conv. 5 Aug. 1588—IX(69).

TEBBOTT, Tebbote, John, 'clericus', of Southwark, Surrey [prisoner][319]. 2 mths recusancy ending 11 Mar. 1582/3, when convicted—III(58v). Debt re-enrolled—V(52v). See TIBBET.

TEDDER, William, 'clericus'; see TYDDER.

TEMPLE, John, gent., of Estgrinsted [East Grinstead], Sussex[320]. 2 mths recusancy from 17 Apr. 1587: conv. 26 Feb. 1587/8—VIII(63v).

TESHE, Teysshe, Edward, gent., of Bishopfeild, city of York. Fine of £50 imposed by High Commissioners (? 1579)—III(10). Debt re-enrolled—V(8). VII(8). IX(8). XII(11).

TESHE, Ann, wife of Edward Teshe, of the city of York. Fine of 100 marks imposed for hearing Mass. Convicted at Guildhall, York: 18 July 1586.— VI(8v). Debt re-enrolled—IX(8). XII(11).

TETON, Robert, 'yeoman', of Irtlingburghe [Irthlingborough], Northants. 12 mths recusancy ending 2 May 1587: conv. 12 Mar. 1587/8—VIII(52v).

THATCHER, James, esq., of Westham, Sussex. 2 mths recusancy from 17 Apr. 1587: conv. 26 Feb. 1587/8—VIII(63v). Record of land-seizure, 17 Jan. 1589/90 [⅔ of Goate manor in Ringmer; Glinde farm and lands in Westham, E. Sussex. Rent charged, £66 – 13 – 4 p.a.]. Thatcher exonerated and lands restored, Hilary term 1590[321]—IX(54v).

THATCHER, Richard, 'yoman', of Sutton, Cheshire[322]. 12 mths recusancy from 26 Sept. 1586: conv. 25 Sept. 1587—VIII(58v).

THIMOLBYE, John, gent., of Irenham [Irnham], Lincs. 3 mths recusancy from 23 June 1581: conv. 22 Sept. 1581—I(37v). Debt re-enrolled—II(45v). Goods, value £17 – 3 – 4, seized Michaelmas 1587—VII(9v)[323]. Record of land-seizure, 23 Aug. 1587 [⅔ of Manor of Corby, Lincs., and of lands & tenements in Irnham, Bulby & Hawthorpe. Rent charged: £37 – 7 – 3 p.a.]—VIII(44v). Rental of lands seized 23 Aug. 1587—IX(40v). X(42). XI(42). XII(41). Seized lands let by Crown to Edward Billesby & Michael Hennage from 23 July 1591. [Rent charged: £51 – 6 – 8 p.a.]—XI(11v). XII(41v).

---

319. John Tebbott (Cf. Anstruther I, p. 360, under Tippet.)
320. John Temple was listed as a recusant of Farleigh in Sussex in Mar. 1588. (Cf. *CRS* XXII, p. 123.)
321. James Thatcher of Priesthawes at Westham, Sussex, conformed in 1590, and his discharge is recorded in M.R., L.T.R., 32 Eliz., Hilary Term, 'Recorda' section. (Cf. Mackenzie J. Urquhart, 'A Sussex Recusant Family', in the *Dublin Review*, no. 512, (1967), pp. 162 – 170.)
322. Richard Thatcher (Cf. Wark, p. 166.)
323. John Thimbolby was discharged in Mar. 1587. (Cf. M.R., L.T.R., 29 Eliz., Michaelmas Term, 'Recorda' section.)

THISTLETON, John, 'merchaunt', of Warton, Kirkham parish, Lancs. 13 mths recusancy from 30 July 1587: conv. 17 Mar. 1588/9—X(35).

THISTLETON, John, 'yom'', of Weeton, Kirkham parish, Lancs. 13 mths recusancy from 14 Aug. 1586: conv. 25 Mar. 1588—VIII(21v).

THISTLETON, Margaret, 'spinster', of Bryning [with Kellamergh], Lancs. 12 mths recusancy from 20 Sept. 1589: conv. 22 Mar. 1590/1—X(39v).

THOMAS, Alice, 'spinster', of Llanarth, Mon. 5 mths recusancy from 24 Mar. 1586/7: conv. 13 Mar. 1587/8—VIII(48).

THOMAS, 'Aloicia' James, wife of Richard Thomas, [ ], of Llanover, Mon. (same recusancy period and conviction date)—VIII(48v).

THOMAS, David William, 'yoman', of Skenfrith, Mon. (same recusancy period & conviction date)—VIII(48).

THOMAS, 'Elnora', wife of John Thomas, [ ], of Llanllowell, Mon. (same recusancy period and conviction date)—VIII(49v).

THOMAS, Henry John, 'yoman' (same parish, recusancy period and conviction date)—VIII(49v).

THOMAS, James, 'yoman', of Llanarth, Mon. (same recusancy period & conviction date)—VIII(48).

THOMAS, James, 'yoman', of Tregare, Mon. (same recusancy period & conviction date)—VIII(49v).

THOMAS, Jane, 'spinster', of Llanarth, Mon. (same recusancy period & conviction date)—VIII(48).

THOMAS, Joan, wife of John Thomas, 'marchent', of Llandenny, Mon. (same recusancy period and conviction date)—VIII(49v).

THOMAS, Lewis, 'laborer', of Llangattock Vibon Avel, Mon. (same recusancy period and conviction date)—VIII(48v).

THOMAS, Isabel, his wife (same parish, recusancy period and conviction date)—VIII(48v).

THOMAS, Mericke, [ ], of Llangibby, Mon. 5 mths recusancy from 24 Mar. 1586/7: conv. 13 Mar. 1587/8—VIII(49v).

THOMAS, Robert, junior, 'yoman' [recusant], of Colston [? Colwinston], Glam., Wales. Lands seized for recusancy let by Crown to John Griffin from 5 Sept. 1590—X(74v).

THOMAS, William, 'yoman' [recusant], of Whitchurch, Glam., Wales. Lands seized for recusancy let by Crown to John Griffin from 5 Sept. 1590—X(74v).

THOMAS, William, 'yoman', of Llanarth, Mon. 5 mths recusancy from 24 Mar. 1586/7: conv. 13 Mar. 1587/8—VIII(48).

THOMAS, William Howell, 'yoman', of Llangattock juxta Caplion [juxta Caerleon], Mon. (same recusancy period & conviction date)—VIII(49v). Record of land-seizure, 24 Oct. 1588 [surname 'THOMAS' omitted]—IX(42v)*. Rental of land seized 24 Oct. 1588, [Rent charged by Crown, 13s.4d. p.a.]—X(50). XI(45).

THOMAS, 'Elnora' John, his wife (of same parish, same recusancy period and conviction date)—VIII(49v).

THOMAS, William Howell, 'yoman', of Llanverchia [Llanfrechfa], Mon.

(Same recusancy period and conviction date)—VIII(49v).
THOMAS, 'Elnora' John, his wife, of Llanfrechfa, Mon. (same recusancy period and conviction date)—VIII(49v).
THOMAS, Winifrid, 'spinster', of Penn, Bucks. 3 mths recusancy from 27 Mar. 1587: conv. 18 Mar. 1587/8—VIII(3).
ap THOMAS, John Thomas, 'yoman', of Llanvihangel Ystern Llewern, Mon. 5 mths recusancy from 24 Mar. 1586/7: conv. 13 Mar. 1587/8—VIII(49v).
ap THOMAS, Jane, his wife (same parish, recusancy period and conviction date)—VIII(49v).
verch THOMAS, Jane, 'spinster', of Grosmont, Mon. (same recusancy period and conviction date)—VIII(49v).
THOMPSON, Thomson, Jane, 'spinster', of St. Margaret's parish, Westminster [prisoner][324]. 1 mth recusancy from 18 May 1581: conv. 26 June 1581 [Pipe Roll entry under 'Oxfords']—I(45v). Debt re-enrolled—III(73v). V(31v).
THOMPSON, Thomson, Jane, 'spinster', of Westminster, Middx. [prisoner]. 3 mths recusancy from 27 June 1581: conv. ? Sept. 1581 [Pipe Roll entry under 'Berks']—II(65v): and four later convictions, ending 16 Mar. 1581/2—II(65v)*.
THOMPSON, John, gent., of Newland, Gloucs. 12 mths recusancy from 1 Apr. 1585: conv. 28 Feb. 1585/6—VI(23v). Debt discharged. Record of land-seizure in Oxfordshire, dated 20 Jan. 1588/9, and lease by Crown to Thomas Bostock & Edward Street. Rent charged, £33 – 10s. p.a.—VII(47v). See TOMPSON, Thompson, John.
THORNEBURIE, Edward, gent., of Chedull [Cheadle], Staffs. 12 mths recusancy from 6 Sept. 1586: conv. 25 Mar. 1588—VIII(78v).
THORNEHILL, John, gent., of Blandford St. Mary, Dorset. 12 mths recusancy from 24 July 1587: conv. 15 July 1588—VIII(19v).
THROCKMORTON, Anthony, esq., of Cheston, *alias* Chestehunte [Cheshunt], Herts. Fine of £40 imposed, in ? 1579, for contempt before John [Aylmer], Bp. of London and other High Commissioners (discharged 1585)—III(29v). Debt re-enrolled—V(27v). VII(26v).
THROCKMORTON, Throgmorton, Anthony, gent., of Westminster, Middx [prisoner][325]. 3 mths recusancy from 18 Jan. 1581/2 to 16 May 1582. Fined £60 by High Commissioners (£30 paid)—V(27).
THROCKMORTON, Throgmorton, Dorothy, wid., of parish of St. Dunstan in the West, Farringdon Ward Without, London. 3 mths recusancy prior to 20 Apr. 1588, when convicted—VIII(38v).
THROCKMORTON, Throgmorton, Margaret, wid., of Fecknam Parke, Hanbury parish, Worcs. 12 mths recusancy from 10 Mar. 1587/8: conv. 25 July 1588—VIII(80v).

---

324. Jane Thompson was discharged from the Gatehouse on 2 Jan. 1582/3. (Cf. *CRS* II, p. 231.)
325. Anthony Throckmorton, a merchant of London, was sent into the Gatehouse by the Lieutenant of the Tower in 1581. He was still there in Mar. 1583/4. (Cf. *CRS* II, pp. 225, 230.)

THROCKMORTON, Throgmorton, Thomas, esq., of [Weston Underwood] Bucks[326]. Summary of debts for continued recusancy from 27 Mar. 1587 to 29 Oct. 1588. Total £220, paid 28 Nov. 1589. Quit.—VIII(2v). Annual Fines for recusancy (£260): first serial payment, covering period 29 Oct. 1588 to 28 Oct. 1589, paid by 28 Nov. 1590. Quit.—IX(1v). X(2). XI(3). XII(2v).

THURGAR, Thurgare, Agnes, wid., of Linton, Cambs. 10 mths recusancy from 1 Sept. 1586: conv. 24 Mar. 1587/8—VIII(7v). Record of land-seizure, 3 June 1588 ($\frac{2}{3}$ of lands & tenements in Linton, occupied by Richard Thurgare. Rent charged, £2 p.a.)—IX(5v). Rental of seized lands—IX(10v). X(6). XI(6). XII(6).

THURLAND, Isabel, 'spr", wife of Edmund Thurland, gent., of Welburne [Welbourn], Kesteven, Lincs. 3 mths recusancy from 10 Oct. 1585: conv.? Jan. 1585/6—VI(9v).

THWAITES, Thwaytes, Margaret, wife of John Thwaites, of Marston in the county of the city of York. 4 mths recusancy from 28 Mar. 1581: conv. 17 July 1581—I(8). Debt re-enrolled—III(10). V(8). VII(8). IX(8).

TIBBETT, Tybbett, John, 'clericus', of Southwark, Surrey [prisoner]. 4 mths recusancy ending 22 July 1583, when convicted—IV(49v): and three later convictions, ending 18 Feb. 1584/5—V(50v), (52v). VI(51). See TEBBOTT (and footnote).

TIBOLD, Robert, 'glacier', of Bury St. Edmund, Suffolk. 3 mths recusancy from 8 Apr. 1587: conv. 27 Mar. 1588—VIII(73).

TICHEBORNE, Tycheborne, Eliz., wid., of Westysted [West Tisted], Hants. 6 mths recusancy from 1 Aug. 1587: conv. 8 July 1588—VIII(68v).

TICHEBORNE, Tycheborne, John, gent., of Somerford, parish of Christchurch, Hants. 6 mths recusancy from 1 Nov. 1586: conv. 26 Feb. 1587/8—VIII(67).

TICHEBORNE, Tycheborne, Nicholas, gent., of Hartley Mawditt [Mauditt], Hants.[327]. 18 mths recusancy ending 13 Aug. 1582, when convicted—II(52): and three later convictions, ending 8 July 1588—IV(53). VI(54). VIII(68v). Debts re-enrolled—IV(52). VI(54)*.

TIDDER, see TYDDER, William, 'clericus'.

TIDDY, Thomas, gent., of Nappa Hall, Ayskarth [Aysgarth] parish, N.R. Yorks. 13 mths recusancy from 3 Sept. 1586: conv. 4 Sept. 1587—VIII(25v).

TILER, Margaret, 'spinster', of Bennacre [Benacre], Suffolk. 6 mths recusancy from 20 Sept. 1588: conv. 2 July 1589—IX(64). Debt re-enrolled—XI(72v).

TILL, Margaret, 'spinster', of Acton, Suffolk. (same recusancy period and conviction date)—IX(64). Debt re-enrolled—XI(72v).

---

326. Thomas Throckmorton was listed as a prisoner after the Babington Plot, Sept. 1586. (Cf. CRS II, p. 257.)

327. Nicholas Ticheborne, martyr, was hanged at Tyburn, 24 Aug. 1601, for rescuing a priest, his own brother Thomas, from prison. Thomas Ticheborne himself was martyred. (Cf. Anstruther I, pp. 358, 359, under Thomas Tichbourne.)

TINDALL, Thomas, 'yoman', of Arlington, Sussex. 3 mths recusancy from
1 Nov. 1588: conv. 27 June 1589—IX(53). Goods, value £4 – 7 – 4,
seized 13 Apr. 1590—X(67).
TIPPER, Marian, 'spinster', of Longdon, Worcs. 6 mths recusancy from
29 Sept. 1587: conv. 25 July 1588—VIII(80v).
TIPPING, Hugh, of Christ Church parish, Farringdon Ward Within,
London. 3 mths recusancy from 18 Mar. 1580/1: conv. 28 July
1581—I(32v). Debt re-enrolled—III(38v). V(35).
TIRRELL, see TYRRELL, Anthony, 'clericus'.
TIRWHITTE, Tyrwhitte, Robert, gent., of Thornton, Lincs. 3 mths
recusancy from 20 June 1581: conv. 22 Sept. 1581—I(37v). Debt re-
enrolled—III(11). 1 mth recusancy from 20 Jan. 1581/2: conv. ? Mar.
1581/2—I(49): and one later period, of 2 mths recusancy, from
20 Mar. 1581/2; conv., at Old Bailey, London, on 20 Dec. 1582[328].—
I(49). Debts re-enrolled—V(9v). VII(9v).
TIRWHITTE, Robert, gent., of Lincolnshire. Fine of 100 marks imposed at
City Guildhall, London, on 11 Apr. 1582, for hearing Mass said on
7 Jan. 1581/2 by Edward Osborne in the Fleet Prison, St. Bride's
parish, Farringdon Ward Without, London[329].—I(49). Debt re-
enrolled—III(11). V(9v). VII(9v). IX(9v).
TIRWHITTE, Tyrwhitte, William, esq., of Kettleby [Thorpe], Lincs.
(a) Summary of pre-1587 debts for recusancy, from 11 Dec. 1582 to
19 Oct. 1586 (63 months, @ 28 days per month). Total £1,260.
Rendering £60 this Trinity term (1587), and £400 yearly at Michaelmas
till total debt cleared: sureties being Sir William John Mounson of
Little Carlton, Lincs., and William FitzWilliams of Mablethorpe,
Lincs—VII(9v). (b) Annual Fines for recusancy (£260): first serial
payment to cover period 29 Oct. 1586 to 28 Oct. 1587— VII(9v).
VIII(12v). IX(9v). X(42v)[330].
TOCKER, see TUCKER, John.
TOCKETTS, Roger, esq., of Dripoole, parish of Swyne, Kingston-on-Hull,
[Yorks]. 12 mths recusancy from 6 Aug. 1581: conv. 6 Aug. 1582—
II(29). Debt re-enrolled—VI(22).
TOFTWOOD, Brigit, 'spinster', of Mellis, Suffolk. 3 mths recusancy from
8 Apr. 1587: conv. 27 Mar. 1588—VIII(73).
TOFTWOOD, Christopher, gent., of Mellis, Suffolk (same recusancy
period and conviction date).—VIII(73). Record of land-seizure,

---

328. Robert Tirwhitte was discharged from the Fleet by warrant from Walsingham to make his further appearance, 22 Nov. 1582. (Cf. *CRS* II, p. 223.) In a note opposite this entry in the margin, it is recorded that, 'he has an annuity in the Manor of Buslingthorpe', Lincs.

329. Cf. footnote 257.

330. William Tirwhitte Although the writ *diem clausit extremum* on William Tirwhitte's death was recorded in the 1st. RR in 1592 (Cf. *CRS* XVIII, p. 151.) no precise date for that event is given. However, his last 'annual fine' (£120) was registered in the Pipe Roll under date, 27 Nov. 1590, when his executors completed the payment of £260 for the year 1589 – 90. A final £40 was recorded as due in 1591. (Cf. *CRS* LXI, p. 46.) and was paid on 21 Nov. 1597. (Cf. RR, 1597 – 8, under 'Linc'.)

7 Oct. 1588—IX(64). XI(65v). Rental of lands seized 7 Oct. 1588 (⅔ of lands in Melles [Mellis]. Rent charged,
£2 – 4 – 5½ p.a.)—IX(45v). X(63v). Seized lands let by Crown to Matthew Crip(p)es from Michaelmas 1589 (Rent charged, £2 – 17 – 9 p.a.)—X(80v). XI(65v)*. XII(66v).

TOFTWOOD, Ethelreda, his wife (same parish, recusancy period and conviction date)—VIII(73).

TOFTWOOD, Dorothy, 'spinster', wife of Thomas Toftwood, gent., of Mellis, Suffolk (same recusancy period and date)—VIII(73).

TOMKINS, James, 'yoman', of St. Dunstan's parish, Canterbury, Kent [? prisoner]. 9 mths recusancy ending 4 Mar. 1582/3, when convicted—III(28v): and two later convictions, ending 22 Feb. 1583/4—III(28v). IV(12). Debts re-enrolled—V(30). VI(12).

TOMLINSON, Ellen, 'spinster', of Chipping, Lancs. 12 mths recusancy from 20 Sept. 1589: conv. 22 Mar. 1590/1—X(39).

TOMPSON, Tomson, Dorothy, 'spinster', of Brodwell [Broadwell], Oxfords. 12 mths recusancy from 26 Sept. 1586: conv. 7 Mar. 1587/8—VIII(35).

TOMPSON, Jane, 'spinster', of Broadwell, Oxfords (same recusancy period and conviction date)—VIII(35).

TOMPSON, Thompson, John, gent., of Brodwell [Broadwell], Oxfords. 12 mths recusancy from 26 Sept. 1586: conv. 7 Mar. 1587/8—VIII(35). Record of land-seizure, 20 Jan. 1588/9—IX(31). X(79). Rental of lands seized 20 Jan. 1588/9, and let by Crown to Thomas Bostock & Edward Street from 5 July 1589 (⅔ of the manor of Broadwell, and of lands in Kelmscott, Over Filkins & Nether Filkins, Oxfordshire. Rent charged, £33 – 10s p.a.)—X(57v). XI(53v). XII(53v). Seizure cancelled, Easter term 1593[331]. See THOMPSON, John.

TOMPSON, Tomson, John, 'yoman', of Astley, Worcs. 6 mths recusancy from 29 Sept. 1587: conv. 25 July 1588—VIII(80v).

TOMPSON, Tomson, Katherine, wid., of Ribby, Lancs. 12 mths recusancy from 20 Sept. 1589: conv. 22 Mar. 1590/1—X(39v).

TOMPSON, Mary, 'spinster', of Asteley [Astley], Worcs. 12 mths recusancy from 20 Sept. 1586: conv. 28 Mar. 1588—VIII(77).

TOMPSON, Tomson, Richard, 'yoman', of Wesham, Lancs. 12 mths recusancy from 20 Sept. 1589: conv. 22 Mar. 1590/1—X(39).

TOMPSON, Tomson, Margaret, his wife (same parish, recusancy period & conviction date)—X(39).

TOMPSON, Robert, gent., of Brodwell [Broadwell], Oxfords. 12 mths recusancy from 26 Sept. 1586: conv. 7 Mar. 1587/8—VIII(35). See THOMPSON.

TONGE, Agnes, wife of William Tonge, 'yoman', of Hamstall Ridware, Staffs. 8 mths recusancy from 1 Aug. 1585: conv. ?13 Mar. 1586/7—VI(63v).

---

331. John Thompson had the seizure of his property cancelled in 1593. (Cf. *CRS* XVIII, p.253, and M.R., L.T.R., 35 Eliz., Easter Term, 'Recorda' section.)

TOOLEY, Margaret, 'spinster', of Marten [Merton], Norfolk. 12 mths recusancy from 10 July 1587: conv. ? 20 July 1588—IX(45): and one later conviction dated 7 July 1589—IX(45v). Debts re-enrolled—XI(48)*.

TORRELL, Frances, wid., of Great Shelford, Cambs. 10 mths recusancy from 1 Sept. 1586: conv. 24 Mar. 1587/8—VIII(7v).

TOWNELEY, John, [   ], of Colne, Lancs., son of Henry Towneley, [   ]. 12 mths recusancy from 20 Sept. 1589: conv. 22 Mar. 1590/1—X(40).

TOWNELEY, John, gent., of St. Margaret's parish, Westminster [prisoner][332]. 1 mth recusancy from 18 May 1581: conv. 26 June 1581—I(9).

TOWNELEY, John, esq., of Salford, in parish of Manchester, Lancs [prisoner]. 5 mths recusancy from 1 Aug. 1582: conv. 16 Jan. 1582/3—II(38v): and one later conviction, dated 22 Jan. 1583/4—II(37). Debt re-enrolled—IV(37). VI(39).

TOWNELEY, John, esq., of Manchester, Lancs. 9 mths recusancy: undated (1583—4) [convicted by informer's suit][333].—IV(46v).

TOWNELEY, John, esq., of Southmyms [South Mimms], Middx. 5 mths recusancy from 1 May 1585 [convicted by informer's suit][334].—V(36).

TOWNELEY, John, esq., of Cheaping [Chipping] Barnet, Herts. 5 mths recusancy from 16 Sept. 1585 [convicted by informer's suit][335].—VI(27).

TOWNELEY, John, esq., of Enfield, Middx. Summary of pre-1587 debts for recusancy (29 Aug. 1582 to 24 Oct. 1586: 54 mths, @ 28 days per month). Total £1,080. By 11 Nov. 1589 the arrears of the remaining £280 had been paid off—VII(33). Annual fines for recusancy (£260): first serial payment covering the period 24 Oct. 1586 to 23 Oct. 1587—VII(33). VIII(38). IX(33). X(37) [This was his last Pipe Roll entry under 'Lancs'].

TOWNELEY, John, esq., of Lancs[336]. Two Annual Fines (of £260) paid and consecutively registered under 'Lancs' (the 5th & 6th of the series):—
21 Oct. 1590 to 20 Oct. 1591: paid 23 Oct. 1591. Quit
20 Oct. 1591 to 19 Oct. 1592: paid 17 Nov. 1593. Quit   —X(40v)*.

TOWNELEY, Lucy, wid., of Parkehill [Whalley], Lancs. 12 mths recusancy from 20 Sept. 1589: conv. 22 Mar. 1590/1—X(40).

---

332. John Townley was a prisoner in the Gatehouse, and was then sent to the New Fleet Prison in Salford by the Privy Council, 11 July 1581. (Cf. *CRS* II, pp. 220, 230.)

333. John Townley (Cf. M.R., L.T.R., 26/27 Eliz. Michaelmas Term, 'Recorda' section, rotulet 203. 9 months recusancy £180, paid 26 May 1585, and he is quit.)

334. John Townley (Cf. M.R., Q.R., 27 Eliz., Michaelmas Term, 'Recorda' section, rotulet 271. The informer was Simon Maxey of Potton, Beds., yeoman. He paid £100 for 5 months recusancy from 1 May 1585 on 10 June 1586. And he is quit.)

335. John Townley (Cf. M.R., Q.R., 28 Eliz., Hilary Term, 'Recorda' section, rotulet 177. The informer was the same, and he paid £100 for 5 months recusancy from 16 Sept. 1585 on 10 Jun. 1586. And he is quit.)

336. References to Enfield cease with this entry, and show that Townley's permanent residence was now probably Townley Hall, in the parish of Burnley, Lancs. (Cf. *CRS* XXII, p. 126.)

TOWNELEY, Robert, esq., of Barneside [Whalley], Lancs. (same recusancy period and conviction date)—X(40).

TOWNELEY, Sarah, 'spinster', of Burnley, Lancs. (same recusancy period and conviction date)—X(40).

TOWNEND, Isabel, 'spinster', of Weeton, Lancs. 12 mths recusancy from 20 Sept. 1589: conv. 22 Mar. 1590/1—X(39v).

TOWNEND, Margaret, wid., of Weton [Weeton], Kirkham parish, Lancs. 13 mths recusancy from 30 July 1587: conv. 17 Mar. 1588/9—X(35): and one later conviction, dated 22 Mar. 1590/1—X(39).

TOWNEND, Margaret, of Plumpton, Lancs., wife of Richard Townend, junior [   ]. 12 mths recusancy from 20 Sept. 1589: conv. 22 Mar. 1590/1—X(39v).

TOWNESHEND, Ann, wife of Edward Towneshend, gent., of Long Stratton, Norfolk. 3 mths recusancy from 13 Apr. 1587: conv. 1 Apr. 1588—VIII(54).

TOWNESHEND, Edmund, gent., of Bennacre [Benacre], Suffolk. 3 mths recusancy from 8 Apr. 1587: conv. 27 Mar. 1588—VIII(73).

TOWNESHEND, Townesend Edmund, gent., of Long Stratton, Norfolk. 3 mths recusancy from 13 Apr. 1587: conv. 1 Apr. 1588—VIII(54). Record of land – seizure, 18 Oct. 1588—IX(45). Rental of seized lands ($\frac{2}{3}$ of a tenement and lands in Long Stratton, Norfolk. Rent charged, 9s. 4d. p.a.)—IX(45). X(52v). XI(46v). XII(47v).

TOWNESHEND, Tounshend, Giles, gent., of Cawkett [? Caldecote], Norfolk. 3 mths recusancy from 13 Apr. 1587: conv. 1 Apr. 1588—VIII(54).

TOWNSHEND, Thomas, gent., of Cocle Claye [Cockley Cley], Norfolk. 1 mth recusancy from 10 June 1582: conv.? July 1582—IV(44v).

TRAVERS, Traverse, Ann, of Natebye [nr Garstang], Lancs., wife of William Traverse, esq. 12 mths recusancy from 20 Sept. 1589: conv. 22 Mar. 1590/1—X(39).

TRAVES, Travers, Matthew, gent., of Salford in the parish of Manchester, Lancs [prisoner]. 12 mths recusancy from 20 Feb. 1582/3: conv. 22 Jan. 1583/4—IV(37): and two later convictions, ending 20 Apr. 1585—VI(40v). Debts re – enrolled—IV(42v). VI(39). Seized property (a messuage in Windle, Lancs) let by Crown to High Cuffe from Michaelmas 1585—VI(33v). VIII(16v). X(35v). XII(9).

TRAVIS, Traves, Travys, Thomas, 'yoman', of Stevington [Steventon], Hants. 2 mths recusancy from 19 Mar. 1580/1: conv. 28 June 1581—I(55): and one later conviction, dated 9 Jan. 1581/2—I(55)*. Debts re – enrolled—III(62). V(56). VII(54).

TRAVIS, William, [   ], of St. George's parish, Southwark, Surrey [prisoner][337]. 5 mths recusancy from 17 Feb. 1586/7: conv. 17 July 1587—IX(54).

---

337. William Travis was a prisoner in the Marshalsea, and described as 'an obstinate recusant' on 25 Sept. 1586. (Cf. *CRS* II, p. 259.)

TREMAYNE, Jane, 'spinster', of Stepney, Middx. 3 mths recusancy from 5 Apr. 1587: conv. 1 Sept. 1587—VIII(38v).
TREMAYNE, Tremane, Mary, 'spinster' (same parish, recusancy period and conviction date)—VIII(38v).
TREMAYNE, Richard, gent. (same parish, recusancy period & conviction date)—VIII(38v).
TREMAYNE, Joan, his wife (same parish, recusancy period & conviction date)—VIII(38v).
TREMAYNE, Tremaine, Richard, gent., of Goreham [St. Goran], Cornwall[338]. 14 mths recusancy ending 20 Apr. 1582: conv. 3 Sept. 1582—II(6v); and one later conviction, ending ? 10 Sept. 1582—III(8). V(6). VI(6). Lands in Cornwall seized and let by Crown to Hugh Cuffe, Michaelmas, 1585 (two tenements called 'Tregannon' and 'Ludcotte'. Rent charged, £8 p.a.)—VI(33v). VIII(16v). X(8). XI(7). XII(7). Summary of debts for recusancy (Total of £320 reduced to £286 – 13 – 4 by payment of £33 – 6 – 8 on 12 Nov. 1584)—III(8). VI(6). Record of land-seizure in Cornwall, 21 Apr.1588—VIII(8). Rental of lands seized on 21 Apr. 1588 ($\frac{2}{3}$ of tenements in Tregonan, Trelissick, Morval and St. Martin. Rent charged, £22 – 4 – 5 p.a.)— VIII(8v). IX(6). Seized lands in Cornwall let by Crown to Hannibal Vivian from 18 Mar. 1588/9—IX(6). X(8). XI(7). XII(7).
TREMAYNE, Tremane, Sampson, gent., of Chideok, Dorset. 12 mths recusancy from 1 Apr. 1583: conv. Lent, 1584—IV(16v).
TREMAYNE, Tremaine, Sampson, 'yom''', of Dorchester, Dorset. 5 mths recusancy from 23 Mar. 1583/4: conv. 24 Aug. 1584—IV(16v).
TREMAYNE, Eleanor, his wife (of same parish). 6 months recusancy from 1 Jan. 1587/8: conv. 15 July 1588—VIII((19v).
TREMAYNE, Tremane, Sampson, gent., of Dorchester, Dorset. 5 mths recusancy from 1 Sept. 1585: conv. 28 Feb. 1585/6—VI(16): and one later conviction, dated 4 Mar. 1587/8—VIII(19).
TRESSHAM, Sir Thomas, knt., of St. Bride's parish, Farringdon Ward Without, London [prisoner][339]. 1 mth recusancy from 7 Dec. 1581: conv. 19 Jan. 1581/2—I(4v): and three later convictions, ending 18 Jan. 1582/3—I(4v). II(41v) [Total debts paid into Treasury:— £100, 21 Nov. 1582; £180, 29 May 1585. And he is quit.]

---

338. Richard Tremayne was born at Mastowe in Devon. He was committed to the custody of the Marshall of the King's Bench Prison by the Sheriff of Cornwall, 4 Feb. 1583/4. (Cf. *CRS* II, pp. 227, 230). Indicted, with his wife Joan, for recusancy in 1577, he was living in Devonshire in 1577, and Bethnall Green in 1588. (Cf. *CRS* XXII, pp. 76, 102, 123.) He was a prisoner in London in 1588. (Cf. *CRS* II, p. 283.)

339. Sir Thomas Tresham, knighted in 1577, was reconciled to the church by Fr. Robert Parsons in 1580. He was summoned to the Privy Council on 18 Aug. 1581, and committed to the Fleet for harbouring St. Edmund Campion. He remained confined for the next seven years, chiefly in the Fleet, later in his own house at Hoxton and then at Ely. He was released on bail on 29 Nov. 1588. He died on 11 Sept. 1605, and was buried at St. Peter's Rushton, Northants. (Cf. *DNB* LVII, p. 204, and *CRS* II, pp. 223, 229.)

Fine of 100 marks imposed on Sir Thomas Tressham at Guildhall, London, sessions of Oyer & Terminer, 11 April 1582, for hearing Mass said on 7 Jan. 1581/2 by Edward Osborne in the Fleet prison, parish and ward aforesaid[340]. Fine [£66 – 13 – 4] paid 21 Nov. 1584.—I(4v).

TRESSHAM, Tresham, Sir Thomas, knt., of Rusheton [Rushton], Northants. Summary of pre – 1587 debts for recusancy [Total debt at Michaelmas 1587 = £953 – 6 – 8, being the remainder of an original debt of £1,260 for 63 mths of recusancy @ 28 days per mth, from 20 Dec. 1582 to 24 Oct 1586; to be settled by a payment to the Exchequer of £353 – 6 – 8 at Michaelmas 1587, and by two further payments of £300 at Michaelmas 1588 and 1589]—VII(42v)[341]. Statement re-enrolled—IX(47). Annual fines for recusancy (£260) paid: first serial payment covering period 29 Oct. 1586 to 28 Oct. 1587—VII(42v). VIII(52v). IX(47). X(54v). XI(50v). XII(49v).

TREVETHEN, Walter, [ ], of Southwark, Surrey [prisoner][342]. 10 mths recusancy ending 17 Feb. 1585/6, when convicted—VI(49v).

TREVIN, Philip, 'yoman', of Leigh, Staffs. 6 mths recusancy from 6 Sept. 1587: conv. 22 July 1588—VIII(58).

TRIME, Thomas, 'lab'', of St. Mary's parish, city of Chester, Cheshire [prisoner][343]. 8 mths recusancy from 1 Sept. 1584 to 26 Apr. 1585, when convicted—VI(48v): and one later period (5 mths) from ? Apr. 1585 to 14 Sept. 1585, when convicted—VI(48v).

TRIME, Thomas, 'yoman', of Chester Castle, Cheshire [prisoner]. 13 mths recusancy from 14 Sept. 1585 to 15 Sept. 1586: conv. 3 Oct. 1586—X(35v): and one later period (7 mths) from 26 Sept. 1586 to 24 Apr. 1587, when convicted—VIII(58v).

TROWELL, Nicholas, [ ], of Ashby Magna, Leics. 9 mths recusancy ending 10 Aug. 1587, when convicted—VIII(45v).

TUCKER, Tocker, John, 'printer', of Southwark, Surrey [prisoner][344]. 10 mths recusancy ending 11 Mar. 1582/3, when convicted—III(58v): and one later conviction, dated 22 July 1583—IV(49v). Debt re-enrolled—V(52v).

---

340. Edward Osborne (Cf. footnote 257.) For Osborne's confession, see *CRS* V, pp. 27, 28. Edward ROGERS and his wife, attended the same mass.

341. Sir Thomas Tressham's first payment of £353 – 6 – 5 was made on 13 May 1588 (VII(42v)), reducing the total debt to £600. His second payment dealt with a number of smaller debts totalling £273 – 6 – 8. (Cf. *CRS* LVIII, pp. 116, 117; and Introd., p.xxxii, footnote 103.) This final debt of £273 – 6 – 8 was not covered until 1592, when Sir Thomas Tresham and his two sureties (Louis, Lord Mordaunt of Drayton and Edward Watson of Rockingham) were discharged, and, by a recognisance before the Exchequer barons dated 12 May 1592, the debt in the sum of £400 was taken over by Jervase Clifton, esq., son and heir apparent of Sir John Clifton of Bassington, Somerset, and Nicholas Farmor of Hardwick, Oxford, as recorded under RR no. 6 (E. 377/6), under 'Northants'.

342. Walter Trevethen was a prisoner (unidentified) in the Clink in Southwark.

343. Thomas Trine (Cf. Wark, p. 166.)

344. John Tucker was one of four printers seized at Stonor Park on 4 Aug. 1581. He was sent to the Tower of London, 13 Aug. 1581, from thence removed to the Marshalsea, 23 Aug. 1581, and was there confined until 30 Sept. 1588. The date of his release was not given. (Cf. *CRS* II, pp. 30 footnote, 233, 283.)

TUCKER, Tocker, John, gent., of Southwark, Surrey [prisoner]. 4 mths recusancy ending 20 July 1584, when convicted—V(50v).

TUCKER, Tocker, John, 'yoman', of Southwark, Surrey [prisoner]. 4 mths recusancy ending 22 July 1583, when convicted—VI(51): and three later convictions, ending 16 Feb. 1586/7—V(52v). VI(49v). VI(50).

TUCKER, Margery, 'spinster', of Clerkenwell, Middx. 6 mths recusancy from 1 Oct. 1587: conv. 19 Apr. 1588—IX(37).

TUCKER, Tocker, William, gent., of Southwark, Surrey [prisoner][345]. 10 mths recusancy ending 11 Mar. 1582/3, when convicted—IV(49v): and two later convictions, ending 15 Feb. 1583/4—IV(49v)*. Debts re-enrolled—VI(51)*. Seized lands in London and Essex let by Crown to Hugh Cuffe from Michaelmas 1585—VI(33v). VIII(16v). Seized lands in the city of London, let by Crown to Hugh Cuffe from Michaelmas 1585 [tenement called 'le Blewbell' in Bread Street, London. Rent charged, £3 p.a.]—X(46). XI(36v). XII(36v). Seized lands in Essex, let by Crown to Hugh Cuffe from Michaelmas 1585 [two cottages, with appurtenances, in Barking, Essex. Rent charged, £1 – 10s p.a.] – X(26v). XII(20v).

TUCKER, William, gent., of St. Sepulchre's parish, Bishopsgate Ward, London. 3 mths recusancy prior to 20 Apr. 1588, when convicted – VIII(38v).

TUKE, Henry, 'yeoman', of Harrowden, Northants[346]. 12 mths recusancy ending 2 May 1587: conv. 12 Mar. 1587/8 – VIII(52v).

TURBERVILE, Lewis, gent., of Llancarvan [Llancarfan], Glam., Wales. Seized lands let by Crown to John Cornewall from Ladyday 1589 [$\frac{2}{3}$ of a messuage & 30 acres of land, with appurtenances in Llanbetherne [Llanbethery], parish of Llancarfan, in tenure of Mary George, wid. Yearly value, £2 – 4 – 5]—X(74v).

TURBERVILE, Thomas, esq., of Beer [Bere] Regis, Dorset. Fine of £100 imposed by High Commissioners, 16 June 1578. £30 due by Michaelmas 1588 (fine paid)—VI(16).

TURBERVILE, Thomasina, his wife, of Bere Regis, Dorset. 9 mths recusancy from 4 Oct. 1586: conv. 4 Mar. 1587/8—VIII(19).

TURBILL, Richard, 'laborier', of Longdon, Worcs. 2 mths recusancy from 7 Apr. 1588: conv. 6 Mar. 1588/9—IX(70v). See TURVILL.

TURNER, 'Jenetta', wid., of Thistleton, Lancs. 12 mths recusancy from 20 Sept. 1589: conv. 22 Mar. 1590/1—X(39).

TURNER, Richard, 'yoman', of Southwark, Surrey [prisoner][347]. 3 mths recusancy ending 15 Feb. 1583/4, when convicted—IV(49v). Debt re-enrolled—VI(51).

---

345. William Tucker was sent to the Marshalsea by the Bishop of London, 28 July 1580, for 'papistry' (Cf. *CRS* I, p. 71.), and, as 'Tocker', was still there in Mar. 1582/3. (Cf. *CRS* II, p. 231.)

346. Henry Tuke, 'serving man and servant to Lord Vaux', was committed to the Poultry Counter, 25 Feb. 1581/2, and discharged 7 July 1582. (Cf. *CRS* II, pp. 223, 229.)

347. Richard Turner was sent to the Marshalsea on 4 Oct. 1583, and was still there in Apr. 1584. (Cf. *CRS* II, pp. 233, 236.)

TURNOR, Brigit, wife of James Turnor, gent., of Killinghall, parish of
　　Ripley, W. R. Yorks. 13 mths recusancy from 3 Sept. 1586: conv.
　　4 Sept. 1587—VIII(25v).
TURNOR, Thomas, 'yom'', of Garwey [Garway], Herefords. Fine of 100
　　marks imposed for hearing Mass. Convicted 8 Aug. 1586—VI(25).
TURVILL, Richard, 'yoman', of Fairend, Worcs. 12 mths recusancy from
　　5 Mar. 1587/8: conv. 14 July 1589—IX(68v). See TURBILL.
TWIFORD, Richard, 'yoman', of Sondon [Sandon], Staffs. 6 mths
　　recusancy from 6 Sept. 1587: conv. 22 July 1588—VIII(58).
TYDDER, Tedder, Tidder, William, 'clericus', of Southwark, Surrey
　　[prisoner][348]. 2 mths recusancy ending 11 Mar. 1582/3, when
　　convicted—III(58v). Debt re-enrolled—V(52v).
TYLLYE, William, 'yoman', of Steyning, Sussex. 2 mths recusancy from
　　17 Apr. 1587: conv. 26 Feb. 1587/8—VIII(63v).
TYLSON, Tilletson, Francis, 'clericus', of Southwark, Surrey [prisoner][349].
　　7 mths recusancy ending 17 Feb. 1585/6, when convicted—VI(49v).
TYRRELL, Tirell, Anthony, 'clericus', of St. Margaret's parish,
　　Westminster [prisoner][350]. 1 mth recusancy from 18 May 1581: conv.
　　26 June 1581—I(19v). Debt re-enrolled—III(22). V(19v).

URMESTON, *alias* RYCHARDSON, Thomas, 'yoman', of Horwich,
　　Lancs. 12 mths recusancy from 24 Aug. 1589: conv. 22 Mar.
　　1590/1—X(40v).
USSHERWOOD, Issherwood, Christoper, 'husb'', of Thornley with
　　Wheatley, Lancs. 12 mths recusancy from 20 Sept. 1589: conv.
　　22 Mar. 1590/1—X(39).
USSHERWOOD, Usherwood, Christopher, 'husb'', of the parish of 'St,
　　Mary on the Hill', Chester, Cheshire [prisoner]. 8 mths recusancy
　　from 1 Sept. 1584: conv. ? 26 April 1585—VI(48v).
USSHERWOOD, Usherwood, Christopher, 'yoman', of Chester Castle,
　　Cheshire [prisoner][351]. 13 mths recusancy from 14 Sept. 1585: conv.
　　3 Oct. 1586—VIII(58v); and one later conviction, dated 24 Apr.
　　1587—X(35v).
UVEDALE, Uvedall, Anthony, esq., of Hambledon, Hants. 6 mths
　　recusancy from 1 Nov. 1586: conv. 25 Feb. 1586/7—VIII(67).
　　Goods, value £100, seized 8 Nov. 1588 (20 acres of woodland, called
　　Beech Wood, and 20 acres of oaks)—IX(58). Record of land-seizure,
　　8 Nov. 1588 (Two thirds of Woodcote farm near Alesford [Old
　　Alresford]. Rent charge, £16 – 4 – 6 p.a.) – IX(58). Rental of seized
　　lands—IX(59v). X(68). Seized lands at Woodcote let by Crown to
　　Charles Pagett from 30 May 1589 for a rent of £16 – 4 – 6 p.a.—
　　X(68v). XI(59v). XII(60v).

---

348. William Tydder (Cf. Anstruther I, pp. 347, 348, under Tedder.)
349. Francis Tylson (Cf. Anstruther I, pp. 359, 360, under Tilletson.)
350. Anthony Tyrrell (Cf. Anstruther I, pp. 361 – 363, under Tirell.)
351. Christopher Ussherwood (Cf. Wark, p. 154, under Isherwood.)

VACHELL, Vachill, Stephen, gent., of Berryton [Buriton], Hants. 18 mths recusancy from 18 Mar. 1580/1: conv. Sept. 1582 – III(50v): and one later conviction, dated 26 Feb. 1587/8 (for 10 mths recusancy)— VIII(67). Debt re-enrolled—V(56). Record of land-seizure, 30 May 1589 (Two-thirds of Heath House farm in Buriton near Petersfeild. Rent charge, £48 – 17 – 10 p.a. [352]). Rental of lands seized 30 May 1589—IX(59v). X(68v). XI(59v). Seized lands at Heath House let by Crown to Charles Pagett for a reduced rent of £18 – 6 – 6 p.a. from 4 May 1593.

VACHELL, Thomas, gent./esq., of Ippesden [Ipsden], Oxfords. 12 mths recusancy from 26 Sept. 1586: conv. 7 Mar. 1587/8—VIII(35). Rental of lands in Berks, seized 24 Apr. 1589 (The whole tenement called 'Beansheaves' in Tilehurst; two-thirds of property at Coley House, Reading, and in Burghfeild, Greshill, North Street and Shinfeild. Rent charged, £24 – 16 – 4 p.a.)—IX(4v). Seized lands in Berks. let by Crown to John Arden and Vincent Coventry from 7 July 1589, for same rent.—IX(4v). X(3). XI(4). XII(4). Rental of lands in Oxfords. seized 23 May 1589 (Two-thirds of a parcel of land called 'Payges', estimated to contain 30 acres, in Mapledurham, Oxon., and two-thirds of the manors of Ipsden Huntercombe & Ipsden Bassett, Oxon. Rent charged, £13 – 14 – 8 p.a.)—IX(31). X(57). Seized lands in Oxfords. let by Crown to Thomas Read from Ladyday 1589, for same rent—IX(31v). XI(53). XII(53v).

VAUGHAN, Edward, gent., of the parish of 'Le Stronde, alias Savoy', London. 3 mths recusancy from 10 Mar. 1588/9: conv. 4 Sept. 1589—IX(37).

VAUGHAN, Jane, wife of William Vaughan, gent., of Welsh Bicnor [Bicknor], Herefords. 12 mths recusancy from 1 Sept. 1586: conv. 18 Mar. 1587/8—VIII(30).

VAUGHAN, Joan, 'spinster', of St. Saviour's parish, Southwark, Surrey [? prisoner][353]. 3 mths recusancy from 29 Sept. 1588: Conv. 30 June 1589—IX(53).

VAUGHAN, Margery, wife of Richard Vaughan, esq., of Kynnersley [Kinnersley], Herefords. 12 mths recusancy from 1 Sept. 1586: conv. 18 Mar. 1587/8—VIII(30).

VAUGHAN, Vaughen, Michael, gent., of Winforton, Herefords (same recusancy period and conviction date)—VIII(30). Record of land-seizure, 23 Aug. 1588 (Two-thirds of the manor of Winferton [Winforton], with appurtenances in Co. Hereford)—IX(25v). Rental

---

352. Stephen Vachell From 1592 the Exchequer decided to reduce the rent of Heath House from £48 – 17 – 10 *per annum*, to £18 – 6 – 6 (two annual payments of £9 – 3 – 3) and prohibited the further charge of £30 – 11 – 4. (Cf. M.R., L.T.R., 31 and 32 Eliz., Michaelmas Term. 'Recorda' section, see *CRS* XVIII, p. 286, and *CRS* LVII, p. 39, footnote.) The yearly payment of £18 – 6 – 6 continued until 1598.

353. Joan Vaughan was a prisoner (unidentified) in the Clink in Southwark.

of seized lands (Rent charged, £22 – 4 – 5½ p.a.: unpaid)—IX(25v). X(28). XI(28). XII(28).[354]

VAUGHAN, Reginald William, gent., of Whitechurche [Whitchurch], Herefords. Two fines of £20 imposed for ignoring the sheriff's summonses after excommunication, 4 Apr. 1581 and 4 Oct. 1581—III(28)*. Debts re-enrolled—V(26), (26v).

VAUX, George, esq., of Great Harrowden, Northants. 12 mths recusancy from 31 July 1587: conv. 4 Mar. 1588/9—IX(47).

VAUX, Henry, gent., of Tottenham, Middx[355]. 3 mths recusancy from 1 Oct. 1583: conv. 1 Jan. 1583/4—IV(32v). Debt re-enrolled—VI(34).

VAUX OF HARROWDEN, William, Lord, of St. Bride's parish, Farringdon Ward Without, London [prisoner][356]. Fine of 100 marks imposed at London Guildhall sessions of Oyer & Terminer, 11 Apr. 1582, for hearing Mass said on 7 Jan. 1581/2 by Edward Osborne in the Fleet prison, parish and ward aforesaid—I(4v). VII(42v).

VAUX OF HARROWDEN, William, Lord, of St. Bride's parish, Farringdon Ward Without, London [Pipe Roll entry under 'Northants']. 6 mths recusancy from 11 Oct. 1581: conv. 11 Apr. 1582—I(4v). Debt re-enrolled—III(48v). V(43v).

VAUX, William, Lord of Harrowden, Northants [3rd Baron]. Summary of pre-1587 debts for recusancy: £853 – 6 – 8 (unpaid)—VII(42v). Debts re-enrolled—IX(47). XII(49v). Seizure of Lord Harrowden's lands in Northants., 3 Oct. 1587 (Two-thirds of manors of Great & Little Harrowden, Isham, Clipston & Mears Ashby etc. Rent charge, £259 – 13 – 4 p.a.)—VIII(52v). IX(46v). XI(49v). XII(49v). Seizure of Lord Harrowden's lands in Beds., 28 Sept. 1587 (Two-thirds of manors of Patenham [? Pavenham] & Eaton Socon. Rent charge, £58 – 5 – 6 p.a. [357])—VIII(lv). IX(1). X(5). XI(1). XII(1). Seizure of Lord Harrowden's lands in Cambs., 14 Oct. 1587 (Two-thirds of manors of Cheynes & Wallinge in Long Stanton & Fendytton, called 'Dytton Hall'. Rent charge, £42 – 14s. p.a.)—VIII(30v). IX(5). X(6). Seizure of Lord Harrowden's lands in Lincs., 22 Aug. 1587

---

354. Michael Vaughan's Manor of Winforton, Herefords., was revalued by the Exchequer, 4 Oct. 1595, and let to Gregory Price, esq., from 31 Jan. 1595/6 for a reduced rent of £8 – 17 – 10 *per annum*. At the same time the previous debts (£166 – 13 – 4) up to Michaelmas 1595 were cancelled, except one debt of £22 – 4 – 5½. (Cf. M.R., L.T.R., 31 Eliz., Hilary Term, 'Recorda' section, see *CRS* LXI, p. 155.)

355. Henry and George Vaux, the elder and younger sons of William, Lord Vaux of Harrowden, were also indicted three times for recusancy between 14 Dec. 1584 and 1 Oct. 1585, as 'of Hackney, Middx.' (Cf. Jeaffreson I, p. 144 *seq*.)

356. William Vaux, Lord Vaux, was imprisoned in the Fleet for a period at this time. (Cf. Godfrey Anstruther, *Vaux of Harrowden*, (1953), p. 225.)

357. Lord Vaux's lands seized on 28 Sept. 1587, were taken to recover his debts of £1,420. (Cf. *CRS* LVII, Introd., p.xxxi, footnotes 97 and 98.)

(Two – thirds of the manor of Brant Broughton. Rent charge, £21 – 2 – 11 p.a.)—VIII(44v). IX(40v). X(42). XI(42). XII(41).[358]

VAVISOR, Vaviser, Frances, 'spinster', of Warton [Wharton] in Lindsey, Blyton parish, Lincs. 10 mths recusancy from 8 Sept. 1586: conv. 28 Mar. 1588—VIII(44v).

VAVISOR, Vaviser, Thomas, gent., of Rushton, Northants. 12 mths recusancy ending 2 May 1587: conv. 12 Mar. 1587/8—VIII(52v).

VERNON, Eliz., wid., of Drayton [in Hales], Salop[359]. 12 mths recusancy from 24 Feb. 1586/7: conv. 18 July 1588—VIII(16v).

VERNON, Robert, gent., (same parish, recusancy period and conviction date)—VIII(16v).

VERNON, Thomas, gent., (same parish, recusancy period and conviction date)—VIII(16v). Goods, value £11 – 10s., seized 9 Oct. 1589—IX(13v). Debt re-enrolled—X(58v). XI(63v). Record of land-seizure, 9 Oct. 1589—IX(13v). Rental of seized lands (Two-thirds of a tenement with appurtenances called 'Ternehill' in Drayton. Rent charge, £2 – 13 – 4 p.a.)—IX(69v). X(59v). XI(62v). Seized lands let by Crown to William Jewett from 16 Apr. 1590[360]—X(58v). XI(62v).

VEYNE, Reginald John, 'yoman', of Grosmont, Mon. 5 mths recusancy from 24 Mar. 1586/7: conv. 13 Mar. 1587/8—VIII(49v).

VIES, Vice, Joan, 'spinster', of Standon, Staffs. 4 mths recusancy from 31 Mar. 1582: conv. 2 Aug. 1582—II(14): and four later indictments ending 1 Aug. 1586—III(64v). IV(62v). VI(63v)*. Debts re-enrolled IV(62). V(66). VI(63). See VYES. VYSE.

VIEZ, Vies, Edmund, 'yoman', of Stoke [upon Trent], Staffs. 6 mths recusancy from 25 Mar. 1588: conv. 14 Mar. 1588/9—IX(69v).

VIVIAN, John, 'clericus', of Southwark, Surrey [prisoner][361]. 1 mth recusancy from 5 June 1588: conv. 5 July 1588—VIII(63).

VOWELL, Thomas, gent., of Ringestead [Ringstead], Norfolk[362]. 3 mths recusancy from 13 Apr. 1587: conv. 1 Apr. 1588—VIII(54).

VYSE, Vyes, Joan, 'spinster', of Stoke [upon Trent], Staffs. 8 mths recusancy from 22 July 1581: conv. 22 Mar. 1581/2—I(13): and two later indictments ending 19 July 1585—V(66)*. Debts re-enrolled—III(71). V(66).

---

358. The only recorded rent payment from Lord Harrowden's seized lands, was the sum of £7 – 19 – 2 paid into the Treasury on 13 May 1594, from the Manor of Brant Broughton, Lincs. (Cf. CRS LVII, p.88.) These four entries in Beds., Cambs., Lincs., and Northants. are annotated by the word 'supersedeas' in 1595 (the year of Lord Harrowden's death) and disappear from the Rolls.

359. Elizabeth Vernon, widow, and her two sons, Robert and Thomas, of the Diocese of Coventry and Lichfield, were reported as recusants in Nov. 1577. (Cf. CRS XXII, p. 94.) The daughter, Margery, was also mentioned.

360. Thomas Vernon's lands were discharged. (Cf. M.R., L.T.R., 33 Eliz., Hilary Term, 'Recorda' section.)

361. John Vivian (Cf. Anstruther I, p. 367).

362. Thomas Vowell was reported as a recusant at Ringstead, Norfolk, in Mar. 1588. (Cf. CRS XXII, p. 121.)

WADDINGTON, Edward, 'scholm[aster]', of Churche, Lancs. 12 mths recusancy from 20 Sept. 1589: conv. 22 Mar. 1590/1—X(40).

WADE, Margery, 'supposed recusant & fugitive', of Staffs. Goods, value £7 – 2 – 2, seized 4 Sept. 1589—X(14).[363]

WAITE, Ann, wife of Henry Waite, gent., of Tittleshall, Norfolk. 3 mths recusancy from 13 Apr. 1587: conv. 1 Apr. 1588—VIII(54).

WAKEMAN, Joan, wife of Richard Wakeman, 'yeoman', of 'the county of Worcester'. 12 mths recusancy from 20 Sept. 1586: conv. 28 Mar. 1588—VIII(77).

WAKEMAN, Wakemane, John, 'yoman', of Steyning, Sussex. 2 mths recusancy from 17 Apr. 1587: conv. 26 Feb. 1587/8—VIII(63v).

WAKEMAN, Roger, 'clericus', of St. Michael's parish, Cripplegate Ward, London [prisoner][364]. 3 mths recusancy from 18 Mar. 1580/1: conv. 28 July 1581—I(32): and two later indictments ending 20 Dec. 1581—I(35)*. Debts re-enrolled—III(38v)*. V(35)*.

WALBANCK, Eliz., wid., of Exelbye [? Eppleby], in Gilling parish, N.R. Yorks. 13 mths recusancy from 3 Sept. 1586: conv. 4 Sept. 1587—VIII(25v).

WALDERN, Richard, [   ], of Aston near Brymyngham [Birmingham], Warwicks. 6 mths recusancy from 1 Sept. 1588: conv. 21 July 1589—IX(11v).

WALDRON, Walrond, Walrand, George, gent., of Alborne [Aldbourne], Wilts. 6 mths recusancy from 2 Jan. 1586/7: conv. 1 Mar. 1587/8—VIII(74v). Record of land-seizure, 8 Oct. 1588—IX(66). Rental of seized lands (Two-thirds of lands & tenements in Aldbourne. Rent charged, £13 – 6 – 8 p.a.)—IX(66). Seized lands let by Crown to Freman Younge from 5 May 1589, for a rent of £13 – 6 – 8 p.a.— IX(66). X(76v). XI(67v). XII(68v).

WALDRON, Walderne, Walderen, Richard, 'linen draper', of Southwark, Surrey [prisoner][365]. 10 mths recusancy ending 11 Mar. 1582/3, when convicted—IV(49v): and three later indictments, ending 16 Feb. 1586/7—IV(49v)*. VI(50). Debts re-enrolled—V(50v). VI(51)*.

WALDRON, Richard, 'linen draper', of Newington, Surrey [prisoner]. 6 mths recusancy ending 18 Feb. 1584/5, when convicted—V(52v): and one later indictment, dated 17 Feb. 1585/6—VI(49v).

WALKER, Charles, 'yom'', of Rawroyd, W.R. Yorks. 2 mths recusancy from 4 Jan. 1585/6: conv. 14 Mar. 1585/6—VI(20v): and one later indictment, dated 18 Mar. 1587/8—VIII(25v).

---

363. Margery Wade of Hamstell Ridware, Staffs., 'a tenant or sevant of Sir Thos Fitzherbert', was listed as a recusant in 1577. (Cf. *CRS* XXII, p. 88.)

364. Roger Wakeman (Cf. Anstruther I, pp. 368, 369.) The Pipe Roll entry in this case has the marginal note, 'fieri faciat vicecomiti Glouc', indicating that the Sheriff of Gloucester was responsible for levying the debt in this case of recusancy.

365. Richard Waldron was committed first to the Poultry Counter by the Commissioners for ecclesiastical causes on 29 April 1580. He was removed to the Tower on 17 May 1580. (Cf. *CRS* I, p. 56.) On 8 Apr. 1584, he was found in the White Lion prison in Newington, Surrey. This 'poor simpleman' spent 15 years in prison, and appears to have been released in 1595. (Cf. *CRS* II, pp. 237, 287.)

WALKER, Eliz., 'spinster', of Kirtleton [? Kirtlington], Oxfords. 12 mths recusancy from 26 Sept. 1586: conv. 7 Mar. 1587/8—VIII(35v).
WALKER, Frances, wid., of Rypley [Ripley], W.R. Yorks. 13 mths recusancy from 3 Sept. 1586: conv. 4 Sept. 1587—VIII(25v).
WALKER, George, 'husb", of Whichnor [Wichnor], Staffs[366]. 12 mths recusancy from 6 Sept. 1586: conv. 25 Mar. 1588—VIII(78v).
WALKER, 'Jennetta' verch Phillippe, [   ], of Skenfrith, Mon. 5 mths recusancy from 24 Mar. 1586/7: conv. 13 Mar. 1587/8—VIII(48).
WALKER, John, gent., of Nether Stowey, Somerset. 7 mths recusancy from 1 Jan. 1586/7: conv. 6 Mar. 1587/8—VIII(65).
WALKER, Ralph, [   ], of [   ], W.R. Yorks. 2 mths recusancy from 4 Jan. 1585/6: conv. 14 Mar. 1585/6—VI(20v).
WALKER, Walter, 'husb", of Kirtleton [Kirtlington?], Oxfords. 12 mths recusancy from 26 Sept. 1586: conv. 7 Mar. 1587/8—VIII(35v).
WALKER, Mary, his wife (same parish, recusancy period and conviction date)—VIII(35v).
WALKER, William, [   ], of [   ], W.R. Yorks. 2 mths recusancy from 4 Jan. 1585/6: conv. 14 Mar. 1585/6—VI(20v).
WALLE, Margaret, 'spinster', of Flixton, Suffolk. 3 mths recusancy from 8 Apr. 1587: conv. 27 Mar. 1588—VIII(73). See WHALLE.
WALMESLEY, Henry, 'cowper', of Billington, Lancs. 12 mths recusancy from 20 Sept. 1589: conv. 22 Mar. 1590/1—X(40v).
WALNE, Wallne, Grace, 'spinster', of Wyresdale, Lancs. (same recusancy period and conviction date)—X(39v).
WALROND, Walrand: see WALDRON, George.
WALTAM, Thomas, gent., of Higham [High Ham], Somerset. 7 mths recusancy from 1 Jan. 1586/7: conv. 6 Mar. 1587/8—VIII(65).
WALTER, Hugh, 'yoman', of Llangattock juxta Caerleon, Mon. 5 mths recusancy from 24 Mar. 1586/7: conv. 13 Mar. 1587/8—VIII(49v).
WALTON, Barnard, 'webster', of Bareford [? Barrowford, near Colne], Lancs. 12 mths recusancy from 20 Sept. 1589: conv. 22 Mar. 1590/1—X(40).
WALWEN, Alice, wife of John Walwen, gent., of Sutton, Herefords[367]. 12 mths recusancy from 1 Sept. 1586: conv. 18 Mar. 1587/8—VIII(30).
WALWEN, Francis, gent., of Tomworthe [? Tanworth-in-Arden], Warwicks. 3 mths recusancy from 12 May 1587: conv. 15 Mar. 1587/8—VIII(76).
WARD, Warde, John, gent., of Ringestead, parish of Denford, Northants. 12 mths recusancy ending 2 May 1587: conv. 12 Mar. 1587/8—VIII(52v). Goods, value £2, seized 29 July 1587—IX(33). Debt re-enrolled—XII(50v). Record of land-seizure, 29 July 1587

---

366. George Walker was said to be worth 40s. in land in the Diocesan Returns of Recusants in 1577. (Cf. *CRS* XXII, p. 91.)
367. Alice Walwen was listed among the principal and most dangerous recusants in the Diocese of Hereford in 1604. (Cf. *CRS* II, p. 294.)

(Two-thirds of one cottage or tenement in Ringstead and of the tithes of grain- and hay-sheaves annually growing there)—IX(33). XII(50v). Seized lands let by Crown to John Newett from 7 Feb. 1588/9 for a rent of £4 p.a.—IX(47). XI(49v). XII(50v).

WARD, Warde, Lucy, 'spinster', wife of William Warde [ ], of Tomworthe [? Tanworth-in-Arden], Warwicks. 3 mths recusancy from 12 May 1587: conv. 15 Mar. 1587/8—VIII(76).

WARD, Robert, gent., of Bowes, N.R. Yorks. 8 mths recusancy from 22 Jan. 1586/7: conv. 4 Sept. 1587—VIII(25v).

WARD, Thomas, 'laborer', of Hamstall Ridware, Staffs. 6 mths recusancy from 6 Sept. 1587: conv. 22 July 1588—VIII(58).

WAREHAM, Robert, 'yom''', of Dorchester, Dorset. 3 mths recusancy from 20 Dec. 1583: conv. Lent 1584—IV(16v): and one later indictment dated 24 Aug. 1584—IV(16v).

WARNEFORD, Oliver, gent., of Farlington, Hants[368]. 7 mths recusancy from 16 Sept. 1583: conv. ? Apr. 1584—V(56v).

WARNEFORD, Oliver, gent., of Chilworth, Hants. 6 mths recusancy from 1 Aug. 1587: conv. 8 July 1588—VIII(68v).

WARNEFORD, Richard, gent., of the city of Winchester, Hants [? prisoner][369]. 6 mths recusancy from 6 May 1581: conv. ? Oct. 1581—I(55). Debt re-enrolled—III(62). V(56). VII(54).

WARNEFORD, Richard, gent., of St. Maurice's parish in the city of Winchester, Hants. 3 mths recusancy from 1 Oct. 1581: conv. 9 Jan. 1581/2—I(55): and one later conviction, dated 8 July 1588—VIII(68v). Debts re-enrolled—III(62). VII(54). Richard Warneford indebted to Queen in £1,540 by the Act of 1586–7. Land seizure in Hants and Wilts for recusancy:—

[1] 23 acres of land called Upbattel in Winchester, seized on 22 Apr. 1588. Rent charge, £12 – 8 – 10 p.a.—VIII(67).

[2] Two-thirds of the manor-farm of Newland in the parish of Southwick, Hants., seized 20 May 1592. Rent charge, £26-13-4 p.a.—VIII(68v). IX(57v). X(68v). XI(59v). XII(60v).

[3] Two-thirds of seized chattels-real in Wilts ['purparty and portion' of the manor of Bury Blunsdon, Wilts., in Blunsdon St. Andrew; seized 27 Jan. 1590/1. Rent charge, £10 – 13 – 4 p.a.]. This Wilts property let by Crown to John Gregory from 22 Mar. 1590/1—XI(68v), (73v). XII(68v).[370]

WARNER, Simon, gent., of Alchurche [Alvechurch], Worcs. 2 mths recusancy from 7 Apr. 1588: conv. 6 Mar. 1588/9—IX(70v).

---

368. Oliver Warnford was described as worth £50 in goods in the Diocesan Returns of Recusants in 1577. (Cf. *CRS* XXII, p. 41.)

369. Richard Warneford of Southwick, Hants., was described as worth £200 in goods in the Diocesan Returns of Recusants in 1577. (Cf. *CRS* XXII, p. 40.) He was committed to the Wood Street Counter, together with his wife Mary, in June 1586. (Cf. *CRS* II p. 252.)

370. Richard Warneford's land seizures and debts are detailed in the *RRs*. (Cf. *CRS* XVIII, p. 287, *CRS* LVII, p. 39, 186, and *CRS* LXI, p. 239.)

WARREN, William, [   ], of St. Bride's parish, Farringdom Ward Without, London [? prisoner]. 1 mth recusancy from 6 Sept. 1581:—I(35); and one later conviction, dated 20 Dec. 1581—I(35)*. Debts re-enrolled—III(38v). V(35).

WARTON, Ellen, of Treyles [Treales: Kirkham], Lancs., wife of William Warton, 'husb''. 12 mths recusancy from 20 Sept. 1589: conv. 22 Mar. 1590/1—X(39v).

WARTON, Thomas, junior, 'tanner', of Kirkbythure [Kirkby Thore], Westmorland. 1 mth recusancy from 1 June 1588: conv. 5 Aug. 1588—IX(69). See WHARTON.

WATERS, Francis, 'yoman', of Bledlowe, Bucks. 3 mths recusancy from 27 Mar. 1587: conv. 18 Mar. 1587/8—VIII(3).

WATERTON, Mary, wife of Thomas Waterton, gent., of Walton, W.R. Yorks. 6 mths recusancy from 3 July 1587: conv. 18 Mar. 1587/8—VIII(25v). Record of land-seizure, 8 Apr. 1589—IX(22v). Rental of lands seized 8 Apr. 1589 [Two-thirds of the manor of Cawthorne, with iron-mills, lands & tenements in Mensthorpe, in the parish of South Kirkby, W.R. Yorks. Rent charge, £34 – 3 – 4 p.a.]—IX(21v). X(21v). XI(24v). XII(23v). Seized lands let by Crown to Edward Birde & John Terrye from 14 Oct. 1590 [Lease discharged—X(13v)].

WATERTON, Thomas, esq., of Walton, W.R. Yorks, and [   ], his wife. 2 mths recusancy from 4 Jan. 1585/6: conv. 14 Mar. 1585/6—VI(20v).

WATKIN, Watkyne, Eliz., wife of John Watkine, gent., of Baysham, parish of Sellock [Sellack], Herefords. 12 mths recusancy from 1 Sept. 1586: conv. 18 Mar. 1587/8—VIII(30).

WATKIN, Eliz., wife of Peter Watkine, 'yom'', of Willington [Swillington], W.R. Yorks. 6 mths recusancy from 3 July 1587: conv. 18 Mar. 1587/8—VIII(25v).

WATKIN, Joan, wife of Roger Watkin [   ], of Llangoven, Mon. 5 mths recusancy from 24 Mar. 1586/7: conv. 13 Mar. 1587/8—VIII(49v).

WATKIN, Watkyne, John, 'yoman', of Raglan, Mon. (same recusancy period and conviction date)—VIII(48). Record of land-seizure, 24 Oct. 1588—IX(42v). Rental of lands seized 24 Oct. 1588 (tenants owe 2s.8d. p.a.)—X(50). XI(45).

WATKIN, 'Jonetta', wife of John Watkyne, [   ], of Raglan, Mon. (same recusancy period and conviction date)—VIII(48).

WATKIN, Katherine, wife of Charles Watkin, [   ], of Llangattock Vibon Avel, Mon. (same recusancy period and conviction date)—VIII(48v).

WATKIN, Philip, [   ], of Llangattock juxta Caerleon, Mon. (same recusancy period and conviction date)—VIII(49v).

WATKIN, Watkyne, William, 'yoman', of Landewye [? Llanthewy], Mon. (same recusancy period and conviction date)—VIII(49v).

WATKIN, 'Alsona', his wife (same parish, recusancy period and conviction date)—VIII(49v).

verch WATKIN, Ann, 'spinster', of Tregare, Mon. (same recusancy period and conviction date)—VIII(49v).

WATSON, Watsone, Christopher, 'yom'', of Ryppon [Ripon], W.R. Yorks. 4 mths recusancy from 28 Mar. 1581: conv. 17 July 1581[371].— I(21v). III(24). V(22).

WATSON, Watsone, Frances, wid., of Killinghall, parish of Ripley, W.R. Yorks. 13 mths recusancy from 3 Sept. 1586: conv. 4 Sept. 1587—VIII(25v).

WATSON, William, 'clericus', of St. George's parish, Southwark, Surrey [prisoner][372]. 5 mths recusancy from 17 Feb. 1586/7: conv. 17 July 1587—IX(54).

WEBLEY, Henry, 'yoman', of Southwark, Surrey[373][prisoner]. 8 mths recusancy ending 16 Feb. 1586/7, when convicted (of recusancy)— VI(50).

WEBSTER, Ellen, of Bryning, Lancs., wife of Laurence Webster. 13 mths recusancy from 20 Sept. 1589: conv. 22 Mar. 1590/1—X(39v).

WEBSTER, Richard, gent./'yoman', of Southwark, Surrey [prisoner][374]. 10 mths recusancy ending 11 Mar. 1582/3, when convicted—IV(49v)*: and 3 later indictments ending 16 Feb. 1586/7, when convicted— IV(49v)*. V(52v). VI(50), (51)*.

WEBSTER, Richard, gent., of St. Botolph's parish, Bishopsgate Ward, Without London. Fine of 100 marks imposed for hearing Mass said on 30 Jan. 1585/6 by William Thompson in the house of Robert Bellamy [*q. v.*]. Convicted at Old Bailey, 18 Apr. 1586—VI(34v).

WEBSTER, William, 'yeoman', of Appulby [Appleby], Westmoreland. 1 mth recusancy from 1 June 1588: conv. 5 Aug. 1588—IX(69).

WEEKELEY, Edward, gent., of Adington [Addington], Northants. 12 mths recusancy from 31 July 1587: conv. 4 Mar. 1588/9—IX(47).

WELLES, Gilbert, esq., of Brambridge, parish of Twyford, Hants.[375]. 18 mths recusancy ending 13 Aug. 1582, when convicted—II(52): and two later convictions ending Apr. 1586—IV(53). VI(54). VIII(68). Goods, value £53 – 5s., seized 8 Nov. 1588—IX(58). Goods, value £136 – 13 – 4, date of seizure unspecified—X(69). Record of land— seizure in Hants, 22 Apr. 1588—VIII(67v). Rental of seized lands in Hants [Two—thirds of the reversion of the manor of Brambridge.

---

371. Christopher Watson, a successsful merchant in Ripon, Yorks., was reconciled by Fr. Henry Comberford. He was arrested at York in 1580, imprisoned in York Castle, and died there in Sept. 1581. (Cf. *CRS* XXII, p. 32 footnote.)

372. William Watson (Cf. Anstruther I, pp. 372–374.)

373. Henry Webley was born into a yeoman family in Gloucester. He was arrested in Chichester Haven on board a ship going to France, and was sent to the Marshalsea on 25 Apr. 1586. (Cf. *CRS* II, pp. 242, 244, 251, 254.) He was convicted at the Old Bailey of aiding William Deane, the priest martyr on 26 Aug. 1588, and was hanged at Mile End.

374. Richard Webster, a schoolmaster, was imprisoned in the Marshalsea from 25 Mar. 1574. (Cf. *CRS* I, p. 61, 70.) He was committed to Newgate for examination, and returned to the Marshalsea on 12 June 1586. (Cf. *CRS* II, p. 244.) Described as 'a great perverter of youth', he was still in the Marshalsea on 30 Sept. 1588, and on 6 July 1602. (Cf. *CRS* II, pp. 231 *seq.*)

375. Gilbert Welles was the brother of St. Swithun Wells. (Cf. *CRS* V, pp. 131, 132.) He was a prisoner in Winchester in June 1582, was sent into Newgate on 21 Dec. 1583, and thence to the Marshalsea, where he still remained on 8 Apr. 1584. (Cf. *CRS* II, pp. 221, 233, 235.)

Rent charge, £68 – 8 – 11 p.a.]—VIII(68v). IX(57v). X(68v). Record of land-seizure in Dorset, 23 Nov. 1588—VIII(83v). Rental of seized lands in Dorset [Two – thirds of the manor of Ranescombe (? or Ravescombe) in the Isle of Purbeck, and lands in Worth (Matravers) in the same Isle. Rent charge, £20 – 13 – 4 p.a.]—VIII(83v). Seized lands let by Crown in Hants and Dorset to Thomas Hixon from 4 Feb. 1588/9—IX(59). X(68v). XI(59v). XII(60v).

WELLES, Henry, gent., of Tychfeild [Titchfield], Hants. 6 mths recusancy from 1 Aug. 1587: conv. 8 July 1588—VIII(68v).

WELLES, Henry, gent., of Goldingstone [Godlingston], Dorset. 3 mths recusancy from 1 Apr. 1587: conv. 4 Mar. 1587/8—VIII(19). Record of land-seizure in Dorset, 1 July 1590 [two-thirds of the manor of Godlingston in the Isle of Purbeck. Rent charge, £6 – 13 – 4 p.a.]—X(83v). Seized lands let by Crown to John Hopkinson from 3 Nov. 1590—X(83v). XI(35v). XII(53v).

WELLES, Thomas, gent., of Brambridge, Hants. 6 mths recusancy from 1 Aug. 1587: conv. 8 July 1588—VIII(68v).

WELLES, Wills, Thomas, 'yeoman', of Home Hale, Norfolk. 3 mths recusancy from 13 Apr. 1587: conv. 1 Apr. 1588—VIII(54). Goods, value £1, seized 18 Oct. 1588—IX(45). Rental of lands seized 18 Oct. 1588 [two-thirds of a messuage, lands & tenements in Hilbrough, Norfolk. Rent charge, £1 – 6 – 8 p.a.]—IX(45). X(52v). XI(46v). XII(47v).

WENFORD, Dorothy, 'spinster', of Longdon, Worcs. 6 mths recusancy from 29 Sept. 1587: conv. 25 July 1588—VIII(80v). See WRINFORD.

WENHAM, John, 'yoman', of Laughton, Sussex. 2 mths recusancy from 17 Apr. 1587: conv. 26 Feb. 1587/8—VIII(63v).

WENTWORTHE, Dorothy, wife of Matthew Wentworthe, esq., of Bretton, W.R. Yorks. 2 mths recusancy from 4 Jan. 1585/6: conv. 14 Mar. 1585/6—VI(20v).

WENTWORTHE, Dorothy, [   ], of Bretton, parish of Silkstone, W.R. Yorks. 6 mths recusancy from 3 July 1587: conv. 18 Mar. 1587/8—VIII(25v).

WENTWORTH, Magdalen (sic, for Matilda) [   ], of Silkstone, W.R. Yorks. 6 mths recusancy from 3 July 1587: conv. 18 Mar. 1587/8—VIII(25v). Record of land-seizure, 8 Apr. 1589 [under MATILDA WENTWORTH]—IX(22v). Rental of seized lands [two-thirds of an annuity of 20 marks issuing from lands at West Bretton Hall, W.R. Yorks. Rent charge, £8 – 17 – 10 p.a.]—IX(21v). X(21v). XI(24v). XII(23v).

WESTBY, Westbie, John, esq., of Mollebrick [Mowbrick], Kirkham parish, Lancs. 4 mths recusancy from 18 Mar. 1580/1: conv. 31 July 1581—VI(40v). Debt re-enrolled—VIII(21v). Goods, value £247, seized 24 Oct. 1587—X(40v). Rental of lands seized by Crown on 24 Oct. 1587 [Two-thirds of the demesne lands of Mowbreck & Burne, and of lands in Mellor]. Rent charge, £77 – 15 – 8 p.a.—X(37). Seized lands let by Crown to Richard Mollyneux for the above rent from 1 May 1588—XII(44).

WESTBY, Ann, his wife, of Mowbrick, Kirkham, Lancs. 12 mths recusancy from 20 Sept. 1589: conv. 22 Mar. 1590/1—X(39).

WESTBY, Westbie, Richard, 'husb', of Torrisholme, in the parish of Lancaster, Lancs. 13 mths recusancy from 30 July 1587: conv. 17 Mar. 1588/9—X(35): and one later conviction, ending 22 Mar. 1590/1—X(39v).

WESTBY, Margaret, his wife, of Torrisholme, Lancaster, Lancs. 12 mths recusancy from 20 Sept. 1589: conv. 22 Mar. 1590/1—X(39v).

WESTON, Thomas, 'yoman', of Tamworthe, Staffs. 6 mths recusancy from 25 Mar. 1588: conv. 14 Mar. 1588/9—IX(69v).

WEVER, Roger, 'yoman', of Llangattock Vibon Avel, Mon. 5 mths recusancy from 24 Mar. 1586/7: conv. 13 Mar. 1587/8—VIII(48v).

WEVER, Joan, his wife (same parish, recusancy period and conviction date)—VIII(48v).

WHALLE, Henry, gent., of parish of SS. Simon & Jude, Norwich, Norfolk. 1 mth recusancy from 1 Nov. 1587: date of conviction not given. Debt re-enrolled—IX(10) and XI(12). See WALL.

WHALLEY, Oliver, 'husb', of Blackburn, Lancs. 12 mths recusancy from 20 Sept. 1589: conv. 22 Mar. 1590/1—X(40v).

WHALLEY, Thomas, 'yeom', of Langford [Longford], Derbys. 10 mths recusancy from 9 Sept. 1586: conv. 22 Mar. 1587/8—VIII(21). Goods, value £1 – 17 – 10, seized 27 Jan. 1588/9—IX(17v).

WHARTON, Cecilia, of Kyrkbythure [Kirkby Thore], Westmoreland. 1 mth recusancy from 1 June 1588: conv. 5 Aug. 1588—IX(69). See WARTON.

WHELER, Ann, wife of Richard Wheler, gent., of Great Malvern, Worcs. 6 mths recusancy from 29 Sept. 1587: conv. 25 July 1588—VIII(80v).

WHETERHOSTE [WHITCROFTE?], Thomas, 'husb', of [   ] in North Wingfeild parish, Derbys. 10 mths recusancy from 2 Sept. 1586: conv. 22 Mar. 1587/8—VIII(21).

WHITCROFTE, Thomas, [   ], of Tupton, Derbys., recusant. Goods, value £21 – 1 – 8, seized 27 Jan. 1588/9—IX(17v).

WHITE, Whyte, Adam, 'yeoman', of Ensham [Eynsham], Oxfords.[376] 12 mths recusancy from 26 Sept. 1586: conv. 7 Mar. 1587/8—VIII(35v).

WHITEACRES, Whitacres, Eliz., wid., of Towneley [Burnley], Lancs. 12 mths recusancy from 20 Sept. 1589: conv. 22 Mar. 1590/1—X(40).

WHITEACRES, Whitacres, Henry, 'taleor', of Burnley, Lancs. (same recusancy period and conviction date)—X(40).

WHITEACRES, Whitacres, Thomas, 'taleor', of Burnley, Lancs. (same recusancy period and conviction date)—X(40).

WHITEHALL, Walter, gent., of Linley [Lindley], in Co. Leics. 3 years recusancy from 1 Mar. 1582/3: conv. 11 Mar. 1585/6—VI(38v).

---

376. Adam White was listed in the Diocesan Return of Recusants in 1577. (Cf. *CRS* XXII, p. 110.)

Rental of lands in Leics, seized 14 Oct. 1587 [Two-thirds of lands in the parish of Linley (Lindley), Leics. Rent charge, £6 – 13 – 4 p.a.]—VIII(45). IX(41). X(41). XI(44). XII(43).

WHITEHALL, Whittall, Walter, gent., of Bloxwich, Staffs. 12 mths recusancy from 6 Sept. 1586: conv. 25 Mar. 1588—VIII(78v). Rental [Two-thirds of lands & tenements in Walsall and Bloxwich (Staffs), and in Linley [Lindley], Leics. Rent charge, £44 – 8 – 10 p.a.]—VIII(78v). See WHITTALL, Walter.

WHITEHEDD, John, 'yom'', of Westminster, Middx [? prisoner]. (Pipe Roll entry under 'Berks')—1 mth recusancy from 6 Feb. 1581/2: conv. 18 Mar. 1581/2.—II(65v).

WHITEINGE, Joan, wife of Walter Whiteinge, gent., of Melton, Norfolk. 3 mths recusancy from 13 Apr. 1587: conv. 1 Apr. 1588—VIII(54).

WHITINGE, Eliz., wife of William Whitinge, 'butcher', of Cirencester, Gloucs. 5 mths recusancy from 26 Mar. 1587: conv. 11 Mar. 1587/8—VIII(82).

WHITFEILD, Robert, 'husb'', of Blackborne [Blackburn], Lancs. 12 mths recusancy from 20 Sept. 1589: conv. 22 Mar. 1590/1—X(40).

WHITFEILD, Isabel, his wife (same parish, recusancy period and conviction date)—X(40).

WHITFORD, Richard, 'yom'', of Charney [Basset], Berks. 3 mths recusancy from 23 Mar. 1580/1: conv. 18 June 1581—II(65v).

WHITFORD, Richard, gent., of Charney [Basset], Berks. 3 mths recusancy from 19 June 1581: and 2 later convictions, ending 23 June 1582—II(65v)*.

WHITMORE, Alice, wife of William Whitmore, esq., of Laiton [Leighton], parish of Neston, Cheshire.[377]. 13 mths recusancy from 25 Sept. 1586: date of conviction omitted—VIII(58v).

WHITMORE, John, esq., of St. Mary's parish, Chester, Cheshire [prisoner][378]. 8 mths recusancy from 1 Sept. 1584: date of conviction omitted—VIII(60v).

WHITMORE, John, esq., of Chester Castle, Cheshire [prisoner]. 7 mths recusancy from 26 Sept. 1586. Convicted 24 Apr. 1587 (after 12 mths imprisonment)—VIII(58v). Record of lands seized on 7 Sept. 1588 [Two-thirds of property in Thurstaston, Cheshire, including five closes there]—X(35v). Rental of seized lands, Nov. 1588 [Rent charge, £15 – 7 – 10 p.a.]—X(35v). Seized lands let by Crown to William Grafton from 18 Nov. [31 Eliz.].—X(35v). XII(9).

WHITMORE, *alias* PRYMROSE, Jane, of Chester Castle, Cheshire, second wife of John Whitmore, esq., of the same Castle[379]. 7 mths recusancy from 26 Sept. 1586: conv. 24 Apr. 1587—VIII(58v).

WHITMORE, Richard, 'yoman', of Sutton, Cheshire.[380] 12 mths recusancy from 26 Sept. 1586: conv. 25 Sept. 1587—VIII(58v).

---

377. Alice Whitmore (Cf. Wark, p. 168.)
378. John Whitmore (Cf. Wark, pp. 169, 170.)
379. Jane Whitmore (Cf. Wark, pp. 168, 169.)
380. Richard Whitmore (Cf. Wark, p. 170.)

WHITMORE, Katherine, his wife (same parish, recusancy period and conviction date)—VIII(58v).
WHITMORE, Thomas, esq., of St. Mary's parish, Chester, Cheshire. 8 mths recusancy from 1 Sept. 1584: date of conviction omitted—VI(48v).
WHITNEY, Ann, 'gentlewoman', of Mytcham [Mitcham], Surrey. 3 mths recusancy from 25 Mar. 1587: conv. 13 Feb. 1587/8—VIII(63).
WHITTALL, Walter, gent., of Bloxwich, Staffs. Record of land-seizure in Staffs and Leics, 4 Sept. 1589—X(78v). rental of seized lands [Two-thirds of lands in Staffs (Walsall & Bloxwich) and Leics (Lindley). Rent charge, £44 – 8 – 11 p.a.] – X(7v). XI(64v). XII(65v). See WHITEHALL, Walter.
WHITTINGHAM, Richard, [ ], of Whittingham, Gosnargh [Goosnargh] parish, Lancs. 13 mths recusancy from 30 July 1587: conv. 17 Mar. 1588/9—X(35).
WHOOPER, Isabel, wife of Thomas Whooper, 'yeoman', of county of Worcester. 12 mths recusancy from 20 Sept. 1586: conv. 28 Mar. 1588—VIII(77).
WHOOPER, Sibyl, wife of William Whoper, 'yoman', of Hanley Castle, Worcs. 6 mths recusancy from 29 Sept. 1587: conv. 25 July 1588—VIII(80v). See HOPER, Isabel.
WHYTE, John, senior, gent., of Chilworth, Hants[381]. 6 mths recusancy from 1 Aug. 1587: conv. 8 July 1588—VIII(68v). See WHITE, Adam.
WIATT, Margaret, wife of John Wiatt, 'yeoman', of Hanley Castle, Worcs. 12 mths recusancy from 26 Sept. 1586: conv. 28 Mar. 1588—VIII(77).
WIBORNE, *alias* of FECKINGHAM, William.
WICKSTEED, Richard, 'yoman', of Marden, Herefords. 9 mths recusancy from 24 June 1583: conv. 2 Mar. 1583/4—V(26v).
WIKES, Alice, wid., of Asheburie [Ashbury], Berks. 12 mths recusancy from 1 Sept. 1586: conv. 4 Mar. 1587/8—VIII(5).
WILBRAM, Wilbraham, Hugh, 'yoman', of Malpas, Cheshire[382]. 12 mths recusancy from 26 Sept. 1586: conv. 25 Sept. 1587—VIII(58v).
WILCOCKES, Robert, 'clericus', of St. George's parish, Southwark, Surrey [prisoner][383]. 5 mths recusancy from 17 Feb. 1586/7: conv. 17 July 1587—IX(54).
WILDE, [ ], wid., of Worthington, Lancs., relict of James Wilde [ ]. 12 mths recusancy from 20 Sept. 1589: conv. 22 Mar. 1590/1—X(38v).
WILDINGE, James, 'yoman', of Plumpton, Lancs. 12 mths recusancy from 20 Sept. 1589: conv. 22 Mar. 1590/1—X(39v).
WILDINGE, Margaret, his wife (same parish, recusancy period and conviction date)—X(39v).

---

381. John Whyte was committed to the Clink by the Bishop of Winchester on 21 Dec. 1585. (Cf. *CRS* II, p. 246.)
382. Hugh Wilbraham (Cf. Wark, p. 170.)
383. Robert Wilcocks (Cf. Anstruther I, p. 381.)

WILDON, Katherine, wife of John Wildon of the city of York[384]. 4 mths recusancy from 28 Mar. 1581: date of conviction omitted—II(8).

WILFORD, Thomas, esq., of Leneham [Lenham], Kent. 15 mths recusancy from 18 Mar. 1580/1: conv. July 1582.—II(28). Debts re-enrolled—IV(12). VI(12v). VIII(34). Record of land-seizure, 4 Oct. 1587—VIII(34). Rental of seized lands, 4 Oct. 1587 [Rent charged, £68 – 2 – 2 p.a.; i.e. two-thirds of the manor & rectory of Lenham, Kent; let by the Crown to Thomas Horseman, from 19 Dec. 1590—XIII(32v).

WILKES, Henry, 'yeoman', of Sandringham, Norfolk. 3 mths recusancy from 13 Apr. 1587: conv. 1 Apr. 1588—VIII(54).

WILKINSON, Wilkingson, Wylkynson, Eliz., of York city, wife of William Wilkinson. 4 mths recusancy from 28 Mar. 1581: conv. 17 July 1581—I(8). Debt re-enrolled—III(10). V(8). VII(8). IX(8). Goods, value £6 – 8 – 2, seized from husband 6 Feb. 1582/3—II(8).

WILKINSON, Isabel, of Thistleton [Kirkham], Lancs., wife of Laurence Wilkinson, 'laborer'. 12 mths recusancy from 20 Sept. 1589: conv. 22 Mar. 1590/1—X(39).

WILKINSON, Nicholas, esq., of Brickles [Breckles] Magna, Norfolk. 3 mths recusancy from 13 Apr. 1587: conv. 1 Apr. 1588[385]—VIII(54).

WILKINSON, Nicholas, gent., of St. Olave's parish, Hart Street, Tower Ward, London. 3 mths recusancy from 25 Mar. 1587: conv. 10 July 1587—VIII(38v).

WILKINSON, Paul, gent., of Shiplack [Shiplake], Oxfords. 5 mths recusancy from 5 Feb. 1584/5: conv. 26 June 1585—VI(11v): and two later convictions, ending 17 Mar. 1586/7—VI(11v)*.

WILKINSON, Margaret, wife of Paul Wilkinson, gent., of Shiplake, Oxfords. 12 mths recusancy from 26 Sept. 1586: conv. 7 Mar. 1587/8—VIII(35).

WILKENSON, Thomas, 'husb'', of [? Thornley], Lancs. 12 mths recusancy from 20 Sept. 1589: conv. 22 Mar. 1590/1—X(39).

WILLES, *alias* WILLIAMSON, Roger.

WILLFORD, Robert, esq., of Hoxton, Middx. 6 mths recusancy from 29 Mar. 1587: conv. 1 Dec. 1587—VIII(38v).

WILLFORD, Mary, his wife (same parish, recusancy period and conviction date)—VIII(38v).

WILLIAM, [ ], wife of Watkin ap John William, [ ], of Llangattock juxta Caerleon, Mon. 5 mths recusancy from 24 Mar. 1586/7: conv. 13 Mar. 1587/8—VIII(49v).

---

384. Katherine Wildon was listed in the Diocesan Returns of Recusants in 1577, where her husband is described as being worth £5 in goods. (Cf. *CRS* XXII, p. 29.) He was later imprisoned for a distress on account of his wife's recusancy. She was reported on 6 June 1586 as saying that she came not to church, 'because there is neither altar nor sacrifice there'. (Cf. *CRS* V, p. 29, footnote.)

385. Nicolas Wilkinson's conviction was cancelled. (Cf. M.R., L.T.R., 41 Eliz., Michaelmas Term, 'Recorda' section.)

WILLIAM, Eliz., 'spinster', of Llanllowell, Mon. 5 mths recusancy from 24 Mar. 1586/7: conv. 13 Mar. 1587/8—VIII(49v).
WILLIAM, 'Evanus', 'yoman', of Llangattock nigh Usk, Mon. (same recusancy period and conviction date)—VIII(49).
WILLIAM, Jane, 'spinster', of Usk, Mon. (same recusancy period and conviction date)—VIII(49).
WILLIAM, Jane verch John, wife of Jenkin William, [ ], of Llanthewy Skirrid, Mon. (same recusancy period and conviction date)—VIII(48v).
WILLIAM, 'Jenava', 'yoman', of Usk, Mon. (same recusancy period and conviction date)—VIII(49).
WILLIAM, Joan, 'spinster', of Llanvihangel Crucorney, Mon. (same recusancy period and conviction date)—VIII(48v).
WILLIAM, Joan Watkin, wife of David ap Jevan William, [ ], of Llanhennock, Mon. (same recusancy period and conviction date)—VIII(49).
WILLIAM, Judith, 'spinster', of Llanllowell, Mon. (same recusancy period and conviction date)—VIII(49v).
WILLIAM, Katherine verch Thomas, wife of Merideth William, 'yoman', of Aburgavenny, Mon. (same recusancy period and conviction date)—VIII(48).
WILLIAM, Matilda John, 'spinster', of Raglan, Mon. (same recusancy period and conviction date)—VIII(48)
WILLIAM, Matilda verch Thomas, wife of Lewis John William, [ ], of Llangattock Vibon Avel, Mon. (same recusancy period and conviction date)—VIII(48v).
WILLIAM, Philip, 'yoman' of Llanvihangel Tomegrose [Llantarnam], Mon. (same recusancy period and conviction date)—VIII(49).
WILLIAM, Philip, 'yoman', of Skenfrith, Mon. (same recusancy period and conviction date)—VIII(48v). Record of land-seizure, 24 Oct. 1588—IX(42v). Rent charge [Two-thirds of lands at 2s. 2d. p.a.]—X(50). XI(45).
WILLIAM, Katherine, his wife (same parish, recusancy period and conviction date)—VIII(48v).
WILLIAM, Richard, 'yoman', of Llanvihangel Tomegrose [Llantarnam], Mon. (same recusancy period and conviction date)—VIII(49).
WILLIAM, Richard David, 'yoman', of Llenvathorne [Llanvetherine], Mon. (same recusancy period and conviction date)—VIII(49).
WILLIAM, Joan Lewis, his wife (same parish, recusancy period and conviction date)—VIII(49).
verch WILLIAM, 'Gwenliana', 'spinster', of Llangoven, Mon. (same recusancy period and conviction date)—VIII(49v).
WILLIAMS, Margaret, [ ], of Herefords. 4 mths recusancy from 30 May 1582: conv. ? 20 Sept. 1582—II(64).
WILLIAMS, Mary, wife of John Williams, gent., of Mary Mawdlyn [St. Mary Magdalene parish], Cornwall. 13 mths recusancy from 20 July 1582: conv. 6 Apr. 1584—IV(6v). Debt re-enrolled—VI(6).

WILLIAMS, *alias* of MILMAN, Elizabeth and Joan.
WILLIAMSON, Eliz., 'spinster', of Midhurst, Sussex. 2 mths recusancy from 17 Apr. 1587: conv. 26 Feb. 1587/8—VIII(63v).
WILLIAMSON, John, 'yoman', of Southwark, Surrey [prisoner]. 4 mths recusancy ending 17 Feb. 1585/6, when convicted—VI(49v).
WILLIAMSON, Margaret, Margery, wid., of St. Clement's parish, Winchester, Hants. 2 mths recusancy ending 16 May 1581, when convicted—I(55): and three later convictions,—III(50v), (62). V(56), ending 24 Apr. 1582.
WILLIAMSON, Margery, 'spinster', of the parish of St. Maurice, Winchester, Hants. 3 mths recusancy from 1 Oct. 1581: conv. 9 Jan. 1581/2—III(62).
WILLIAMSON, Mary, wife of Robert Williamson, gent., of Crowmarsh [Gifford], Oxfords. 12 mths recusancy from 26 Sept. 1586: conv. 7 Mar. 1587/8—VIII(35).
WILLIAMSON, Thomas, 'clericus', of Salford in the parish of Manchester, Lancs. [prisoner][386]. 12 mths recusancy from 20 Feb. 1582/3: conv. 22 Jan. 1583/4—IV(37). Debt re-enrolled—IV(42v). VI(39).
WILLIAMSONNE, Thomas, 'yoman', of Edge, in parish of Malpas, Cheshire[387]. 13 mths recusancy from 25 Sept. 1586: conviction date omitted—VIII(58v).
WILLIAMSON, *alias* WILLES, Roger, 'husb", of Cople [Coppull], Lancs. 12 mths recusancy from 20 Sept. 1589: conv. 22 Mar. 1590/1—X(38).
WILLIAMSON, *alias* WILLES, Joan or Jenetta, his wife (same parish, recusancy period and conviction date)—X(38).
WILLINGTON, Ellen, wife of William Willington, 'husband", of St. Mary's parish, Stafford, Staffs. 8 mths recusancy from 1 Aug. 1585: conv. 13 Mar. 1585/6:—VI(63v): and one later conviction, dated 1 Aug. 1586—VI(63v).
WILLINGTON, Joan, 'spinster', of Meare [Maer], Staffs. 4 mths recusancy from 21 July 1589, when convicted—IX(69v).
WILLINGTON, William, 'yoman', of Stafford, Staffs. 6 mths recusancy from 6 Sept. 1587: conv. 22 July 1588—VIII(58).
WILLOUGHBIE, George, esq., of Wigenhall [Wiggenhall St. Mary] Magdalene, Norfolk. 3 mths recusancy from 13 Apr. 1587: conv. 1 Apr. 1588—VIII(54). Goods, value £14 – 3s., seized 18 Oct. 1588—IX(45). Lands seized, 18 Oct. 1588—IX(45). Rental of seized lands [Two-thirds of seized lands in Tilney and Islington, Norfolk

---

386. Thomas Williamson was one of three priests (James Bell, Richard Hatton and Thomas Williamson) and one layman (John Finch) who were committed to Manchester Gaol for the Lent Assizes of 1584. On 9 Apr., the day before the Sessions began, all the prisoners were removed from Salford to Lancaster, and were there and then condemned to death for denying the Royal Supremacy in spiritual matters. The Judge, however, had instructions to sentence to death no more than two (Bell and Finch). The lives of the remaining two (Hatton and Williamson) were spared, but they suffered perpetual imprisonment and the loss of all their goods, 'as in cases of praemunire'. (Cf. *CRS* V, pp. 70, 74 – 87.)

387. Thomas Williamson (Cf. Wark, p. 171.)

(including Easthall manor in Denver, Norf.), all let by the Crown to Rice Maunsell for a rent of £20 p.a., from 10 Sept. 1591]—IX(45). X(52v). XI(46v). XII(48).

WILLOUGHBIE, Eliz., his wife (same parish, recusancy period and conviction date)—VIII(54).

WILLOUGHBIE, Raphael, esq., (same parish, recusancy period and conviction date)—VIII(54).

WILLOWES, Agnes, wife of Robert Willowes, gent., of Bareford [Barford], Beds. 3 mths recusancy from 29 Mar. 1587: conv. 20 Mar. 1587/8—VIII(1).

WILLS, see WELLES, Thomas.

WILLYS, David, 'yom''', of Didlaston [Dudleston], Salop. 12 mths recusancy from 24 Feb. 1586/7: conv. 18 July 1588—VIII(16v).

WILLYS, 'Jonetta', his wife (same parish, recusancy period, and conviction date)—VIII(16v).

WILMOTT, Cicilia, wife of William Wilmott, 'tanner', of Wantage, Berks. 12 mths recusancy from 1 Sept. 1586: conv. 4 Mar. 1587/8—VIII(5).

WILMOTT, Nicholas, gent., of Northmerden [Northmarden], Sussex. 2 mths recusancy from 17 Apr. 1587: conv. 26 Feb. 1587/8—VIII(63v).

WILSON, Willson, William, 'sacerdos'/'clericus', of Salford in the parish of Manchester, Lancs. [prisoner][388]. 3 mths recusancy from 10 Oct. 1581: convicted 18 Jan. 1581/2—II(38v). 3 mths recusancy from 17 Jan. 1581—II(38v). 4 mths recusancy from 2 Sept. 1582—II(38v). 12 mths recusancy from 20 Feb. 1582/3—IV(37): convicted 22 Jan. 1583/4. Debts re-enrolled—VI(39). VIII(46).

WINBOROUGHE, Ann, 'spinster', of Boughton, Norfolk. 3 mths recusancy from 13 Apr. 1587: conv. 1 Apr. 1588—VIII(54).

WINNALL, John, 'fysher', of Ripple, Worcs. 6 mths recusancy from 29 Sept. 1587: conv. 25 July 1588—VIII(80v).

WINTERTON, Joan, 'spinster', of Ashby Magna, Leics. 9 mths recusancy ending 10 Aug. 1587, when convicted—VIII(45v).

WIRDNAM, Alice, wife of Robert Wirdnam, gent., of Wantage, Berks. 12 mths recusancy from 1 Sept. 1586: conv. 4 Mar. 1587/8—VIII(5).

WIRDNAM, Martha, wife of John Wirdnam, gent., of Wantage, Berks. (same recusancy period and conviction date as preceding)—VIII(5).

WITHERINS, Margaret, 'spinster', of Checkley, Staffs. 4 mths recusancy (un-dated): convicted 21 July 1589—IX(69v).

WOLFE, Woolfe, Nicholas, gent., of Ashington, Sussex[389]. 3 mths recusancy from 8 Jan. 1581/2: conv. 21 July 1582 (and nine consecutive convictions, ending 1 Oct. 1584)—VI(49v)*. One final indictment: 2 mths recusancy from 17 Apr. 1587: conv. 26 Feb. 1587/8—VIII(63v). Goods, value £13, seized 17 Jan. 1589/90—IX(54v). Record of land-seizure, 17 Jan. 1589/90 [Two-

---

[388]. William Wilson (Cf. Anstruther I, p. 383.)

[389]. Nicholas Woolf was a prisoner in the Marshalsea on 7 Dec. 1583. He was still there on 8 Apr. 1584, and again on 3 Apr. 1585. (Cf. CRS II, pp. 233, 235, 240.)

thirds of lands in Ashington, Warminghurst and
Thakeham]—IX(54v). Rental of seized lands [Rent charge,
£15 – 11 – 1 p.a.]—X(65v). XI(55v). XII(56v).
WOLFE, Woolfe, Mary, his wife (same parish, recusancy period and
conviction date)—VIII(63v).
WOLFE, Richard, 'yeoman', of Welton, Northants. 12 mths recusancy
ending 2 May 1587: conv. 12 Mar. 1587/8—VIII(52v).
WOLLASCOTT, Richard, gent., of Richard's Castle, Herefords. Two fines
of £20 imposed for ignoring sheriff's summonses after
excommunication, 27 May 1581 and 4 Oct. 1581—III(28)*. [Fines
discharged in Memoranda Roll, L.T.R., 25 Eliz. (1583), Michaelmas
term, 'Recorda' section].
WOLSEY, Thomas, 'clericus', of Marsham, Norfolk[390]. 7 mths recusancy
from 1 Aug. 1582: conv. 18 Mar. 1582/3—III(72v). Debt re-
enrolled—V(46v).
WOLSELEY, Erasmus, esq., of Colwich, Staffs.[391]. 8 mths recusancy from 4
July 1581: conv. 19 Mar. 1581/2—IV(62v)*: and six later convictions,
ending 1 Aug. 1586 [refs. IV(62v). V(66)*. VI(63v)*.]. Debts re-
enrolled—VI(63).
WOLSELEY, Erasmus, esq., of Wolseley Bridge, Staffs. 12 mths recusancy
ending 1 Apr. [? 1582], when convicted—VI(63v): and one later
conviction, dated 25 Mar. 1588—VIII(78v). Lands seized and let by
Crown to Thomas Greysley from Michaelmas 1585—VII(57).
VIII(70). IX(62). XI(64). XII(65). Seized lands specified [The whole
manor of Wolseley with all lands, tenements & hereditaments
belonging to the said manor in Staffs; and also all the lands, tenements
& hereditaments, with appurtenances, in Parheywood [Little (Parva)
Haywood], Staffs:...! for the satisfaction of the said Erasmus
Wolseley's debt of £500'. Rental, £15 p.a.
WOLSELEY, John, gent., of Colwich, Staffs. 6 mths recusancy from
6 Sept. 1587: conv. 22 July 1588—VIII(58).
WOLSTENHOLME, Richard, 'yoman', of Wedacre, Lancs. 12 mths
recusancy from 20 Sept. 1589: conv. 22 Mar. 1590/1—X(39).
WOOD, John, 'tailor', of the city of York. 4 mths recusancy from 26 Mar.
1582: conviction date missing.—II(8). Debt re-enrolled—V(8). VII(8).
IX(8).
WOODEHOWSE, Eleanor, wife of Francis Woodehowse, esq., of Breckles
Magna, Norfolk. 3 mths recusancy from 13 Apr. 1587: conv. 1 Apr.
1588—VIII(54).
WOODES, Thomas, 'clericus', of Salford in parish of Manchester, Lancs
[prisoner][392]. 3 mths recusancy from 17 Jan. 1581/2: conv. 2 May

---

390. Thomas Wolsey, an unidentified cleric.
391. Erasmus Wolseley was described as worth £200 in lands and goods in The Diocesan Returns
of Recusants in 1577. (Cf. *CRS* XXII, p. 89.)
392. Thomas Woods was one of the priests listed as being imprisoned in the New Fleet prison in
Salford in 1582. (Cf. *CRS* V, pp. 23, 24.)

1582—II(38v): and one later conviction, ending 22 Jan. 1583/4—IV(37). Debts re-enrolled—IV(42v). VI(39). VIII(46).

WOODFALL, Eliz., wid., of Sutton, Prescott parish, Lancs. 13 mths recusancy from 30 July 1587: conv. 17 Mar. 1588/9—X(35).

WOODROFE, Ann, of Haberchany Eves [Habergham Eves: Burnley], Lancs., wife of Richard Woodrofe, gent. 12 mths recusancy from 20 Sept. 1589: conv. 22 Mar. 1590/1—X(40).

WOODROFE, 'Jenetta', wid., of Bancketofte [? Burnley], Lancs. 12 mths recusancy from 20 Sept. 1589: conv. 22 Mar. 1590/1—X(40).

WOODWARD, Margaret, wife of Thomas Woodward, 'husb'', of Kirtleton [? Kirtlington], Oxfords. 12 mths recusancy from 26 Sept. 1586: conv. 7 Mar. 1587/8—VIII(35v).

WOODWARD, Thomas, 'yoman', of Bunbury, Cheshire. 13 mths recusancy from 25 Sept. 1586: date of conviction omitted.—VIII(58v).

WOODISON, Woddison, Eliz., 'spinster', wife of William Woodison of St. Michael's parish, Soke of Winton, Hants. 5 mths recusancy from 16 May 1581: conv. Oct. 1581—I(55)*: and two later convictions, ending 24 Apr. 1582. Debts re-enrolled—III(50v). III(62). V(56).

WORMINGTON, Warmington, William, 'clericus', of Southwark, Surrey [prisoner][393]. 2 mths recusancy ending 11 Mar. 1582/3, when convicted—III(58v). Debt re-enrolled—V(52v).

WORSELEY, Woursley, Ralph, esq., of Salford in the parish of Manchester, Lancs [prisoner][394]. 3 mths recusancy from 17 Jan. 1581/2: conv. 2 May 1582—II(38v)*: and two later convictions, ending 22 Jan. 1583/4—IV(37).

WORSELEY, Ralph, gent., of Chester Castle, Cheshire [prisoner][395]. 13 mths recusancy from 14 Sept. 1585: conv. 3 Oct. 1586—X(35v): and one other conviction, ending 24 Apr. 1587—VIII(58v).

WORTHINGTON, Agnes, of Shevington, Lancs., wife of Nicholas Worthington [   ]. 12 mths recusancy from 20 Sept. 1589: conv. 22 Mar. 1590/1—X(38).

WORTHINGTON, Ann, wid., of Worthington, Lancs., relict of Thomas Worthington [   ]. 12 mths recusancy from 20 Sept. 1589: conv. 22 Mar. 1590/1—X(38v).

WORTHINGTON, Margaret, 'spinster', of Heath Charnock, Lancs. (same recusancy period and conviction date)—X(38v).

WORTHINGTON, Richard, [   ], of Blaynstowe, in Standish parish, Lancs. 4 mths recusancy from 18 Mar. 1585/6: conv. 8 Aug. 1586—X(35).

WORTHINGTON, Richard, gent., of Coppull, Lancs. 12 mths recusancy from 20 Sept. 1589: conv. 22 Mar. 1590/1—X(38).

---

393. William Wormington (Cf. Anstruther I, pp. 370, 371, under Warmington.)
394. Ralph Worsley was one of the priests listed as being imprisoned in the New Fleet prison in Salford in 1582. (Cf. *CRS* V, pp. 23, 24.)
395. Ralph Worsley (Cf. Wark, p. 172.)

WORTHINGTON, Dorothy, his wife (same parish, recusancy period and conviction date)—X(38).

WORTHINGTON, William, gent., of Westby [with Plumpton], Kirkham parish, Lancs. 13 mths recusancy from 30 July 1587: conv. 17 Mar. 1588/9—X(35).

WOTLEY, Morgan, 'yoman', of Clapham, Sussex. 2 mths recusancy from 17 Apr. 1587: conv. 26 Feb. 1587/8—VIII(63v).

WOTTON, Humphrey, [ ], of Rocester, Staffs. 6 mths recusancy from 25 Mar. 1588: conv. 14 Mar. 1588/9—IX(69v).

WRATHE, *alias* of BUTCHER, Adrian.

WRIGELEY, Ralph, [ ], of Langford [Longford], Derbys. 10 mths recusancy from 9 Sept. 1586: conv. 22 Mar. 1587/8—VIII(21).

WRIGELEY, Margaret, his wife (same parish, recusancy period and conviction date)—VIII(21).

WRIGHT, Jane, wife of John Wright, 'yom'', of Pikeringe [Pickering], N.R. Yorks. 6 mths recusancy from 3 July 1587: conv. 18 Mar. 1587/8—VIII(25v).

WRIGHT, John, 'husb'', of Charnock Richard, Lancs. 12 mths recusancy from 20 Sept. 1589: conv. 22 Mar. 1590/1—X(38).

WRIGHT, Cicily, his wife (same parish, same recusancy period and conviction date)—X(38v).

WRIGHT, Ellen, 'spinster', his daughter (same parish, recusancy period and conviction date)—X(38v).

WRIGHT, Roger, 'laborer', his son (same parish, recusancy period and conviction date)—X(38v).

WRIGHT, Oliver, [ ], of West Hallam, Derbys. 10 mths recusancy from 9 Sept. 1586: conv. 22 Mar. 1587/8—VIII(21). Goods, value (with goods of William Staveley, *q.v.*) £18 – 4 – 2, seized 27 Jan. 1589/90—IX(17v).

WRIGHT, [ ], wife of Oliver Wright of West Hallam, Derbys (recusancy period and conviction date as preceding entry)—VIII(21).

WRIGHT, Thomas, 'yeom'', of Ragdale, Leics. 10 mths recusancy from 9 Sept. 1586: conv. 19 Mar. 1587/8—VIII(45v).

WRINFORD, [ ], wife of Thomas Wrinford, gent., of Longdon, Worcs. 12 mths recusancy from 20 Sept. 1586: conv. 28 Mar. 1588—VIII(77).

WROE, John, 'yoman', of Attleborough, Norfolk. 12 mths recusancy from 12 Sept. 1585: conv. 6 Sept. 1586—VI(25v).

WROE, Joan, his wife, of Attleborough, Norfolk. 3 mths recusancy from 13 Apr. 1587: conv. 1 Apr. 1588—VIII(54).

WROTH, William, 'yoman', of Abergavenny, Mon. 5 mths recusancy from 24 Mar. 1586/7: conv. 13 Mar. 1587/8—VIII(48). Record of land-seizure, 24 Oct. 1588—IX(42v). Rental of seized land [Two-thirds of property in Abergavenny. Rent charged, 13s. 4d. p.a.]—IX(42), (42v). Seized property (unspecified) let by Crown to Hugh Williams from 6 July 1590—XI(45). XII(46).

WROTH, Matilda Jenkyn, his wife (same parish, recusancy period and conviction date)—VIII(48).

WYNDLE, John, 'yoman', of Cronton, parish of Farnworth, Lancs. 13 mths recusancy from 30 July 1587: conv. 17 Mar. 1588/9—X(35).

WYNSTANLEY, Humphrey, gent., of Higfeild [Highfield], Wigan parish, Lancs. 13 mths recusancy from 14 Aug. 1586: conv. 25 Mar. 1588—VIII(21v).

WYNSTANLEY, Humphrey, gent., of Markeland Mylne, Wigan parish, Lancs. 13 mths recusancy from 14 Aug. 1586: conv. 25 Mar. 1588—VIII(21v).

YARDLEY, Roger, gent., of St. Saviour's parish, Southwarck, Surrey [prisoner][396]. 5 mths recusancy ending 17 Feb. 1586/7, when convicted.—VI(50).

YATE, Yatte, Edward, gent., of Westminster, Middx [prisoner][397]. [Pipe Roll entry under 'Berks'] 1 mth recusancy from 6 Feb. 1581/2: conv. 18 Mar. 1581/2—II(65v): and seven later convictions, ending 17 Nov. 1583—IV(46)*. Debts re-enrolled—VI(3v)*.

YATE, Jane, wife of Edward Yate of Buckland, Berks., gent. 12 mths recusancy from 1 Sept. 1586: conv. 4 Mar. 1587/8—VIII(5).

YATE, Francis, esq., of Lyford, Berks. 5 mths recusancy from 8 Feb. 1581/2: conv. 9 July 1582—II(3v).

YATE, Francis, esq., of Berks.; Property, value £260, seized 29 Nov. 1584—VIII(5). Debt re-enrolled—X(4v).

YATE, Francis, gent., of St. Mary's parish, Reading, Berks [prisoner][398]. 8 mths recusancy from 30 June 1582: conv. 12 Feb. 1582/3—II(3v).

YATE, Jane, wife of Francis Yate, gent., of St. Mary's parish, Reading, Berks. [prisoner]. 8 mths recusancy from 30 June 1582: conv. 12 Feb. 1582/3—II(65v): and one later conviction after 4 mths recusancy from 11 Feb. 1582/3, ending 4 June 1583—III(50v). Debt re-enrolled—V(4v).

YATE, Eliz., wife of Francis Yate, gent., of Kencott, Oxfords. 12 mths recusancy from 26 Sept. 1586: conv. 7 Mar. 1587/8—VIII(35).

YATE, Eliz., 'spinster', of Kencott, Oxfords (same recusancy period and conviction date)—VIII(35v).

YATE, John, gent., of Kencott, Oxfords. 5 mths recusancy from 27 Feb. 1583/4: conv. 23 July 1584—IV(29): and one later conviction, ending 5 Feb. 1584/5—V(47). Debt re-enrolled—VI(30v).

---

396. Roger Yardley, servant to the Earl of Westmoreland, arrived from overseas, and was suspected of spying. He was therefore imprisoned in the Clink from 25 Sept. 1586, but disappears from the Prison Lists after Sept. 1588. (Cf. *CRS* II, pp. 260, 262, 264, 268, 283.)

397. Edmund Yate was a prisoner in the Westminster Gatehouse. The son and heir apparent of John Yate of Buckland, Berks., esq., he appears in the Temple Certificate of those not willing to attend church, in the Diocesan Returns of Recusants in 1577. (Cf. *CRS* XXII, p. 106.)

398. Francis Yate, the husband of Jane Yate (officially a prisoner in the Westminster Gatehouse), would seem for 8 months at least, to have shared imprisonment with her in Reading Gaol.

YATE, Henry, 'laborer', of Hapton, Lancs. 12 mths recusancy from
   20 Sept. 1589: conv. 22 Mar. 1590/1—X(40).
YATE, Isabel, of Blackborne [Blackburn], Lancs., wife of Laurence Yate,
   'scolemaster'. 12 mths recusancy from 20 Sept. 1589: conv. 22 Mar.
   1590/1—X(40v).
YATE, John, 'servingman', of Towneley [in Burnley], Lancs. 12 mths
   recusancy from 20 Sept. 1589: conv. 22 Mar. 1590/1.—X(40).
YATES, Francis, gent., of Highgate, Middx. 6 mths recusancy from 29 Mar.
   1587: conv. 1 Dec. 1587—VIII(38v).
YATES, Margaret, wife of John Yates, gent., of Deddington, Oxfords. 12
   mths recusancy from 26 Sept. 1586: conv. 7 Mar. 1587/8—VIII(35).
YAXLEY, Yaxeley, Eve, wife of William Yaxeley, esq., of Yaxley, Suffolk.
   3 mths recusancy from 8 Apr. 1587: conv. 27 Mar. 1588—VIII(73).
YAXLEY, Eve, widow, of Yaxley, Suffolk. Record of land-seizure, 21 Apr.
   1591 [The whole manor of Pountney Hall, *alias* Lancasters, *alias*
   Warkes in Melles [Mellis] Burgate, and Yaxley etc: the whole manor of
   Fithiones in Over and Nether Rickinghall: and the whole manor of
   Mabisons in Thrandeston, all in Suffolk; being two-thirds of the lands
   and possessions of Eve Yaxley]. Seized on 21 Apr. 1591. Rent charge,
   £21 – 3 – 4 p.a.—XI(72v). Let by Crown to Ralph Lathome from
   5 July 1591 for the above rent—XI(72v).
YAXLEY, Yaxeley, John, gent., of Brandon Parva, Norfolk. 3 mths
   recusancy from 13 Apr. 1587: conv. 1 Apr. 1588—VIII(54). Goods,
   value £16 – 6s., seized 18 Oct. 1588—IX(45). Record of land – seizure,
   18 Oct. 1588 [Two-thirds of the manor of Brandon Parva, Norfolk.
   Rent charge, £19 – 19 – 4 p.a.] Seized lands let by Crown to Thomas
   Palgrave and John Murfyne from 2 Dec. 1590 for a rent of £20 p.a.—
   XI(45).
YAXLEY, William, esq., of Intwood, Norfolk. 11 mths recusancy from
   1 Aug. 1581: conv. 23 July 1582—II(40): and two later convictions,
   ending 31 Mar. 1584—III(72v). IV(44v). Debts re-enrolled—IV(40).
   V(41v), (46v). VI(41v). VII(44v). Record of land-seizure, 26 Sept.
   1587 [Two-thirds of the manor at Bowthorpe, Norfolk. Rent charged,
   £43 – 10s., p.a.]—VIII(51).
YAXLEY, Yaxeley, William, senior, esq., of Coulney [Colney], Norfolk. 3
   mths recusancy from 13 Apr. 1587: conv. 1 Apr. 1588—VIII(54).
   Rental of seized land [Recorded in Pipe Roll under 'Civitas Ebor']
   Two-thirds of a messuage with a grain-mill and a cottage belonging to
   the City of York, and to the manor of Bickerton (Ainsty). Property
   seized 8 Apr. 1589 for the recusancy of the above William Yaxley,
   senior. Rent charged, £24 p.a.—IX(21v), (22v), X(13).
   Bickerton is a township in the parish of Bilton, Norwich, in the ainsty
   of the City of York.
YELVERTON, Edward, gent., of Rougham, Norfolk. 3 mths recusancy
   from 13 Apr. 1587: conv. 1 Apr. 1588—VIII(54). Record of land-
   seizure, 7 Jan. 1590/1 [Two-thirds of the manor of Morleys in
   Grimston, Norfolk, with a messuage and certain lands and meadows

pertaining thereto, and a close in Grimston called 'Bartons'; also three cottages with a parcel of land in Congham, Norfolk]. Rent charged, £10 p.a. Seized lands let by Crown to William Cobbe and John Dover from 2 Mar. 1590/1—XI(48v).

YERWORTH, Ann Morgan, wife of John Morgan Yerworth, [   ], of Raglan, Mon. 5 mths recusancy from 24 Mar. 1586: conv. 13 Mar. 1587/8—VIII(48).

YONGE, Richard, 'yeom'' of Haseley, Oxfords. 12 mths recusancy from 26 Sept. 1586: conv. 7 Mar. 1587/8—VIII(35v).

YORKE, Joan, 'spinster', of the parish of St. Mary Magdalene, borough of Southwark, Surrey. 12 mths recusancy from 10 Sept. 1586: conv. 5 July 1588—VIII(63).

YORKE, Margaret, wife of Humphrey Yorke, gent., of Kempsford, Gloucs. 5 mths recusancy from 26 Mar. 1587: conv. 11 Mar. 1587/8—VIII(82).

YOUNGE, Henry, 'husb'', of Wimborne Minister, Dorset. 6 mths recusancy from 15 Jan. 1586/7: conv. 4 Mar. 1587/8—VIII(19).

INDEX

1. More than one entry on a page is not noted in the index.
2. The Counties in the index are the pre- Local Government Re-Organization counties.

Abergavenny, Monmouthshire, 49, 95, 112, 123, 139, 148, 192, 197
Abingdon, Berkshire, 26, 82; Norcott, 82
Accrington, Lancashire, 144
Acton, Suffolk, 47, 48, 51, 52, 170
Acton Reynold, Shropshire, 55
Addingham, Yorkshire, 103
Addington, Northamptonshire, 186
Addington, Yorkshire, 144
Adwell, Oxfordshire, 21
Aintree, Lancashire, 116
Alborough, Norfolk, 79
Alby, Norfolk, 162
Alciston, Sussex, 60, 63, 65, 106, 124
Aldbourne, Wilts, 182
Aldeby, Norfolk, 9
Allensmore, Herefordshire, 151
Old Alresford, Hampshire; Woodcote Farm, 178
Alton, Hampshire, 149
Alvechurch, Worcestershire, 23, 80, 81, 129, 136, 152, 184
Alvediston, Wiltshire, 71
Antwerp, 54
Appleby, Westmoreland, 186
Arborfield, Berkshire, 103
Arlington, Sussex, 171
Arneforth, Yorkshire, 140
Arthington, Yorkshire, 11
Arthingworth, Northamptonshire, 117
Arundel, Sussex, 43, 153; Almshouse of the Holy Trinity, 153
Ashburnham, Sussex, 11, 61, 76

Ashbury, Berkshire, 190
Ashby Folville, Leicestershire, 156
Ashby in Bottesford, Lincolnshire, 112
Ashby Magna, Leicestershire, 13, 90, 96, 153, 155, 156, 176, 194
Ashby St. Ledgers, Northamptonshire, 31
Ashington, Sussex, 194, 195
Ashmore, Dorset, 40
Ashover, Derbyshire; Lee, 44
Ashperton, Herefordshire, 42
Askham, Westmoreland, 167
Aspull, Lancashire, 80
Astley, Worcestershire, 22, 23, 64, 75, 172
Aston, Staffordshire, 41
Aston, Warwickshire, 30, 182
Aston Rowaunt, Oxfordshire, 58
Astwick, Bedfordshire, 10
Attleborough, Norfolk, 197
Audlem, Cheshire, 58
Aughton, Lancashire, 67
Aylesham, Norfolk, 26, 129
Aysgarth, Yorkshire; Berry Park, 132; Heming, 120; Nappa Hall, 47, 170; Thoralby, 147

Baguley, Cheshire, 109
Baldon Toot, Oxfordshire, 160
Bamfurlong, Lancashire, 12
Barford, Bedfordshire, 194
Barking, Essex, 177
Barlborough, Derbyshire, 63
Barlow Hall, Lancashire, 109
West Barming, Kent, 74
Barnaby Hall, Yorkshire, 15
Barnborough, Yorkshire, 121
Barnby, Suffolk, 96

Barnby-Upon-Don, Yorkshire, 15
Chipping Barnet, Hertfordshire, 173
Barton Roo, Lancashire, 16
Barrow On Soar, Leicestershire, 142
Barrowby, Yorkshire, 133
Barrowford, Lancashire, 183
Basing, Hampshire, 46
Basingstoke, Hampshire, 129
Bassington, Somerset, 176
Bathampton, Wiltshire, 132
Baverstock, Wiltshire, 67
Beaghall, Yorkshire, 129
Beaulieu, Hampshire, 44
Beccles, Suffolk, 78
Beckford, Gloucestershire, 44
Beddingham, Sussex, 68
Bedford, Bedfordshire; St. Marys, 69
Bedfordshire, 180, 181
Bedhampton, Hampshire, 9, 159
Beechamwell, Norfolk, 107, 114
Beighton, Derbyshire, 108
Beltoft, Lincolnshire, 29
Benacre, Suffolk, 170, 174
Bentham, Yorkshire, 37, 69, 144
Beoley, Worcestershire, 152
Bere Regis, Dorset, 177
Berkshire, 26, 27, 91, 93, 101, 125, 169, 179, 189, 198
Berkswell, Warwickshire, 82
Bermondsey, Surrey; St. Mary Magdalen, 66
Berrington, Shropshire, 119
Berrington, Worcestershire, 75
Berwick St. John, Wiltshire, 153
Besthorpe, Norfolk, 145
Bethnall Green, London, 175
Bettws Newydd, Monmouthshire, 112, 131, 134
Beverley, Yorkshire, 105
Biddulph, Staffordshire, 21
Bidford-on-Avon, Warwickshire, 21, 164
Billington, Lancashire, 183; Butterworth, 36

Bilton, Norwich; Bickerton, 199
Bircholt, Kent, 74
Birmingham, Warwickshire, 182
Birtsmorton, Worcestershire, 126
Bishops Frome, Herefordshire, 52
Bishopsthorpe, Yorkshire, 15
Blackburn, Lancashire, 24, 61, 156, 158, 188, 189, 199; Billington, 37; Livesey, 125; Salesbury, 23, 24, 108, 155, 158, 165
Blandford St. Mary, Dorset, 169
Bledlow, Buckinghamshire, 21, 55, 185
Bletchington, Oxfordshire, 137
Blickling, Norfolk, 107
Blithbury, Staffordshire, 23
Blount, Derbyshire, 10
Bloxwich, Staffordshire, 189, 190
Bloxworth, Dorset, 27
Blyton, Lincolnshire; Wharton, 181
West Boarhunt, Hampshire, 81
Boarstall, Buckinghamshire, 12
Bolton on Swale, Yorkshire; Uckerby, 26
Boroughbridge, Yorkshire, 133, 157
Boughton, Norfolk, 52, 137, 194
Bowes, Yorkshire, 184
Bowthorpe, Norfolk, 199; Manor of Bowthorpe, 199
Bradley, Staffordshire, 161; Littlewood, 161
Brambridge, Hampshire, 187
Bramhope, Yorkshire, 55
Brampton Brian, Herefordshire, 77
South Bramwith, Yorkshire, 75
Brand, Shropshire, 70
Brandon Parva, Norfolk, 199
Brandsby, Yorkshire, 141
Brant Broughton, Lincolnshire, 181
Branton, Yorkshire, 133; Branton Grange, 133
Breckles Magna, Norfolk, 44, 122, 191, 195

Bredon, Worcestershire, 88
Brentingby, Leicestershire, 156
Bretton, Yorkshire, 187
West Bretton, Yorkshire, 28; West Bretton Hall, 187
Bright Walton, Berkshire, 26
Brill, Buckinghamshire, 20, 32
Broadwater, Sussex, 66
Broadwell, Oxfordshire, 13, 172
Brockholes, Lancashire, 159
Bromfield, Kent, 127
Bromley Hurst, Staffordshire, 62
Bromyard, Herefordshire, 9
Brotherton, Yorkshire, 10, 70
Brough under Stainmore, Westmoreland, 21
Broughton, Lancashire; Barton, 17, 158
Bruisyard, Suffolk, 76
Bryning, Lancashire, 25, 26, 46, 168, 186
Bryning with Kellamersh, Lancashire, 120
Old Buckenham, Norfolk, 64
Buckinghamshire, 55, 131
Buckland, Berkshire, 61, 62, 87, 198
Bulby, Lincolnshire, 167
Bunbury, Cheshire, 42, 92, 196
Bungay, Suffolk, 70
Bupton, Derbyshire, 10
Burgate, Suffolk, 24
Burghfield, Berkshire, 179
Buriton, Hampshire, 179; Heath House Farm, 179
Burnley, Lancashire, 77, 143, 149, 173, 174, 188, 196; Habergham Eves, 196; Hurstwood, 14; Townley, 90, 173, 188, 199
Burton on Trent, Staffordshire, 120
Burton in Warcop, Westmoreland, 84
Burton Constable, Yorkshire, 42
Burton Latimer, Northamptonshire, 95
Bury, Lancashire, 166
Bury Blunsden, Wiltshire, 184
Bury St. Edmunds, Suffolk, 12, 89, 136, 163, 170; High Street, 163; Old Baxters Street, 163; St. Marys, 25
Buscot, Berkshire, 132
Buslingthorpe, Lincolnshire, 171

Caldecote, Norfolk, 174
Callow, Herefordshire, 78
Calverley, Yorkshire, 33
Cambridge, Cambridgeshire; Christ's College, 45; St. John's College, 39; Trinity College, 68
Cambridgeshire, 118, 180, 181
Canfield, Essex, 71
Canterbury, Kent, 33, 38, 57; St. Dunstans, 9, 14, 17, 57, 71, 123, 172
Carbrooke, Norfolk, 72
Carlisle, Cumberland, 58, 84, 105; St. Marys, 84
Little Carlton, Lincolnshire, 171
Carlton Colville, Suffolk, 96
Carr, Lancashire; Carr Hall, 165
Carreside, Lancashire, 22
Cartuther, Cornwall, 17
Castle Frome, Herefordshire, 36
Castlemorton, Worcestershire, 63
Catesby, Northamptonshire, 43
Catmore, Berkshire, 27
Catterick, Yorkshire; Brough, 107
Catton, Yorkshire, 35
Cawthorne, Yorkshire, 15
Chaddesley Corbett, Worcestershire, 130; Harvington Hall, 130
Charlbury, Oxfordshire, 62, 158
Charney Basset, Berkshire, 189
Charnock Richard, Lancashire, 15, 16, 24, 28, 45, 89, 100, 145, 197
Charsfield, Suffolk, 22, 128
Chastleton, Oxfordshire, 10, 129
Cheadle, Staffordshire, 169
Checkley, Staffordshire, 42, 194

Cheddington, Buckinghamshire, 56, 103
Cheddleton, Staffordshire, 69, 84
Chediston, Suffolk, 128
Chelsea, Middlesex, 86, 122
Cheriton Fitzpaine, Devon, 44
Chertsey, Surrey, 162
Cheshire, 81, 85, 87, 89, 118, 120
Cheshunt, Hertfordshire, 169
Chester, Cheshire, 140, 144;
  Chester Castle, 37, 89, 118, 119, 139, 144, 159, 176, 178, 189, 196; St. Marys, 37, 116, 118, 159, 176, 178, 189, 190
Chesterfield, Derbyshire, 42
Chesterton, Oxfordshire, 24
Chichester, Sussex, 137, 166;
  Cathedral, 68, 99; Haven, 45, 186; Kingsham, 153;
  St. Pancras, 153
Chickerell, Dorset, 96
Chideock, Dorset, 29, 81, 175
Chillington, Staffordshire, 67
Chilton, Berkshire, 44
Chilworth, Hampshire, 184, 190
Chinnor, Oxfordshire, 82
Chippenham, Cambridgeshire, 16, 63
Chipping, Lancashire, 21, 81, 155, 172
Cholmondeley, Cheshire, 138
Christchurch, Hampshire;
  Somerford, 170
Christchurch-Twinham, Hampshire, 34
Church, Lancashire, 54, 73, 103, 143, 144, 182
Church Eaton, Staffordshire, 23
Church Lawton, Cheshire, 108
Cirencester, Gloucestershire, 25, 32, 189
Clapham, Sussex, 143, 153, 158, 197; Michelgrove, 51
Claughton, Lancashire, 64
Claughton-on-Brock, Lancashire, 28
Claverley, Shropshire, 66

East Claydon, Buckinghamshire, 120
Clerkenwell, Middlesex, 67, 69, 92, 93, 108, 141, 148, 177
Clipston, Northamptonshire, 180
Clothall, Hertfordshire, 31
Cockfield, Suffolk, 157
Cockley Cley, Norfolk, 38, 174
Coleshill, Warwickshire, 126;
  Kingshurst, 126
Colne, Lancashire, 14, 21, 86, 173, 183
Colney, Norfolk, 90, 199
Colwich, Staffordshire, 195
Colwinston, Glamorgan, 168
Comberton, Worcestershire, 17, 54, 144, 148
Compton Pauncefoot, Somerset, 101, 102
Congham, Norfolk, 200
Coppull, Lancashire, 131, 193, 196, 197
Corby, Lincolnshire, 167
Cornwall, 11, 175
Corse, Gloucestershire, 26
Costessey, Norfolk, 50
Cottisford, Oxfordshire, 11, 133, 146
Coughton, Warwickshire, 11
Coventry and Lichfield, Diocese, 181
Cowley, Gloucestershire, 33
Great Coxwell, Berkshire, 58, 125
Cradley, Herefordshire, 31
Cranborne, Dorset, 68
Cranleigh, Surrey, 137
Cranworth, Norfolk, 79
Long Crendon, Buckinghamshire, 27; Lovedens, 27
Cridling Stubbs, Yorkshire, 147
Crondall, Hampshire, 133, 150
Crosby, Lancashire, 22, 34, 116
Great Crosby, Lancashire, 16, 99, 119
Much Crosby, Lancashire, 22, 35
Crosthwaite, Westmoreland, 135, 140

Croston, Lancashire, 81; Bispham, 62
Croughton, Northamptonshire, 54
Crowmarsh, Oxfordshire, 21, 91, 93, 100; Crowmarsh Gifford, 83, 93
Croydon, Surrey, 65
Cumberland, 146

Danby, Yorkshire, 135, 147
Darton, Yorkshire, 149
Deane, Lancashire; Over Hulton, 23; Parke, 84
Debenham, Suffolk, 45
Deddington, Oxfordshire, 117, 199
North Deighton, Yorkshire; North Deighton Manor, 111, 164
Denford, Northamptonshire; Ringstead, 182, 183, 184
Denham, Buckinghamshire, 51, 133, 161
Dennington, Suffolk, 84, 146
Denver, Norfolk; Easthall Manor, 194
Deopham, Norfolk, 18
Derby, Derbyshire; Querndon in All Saints, 151
Derbyshire, 106
West Dereham, Norfolk, 36
Devonshire, 175
Dewsbury, Yorkshire, 28
Dilwyn, Herefordshire, 64
Dinckley, Lancashire, 10, 23, 148, 166
Donhead St. Andrew, Wiltshire, 73, 153; Manor of Easton Bassett, 153
Dorchester, Dorset, 13, 40, 51, 76, 96, 113, 119, 123, 175, 184
Dormington, Herefordshire, 111
Dorrington, Shropshire, 130
Dorset, 34, 37
Douai, 68, 101
Dover, Kent, 122, 154

Draycott, Staffordshire, 53; Paynesley, 53
Drayton, Oxfordshire, 165
Drayton, Shropshire, 30, 33, 63, 71, 76, 87, 131, 138, 166, 176, 181; Ternhill, 181
Droitwich, Worcestershire, 32
Dronfield, Derbyshire; Dore, 15
Dublin, 166
Dudleston, Shropshire, 33, 57, 73, 142, 143, 144, 194
Dufton, Westmoreland, 24
Dunwich, Suffolk, 108
Durham, Durham, 166
Dutton, Shropshire; Ditton Priors, 130
Duxbury, Lancashire, 47, 128

Earnley, Sussex, 25, 152
Eastbourne, Sussex, 68
Easton, Hampshire, 74
Eaton Socon, Bedfordshire, 180
Eccles, Lancashire; Clifton, 86; Woodend, 86
Eccles, Norfolk, 93
Eccleston, Lancashire; Wrightington, 14, 75
Eckington, Derbyshire; Spinkhill, 137
Edlaston, Derbyshire, 128
Edmonton, Middlesex, 108, 130
Eldersfield, Worcestershire, 25
Ellerker, Yorkshire, 58
Ellesmere, Shropshire; Welsh Hampton, 102
Ellisfield, Hampshire, 129, 132
Elswick, Lancashire, 99
Eltham, Kent, 59
Ely, Cambridgeshire, 175
Enfield, Middlesex, 173
England, 101, 149
Englefield, Berkshire, 148
Enville, Staffordshire, 127
Eppleby, Yorkshire, 67, 129
Essex, 47, 96, 117, 118, 177
Etwall, Derbyshire, 21, 48, 56, 83

Euston, Suffolk, 145
Euxton, Lancashire, 10
Everton, Cambridgeshire, 87
Evesham, Worcestershire, 22, 102, 158
Ewell, Surrey, 28
Ewyas Harold, Herefordshire, 110
Exelby, Yorkshire, 12
Eynsham, Oxfordshire, 23, 50, 188
Eyworth, Bedfordshire, 61, 63

Fairend, Worcestershire, 178
Little Fakenham, Suffolk, 29
Fareham, Hampshire, 92, 114; Cames Eysell, 114
Farlington, Hampshire, 137, 184
Farnham, Dorset, 120
Farnworth, Lancashire; Cronton, 153, 198
Faversham, Kent, 77
Fawdon, Northamptonshire, 40
Featherstone, Yorkshire; Monkroyd, 75
Felmingham, Norfolk, 18, 19
Feltwell, Norfolk, 30
Fenny Bentley, Derbyshire, 20
Fernley, Yorkshire, 60, 131
Ferry Frystone, Yorkshire, 116
Fifield Bavant, Wiltshire, 39
Nether Filkins, Oxfordshire, 172
Over Filkins, Oxfordshire, 172
Fillongley, Warwickshire, 138
Fincham, Norfolk, 155
West Firle, Sussex, 65, 153; Firle Place, 43
New Fishbourne, Sussex, 84, 92, 106
Fisherton Anger, Wiltshire, 66, 67
Fladbury, Worcestershire, 28
Flixton, Suffolk, 96, 183
Fordingbridge, Hampshire, 34
France, 162
Frickley, Yorkshire, 10
Fulham, Middlesex, 80, 106, 107

Fulmer, Buckinghamshire, 66
Funtington, Sussex; Densworth, 68

Garboldisham, Norfolk, 114
Gargrave, Yorkshire, 139
Garsington, Oxfordshire, 64
Garstang, Lancashire, 18, 31, 32, 47, 143, 174; Byreworth, 89; Nateby, 32, 174
Garway, Herefordshire, 121, 134, 178
Gayton, Staffordshire, 45
Gifford, Oxfordshire, 193
Gilling, Yorkshire, 87; Barforth Dykes, 51, 87, 127, 140; Eppleby, 182; Littlehorton, 150; Sedbury, 66
Gisburn, Yorkshire; Westby Hall, 115
Glamorganshire, 72
Gloucester, Gloucestershire, 182, 186; Diocese of, 125; Tedenham Farm, 158; Wollaston Grange, 158
Gloucestershire, 158
Gnosall, Staffordshire; Coley Hall, 25
Godlingstone, Dorset, 187
Godstowe, Oxfordshire, 129
Golborne, Lancashire, 19, 159
Goosey, Berkshire, 160
Goosnargh, Lancashire, 159; Whittingham, 190
Goudhurst, Kent, 123
Grace Dieu, Leicestershire, 72
Grafton, Worcestershire, 165
Grange over Sands, Lancashire, 36, 51, 80, 90, 93, 107
Grantley, Yorkshire, 88
Grays Inn, Middlesex, 74
Grayrigg, Westmoreland, 58
Gretton, Northamptonshire, 146
Grimston, Norfolk; Bartons, 200; Manor of Morleys, 199

Grimthorpe, Yorkshire, 113
Grindon, Staffordshire, 44
East Grinstead, Sussex, 167; Farleigh, 167
Grinton, Yorkshire, 103, 144,
Grosmont, Monmouthshire, 35, 65, 78, 85, 95, 169, 181
Guildford, Surrey, 152; Castle, 59
Guiseley, Yorkshire, 128

Hackney, Middlesex, 180
Hadfield, Gloucestershire, 133
West Hallam, Derbyshire, 14, 26, 29, 68, 138, 161, 197
Halselmore, Lancashire, 51
Halton, Buckinghamshire, 131
Hambledon, Hampshire, 178
Hamphall Stubbs, Yorkshire, 147
Hampshire, 14, 34, 85, 88, 138, 186, 187
Hampstead Norris, Berkshire, 101, 102, 104; Hawe Court, 104
Hampton, Oxfordshire, 122
Hampton Lovett, Worcestershire, 163
Hamstall Ridware, Staffordshire, 10, 11, 13, 15, 29, 39, 40, 42, 44, 45, 62, 104, 105, 126, 172, 182, 184; Heartsmere, 39, 62
Hamworthy, Dorset, 34
Hanley, Worcestershire, 17, 124; Fecknam Park, 169
Hanley Castle, Worcestershire, 13, 16, 25, 47, 87, 93, 109–112, 121, 127, 140, 148, 155, 162, 163, 190
Hapton, Lancashire, 199
Hardwick, Oxfordshire, 30, 33, 120, 156, 176
Harley, Shropshire, 36
East Harling, Norfolk, 29, 46, 69, 104, 114
Harlington, Middlesex, 141
Harmondsworth, Middlesex, 59
Harrow, Middlesex, 9, 19, 102, 153, 157, 162

Harrowden, Northamptonshire, 34, 138, 177, 180; Great Harrowden, 180; Little Harrowden, 34; Manors of Great and Little Harrowden, 180
Harting, Sussex, 65, 147
Hartley Mauditt, Hampshire, 170
Hartshorne, Derbyshire, 151
Haseley, Oxfordshire, 89, 109, 200
Hatherop, Gloucestershire, 22
Hathersage, Derbyshire, 15, 21, 61
Hawksworth, Yorkshire, 80
Hawthorpe, Lincolnshire, 167
Hayton, Yorkshire, 147
Little Haywood, Staffordshire, 195
Heath Charnock, Lancashire, 166, 196
Hemingbrough, Yorkshire, 55, 127
East Hendred, Berkshire, 118
West Hendred, Berkshire, 92
Hereford, Herefordshire, 48, 58, 69, 109, 110, 111, 134, 150, 192; Bullingham, 16; Diocese, 121, 183; Gaol, 111; All Saints, 38, 68, 77, 100, 111; St. John Baptist, 127, 157; St. Martins, 16; St. Nicholas, 16; St. Owens, 48, 58, 110; St. Peters, 58, 68, 110, 140, 165
Herefordshire, 38, 72, 151
Herringfleet, Suffolk, 78
Heslerton, Yorkshire, 49, 50
Heston, Middlesex, 39
High Ham, Somerset, 183
Higham Gobion, Bedfordshire, 10
Hilborough, Norfolk, 187
Hillesden, Buckinghamshire, 99, 134
Hindringham, Norfolk, 35
Hinton on the Green, Worcestershire, 158
Hitcham, Suffolk, 119

Hockering, Norfolk, 148
Hoggeston, Buckinghamshire, 119
Holborn, Middlesex, 15; St. Andrews, 69
Holme, Lancashire, 159
Holme Hall, Norfolk, 18, 45, 187
Holton, Oxfordshire, 161
Holton, Suffolk, 117
Hooe, Sussex, 135
Hopton, Shropshire, 130
Hordle Breamore, Hampshire, 34
Hornby, Yorkshire, 48
Hornsey, Middlesex, 100, 116
Horsham, Sussex, 42, 55, 137
Horsham St. Faith, Norfolk, 33
Horsley, Derbyshire, 29, 50, 100; Denbie, 53
Horwich, Lancashire, 178
Houghton, Middleton and Arbury, Lancashire, 159
Hoxton, Middlesex, 175, 191
Huddwick, Shropshire, 130
Hunsingore, Yorkshire, 50
Hunstanton, Norfolk, 73
Hunston, Suffolk, 164

Ibstone, Buckinghamshire, 82
Iden, Sussex, 76, 149, 150
Idsworth, Hampshire, 14
Iffley, Oxfordshire, 13, 135
East Isley, Berkshire, 83, 92, 132
Ince, Lancashire, 67, 93
Ince Blundell, Lancashire, 22, 48
Intwood, Norfolk, 107, 199
Ipsden, Oxfordshire, 179; Manor of Ipsden Bassett, 179; Manor of Ipsden Huntercombe, 179
Ipswich, Suffolk, 76
Irnham, Lincolnshire, 167
Irthlingborough, Northamptonshire, 36, 85, 119, 131, 167

Isham, Northamptonshire, 180
Islington, Middlesex, 67, 135, 142, 161
Itchen Abbas, Hampshire, 104
Itchen Stoke, Hampshire, 150

Kelmscott, Oxfordshire, 172
Kempley, Gloucestershire, 165
Kempsford, Gloucestershire, 200; Whelford, 84
Kencott, Oxfordshire, 198
Kenderchurch, Herefordshire, 150, 151
Kent, 71, 119
Kentchurch, Herefordshire, 150, 151
Kettleby, Lincolnshire, 171
Kexborough, Yorkshire, 149
Keyhaven, Hampshire, 34
Kiddal, Yorkshire, 58
Kings Norton, Worcestershire, 121
Kings Somborne, Hampshire, 33
Kingston, Dorset, 113
Kingston, Herefordshire, 124; Arkeston, 124
Kingston upon Hull, Yorkshire, 107, 129; Swine, Drypool Ward, 105, 109, 129, 171
Kinnersley, Herefordshire, 37, 170
Kippax, Yorkshire, 133, 140
West Kirby, Cheshire, 116; Woodhouse, 64
Kirk Deighton, Yorkshire, 21
Kirk Langley, Derbyshire, 14
South Kirkby, Yorkshire; Manor of Cawthorne in Mensthorpe, 185
Kirkby Fleetham, Yorkshire, 120
Kirkby Mallory, Leicestershire, 32
Kirkby Ravensworth, Yorkshire; Newsham, 158
Kirkby Thore, Westmoreland, 116, 185, 188

Kirkham, Lancashire, 28, 81, 85, 145, 155; Ballow, 38, 113; Clifton, 76; Greenhalgh, 46; Mowbrick, 187, 188; Plumpton, 37, 108, 197; Preesall, 156; Ribby, 152; Swarbrick, 51; Thistleton, 42, 69, 191; Treales, 185; Warton, 168; Weeton, 144, 168, 174; Wesham, 34, 94, 118, 155; Westby, 38, 85, 197
Kirkland, Lancashire, 32
Kirkless, Lancashire, 80
Kirtlington, Oxfordshire, 16, 183, 196
Kirton, Suffolk, 59
Knaresborough, Yorkshire; Arkendale, 24
Knottingley, Yorkshire, 54
East Knoyle, Wiltshire, 68

Laleston, Glamorgan, 97
Lambeth, Surrey, 56; Kennington, 42
Lambourn, Berkshire, 113
Lancashire, 74, 81, 85, 106, 149, 173
Lancaster, Lancashire, 90, 193; Torrisholme, 188
Hanging Langford, Wiltshire, 132
Lanherne, Cornwall, 11
Laughton, Lincolnshire, 47
Laughton, Sussex, 187
Launceston, Cornwall, 132
Laverstock, Wiltshire, 60
Lawshall, Suffolk, 53, 54; Manor, 54
Lawton, Lancashire, 159
Layland, Lancashire; Euxton, 10
Layton, Lancashire, 120
Leckhampton, Gloucestershire, 50, 82, 126
Ledbury, Herefordshire, 10, 58; Weathers, 156
Ledstone, Yorkshire, 19
Leeds, Kent, 127
Leeds, Yorkshire, 156

Leek, Staffordshire, 155
Leicestershire, 189
Leigh, Lancashire; West Leigh, 161
Leigh, Staffordshire, 42, 60, 80, 108, 147, 154, 165, 176
Leighton, Cheshire, 58, 89
Lenham, Kent, 191; Manor and Rectory, 191
Letcombe Regis, Berkshire, 69, 82
Lewes, Sussex; St. Marys Westout, 159; St. Michaels, 24
Leyland, Lancashire; Whittle-le-Woods, 56
Leyton, Essex, 122
Lichfield, Staffordshire; Cathedral, 36
Lincolnshire, 135, 171, 180, 181
Lindley, Leicestershire, 188–190
Lindsey, Lincolnshire; Langton, 29
Linsted, Suffolk, 59
Linstead Magna, Suffolk, 59
Linstead Parva, Suffolk, 59
Linton, Cambridgeshire, 34, 65, 131, 132, 170
Lisbon, 131
Litcham, Norfolk; Godwick Hall, 54
Litherland, Lancashire, 23, 46, 119
Llanarth, Monmouthshire, 90, 97, 98, 110, 123, 134, 135, 168
Llancarvan, Glamorgan, 73, 177; Llanbethery, 177
Llandegveth, Monmouthshire, 86
Llandenny, Monmouthshire, 57, 79, 98, 120, 125, 168
Llanforda, Shropshire, 112, 113
Llanfrechfa, Monmouthshire, 168, 169
Llangattock Nigh Usk, Monmouthshire, 48, 110, 111, 123, 192
Llangattock Iuxta Caerleon, Monmouthshire, 168, 183, 185. 191

Llangattock Vibon Avel,
  Monmouthshire, 36, 48, 49, 86,
  97, 111, 134, 168, 185, 188, 192
Llangibby, Monmouthshire, 68,
  97, 168
Llangoven, Monmouthshire, 49,
  78, 98, 185, 192
Llanhennock, Monmouthshire,
  110, 192
Llanishen, Monmouthshire, 67,
  78, 97, 99
Llanllowell, Monmouthshire, 67,
  87, 129, 141, 161, 168, 192
Llanover, Monmouthshire, 110,
  168
Llantarnam, Monmouthshire, 192
Llanthewy Rytherch,
  Monmouthshire, 49, 57, 98, 110
Llanthewy Skirrid,
  Monmouthshire, 17, 48, 49, 78,
  90, 95, 97–99, 105, 110, 123,
  124, 138, 142, 161, 185
Llanthewy Vach, Monmouthshire,
  92
Llantilio Crosseney,
  Monmouthshire, 44, 90
Llantilio Pertholey,
  Monmouthshire, 29, 49, 57, 67,
  73, 97, 98, 100, 102, 105, 123,
  124, 129, 131, 139, 141, 160
Llanvair Kilgedin,
  Monmouthshire, 49, 98
Llanvair Waterdine, Shropshire,
  119
Llanvetherine, Monmouthshire,
  105, 125, 138, 161, 192
Llanvihangel Crucorney,
  Monmouthshire, 48, 73, 124,
  138, 192
Llanvihangel Llantarnam,
  Monmouthshire, 49,
Llanvihangel Pontymoile,
  Monmouthshire, 143
Llanvihangel Ystern Llewern,
  Monmouthshire, 48, 49, 59,
  146, 161, 169

Llwynmaen, Shropshire, 113;
  Loynneman, 113
Londesborough, Yorkshire, 126
London, 29, 54, 81, 100, 108,
  126, 131, 133, 135, 146, 148,
  169, 175, 177; 'Le Blewbell,
  Bread Street, 177; Christchurch,
  Faringdon Ward Within, 34,
  61, 88, 110, 171; City
  Guildhall, 171, 176, 180;
  Lincolns Inn, 71, 72, 96; Le
  Stronde *alias* Savoy, 179;
  Middle Temple, 156; Mile End,
  186; Prisons:— The Clink, 26,
  49, 51, 68, 69, 74, 75, 94, 100,
  102, 107, 109, 115, 126, 133,
  137, 141, 142, 152, 161, 176,
  179, 190, 198; The Fleet, 43,
  57, 60, 72, 75, 80–82, 125, 129,
  145, 147, 158, 163, 166, 171,
  175, 176, 180; The Gatehouse,
  26, 27, 39, 41–43, 56, 57, 59,
  80, 82, 99, 101, 109, 111, 122,
  124, 127, 146, 149, 154, 158,
  169, 173, 198; The Kings Bench
  Prison, 39, 68, 85, 175; The
  Marshalsea, 15, 34, 36, 45, 54,
  61, 69, 71, 72, 78, 79, 83, 85,
  87, 93, 94, 106, 108, 119, 122,
  126, 127, 135, 137, 142, 143,
  148, 151, 152, 154, 162, 166,
  174, 176, 177, 186, 194;
  Newgate, 17, 56, 60, 88, 111,
  122, 126, 133, 137, 146, 162,
  163, 186; The Old Bailey, 19,
  41, 83, 101, 102, 115, 129, 135,
  137, 142, 148, 158, 162, 171,
  186; The Poultry Counter, 13,
  133, 177, 182; The Queens
  Bench Prison, 85, 154; The
  Tower of London, 27, 78, 102,
  109, 146, 162, 169, 176, 182;
  The White Lion, 28, 66, 96,
  114, 148, 150, 152, 156, 166,
  182; The Wood Street Counter,
  52, 55, 60, 68, 83, 88, 115, 129,

London—*continued*
131, 184; St. Anthonys in the Ward of Cheap, 75; St. Botolphs, Bishopsgate Ward Without, 13, 19, 115, 142, 186; St. Brides, Faringdon Ward Without, 9, 17, 25, 31, 32, 43, 57, 58, 72, 75, 76, 80, 81, 82, 94, 119, 125, 129, 135, 144–149, 152, 158, 163, 166, 171, 175, 180, 185; St. Clement Danes, 80, 96; St. Dunstans in the West, Faringdon Ward Without, 59, 169; St. Faiths in St. Pauls Cathedral, 74; St. Margarets, Friday Street, 13; St. Marys Steyning, Aldersgate Ward, 61; St. Marys in Wolchurch, Broadstreet Ward 127; St. Michaels, Cripplegate Ward, 182; St. Olaves, Hart Street, Tower Ward, 191; St. Pauls Cathedral, 30, 39, 70, 84, 85, 129; St. Sepulchres, Bishopsgate Ward, 76; St. Sepulchres, Faringdon Ward Without, 16, 45, 71, 100, 101, 126, 177; St. Swithuns, Walbroke Ward, 94; Thavies Inn, 111; Tyburn, 16, 19, 115, 152, 170

Long Coombe, Oxfordshire, 9
Longdon, Worcestershire, 125, 171, 177, 187, 197
Longford, Derbyshire, 13, 20, 28, 51, 61, 106, 124, 188, 197; Rodsley, 153
Longparish, Hampshire, 31, 32
Long Stanton, Cambridgeshire; Dytton Hall, Manor of Cheynes and Wallinge, 180
Lopham, Norfolk, 96, 121
Lowesby, Leicestershire, 91
Lowestoft, Suffolk, 96
Lugwardine, Herefordshire, 36, 142

Lyford, Berkshire, 12, 26, 77, 91, 101, 102, 103, 198
Lymington, Hampshire, 162

Mablethorpe, Lincolnshire, 171
Madley, Herefordshire; Chilston, 78
Maer, Staffordshire, 115, 116, 119, 193
Magna Over, Derbyshire, 53
Maidstone, Kent, 57, 77, 127
Mallory, Leicestershire, 79
Malpas, Cheshire, 79, 116, 133, 139, 190; Edge, 193; Hampton, 28; Whichalgh, 139, 144
Great Malvern, Worcestershire, 14, 188
Manchester, Lancashire, 19, 79, 106, 173; Manchester Fleet, 89, 193; Salford, 11, 12, 15, 19, 27, 31, 34, 35, 46, 62, 74, 76, 79, 85, 86, 89, 93, 99, 105, 109, 120, 126, 136, 149, 158, 173, 174, 193–196; Salford Gaol, 74, 79, 86, 89, 94, 99, 109, 136, 149, 158, 173, 195, 196
Manton, Lincolnshire, 81
Manuden, Essex, 45
Mapledurham, Oxfordshire, 179
Marcham, Berkshire, 25
Marden, Herefordshire, 166, 190
North Marden, Sussex, 194
Marham, Norfolk, 131, 132
Marleston Manor, Berkshire, 26
Great Marsden, Lancashire, 108
Marsham, Norfolk, 195
Marston, Derbyshire; Hilton, 46
Marston, Yorkshire, 170
Martham, Norfolk, 41
Martin, Yorkshire, 118
Masham, Yorkshire, 106
Mayfield, Staffordshire, 20
Meaddowes, Lancashire, 44, 68, 83, 105

Mears Ashby, Northamptonshire, 180
Long Melford, Suffolk, 117, 118
Mellis, Suffolk, 171, 172; Pountney Hall Manor, 199
Mellor, Lancashire, 159, 187
Melsonby, Yorkshire, 157; Diddersley Grange, 66
Melton Magna, Norfolk, 52, 72, 189; Haggines, 52; Peverelles, 52
East Meon, Hampshire, 60, 100
Merton, Norfolk, 16, 17, 27, 34, 72, 76, 114, 132, 139, 173
Merton, Surrey, 28, 56
Michaelston-on-Avon, Glamorgan, 97
Mickfield, Suffolk, 65
Micklethwaite, Yorkshire, 133
Mickleton, Gloucestershire, 79, 137
Middlesex, 128
Middleton *alias* **Longparish**, Hampshire, 31
Middleton, Lancashire, 159
Middleton, Shropshire, 130
Middleton Tyas, Yorkshire; Cowton Grange, 157; Gatherley, 30, 31, 59
Midhurst, Sussex, 193
Milford, Hampshire, 34
Milford-on-Sea, Hampshire, 34
North Milford, Yorkshire, 109
Milbrook, Bedfordshire, 90
Milton, Cambridgeshire, 42
Milton, Kent, 127
Milwich, Staffordshire, 45, 76, 116, 195
South Mimms, Middlesex, 173
Mitcham, Surrey, 190
Mitton, Yorkshire, 80
Monckton, Dorset, 37, 134
Monmouthshire, 95, 124
Morganstown, Glamorgan, 97
Morley, Norfolk, 24
Morval, Cornwall, 175
Moseley Tilt, Yorkshire, 122

Motcombe, Dorset, 92
Mucklestone, Staffordshire, 51, 52, 72
Murston, Kent, 77

Naburn, Yorkshire, 15, 131
Nassington, Yorkshire, 80
Neston, Cheshire; Leighton, 189
Netherbury, Dorset, 165
Nether Stowey, Somerset, 183
Nettlestead, Kent, 74
Newbald, Yorkshire, 15, 64
Newbury, Berkshire, 130
Newington, Middlesex, 17, 66, 156
Newington, Surrey, 148, 155, 166, 182
New Inn, Middlesex, 146
Newland, Gloucestershire, 35, 169
Newnham Murren, Oxfordshire, 93
Newport, Monmouthshire, 143
Newton, Lancashire, 159; Scales, 29
Newton, Shropshire, 125, 135
Newton by Toft, Lincolnshire, 124
South Newton, Oxfordshire, 151
Nidd, Yorkshire, 73
Norfolk, 72
Normanton, Yorkshire, 116
North Weald Bassett, Essex, 42
Northampton, Northamptonshire; St. Sepulchres, 32, 44
Northamptonshire, 146, 147, 176, 180, 181
Norton, Derbyshire, 114
Norton, Kent, 77, 127
Norton, Suffolk, 164
Norton in Hales, Shropshire, 70
Northwold, Norfolk, 133
Norwich, Norfolk, 13; St. Georges, Colgate, 136; St. Martins before the Gate of the Bishops Palace, 58; St. Peters Mancroft, 90; Sts. Simon and Judes, 115, 188

Nottingham, Nottinghamshire, 123; St. Marys, 40, 47, 62, 77, 79, 123
Nutley, Hampshire, 88

Oakley, Bedfordshire, 123, 140
Oakley, Buckinghamshire, 19, 20, 82; Ixhill Lodge, 19, 20
Orcop, Herefordshire, 68
Ormesby, Norfolk, 165
Ormskirk, Lancashire; Bickerstaff, 12; Lathom, 12
Orwell, Cambridgeshire, 33
Osgodby, Yorkshire, 13
Oswaldtwistle, Lancashire, 159
Oswestry, Shropshire, 112
Otterbourne, Hampshire, 44
South Otterington, Yorkshire, 166
Ottringham, Yorkshire, 162
Oundle, Northamptonshire, 92, 107
Over, Cheshire; Wettenhall, 140
Oving, Sussex, 153
Oxborough, Norfolk, 18, 19, 73, 155
Oxford, Oxfordshire, 59, 99; All Saints, 50, 79, 81, 84, 99; St. Ebbes, 47; St. Mary Magdalens, 14, 90, 134
Oxfordshire, 43, 54–56, 91, 93, 122, 129, 145, 169, 179

Padworth, Berkshire, 132
Passenham, Northamptonshire, 117, 156
Patching, Sussex, 153
Patrington, Yorkshire, 162
Patshull, Staffordshire, 127
Pavenham, Bedfordshire; Manor of Pavenham, 180
Pemberton, Lancashire, 44, 68, 83
Pembridge, Herefordshire, 80, 93
Penn, Buckinghamshire, 134, 169
Peterchurch, Herefordshire, 151
Petersfield, Hampshire, 179

Petworth, Sussex, 27
Pickering, Yorkshire, 197
Pipe Ridware, Staffordshire, 82
Pirton, Worcestershire, 63
Pitstone, Buckinghamshire, 44
Plas Ulcha, Shropshire, 112
Pleasington, Lancashire, 86, 159
Plumpton, Lancashire, 174, 190
Podington, Bedfordshire, 84
Pokesmore, Shropshire, 130
Pontefract, Yorkshire, 147
Poole, Dorset; Harbour, 34
Potton, Bedfordshire, 173
Poulton, Lancashire, 120, 159
Little Poulton, Lancashire, 81
Poynings, Sussex, 43
Preese, Lancashire, 144, 155
Prescott, Lancashire; Mesborough, 107; Sutton, 196
Preston, Lancashire, 22, 56, 62; Cottam, 80; Fishwick, 60
Preston Candover, Hampshire, 88, 133
Pudding Norton, Norfolk, 132
Isle of Purbeck, Dorset, 187
Purston Jaglin, Yorkshire, 75
Pyrton, Oxfordshire, 163

Quarndon, Derbyshire; All Saints, 70
Quidenham, Norfolk, 18

Racton, Sussex, 55, 63, 75, 95, 137, 144
Radford, Nottinghamshire, 63
Ragdale, Leicestershire, 197
Raglan, Monmouthshire, 9, 13, 40, 48, 49, 73, 86, 89, 95, 99, 101, 110, 112, 125, 131, 134, 144, 146, 157, 185, 192, 200
Rainham, Essex, 77
Rainham, Kent, 127
Ravescombe, Isle of Purbeck, Dorset, 187
Rawroyd, Yorkshire, 182

Reading, Berkshire, 57, 101; Reading Castle, 77, 83, 91, 101, 103, 113, 118, 125, 130, 160, 198; Coley House, 179; St. Marys, 59, 77, 83, 91, 101–103, 114, 118, 125, 130, 144, 160, 198
Redenhall, Norfolk; Harleston, 126
Redlingfield, Suffolk, 18
Renhold, Bedfordshire, 150
Revingham, Norfolk, 148
Rheims, 125
Ribbesford, Worcestershire, 110
Ribby, Lancashire, 152, 172
Ribchester, Lancashire, 159
Richard Castle, Herefordshire, 195
Richmond, Yorkshire, 12
Rickinghall, Suffolk, 50; Manor of Fithiones, 199
Ringmer, Sussex; Goate Manor, 167
Ringstead, Norfolk, 181
Ripley, Yorkshire, 93, 183; Clint, 47; Killinghall, 17, 140, 147, 178, 186
Ripon, Yorkshire, 186; Brimham Hall, 111
Ripple, Worcestershire, 61, 123, 194; Queenhill, 26
Rochester, Staffordshire, 28, 197
Rockingham, Northamptonshire, 176
Rokeby, Yorkshire, 145; Moreton, 145
Romsey, Hampshire, 37, 135, 159, 160
Ross on Wye, Herefordshire, 127
Rouen, 149
Rougham, Norfolk, 199
Rowington, Warwickshire, 12
Royston, Cambridgeshire, 132
Rushton, Dorset, 55, 106, 113
Rushton, Northamptonshire, 176, 181; St. Peters, 175
South Rushton, Norfolk, 127
Rutland, 71
Ryall, Northumberland, 121
Ryburgh Magna, Norfolk, 143

St. Clement Danes without Temple Bar, Middlesex, 83, 162
St. Decumans, Somerset, 92
St. Devereux, Herefordshire, 124, 150, 157
St. Giles in the Field, Middlesex, 14, 82
St. Goran, Cornwall, 175
St. Mary Magdalen, Cornwall, 192
St. Maughans, Monmouthshire, 98, 160
St. Martin, Cornwall, 175
St. Michael on Wyre, Lancashire, 32; Inskipp, 121
St. Miniver, Cornwall, 101
Salesbury, Lancashire, 33
Salford Priors, Warwickshire, 61
Samlesbury, Lancashire, 158, 159
Great Sampford, Essex, 71
Little Sampford, Essex, 71
Sandbarrow, Staffordshire, 40
Sandon, Staffordshire, 58, 178
Sandringham, Norfolk, 191
Sarnesfield, Herefordshire, 121, 132
New Sarum, Wiltshire, 66, 67, 159
Saunderton, Buckinghamshire, 17
Scarliffe, Derbyshire, 76
Scotland, 109
Scruton, Yorkshire, 47
Sedbury, Yorkshire, 66
Sefton, Lancashire, 117; Crosbie, 22, 161
Sellack, Herefordshire, 121; Baysham, 185
Sharleston, Yorkshire, 66, 94
Shawbury, Shropshire, 55
Shaw, Berkshire, 130
Great Shelford, Cambridgeshire, 145, 173

Shelley, Essex, 79
Sherburn in Elmet, Yorkshire, 105
Sheringham, Norfolk, 46, 148
Shevington, Lancashire, 138, 196
Shifnal, Shropshire, 70
Shinfield, Berkshire, 179
Shiplake, Oxfordshire, 191
Shropshire, 30, 66, 134, 138
Sidlesham, Sussex, 99
Silkstone, Yorkshire, 187; Bretton, 187
Great Singleton, Lancashire, 87
Sion, Middlesex, 149
Sittingbourne, Kent, 77, 127
Skelton, Yorkshire; Kate Ridding, 95
Skenfrith, Monmouthshire, 86, 90, 95, 123, 134, 138, 168, 183, 192
Smithfield, London, 88
East Smithfield, Middlesex, 108
Snaith, Yorkshire; Goole, 162
Snowswick, Berkshire, 132
Somerset, 67, 92, 101
Somerton, Oxfordshire, 64, 74, 119, 140, 141, 156
Sotterley, Suffolk, 136
Souldren, Oxfordshire, 163
Southmead, Buckinghamshire, 51
Southminster, Essex; Bacons at Dengie, 96
Southover, Sussex; St. Johns, 44, 50
Southwark, Surrey, 9, 15, 17, 23, 26, 28, 30, 34–36, 38, 41, 45, 46, 49–52, 57, 61, 62, 64, 66–69, 71–74, 78, 79, 87, 96, 101, 102, 107–109, 112, 117, 119, 122, 126–128, 133, 135, 136, 138, 142, 143, 146–148, 150–157, 159, 162, 166, 167, 170, 176–179, 181, 182, 186, 193, 196; St. Georges, 11, 12, 23, 26, 33, 36, 38, 45, 54, 57–59, 69, 83, 95, 101, 104, 115, 128, 137, 148, 151, 157, 174, 182, 186, 190; St. Mary Magdalens, 13, 52, 200; St. Olaves, 140, 157; St. Saviours, 21, 23, 29, 43, 68, 70, 83, 94, 100, 102, 109, 133, 134, 147, 164, 165, 179, 198
Southwick, Hampshire, 82; Newland, 184
Southworth with Croft, Lancashire, 159
Manor upon Sowe, Staffordshire, 64
Speen, Berkshire, 130
Spofforth, Yorkshire, 121
Sporle, Norfolk, 12
Stafford, Staffordshire, 15, 193; St. Marys, 36, 106, 193
Staffordshire, 15, 39, 62, 66, 72, 81, 127, 132, 136, 138, 182
Stainfield, Lincolnshire, 9
Standish, Lancashire, 75, 78, 99, 119, 143, 161; Blaynstowe, 196
Standon, Staffordshire, 181
Stanford upon Soar, Nottinghamshire, 142
Stanley, Derbyshire, 79
Great Stanmore, Middlesex, 128
Stanningfield, Suffolk, 63, 145
Stanton Harcourt, Oxfordshire, 15
Stanton St. John, Oxfordshire, 56
Stanwick St. John, Yorkshire, 106; Aldburgh, 132; Carleton, 35
Staplehurst, Kent, 119
Startforth, Yorkshire, 66
Staveley, Derbyshire, 120, 159
Steeple Langford, Wiltshire, 75
Stepney, Middlesex, 13, 27, 29, 50, 86, 93, 115, 131, 175
Steventon, Hampshire, 174
Steyning, Sussex, 30, 109, 178, 182
Stockton Yate, Cheshire, 79
Stoke, Staffordshire, 181
Stoke, Suffolk, 39, 117
Stoke Meon, Hampshire, 40
Stoke Poges, Buckinghamshire, 62, 76

Stokenchurch, Oxfordshire, 135
Stokesley, Yorkshire, 157
Stone, Staffordshire, 25, 41, 53, 82
Stonehouse, Gloucestershire, 20
Stonor, Oxfordshire, 163; Broundesden, 163; Hollandridge Farm, 163; Manor of Stonor or Pishill with Warmodescombe, 163; Stonor Park, 78, 79, 176
Storrington, Sussex; Bartholemews, 153; Les Downes, 153
Stoughton, Sussex, 33
Stowe, Staffordshire, 156
Stowe Bedon, Norfolk, 12
Stowe Langtoft, Suffolk, 164
Long Stratton, Norfolk, 134
Stretford, Herefordshire, 100
Sudbury, Derbyshire, 20
Suffolk, 47, 72, 117, 118, 136, 137, 164
Sugton, Yorkshire, 163
Sulhampstead, Berkshire, 132
Surrey, 87, 137, 150
Sussex, 14, 35, 43, 46, 49, 87, 100, 137, 138, 150, 151, 153
Sutton, Cheshire, 118, 139, 167, 189, 190
Sutton, Herefordshire, 183
Sutton Courtney, Berkshire, 82, 90, 91
Sutton St. Michael, Herefordshire, 151
Sutton Valence, Kent, 127
Swarraton, Hampshire; Godsfield, 104
Swilland, Suffolk, 11, 128
Swillington, Yorkshire, 185
Swinden, Lancashire, 14, 86
Swyncombe, Oxfordshire, 144
Swynnerton, Staffordshire, 15

Taddisford, Hampshire, 34
Tamworth, Staffordshire, 132, 153, 188; Comberford Hall, 41
Tamworth, Warwickshire, 71
Tansor, Northamptonshire, 10, 163
Tanworth in Arden, Warwickshire, 183, 184
Taplow, Buckinghamshire; Amerden, 116, 117
Tardebigg, Worcestershire, 109
Tarvin, Cheshire, 85
Tempsford, Bedfordshire, 39
Tenbury, Worcestershire, 39, 106
Tewkesbury, Gloucestershire, 75
Teynham, Kent; Frognall, 70
Thakeham, Sussex, 195
Thame, Oxfordshire, 65
Thistleton, Lancashire, 46, 56, 69, 103, 177
Thornage, Norfolk, 16
Thorndon, Suffolk; All Saints, 155
Thorneton, Cheshire, 89, 92
Thornham, Lancashire, 56
Thornley with Wheatley, Lancashire, 178, 191
Thornton, Lincolnshire, 171
Bishop Thornton, Yorkshire, 115
Thrandeston, Suffolk; Manor of Mabisons, 199
Thrapston, Northamptonshire, 54
Thurstaston, Cheshire, 189
Tideswell, Derbyshire, 25, 38
Tidworth, Wiltshire, 60
Tilehurst, Berkshire; Beansheaves, 179
Tilney with Islington, Norfolk, 122, 193
Tingrith, Bedfordshire, 27
West Tisted, Hampshire, 170
Titchfield, Hampshire, 187
Tittleshall, Norfolk, 182
West Tofts, Norfolk, 101
Tolpuddle, Dorset, 64
Tonge, Kent, 77
Torrisholme, Lancashire, 35, 36, 90
Totford, Hampshire, 91
Tottenham, Middlesex, 26, 57, 74, 75, 180
Treales, Lancashire, 74

Tredunnock, Monmouthshire, 57, 95, 112, 124, 134, 138
Tregare, Monmouthshire, 14, 168, 185
Trellissick, Cornwall, 175
Trelleck, Monmouthshire, 139
Trostrey, Monmouthshire, 49
Tupton, Derbyshire, 187
Tutbury, Derbyshire, 64
Tuxford, Nottinghamshire, 33
Twyford, Buckinghamshire, 45
Twyford, Hampshire, 111; Brambridge, 186

Uffington, Berkshire, 62
Ufton, Berkshire, 132
Uppingham, Rutland, 39
Upsall, Yorkshire, 24
Upton-on-Severn, Worcestershire, 83, 164
Usk, Monmouthshire, 17, 49, 95, 124, 125, 134, 135, 161, 192
Uttoxeter, Staffordshire, 53; Kingston, 23

Wales, 90, 149
Walkingham Hill, Yorkshire, 104
Walkington, Yorkshire, 154
Walsall, Staffordshire, 21, 189, 190
Walsham, Norfolk, 93
Walthamstow, Essex, 74
Walton, Yorkshire, 185
East Walton, Norfolk, 103
Wantage, Berkshire, 194
Warblington, Hampshire, 30, 43, 44
Warborough, Oxfordshire, 137
Warnham, Sussex, 50
Warrington, Lancashire, 159; Orford, 12, 159; Rixton, 118; Great Sankey, 158
Warwickshire, 138
Washingley, Huntingdonshire, 10, 74, 166

Wateringbury, Kent, 66, 81, 157
Watford, Northamptonshire, 40, 41
Watlington, Oxfordshire, 23
Wedacre, Lancashire, 142, 195
Weeton, Lancashire, 12, 36, 46, 51, 78, 127, 174
Welbourn, Lincolnshire, 170
Welland, Worcestershire, 147
Wellington, Herefordshire, 38
Welsh Bicknor, Herefordshire, 179
Welton, Northamptonshire, 195
Wendlebury, Oxfordshire, 10, 21, 24, 29, 84, 94, 133, 139, 157
Wentlooge St. Bride, Monmouthshire, 49
Weobley, Herefordshire, 29, 109, 155
Wereham, Norfolk, 128
Wesham, Lancashire, 33, 36, 88, 94, 99, 107, 136, 140, 172
West Ashall, Yorkshire, 11
Westbury Manor, Hampshire, 60
Westby, Lancashire, 10, 14, 20, 30, 38, 42, 46, 58, 63, 85–87, 103, 104, 113, 141, 143, 144, 158, 159, 166
Westham, Sussex, 128, 167; Glynde Farm, 167; Priesthawes, 167
Westhampstead, Berkshire, 83
Westhorpe, Suffolk, 125
Westleton, Suffolk, 18
Westminster, Middlesex, 13, 16, 26, 27, 33, 39, 41, 42, 54, 57, 59, 60, 63, 66, 80, 82, 99, 101, 108, 115, 122, 124, 137, 141, 147, 157, 162, 164, 169, 189, 198; Westminster Abbey, 60; Westminster Gatehouse, 26, 27, 56, 57, 109; St. Margarets, 41, 43, 54, 56, 138, 146, 169, 173, 178
Westmoreland, 85
Weston Underwood, Buckinghamshire, 170

Wetherden, Suffolk, 164
Whaddon, Cambridgeshire, 122
Whalley, Lancashire, 10, 28, 71, 89, 107, 132, 148; Barneside, 174; Haslingden, 54; Great Marsden, 144; Milton, 35; Parkhill, 14, 147, 173; Wiswell, 51, 89
Wheatley, Lancashire, 25; Thornley, 56, 117
Whitchurch, Glamorganshire, 168
Whitchurch, Herefordshire, 180
Whitechapel, Middlesex, 140
Whiteparish, Wiltshire. 12, 33
Whitford, Flintshire, 90
Whitgift, Yorkshire; Reednes, 162; Swinefleet, 162
West Wickham, Cambridgeshire, 135
Wichenor, Staffordshire, 141, 183
Wigan, Lancashire, 35, 37, 70, 87, 92, 93, 105, 117, 133, 136, 143, 154; Highfield, 198; Markland Milne, 198; Pemberton, 105, 121
Wigenhall St. Mary Magdalen, Norfolk, 193
Isle of Wight, Hampshire, 84
Wigmore, Herefordshire, 45, 46
Wilbarston, Northamptonshire, 70
Wilpshire, Lancashire, 10
Wilton, Wiltshire, 21
Wiltshire, 153, 184
Wimborne Minster, Dorset, 78, 96, 165, 200
Winchester, Hampshire, 30, 87, 88, 130, 131, 135, 160, 184, 186; Cheeshill St. Peter, 17, 18; Winchester Gaol, 149; St. Clements, 27, 29, 116, 128, 149, 193; St. Maurices, 88, 184, 193; St. Michaels, 196; Upbattle, 184
Windle, Lancashire, 174
Winforton, Herefordshire, 179, 180; Manor of Winforton, 179
Wingfield, Suffolk, 51

North Wingfield, Derbyshire, 38, 44, 63, 64, 103, 188
Winterbourne St. Martin, Dorset, 9, 11, 165
Winterburn, Yorkshire, 139
Winwick, Lancashire; Haydock, 11; Highley Carr, 119, 120; Hollynhey, 67; Lightshawe, 102; Middleton, 159
Wiswell, Lancashire, 47, 56, 89, 93, 114, 148
Withington, Lancashire, 106
Woking, Surrey, 70
Wolseley Bridge, Staffordshire, 195; Wolseley Manor, 195
Wolvercote Manor, Oxfordshire, 129
Wonastow, Monmouthshire, 95, 112, 142
Woodchurch, Cheshire, 85; Prenton, 85
Woodhay, Berkshire, 36, 37
Woolston, Lancashire, 159
Worcester, Worcestershire, 61, 158, 159
Worcestershire, 31, 49, 182, 190
Worfield, Shropshire, 36
Worminghurst, Sussex, 133, 152, 195
Worsall, Yorkshire, 148, 149
Worth Matravers, Dorset, 187
Worthington, Lancashire, 43, 190, 196
West Wratting, Cambridgeshire, 63
Wraxhall, Wiltshire, 28
Wrenbury, Cheshire, 89
Wrightington, Lancashire, 159
Wye, Kent, 57
Wykeham, Yorkshire, 79
Wyresdale, Lancashire, 9, 54, 165, 183

Yarkhill, Herefordshire, 31
Yate, Gloucestershire, 125

Yaxley, Suffolk, 199
Yedingham, Yorkshire, 105
Yetminster, Dorset, 13, 131
York, Yorkshire, 12, 24, 25, 42, 55, 67, 75, 115, 118, 155, 165, 167, 186, 191, 195, 199; Bishopfield, 167; York Castle, 81, 94, 95, 128, 130, 186; St. Johns, 115, 130; St. Marys, 94
Yorkshire, 25, 41, 50, 80, 100, 112, 123, 147, 154, 183
Yoxall, Staffordshire, 92